THE 9/11 GENERATION

The 9/11 Generation

*Youth, Rights, and Solidarity
in the War on Terror*

Sunaina Marr Maira

NEW YORK UNIVERSITY PRESS
New York

NEW YORK UNIVERSITY PRESS
New York
www.nyupress.org

References to Internet websites (URLs) were accurate at the time of writing. Neither the author nor New York University Press is responsible for URLs that may have expired or changed since the manuscript was prepared.

Library of Congress Cataloging-in-Publication Data
Names: Maira, Sunaina, 1969– author.
Title: The 9/11 generation : youth, rights, and solidarity in the war on terror / Sunaina Marr Maira.
Description: New York : New York University Press, [2016] | Includes bibliographical references and index.
Identifiers: LCCN 2016010270| ISBN 978-1-4798-1769-6 (cl : alk. paper) | ISBN 978-1-4798-8051-5 (pb : alk. paper)
Subjects: LCSH: Youth—Political activity—California. | Civil rights—California. | Islamophobia—California. | Muslims—California—Social conditions—21st century. | Minority youth—California—Social conditions—21st century. | September 11 Terrorist Attacks, 2001—Social aspects. | War on Terrorism, 2001-2009—Social aspects.
Classification: LCC HQ799.2.P6 M345 2016 | DDC 320.40835/09794—dc23
LC record available at https://lccn.loc.gov/2016010270

New York University Press books are printed on acid-free paper, and their binding materials are chosen for strength and durability. We strive to use environmentally responsible suppliers and materials to the greatest extent possible in publishing our books.

Manufactured in the United States of America

10 9 8 7 6 5 4 3 2 1

Also available as an ebook

For Layla

CONTENTS

ACKNOWLEDGMENTS

This book project has evolved over more than a decade, since I found myself settled in the Bay Area in 2003–2004 and immersed in post-9/11 political organizing. It was driven by my own curiosity and concerns about the shape that community activism, antiwar, and solidarity campaigns were taking after 9/11 and during the wars in Afghanistan and Iraq, and so its critiques are directed as much at my own engagements as anything else. The book owes a great debt to the many young activists who spearheaded or were involved in these campaigns and to the movements that emerged to resist the violent and repressive policies of the U.S. as well as its allies. I appreciate their dedication and efforts and though there are too many names to list here, I would like to thank comrades from the Alliance for South Asians Taking Action, Justice in Palestine Coalition, Asian Pacific Islander Coalition against the War, Friends of South Asia, (then) St. Peter's Housing Committee and Deporten a la Migra, and Pakistanis for Palestine (in Lahore), among others. I also continue to be sustained and supported by the commitment and vision of fellow organizers in USACBI (U.S. Campaign for the Academic and Cultural Boycott of Israel). In a U.S. academy where professionalized scholars keep a safe distance from "risky" causes, their courage and persistence stands out.

I am grateful for the intellectual support and inspiration of many colleagues and mentors, again too numerous to mention here, who have given me space to share my ideas through talks and conference papers along the way. I would be remiss not to mention in particular the support and inspiration of Natalia Deeb-Sossa, Veena Dubal, Lisa Duggan, David Eng, Robin Kelley, George Lipsitz, Curtis Marez, Sherene Razack, Chandan Reddy, Roshni Rustomji-Kerns, and Howard Winant. At UC Davis I especially appreciate the encouragement I have received from Wendy Ho, Robert Irwin, Richard Kim, Susette Min, Kriss Ravetto, Robyn Rodriguez, and Baki Tezcan. I also want to thank May Jayussi and Nadera Shalhoub-Kevorkian in Palestine for providing me with feedback and intellectual community while I was doing research in the West Bank.

Earlier versions of portions of chapters have appeared in the edited volumes *Gender, National Security, and Counter-Terrorism: Human Rights Perspectives* (2012), edited by Margaret L. Satterthwaite and Jayne C. Huckerby;

At the Limits of Justice: Women of Color on Terror (2014), edited by Suvendrini Perera and Sherene H. Razack; and *The War of My Generation: Youth Culture and the War on Terror* (2015), edited by David Kieran. I have also had the opportunity to present this research at several conferences where the feedback I have received has been very valuable. This book would not have happened without the diligent efforts and resourcefulness of my many able student research assistants who have worked with me over the years: Amena, Amir, Asra, Duaa, Madeline, Marjan, Meena, Najia, Nurges, Sabrena, Safura, Summer, Tanya, and Trisha. Their insights, hard work, and commitment made it possible for me to persist with this ethnographic research and their help with the interviews and field work is an incredibly important part of this study. I also want to give a shout out to the courageous participants in Students for Justice in Palestine–Davis and to my faculty and graduate student colleagues in Faculty for Justice in Palestine.

My deep thanks to my editor, Eric Zinner, for his enthusiastic commitment to this book project and for supporting my work, and to Alicia Nadkarni and Dorothea Halliday at NYU Press for their editorial and production assistance. I am also grateful to Dan Geist for his superb copy editing of the manuscript and knowledgeable review of details.

Last but not least, I want to express my deep thanks to my family and especially my parents, Shama and Arun, for their love and generosity; and my partner, Magid, for his support, feedback, and vision. This book is for my daughter, Layla, whose resilience, sense of fairness, sensitivity, and joy is astonishing and who is the reason for everything.

Introduction

Since the events of September 11, 2001, the intensified concern with national security and the U.S.-led global War on Terror has led to a preoccupation with monitoring, policing, and regulating the political affiliations and engagement of Muslim American and Middle Eastern communities. Under the PATRIOT Act and with the expanded powers given to law enforcement and intelligence agencies to hunt down potential terrorists and "preempt" terrorism, Arab, South Asian (particularly Pakistani), Afghan, Iranian, and Muslim Americans in general have been subjected to surveillance as well as detention and deportation. Youth from these communities who are defined as objects of the domestic as well as global War on Terror have come of age in a moment when the question of political engagement for Muslim youth is extremely pressing but also incredibly fraught.

This book uses ethnographic research to explore the forms that politics takes for South Asian, Arab, and Afghan American youth in Silicon Valley, addressing the overarching question: how is "politics" defined and what forms of politics are viewed as important, effective, and desirable by this generation of youth, the so-called 9/11 generation? And what happens when we decouple "9/11" as a signifier of identification from this generational category to understand the range of political critiques and shifting identifications among South Asian, Arab, and Afghan American youth? The 9/11 generation, of course, includes not only Muslim and Middle Eastern Americans but also young people from other communities who have entered adolescence since 9/11 and have been deeply shaped by the aftermath of this historical event; but it is Muslim and Middle Eastern American youth who have been construed as objects of the War on Terror and so especially impacted by the shifts in national culture.

The U.S.-led War on Terror is now a globalized regime of biopolitics, or regulating and managing populations, from Lackawanna and Lodi to London and Lahore. Youth politics is a central target of this regime as the religious and political "radicalization" of youth variously defined as Muslim, Middle Eastern, Arab, Afghan, or South Asian has come to embody a threat to Western, secular, liberal democracy and U.S. military as well as economic interventions. But this regime also assumes that the politics of Muslim American youth are knowable, within the framework of securitization that views this generational cohort as bedeviled by disaffection, cultural and political alienation, and psychological and social maladjustment (Grewal 2014, 7). Muslim and Arab American youth, especially young males, have become primary objects of the counterterrorism regime, which views them as susceptible to "radicalization" and violent extremism, that is, as ripe for becoming enemies of the state. This focus on "homegrown terrorism" has occurred in tandem with shifts in U.S. wars and counterterrorism operations in Afghanistan, Pakistan, Yemen, and other sites that are mapped onto a transnational jihadist network. The homeland War on Terror has become an increasingly central part of the planetary war and, in the decade since 9/11, increasingly focused on monitoring and prosecuting ideological and religious beliefs, not just terrorist activities. The strategy of preemptive prosecution thus mirrors the doctrine of "preemptive war." In all these debates, the figure of the young Muslim or Arab American is central, given the notion that youth are vulnerable subjects particularly susceptible to indoctrination and radicalization.

While the crackdown on Muslim Americans and backlash against Muslims and "Muslim-looking" people was most intense and violent in the immediate aftermath of 9/11, the scapegoating and repression of Muslim and Middle Eastern communities has persisted well beyond 9/11 and under the Obama administration, with Islamophobic and anti-Arab discourse continuing to appear in the U.S. mainstream, not just right-wing, media. Incidents such as the "Ground Zero" mosque controversy in New York that erupted in 2010, as well as less publicized incidents involving FBI entrapment of Muslim American youth from Lodi to Brooklyn, underscored that Muslims continue to be framed through the lens of the War on Terror, and that their politics, more than that of any other religious group, are viewed as necessary to surveil and contain. This constitutes what some call the "new order of War on Terror" that has been established under the Obama regime, which has relied on mass surveillance, clandestine cooperation between various arms of law enforcement and intelligence, and a counterterrorism discourse that uses the lexicon of counterradicalization to police political and social lives and monitor the "enemy within" (Kumar 2012, 158). Furthermore, the ongoing debate over the prolonged war in Afghanistan—the longest in U.S. history, which was revived by Obama—and the Muslim men incarcerated in Guantanamo without charge or trial in a prison that has endured beyond the Bush regime, not to mention the drone wars in "Af-Pak," has meant that the figure of the (Muslim, Arab, or South/Southwest Asian) enemy continues to represent a flash point where anxieties about U.S. military violence, legal justice, and human rights collide.

Given that state repression has made collective mobilization fragile, what kinds of collectivities and political imaginaries do young people targeted by the state produce? This book interrogates the meaning of political subjecthood for Arab, South Asian, and Afghan American youth in Silicon Valley and new forms of mobilization, especially new cross-racial alliances, that have emerged in the decade since the attacks of 9/11. There has been a turn to civil rights and engagement with human rights activism as the 9/11 generation has created cross-ethnic coalitions and participated in transnational solidarity campaigns. I am interested in how young South Asian, Arab, and Afghan Americans in Silicon Valley engage with the notion of "rights," domestically and globally, in the post-9/11 moment. The study focuses primarily on Muslim American youth, but it also includes non-Muslim youth, in an ethnically and racially diverse region where there are well-established South Asian, Arab, and Afghan American communities and Muslim American institutions and political organizations. While the San Francisco Bay Area is a hub of progressive politics and liberal multiculturalism, at least in the cultural imaginary, less attention has been paid to the post-9/11 political experiences of youth in Silicon Valley, an area that emblematizes American entrepreneurial capitalism but is bedeviled by class inequality and racial tensions.

Young people from communities that have been targeted in the War on Terror, both within and beyond U.S. borders, have increasingly crossed racial and ethnic boundaries, and in some cases religious ones, to forge coalitions in opposing U.S. domestic and global policies. Some of these cross-ethnic and interfaith alliances are oppositional while others seem to shore up a politics of inclusion and recognition, and there is also an important politics of international solidarity that underlies movements linking Muslim and Middle Eastern immigrant communities to overseas homelands and war zones. The South Bay is a fascinating site to examine these cross-racial alliances given the ethnic and racial diversity of the local Muslim population as well as looming anxieties about class mobility and multicultural inclusion. The research explores the possibility of alternative forms of politics that can provide a critique of Islamophobia, racism, and imperial violence as well as of neoliberal multiculturalism, rights-based politics, and humanitarianism.

Since 9/11, political movements among South Asian, Arab, and Afghan American communities have visibly emerged on the terrain of rights—particularly civil rights or human rights—and Muslim American activists have increasingly resorted to rights to challenge racial and political exclusion and violence. The turn to rights takes place in a moment in which what is "civil" and who is "human" is increasingly defined through the language of rights (Eng 2012). This turn is also shadowed by debates about women's rights and gay rights in Muslim and Middle Eastern societies that are deemed inherently patriarchal and homophobic and in need of humanitarian intervention in the War on Terror, so there is a deeply racialized logic underlying the liberation of "others" through the promise of liberal rights (Atanoski 2013, 5). Furthermore, while rights often provide a "normative legal framework," one associated with Western governmentalities, I am also interested in exploring how the "practice of claim making is generative of new understandings and subjects of rights," and also of politics, what Ajantha Subramaniam calls "structures of feeling" using a "historical, processual" approach to rights (cited in Allen 2013, 13). The book explores the engagement of South Asian, Arab, and Afghan American youth in transnational as well as U.S.-based politics, variously framed around questions of civil rights, human rights, women's rights, and gay rights—the rights-based paradigms that have been invoked by the U.S. in its War on Terror and also infused mobilization *against* the U.S. state. In this sense, the book pivots on the question of how rights claims are deployed by youth, but it also speaks to broader questions of justice, accountability, belonging, and violence that these young people grapple with and that are animated, or suppressed, by the notion of rights.

The Long War on Terror

"Terrorism" has been conflated with the notion of Muslim "radicalism" or "extremism," as well as the recent concept of "jihadism," all deeply racialized code words for a broader set of assumptions about who is at war with the United States. As Talal Asad (2003) and other critics have argued, terrorism is a concept embedded in liberal modernity, an object that Western as well as non-Western modern states require to define their Other in what is constructed (and marketed) as an existential battle for the survival of Western civilization and secular, liberal democracy on a global, not just national, scale. The lexicon of counterterrorism has continued to evolve in conjunction with shifts in military strategy in overseas wars and surveillance strategies on the homefront, and as Arun Kundnani (2014) observes, "radicalization became the lens through which Western societies viewed Muslim populations by the first decade of the twenty-first century" (9–10). Within this national security framework and counterterrorism regime, those resisting U.S. policies of global hegemony, especially its wars in West and Southwest Asia, are demonized as "anti-American" militants and anti-Western fanatics defined primarily through the lens of Islam and national security. This imperial narrative of a war on Islam, or Islamists, ignores the complexities on the ground, of course, and its easy categorizations and convenient slippages must be disentangled, yet as I argue in this book, in some cases targeted groups reproduce the dominant framework embedded in religious and cultural discourse even as they try to challenge it.

This book is based on the premise that racism and surveillance targeting Muslim and Arab American youth did not begin on September 11, 2001, and is not exceptional, but must be situated in the longer, global history of U.S. imperial policies in West and South Asia and in relation to other, domestic processes of criminalization, regulation, and elimination of racialized peoples by the U.S. state. This is a key issue that both mainstream discourse and liberal scholarly analysis ignore, conveniently choosing to situate Islamophobia only in relation to the contemporary War on Terror and debates about national security and civil liberties, thus evading the core imperial nature of the warfare state and the longer history of state regulation and repression of groups defined as "enemy aliens" or "anti-American." Post-9/11 repression extends the imperial state's policies of surveilling and containing radicals or leftist "subversives," especially during wartime and through the Cold War, as well as a history of suppressing Arab American activism that precedes the current War on Terror—what Alain Badiou (2011) calls the "long war against terrorism" (20).

The focus on the "Muslim terrorist" as political enemy did not begin under the Bush regime but has evolved since at least the Iranian revolution of 1978–1979 and the Reagan administration's and U.S. media's focus on the threat of Islamist politics to U.S. power. This occurred even as the U.S. covertly supported the Afghan mujahideen in a proxy war against the USSR and celebrated them as "freedom fighters," underscoring the deeply paradoxical history that is buried beneath the trope of the "jihadist" enemy today. It is important to note that the template for the War on Terror was manufactured in the 1980s to demonize those resisting U.S. hegemony and U.S. allies in the Middle East, particularly Israel, and led to the "suturing of Israel and the U.S. as defenders of 'Western' values against 'Islamic fanaticism'" (Kundnani 2014, 45). So Zionist ideology and the Palestine question have long been a "shadow" in U.S. imperial culture and race matters even if they have not always been acknowledged as constitutive of debates about "liberal freedom and colonial violence" and key to U.S. domestic as well as foreign policies in relation to Arabs, Muslims, and anticolonial resistance, as argued by Keith Feldman (2015, 2). This book recenters the question of Palestine in theorizing the long War on Terror and the politics of solidarity with the Palestinians as a crucial site for the production of an anti-imperial politics.

Empire always works on two fronts, the domestic and the global; the War on Terror is an extension of earlier processes of disciplining and subjugating marginalized and dissenting groups at home while consolidating hegemony overseas (Pease 1993; Rogin 1993). The national consensus for U.S. foreign policies is strengthened through historical processes of scapegoating "outsiders" and conflating internal and external enemies (Stoler 2006, 12), as is only too apparent with the domestic as well as global crackdown on and regulation of Muslim and Arab political movements, not to mention alliances with groups and regimes that serve U.S. strategic interests. The current "state of emergency" affecting Muslims and Arabs in the U.S., the suspension of civil rights and targeting of certain groups by sovereign violence, has also affected other immigrant and minority communities (Benjamin 1988). In other words, this exclusion of certain categories of people—defined according to race, religion, or citizenship—is not exceptional but the norm. This "state of exception" is constitutive of an imperial governmentality that rests on the exclusion of certain groups from citizenship and civil rights at different historical moments (Agamben 2005; Ganguly 2001). Exceptionalism is the rule of empire, and U.S. imperialism has also always established its hegemony by creating new, ambiguous, or "exceptional" categories and designations for territories, peoples, and political activities resisting its rule (Kaplan 2005). This everyday "state of exception" is particularly acute for groups of young people who are labeled as culturally antithetical to Western modernity and liberal democracy, given that youth are always already seen as potentially deviant and threatening to the social order. Thus, political activism among the 9/11 generation is a crucial site for understanding the workings of U.S. imperial statecraft as well as shape-shifting movements of political dissent.

Youth as Enemy

In the current moment, the image of immigrant or minority youth and the specter of "militant" or "fundamentalist" Muslims and Arabs threatening "the American way of life" or European and "Western values" reveals a particular global and racial imaginary about Muslim, Arab, Afghan, Iranian, and South Asian youth. This imaginary is embedded in technologies of nation and empire that use a colonialist logic of projection to invert the threat of imperial invasion and intervention that have destroyed other peoples' ways of life and means of livelihood. This devastation of other societies is justified by a discourse of liberal democracy and individual freedom intertwined with neoliberalist notions of individual autonomy and "choice" embedded in free-market rationalities, a discourse that often targets youth (Ong 2006; Salime 2011). Young people, it is assumed, must choose between the "American way of life" (self-realization through capitalism/consumption) and "anti-Americanism" (self-annihilation through militancy/resistance to "the West"). I argue that we must reframe the debate about Muslim American youth to show that their subjectification is not just in response to Islamophobia but also the battle over neoliberal capitalism, racial violence, and imperial democracy.

The War on Terror is a technology of nation making that produces youth as subjects that must be preserved and protected, as well as monitored, contained, repressed, or removed, if necessary through violence. The specter of Muslim or Arab youth who are inherently anti-American has been used to legitimize policies of surveillance, detention, and deportation that have swept unknown numbers of minors into the dragnet of counterterrorism operations. A few years after 9/11, and particularly after the July 7, 2005, bombings by British Muslims in London, the focus of the domestic War on Terror shifted to "homegrown" terrorism and to ferreting out this fifth column in the U.S., with the deployment of undercover FBI informants recruited to infiltrate mosqued communities and networks of Muslim American youth (see Kumar 2010; Maira 2007). These regimes of surveillance and the mass detentions and deportations of individuals after 9/11, involving the use of secret evidence and predatory prosecution policies, as well as revelations of torture in Guantanamo, extraordinary rendition (transnational abduction), and secret prisons overseas have had a chilling effect on political activism in Muslim and Middle Eastern communities in the U.S., particularly in the early years after 9/11. But the slowly growing outrage about the excesses of the security state, exposed through investigative journalism and alternative media as well as leaks by whistleblowers, was also accompanied by an expansion of political mobilization and dissent, both by targeted communities as well as others challenging the domestic and global regimes of repression and removal.

In the cultural imaginary of the War on Terror, which is an important front for the military offensive waged by the U.S., Islam, gender, and human rights are key tropes. This book discusses questions of women's rights and gay rights as part of the post-9/11 culture wars and the ways these are deployed by dissenting movements. It is indeed the case that there are groups that are opposed to the U.S. state and its policies who are misogynist and homophobic, some of which (but not all) are Muslim or have a pan-Islamic ideology. But as the "green menace" of Islamist movements replaced the Red Scare in justifying U.S. warfare and the curtailment of civil rights in the U.S., the imperial policies of the U.S. have been cast in cultural and racial terms as a war *for* democracy, women's rights, and social and economic freedoms—what Neda Atanoski (2013) aptly calls "postsocialist imperialism" (3).

The post-9/11 culture wars have emerged from the blurring of the Cold War into the global War on Terror and are embedded in U.S. interests in dominating and remaking West Asia (otherwise known as the Middle East) and consolidating the status of the U.S. as the lone superpower since the fall of the Soviet Union in 1989. The postsocialist imperial project replaced the "Communist" with the "terrorist," as a state of permanent war is required to make the world safe for neoliberal capitalism and the penetration of free market rationalities—a state of "democratic peace/war" (Badiou 2011, 39). This is why Arab political activists who were leftist *and* militant, such as Palestinian Marxists, have always been targeted as the enemy of the U.S., as illustrated by the case of the L.A. Eight that extended from 1987 to 2007 and so bridged the Cold War and the War on Terror, as will be discussed later in the book.

What is different about the form of warfare waged by the U.S. today is that the fight against terrorism is a battle against an ambiguously defined enemy that is neither a nation-state nor a specific set of nonstate actors, and its (deliberate) ambiguity allows it to target a shape-shifting constellation of enemies, within and beyond the borders of the United States. The War on Terror, in a sense, *must* be a war on Islam, so that complex questions of national sovereignty and resistance to neoliberal capitalism disappear into the monolithic threat of the Islamist terrorist who "hates our freedom." This is an ongoing war against a racialized enemy and against states or networks that are deemed to be outside the bounds of proper, Western national sovereignty— whether it is the ostensibly "failed" state of Afghanistan or the non-national Al Qaeda—thus legitimizing invasion and occupation by nation-states whose own sovereignty must be defended from terror attacks. Badiou (2011)—like others—has observed that "the very category of war has become considerably obscured . . . these wars are never *declared*. Ancient capitals are bombed (Baghdad, Kabul, Belgrade . . .) without serving notice to anyone that war has been declared on them" (39). New territorial designations are created in geographic spaces, such as "Af-Pak," where the U.S. has used new kinds of warfare (such as unmanned drones) and proxy or secret forces in an ongoing war to defend "civilization" and "democracy" against the forces of barbarism, fundamentalism, and misogyny. The book takes up the question of these imperial cartographies, such as the mapping of "Af-Pak" or "Israel-Palestine," as they produce transnational solidarities and "geographies of liberation" as well as evasions and silences about forgotten wars and repressed imperial histories (Lubin 2014).

Furthermore, in this planetary war, a primary target is the young Muslim, for it is the category of youth that is perceived as being vulnerable to indoctrination and recruitment by Islamist movements and terrorist networks, or to "self-radicalization," as in the case of the Chechen youth charged with the Boston Marathon bombings in 2013. The counterradicalization regime that has emerged in the U.S., as well as in the UK and across Europe, is increasingly preoccupied with Muslim youth culture and with cultural codes that presumably signify "radical dissent" and "youth alienation" from Western liberal democracy (Kundnani 2014, 120). South Asian, Arab, and Afghan American youth politics is thus an important node of the post-9/11 culture wars. At the same time, the Arab revolutions that overthrew U.S.-backed dictatorships and U.S.-friendly economic regimes shocked Western media and audiences with images of young Arab and Muslim activists, male and female, who took to the streets and utilized the cybersphere to struggle for democracy and against the ravages of neoliberal globalization, inspiring young Americans in the Occupy movement who struggled to claim their own public spaces. Yet these images were increasingly fraught with ambivalence as the so-called Arab Spring unfolded and U.S. politicians and pundits cast doubts on the political motivations and democratic possibilities of these popular, revolutionary struggles; the specter of Arab/Muslim youth as identifiable icons of popular democracy dissolved into the image of the fundamentalist and militant once again as new waves of protest, violence, and counterrevolution emerged in Egypt, Bahrain, Libya, Syria, and across the region. The Arab uprisings marked a new phase in the War on Terror, for the revolutionary potential of these mass movements (and later the Gezi Park protests in Turkey) fundamentally challenged the alibi of democracy and human and civil rights used in the U.S.-led War on Terror. They also altered the mainstream discourse about Arab and Muslim youth—if only for a second—by shifting from the paradigm of national security and counterterrorism to tropes of youthful activism and cyberprotest, which had ripple effects on movements here and for the youth described in this book.

"Radical" Politics, Rights-Talk, and New Coalitions

Post-9/11 political engagement for Arab, South Asian, and Afghan American youth, and Muslim American youth more broadly, has been shadowed by the trope of "radicalization" produced by the surveillance-security state. This makes it particularly important to understand what a genuinely *radical* politics might actually look like. Muslim American politics underwent a significant transformation after 9/11 with an increasing push by national Muslim organizations to engage in the "public square" and with U.S. politics. This was generally driven by a rationale for greater participation in liberal democratic citizenship and "civic integration," but also the result of a decision by national Muslim American leaders and organizations that political participation in a non-Muslim state could be reconciled with adherence to Islam (Nimer

2005, 9). New coalitions emerged, as Muslim Americans became engaged in or led civil rights campaigns and antiwar organizing, in addition to forming interfaith coalitions and public affairs groups (Afzal 2015). National Muslim American organizations sprang into action after 9/11, launching campaigns based on civil rights and for mobilizing Muslim American voters, drawing many from the 9/11 generation into this activism.

A shift in leadership occurred after 9/11 from immigrant Muslims and Middle Easterners to second- or third-generation activists who became the public face of some of these organizations, as young Muslim Americans also entered new fields and became lawyers, advocates, and activists. A new generation of Muslim American activists became increasingly involved in mainstream or liberal political movements and in interfaith or multiracial coalitions, as well as in progressive/left alliances and human rights activism. "Muslim" youth in the U.S., however, are still defined as the site of potential political "radicalization," defined as based on Islamist politics and thus extracted by counterterrorism discourse from any associations with left "radicalism" or a politics based on solidarity with other movements or other groups. At such a moment, is it possible for young people from these groups to rethink the meaning of "radical" politics?

Furthermore, it is important not to have a narrow definition of what it means to be "political," which is conventionally tied to electoral politics or to organized political activity, but to explore how politics is expressed in a range of realms, especially for young people and in a climate of political repression where "politics" is viewed with anxiety or suspicion, especially for certain racial and religious groups. If politics is "a deviation from the normal order of things," that has "no proper place nor any natural subjects," as Rancière argues (2010, 35), but in fact, creates new political subjects and challenges the boundary of the "political," then the political expression and mobilization of Arab, South Asian, and Afghan American youth in the post-9/11 era is crucial to consider as a site of doing politics. There is a danger in romanticizing the politics of this generation, or of looking to those who bear the brunt of the state's policing as vanguardist subjects of a "return to politics" in a climate of political stagnation (Rancière 2010). In this book, I demonstrate the radical possibilities as well as the contradictions, absences, and cleavages in the politics of Arab, South Asian, and Afghan American youth. The political dissent of this generation has taken many forms, and has been staged on the terrain of rights—civil, political, economic, religious, cultural, immigrant, and human—as well as in alliance with other movements—antiwar, immigrant rights, anti-imperialist, civil rights, or prison abolition—both in domestic and global arenas. There are paradoxes and fissures within and among these sites of mobilization, and it is these tensions that are explored in the following chapters.

This generation of South Asian, Arab, and Afghan American youth participate in political activism based on rights and identities, as well as issue-based struggles, and that is framed by the nation-state as well as transnational in scope. I found in my research that there are two major axes of political mobilization for these youth that cross ethnic, racial, and national boundaries. One is pan-Islamic, and produced mostly in the context of Muslim student groups and Muslim civil rights organizing that involves ethnically and racially diverse groups of youth. The other form of coalition building is framed around issues of imperialism, war, and occupation spanning Iraq, Afghanistan, Pakistan, and Palestine, and focused on issues of national sovereignty and human rights. The research demonstrated that the Palestine question serves as a unifying hub for various communities, including youth who are neither Arab, South Asian, Afghan, nor Muslim, and is a central node for both forms of mobilization. Some might differentiate between these two kinds of politics as being broadly located either in the realm of faith-based activism or secular left critique, a complex distinction that I discuss in Chapter Two. However, in reality there is a great deal of overlap that blurs the boundaries of what is sometimes easily glossed as "religious" and "secular" activism: many Muslim-identified student activists are deeply engaged in antiwar and anti-imperial politics and solidarity movements and civil rights campaigns often include Muslim, Christian, Hindu, Sikh, or other youth who are religiously identified as well as non-Muslims and atheists. These strands of activism cannot be easily divided between a focus on domestic and global issues, for pan-Islamic solidarity provides the basis for a global justice or "Muslim human rights" framework, particularly focused on Muslim societies, and antiwar and Palestine solidarity groups make linkages to domestic movements focused on racism, policing, incarceration, torture, immigration, or indigeneity. But what became evident in my research is that there are different if intertwined currents of political mobilization and forms of solidarity that have been intensified since 9/11: one that mobilizes the notion of Islam, and another that invokes notions of national self-determination and sovereignty, and that there are sometimes tensions between these axes of protest politics. Yet both of these political currents utilize a rights-based framework and often spill over into each other in interesting and sometimes conflicted ways, as I will demonstrate.

The post-9/11 backlash and the assault on the civil, immigrant, and human rights of Muslim, Arab, Iranian, South Asian, Afghan, and "Muslim-looking" people in the U.S. and elsewhere has led to the emergence of new, interracial coalitions and shifting racial formations. The recodification of race, or the intensified codification of the racialization of Muslimness and Arabness, has compelled a turn to the language of antiracism and also generated new forms of solidarity that are cross-racial, interfaith, and transnational. As U.S. nationalism has become multicultural, if not "postracial," and invested in a liberal religious pluralism, Islam has been inserted into the contemporary culture wars over race, religion, and national identity. Islamophobia continues to be manifested in virulent forms, a decade after the 9/11 attacks, and at the same time, there is a growing, and increasingly institutionalized, attempt to carve out a place for an "American Islam" and for the incorporation of Muslim Americans into the national citizenry (for example, see Abdullah 2013). My research reveals that this effort sometimes happens in ways that authorize a "Muslim American" identity that is compatible with liberal multiculturalism and neoliberal democracy, if performed by the "good" Muslim subject—who is virtuous, productive, and peace loving—as distinguished from the "bad" Muslim—who is anti-American and "radical" in opposition to the U.S. War on Terror, as I discuss in Chapter One.

Against the backdrop of this incorporability of "good" Muslim subjects and regulation of "proper" Muslim and Arab American politics, the book explores how the political imaginaries and mobilization of Arab, South Asian, and Afghan American youth in Silicon Valley cross ethnic, racial, national, and religious boundaries. I am interested here in examining the production by youth of what some might call counterpublic spheres, and the formation of identities that are intertwined with the consumption and production of religious, racial, and national difference but also of political dissent. The problem is that it has become increasingly difficult for young people targeted for surveillance, suspicion, and profiling to constitute what might look like a "public" in the post-9/11 era, let alone what could be called a "counterpublic," which raises the question of how useful this terminology is for understanding political dissent. Studies of progressive political culture and organizing, such as Cynthia Young's (2006, 146–147) work on Third Worldist, anti-imperialist formations, demonstrate how radical publics are constituted through "ideological and political work" that defines their object of activism, for example, "resistance to violence," against the grain of dominant political thinking. My research explores the various objects of activism, such as civil rights and human rights, produced in and imagined by the political spheres in which South Asian, Arab, and Afghan American participate in Silicon Valley. In some cases, these counter what Antonio Gramsci (2000) called the "common sense" of the dominant ideology but there are also instances in which these movements end up drawing on commonsensical notions of inclusion or recognition; there are active internal debates and conflicts about whether a truly radical politics that exceeds the terms set by the multicultural, liberal state is possible and effective (Reddy 2011). There is an urgency to the deployment of "rights" for these young people, whether civil rights or human rights, but there is also a cost to defining these as the object of their activism as they struggle to stake out a politics in the "public" sphere and in alliance with various counterpublics (Young 2006, 13). These are some of the key tensions that emerged in this ethnographic study of youth activism in Silicon Valley.

There are two major questions on which this book pivots and that provide a thread linking its chapters. The first is whether rights-based politics can constitute a genuinely subversive or oppositional politics when human rights, women's rights, and gay rights have been used as an alibi for U.S. military interventions in Iraq, Afghanistan, and Pakistan, and U.S. support for the Israeli military occupation in Palestine. Do civil rights coalitions and human rights campaigns opposing the War on Terror and the assault on civil liberties constitute an *alternative* or *arrested politics*? The research explores the possibilities, pitfalls, and contradictions of using rights-talk at a moment when the vocabulary of rights, and of democracy, has been used to justify imperial interventions as humanitarian projects, such as the U.S. invasions and occupations of Iraq and Afghanistan and drone warfare in Pakistan.

Second, the research also examines the nature of political solidarity and cross-racial alliances, in a moment when U.S. nationalism is understood as not just multicultural but also postracial, particularly since the election of the first African American president. Is it possible for cross-racial solidarity to become anti-imperial when the liberal, multicultural state seems to have so successfully co-opted movements challenging the state through a framework of political recognition and cultural and legal inclusion? What kinds of political community are constituted by youth in these new coalitions, and what are the possibilities and also costs of particular alliances? How does the politics of gender shape the mobilization of these young men and women in a moment when Islam, gender, sexuality, and race are deeply conjoined in the contemporary culture wars? How does the class politics of Silicon Valley shape notions of activism and coalition building?

Questions of rights-based activism and cross-racial alliances, and the ways they are shaped by the politics of neoliberal democracy, national sovereignty, and imperial humanitarianism have not been fully addressed in the context of the regulation, classification, and surveillance of Muslim and Arab American youth. I am interested in thinking through the contradictions of neoliberal democracy and liberal rights as they contain resistance by the 9/11 generation. The tension between liberal multiculturalism and U.S. imperialism is one that

I explore in relation to Arab, South Asian, and Afghan American youth, in the context of the accommodation of "good" Muslim subjects and containment of "bad" Muslims in the U.S. and the use of humanitarian discourse to rationalize warfare to save lives considered worth rescuing overseas. These are questions that need much more exploration in discussions of Muslim and Arab American youth, or indeed Muslim and Arab Americans in general, and there is much that research in this area could contribute to theoretical debates about neoliberal multiculturalism and rights-talk. These debates, I would argue, are being staged most centrally in communities currently targeted by the politics of securitization and humanitarianism, yet they have not been fully explored.

Resistance to the post-9/11 backlash generated an important political as well as discursive question: how to define the population that was primarily targeted by the War on Terror? Given the range of groups that were targeted in the post-9/11 backlash, it was virtually impossible to name a single category for political mobilization that could encompass Muslims as well as non-Muslims, Arabs and non-Arabs, Middle Easterners and non–Middle Easterners. Coalitional categories such as Arab, Muslim, and South Asian (AMSA), Middle Eastern, Arab, Muslim, and South Asian (MASA), and other acronyms have been coined by activists in civil and immigrant rights and antiwar movements to index solidarity among communities who increasingly experienced similar processes of disciplining, exclusion, and violence in the aftermath of 9/11. These axes of identification have taken hold largely in the context of political activism and index a certain racial politics in the context of faith-based as well non-faith-based activism, but are not common in everyday parlance or even within these communities. For example, feminist and queer coalitions created the category SWANA (South West Asian and North African) (Naber 2008, 8). The rather unwieldy acronym AMEMSA, or Arab, Middle Eastern, Muslim, and South Asian, was introduced by community organizers in the Bay Area around 2003 and has since then been used by civil and immigrant rights groups across the U.S. as well as community foundations such as the Silicon Valley Community Foundation, which supports interfaith projects through its FAITHS program.[1] These labels were an uneasy conjoining of both religious and ethnic/national categories and are also often problematic in their exclusionary inclusion: Iranians were generally subsumed under the category of Muslims or Middle Easterners; Central Asians and groups who are neither Arab nor Muslim but who are from the geographic region of West Asia fell between the cracks; Afghans disappeared between the boundaries of Central and South Asia; and the label "Muslim" was generally used to encompass those of Muslim background but who may not identify as such.

Much discussion has focused on whether these new pan-ethnic labels represent a new racial categorization and how Muslimness itself has been re-racialized in the post-9/11 era (Rana 2011). Racial thinking is at work in the production, suppression, and suspicion of Muslim identity, which is associated with racialized markers (most obviously, "the Muslim terrorist" but also the "oppressed Muslim woman"); "the Muslim" is considered an exemplary Other in the American nation, defined as (Judeo-)Christian (Esposito 2011). The racialization of Muslim Americans, it must be noted, overlaps with that of Arabs, South Asians, and Central Asians, not to mention African Americans (who constitute one third of the Muslim American population), and so their othering is deeply intertwined with images of the immigrant, the militant, the uncivilized, and the Blackamerican, to use Sherman Jackson's (2011) terminology, variously straddling the divide of American/un-American or "anti-American." Racial thinking is at work in both the repression *and* resistance of Arab, South Asian, Iranian, and Afghan American communities and movements, and it is intertwined with a politics of gender, sexuality, and class in complex ways, as I will explore in the following chapters.

However, while liberal and progressive activists often focused on the question of post-9/11 racial and religious profiling, and faith-based activists challenged an intensified and virulent Islamophobia and the right-wing war on Islam, it was sometimes more difficult—at least in the first few years after 9/11—to acknowledge that it was *political profiling* that was also at work in the imperial surveillance state. One of the interventions this book makes is to critique the turn to a liberal, nation-based framework of civil rights that sidesteps more difficult questions of U.S. nationalism, sovereignty, and hegemony. This liberal nationalist variant of civil rights elides the role of U.S. foreign policy in the Middle East and South Asia and counterterrorism policies that drive much of the suspicion and scrutiny directed against Muslim, Arab South Asian, and Afghan American youth in the post-9/11 homeland security regime. The book also reflects on the contradictions of utilizing the language of human rights and the difficulties of invoking a critical human rights discourse for segments of humanity in war zones such as Afghanistan, Pakistan, or Palestine.

Going beyond the existing liberal framework of Islamophobia, then, the book proceeds from the premise that there are various wars that are being fought since 9/11—a war against terrorism legitimized by Islamophobic discourse, and an increasingly liberal offensive under the Obama regime that targets "Muslim extremists" but aims to incorporate other Muslim subjects; a war on migrant populations who are key to the neoliberal economy but remain in a state of precarity; a war on the poor and working poor who are the detritus of global capitalism; a war on racialized and insurgent movements, from Occupy to Palestine solidarity activists, who are surveilled, entrapped, and incarcerated; and a war on the planet itself whose resources are ravaged for the benefit of the 1%.

I come to this research as someone who is concerned about and personally and politically invested in challenging all of these wars, and troubled by the metaphor of "war" itself, and as someone who grew up and has lived in parts of the world targeted by the war machine and in militarized zones. My time in India, and later in Pakistan and Palestine, as well as my years in the U.S., have allowed me to engage with various movements that resist war, occupation, surveillance, and racialized annihilation and displacement. It is my own experiences as both "insider" and "outsider" to these issues that has in many ways led me to think seriously about the limits and potential of resistance by those whose bodies are marked as disposable or kept alive to embody an ever lurking threat.

Youth and Exceptionalisms

By now, there is a generation of youth for whom the events of September 11, 2001, were a formative experience and one that marked the beginning, rather than a rupture, of the development of their political subjectivity in adolescence. For the 9/11 generation who were in high school in 2001, the attacks of September 11 are not too distant to be recollected and represent a dramatic historical event that made a dent on their early political consciousness. The historical and political worldview of this generation has emerged in the post-9/11 landscape: the era of the Bush-Cheney neoconservative regime, the PATRIOT Act and its reauthorizations, the invasion of Afghanistan and the occupation of Iraq, the revelations of torture at Abu Ghraib and Guantanamo, the election of Barack Obama, the covert and drone warfare in Pakistan, the U.S.-backed wars on Gaza, the ongoing surveillance of Muslim Americans, and the repression of political dissent—not to mention the economic insecurities of the recession years. It should also be noted that the Muslim American population is a particularly youthful one, compared to other religious groups in the U.S.; it is estimated that more than a third of Muslim Americans are young adults between the ages of eighteen and twenty-nine (the proportion of this cohort in the U.S. population at large is 18% and among Protestant Americans, only 9%) (Gallup 2009, 22.).

The label "9/11 generation" emerges from a periodization that links generational categories with historical events and also with a particular notion of social and political development. Adolescence and young adulthood is considered a critical time for the development of political commitments—in part because of the imagining of this period as a formative stage for identity, particularly in Western developmental psychology, and in part due to the empirical realities of cognitive and psychosocial development at a time when individuals are generally in transition to full-time employment, marriage, and establishing their own households. Political thinking is a process that begins early in life, but for youth who could be considered "college age," between seventeen and twenty-three years old, this is a period that has traditionally been conceptualized as a crucial time for testing political commitments and exploring social identities. It is also a time when many youth are in college and have the opportunity to engage in political mobilization or with larger collectives beyond their families or communities. But thinking about the War on Terror through the lens of "youth" also allows for a critique of a deeper set of questions, such as, why is the category of youth so central to defining the threat to national security or Western imperial modernity?

The answer to this lies partly in the view that youth are viewed as key to movements for social change, not just in the U.S. but in many cultural contexts, and simultaneously viewed as incomplete subjects of nationhood or citizenship. The imagining of youth as a site that is simultaneously threatening and hopeful, or deviant and liberating, is fundamentally tied to the conceptualization of youth as a transition between "childhood" and "adulthood." American and European notions of adolescence and psychological theories of stage-based development have produced an association of youth with liminality and identity crisis (Erikson 1968). This notion of in-betweenness and instability is at the heart of the ambivalence with which youth are often associated and the exceptionalism that sometimes overdetermines this category. Youth are assumed to fall between the cracks of "innocent" childhood and "stable" adulthood, dangerously outside of normative social structures and always teetering on the brink of revolt. The romanticization of young people as rebellious agents of social change is the other side of the fear of that very change—the association of youth with not just identity crisis but also social crisis (Lesko 2001; Maira and Soep 2004). This dialectic underlies what scholars of youth studies have critiqued as moral panics about youth, which express a deeper anxiety about threats to the status quo (Cohen 1997).

For Muslim, Arab, Afghan, or South Asian youth, there is another layer of social anxiety and ambivalence that they must confront: the fear that they potentially pose a threat to the U.S. state, Western civilization, and secular liberal democracy, and so must be surveilled, contained, regulated, and also studied, analyzed, and documented by scholars and policy makers. Young people from immigrant communities are often suspected of harboring "divided" national allegiances or being "improper" national subjects. Muslim American and second-generation youth from immigrant communities thus experience a double, if not triple, layer of exceptionalism: as youth, as Muslim, *and* as diasporic. How, then, can one speak of the political concerns or aspirations of this particular group of young people outside of the framework of the security state? This book offers an account of the lived and diverse experiences of South Asian, Arab, and Afghan American youth in the post-9/11 era, and of their political struggles and nuanced critiques as well as of the repression, surveillance, and censorship they face on a daily basis. In addition, it is important to consider how Muslim youth engage in both formal as well as informal politics, participating in public activism as well as in everyday forms of "quiet encroachment" in their daily lives, in ways that may be dispersed and unorganized, but that nonetheless pose a challenge to repressive governmentalities, as argued by Asef Bayat (2013, 46). These ordinary and fluid practices by large numbers of people "establish new norms" and interrupt the dichotomies of "active/passive," "individual/collective," and "civil/political" resistance, an approach that is very relevant to young people for whom spectacular protest and easily identifiable collectives may be risky (Bayat 2013, 28); it is this broader perspective on youth politics that I use in my analysis.

This book discusses the politics of Muslim American youth through a critical lens that has not always been used in existing research, which has tended to focus largely on issues of religious identity and the impact of Islamophobia on Muslim American youth within a narrow framework. Sadia Abbas (2014, 2, 4, 5) offers a trenchant critique of the ways in which Muslims are "repeatedly figured as constituted by injury" and representations of "the injured Muslim, the militant, and the pious woman" dominate what she calls an "economy of collaboration and treachery" as well as research in the Western academy. The studies of Muslim American youth that have proliferated since 9/11 have emerged, in general, from a position of solidarity but not always from a position of critique, and in my view this approach has lacked a complex analysis, often reinscribing a liberal framework for analyzing Islamophobia that stops short of grappling with the politics of imperialism, neoliberal multiculturalism, faith-based inclusion, and national sovereignty. This gap in current frameworks in U.S. academic discourse arises, in part, from a reluctance to interrogate the production of the category of "the Muslim" itself. In some cases, it seems, studies are unable to move beyond the core paradigm of the "war on Islam" by expanding the focus to include categories other than that of "Muslim" or "Muslim American," on the one hand, and to consider the complex and painful contradictions of the U.S. state's historical relationship to Muslim and Arab American communities and Islamist movements, on the other. The sensitivity to Islamophobia among liberal and progressive intellectuals has led to a conjuncture in which a postcolonial, left, feminist secular critique has also been arrested, recreating simplistic binaries of secularity and religion and reductively defining "the Muslim" as inherently and always antisecular, thus creating new lacunae in scholarship. The arrested politics on the ground is paralleled by an arrested critique, a condition that we need to confront as it has serious implications for our theorizing as well as resistance.

For one, the Arab American community includes Muslims as well as non-Muslims and those who identify as secular or atheist, as does the South Asian and Afghan American community, and so subsuming all of these groups under the label "Muslim" or "Muslim American" can be problematic. In fact, much of the research in the new field of Muslim American/American Muslim studies does not acknowledge or examine this complexity, generating the image of a community that has an internal diversity in sectarian affiliations and practices of Islam but that is always and already uniformly identified with Islam (with some exceptions, see Afzal 2015; Mir 2014). In this, furthermore, there is an odd mirroring of the very framework used by the state in the discourse of the War on Terror—if with a more liberal and progressive orientation—that relies solely on the lens of Islam to define Middle Eastern and Muslim communities and evades discussion of those whose lives and identities are not entirely or primarily defined by faith, or who represent a "dissensus" that troubles taken-for-granted assumptions about Muslim Americans (Rancière 2010). Who represents and who gets to speak *on behalf of* Muslim, Arab, South Asian, and Afghan Americans? These are complex and charged issues, surely, given the climate of Islamophobia and the state's assaults on Muslim American communities, and the sense of siege within these communities can lead to a defensive or apologetic position as is the case with many other issues and groups. But a liberal approach that remains uncritical of ontological assumptions about the category "Muslim" or of actually existing politics is intellectually limiting and it simply does not go far enough to challenge the state's policies as well as homogenizing identity politics and internal orthodoxies.

This book, I want to emphasize at the outset, is not a book about Islam nor just about "Muslim Americans"; neither is it about the Islamic practices or religious life of youth. Many other works have addressed these topics (for example, Afzal 2015; Garrod and Kilkenny 2014; Hammer and Safi 2013; Mir 2014; Muhammad-Arif 2002) but in my view, less attention has been paid to political activism by young people from Muslim and Arab American communities, and they ways they move between spaces defined by religion, ethnicity, and nationalism, or between racial and class politics. I am interested here in the attempt by the 9/11 generation to craft alliances between religious and ethnic/racial communities, between different forms of mobilization against the imperial and racial violence of the U.S. state, and the implications this has for an anti-imperialist politics and the politics of liberal inclusion. The sections that follow provide some historical and social context for the ethnographic research on South Asian, Arab, and Afghan American youth in Silicon Valley.

South Asian, Arab, and Afghan American Communities in Silicon Valley

This research focuses on three groups of youth—Afghan, South Asian (in this case, Pakistani and Indian), and Arab (Iraqi, Lebanese, Egyptian, Libyan, and Palestinian, among other nationalities)—both Muslim and non-Muslim, in Silicon Valley.[2] There are no published studies on Arab Americans in Silicon Valley and negligible research on Pakistani Americans and (even more so) Afghan Americans, both groups that tend to slip between the arbitrary geographic and cultural boundaries demarcating West, Central, and South Asia, and that are variously included in "the Middle East" and "the Muslim world" in U.S. mainstream and academic discourse. While I also interviewed some Indian Muslim American youth, my interviews with South Asians were largely focused on Pakistani American youth to fill this glaring gap in the research, and because of the massive media attention given to and state scrutiny of Pakistan, Pakistanis, and Pakistani Americans in the War on Terror. The politics of South Asian, Arab, and Afghan American communities in Silicon Valley are complex and intertwined with the particular immigrant and refugee histories of the diverse groups that make up each of these communities, which are not a monolithic block but highly differentiated.

The South Asian community in the South Bay, as the region where Silicon Valley is located is called, is largely comprised of Indian and Pakistani immigrants, with very few Bangladeshis, and even fewer Sri Lankans. Most of these immigrants came to California after the Immigration Act of 1965, which introduced visa categories promoting the influx of highly educated, technically skilled immigrants to work in technology as well as in other industries. But the migration of South Asian immigrants, particularly from what is now Pakistan and north India, to the larger region of northern California began much earlier, in the first decades of the twentieth century, when male migrants from the Punjab, in particular, came to work in agricultural labor in the Sacramento Valley and to a lesser extent, to study at UC Berkeley and other universities (Prashad 2000; Shah 2012). These labor migrants (who were Sikh, Hindu, and Muslim) worked on farms and railroads and formed communities that later expanded in towns such as Fresno, Stockton, and Lodi and established religious institutions such as the Muslim Association of America, founded by Pakistani immigrants in Sacramento as early as 1920 (Khan 1981). These South Asian migrants were also engaged in radical political movements, such as the anti-imperialist, transnational Ghadar movement that mobilized against British colonialism and forged alliances with other leftists on the West Coast (Prashad 2000; Ramnath 2011). However, the communities formed by these early migrants remain largely distinct from the later migration streams to the Silicon Valley after 1965, although these newer waves included Punjabi (Pakistani and Indian) migrants who were similarly a mix of Muslim, Sikh, and Hindu. The post-1965 immigrants are heterogeneous in terms of class, as mentioned earlier, including both highly educated professionals and scientists as well as technical workers on H-1B visas and others employed in the taxi industry, small businesses, and factories.

The Arab American community in northern California is a historic and diverse one, consisting mainly of Egyptians, Lebanese, Palestinians, Iraqis, Syrians, Yemenis, and Jordanians. Some of these families have lived in the Bay Area for three generations, since the early 1900s, and migrated from what was known as Greater Syria (now Lebanon, Syria, Jordan, and Palestine) at the time (Naff 1985; Sifri 1984). Political upheaval in the Arab region in the 1950s and 1960s fueled much of the migration to the U.S. and early migrants and refugees were mainly peddlers, merchants, or agricultural and blue-collar workers (Sifri 1984, 81). Some Arab immigrants worked in fruit and vegetable farms with South Asian laborers, for example, in Stockton and Fresno; Yemeni migrants who left due to political turmoil in Yemen worked in the Delano area and became involved in organizing with Chicanos in the United Farm Workers (UFW) (Friedlander 1994; Sifri 1984, 83, 85). Eventually some of these Arab immigrants opened grocery and convenience stores in towns such as Bakersfield, Stockton, Merced, and Oakland; the legacy of their early labor activism lives on in a union hall in San Francisco named after Nagi Daifullah, a Yemeni worker active with the UFW who was killed by a California sheriff (Friedlander 1994, 431–433; Malek 2009, 69). Arab immigration to the Bay Area increased with the displacement of Palestinian refugees in 1948, when Israel was established, and after the 1967 Arab-Israeli war as well as the Immigration Act of 1965. In the 1960s and 1970s, Arab immigrants in the Bay Area were largely Christian (and had established Orthodox, Maronite, and Melkite churches), but there was an expansion of Muslim Arab immigration beginning in the 1980s, including from North Africa and the Gulf states, leading to the growth of Muslim community institutions and coinciding with the "Islamic resurgence" in the Arab and Muslim region (Naber 2012, 114–116).

According to Vic Zikoor, an Iraqi American engineer who came to the U.S. in the late 1970s and lives in the South Bay, where he was vice president of the Arab American Cultural Center (AACC) at the time, most Arab immigrants arrived in Silicon Valley in the 1960s and 1970s; many, particularly those who were refugees such as Iraqis, had professional backgrounds but were relatively lacking in economic or social capital and so some worked in gas stations or opened small businesses, as is true of other Arab immigrants in the area. Many Iraqi refugees who have been coming to San Francisco since the first Gulf War, as well as Yemeni immigrants, live in the Tenderloin, a racially mixed, working-class and working-poor neighborhood in San Francisco. As Arab immigrants, some of whom had owned grocery or liquor stores in the city, became more affluent they moved into what is known as "the peninsula" south of San Francisco, settling in towns such as San Mateo, Redwood City, Burlingame, Milbrae, and Daly City (Naber 2012, 44). More recently arrived Arab and South Asian immigrants who work in low-wage jobs—as taxi drivers, janitors, or restaurant workers—as well as small business owners and their families generally live in San Francisco; there are also pockets of working- to middle-class Arab, South Asian, and Afghan immigrants in towns in the East Bay and South Bay such as Alameda, Emeryville, Sunnyvale, Union City, and Newark. There is a great deal of crisscrossing between these towns and cities in the larger Bay Area, with youth as well as adults commuting for work, education, entertainment, and social life, so Silicon Valley is embedded in the cultural geography of what is called "the Bay."

The Afghan American community does not have much of a presence in Silicon Valley but is centered in the adjacent towns of Fremont and Hayward to the north—which are home to the largest Afghan community outside Afghanistan (Omidian and Lipson 1996). The Afghan community consists mainly of refugees, who constitute one of the largest refugee populations in the world, and who are less affluent and less highly educated than South Asian and Arab Americans in the Bay Area; Afghans came in two waves, one after the Soviet invasion of Afghanistan in 1979 and the second after the rise of the Taliban in the 1990s.[3] The community includes "the formerly wealthy and highly educated urban elite" as well as those described as "less educated" and more socially conservative (Omidian and Lipson 1996, 355). Ali Mardanzai, the director of the Afghan and International Refugee Services center in Hayward and a refugee from Kabul, said that the reason that many Afghans initially flocked to Hayward in the 1980s and later to Fremont was because the cost of living there was relatively low at the time, there were already two mosques established, and the Hayward Unified School District received a grant to teach Farsi and Pashto (as well as Hindi/Urdu and Arabic). All of these factors were appealing to the newly arrived refugees, many of whom lived in what came to be known as the "Afghan Village," an apartment complex in Hayward, and formed a burgeoning community in nearby cities that drew other Afghans from all over the United States. The director of the Afghan Coalition—a community organization in Fremont—Rona Popal, also observed that since Afghan refugees came to the U.S. with "very little money or nothing at all," they settled in towns where there was low-income housing and social services that offered some support, including Union City and Alameda.

Estimates of the Afghan population in Fremont and Hayward vary widely—the Census actually counted only 3,421 Afghans in Fremont in 2010, clearly an underestimate (and not unusual for immigrant or refugee communities, where many are undocumented or simply wary of data collection). Mardanzai estimated that there were 8,000–10,000 Afghans in Fremont and 1,500 families in Hayward in 2008, while Popal estimated that there were 15,000 Afghans in Fremont. As housing costs increased in Fremont and Hayward during the boom years of the 1990s, Afghans moved out to Alameda and Livermore in the East Bay, where Section 8 housing became available. Afghan Americans were also hit hard by the subprime mortgage crisis in the late 2000s, which affected both those employed in the real estate sector and home owners, and some ended up moving out of Fremont and Hayward to towns in the Central Valley such as Tracy, Stockton, Modesto, and Antioch.

The growth of the Afghan enclave in Fremont/Hayward has not been without resistance in this presumably "liberal" area, according to Anu Natarajan, an Indian American city council member in Fremont. For example, she recalled the campaign to name a section of Fremont where there is a cluster of Afghan businesses, in the neighborhood of Centerville, as "Little Kabul" and commented that the proposal was met with a "push back" from white residents. This incident is linked to the racial tensions that have surfaced over the years between whites and the expanding Asian American population in the area. There has been controversy over the presumed "new white flight" from Fremont, centered in part on nationally recognized public high schools such as Mission San Jose, which in 2007 had an Asian American student population of 77% while the white student population apparently declined by 61% between 1995 and 2005 (Gokhale 2007). There appeared to be a dramatic rejection by white students and families of this predominantly Asian American high school, whose highly competitive image has been at the center of a debate with racialized undertones fueled by concerns about model minority youth. However, this was situated by some local residents and school officials in the context of the real-estate boom in this period, when many white residents sold their homes and moved out as Asian immigrant communities, mainly Indian and Chinese, were moving in and expanding in size (Gokhale 2007). So interracial and cross-ethnic relations in this area are complex and layered with struggles over class, race, education, and immigration that emerge from the economic context of employment and housing.

These structural and historical contexts need to be considered in understanding local racial economies and interethnic affiliations. South Asian, Afghan, and Arab American youth from this area grow up interacting in a variety of ways with other youth of color, Latino/as, Asian Americans, and, to a much lesser extent, African Americans, who are a small minority—forging cross-racial alliances and negotiating tensions embedded in historical and material contexts. For example, in Fremont and Hayward, as well as Union City, Afghan American youth have grown up with Latinos, and as a few older Afghan Americans from Hayward told me, they often pass as or identify with Latino/as but also find themselves in engaged in turf battles with Latino/a youth. One Afghan American graduate of California State University East Bay (CSUEB) in Hayward, who was president of the Afghan Student Association while at Chabot College, commented that Afghan youth in Fremont created a "gang," A.L.T.—whose full name translates as "Wild Afghan Tribe"—in response to Latino/a gangs. This also seemed to be an effort to mark themselves as distinct from Latino/a youth, their proximate ethnic/immigrant group. Young South Asian, Afghan, and Arab Americans attend the same high schools, or in some cases the same Islamic schools, and are involved in creating and developing Muslim and Middle Eastern groups and engaging in political mobilization together when they go to college. The relationships between various immigrant and racial groups in this area are complex and often fraught and the context for cross-ethnic solidarity and coalition building, either before or after 9/11, should not be idealized.

Furthermore, youth activism needs to be considered in the context of the increasingly visible and organized Muslim American community in Silicon Valley that has grown since the 1980s, when there was a spurt of Muslim immigration to the Bay Area.[4] In 2013, 30% of Muslims were South Asian, 23% were Arab, 17% Afghans, and 9% African American in the Bay Area's six counties, including Santa Clara County, where San Jose is located, and Alameda County, where Fremont and Hayward are located (Senzai and Bazian 2013). The Muslim immigrant professionals who came to work in Silicon Valley had the economic resources to establish Muslim community institutions, including mosques. There was a "mosque movement" in the 1990s in the Bay Area, including in the San Jose area, led by South Asian, especially Pakistani, and Arab Muslim professionals who had migrated to the U.S. after 1965, and less so by Afghan Americans, who as noted earlier, were generally less affluent and established their own mosques in Hayward and Fremont. Silicon Valley is home to the Muslim Community Association (MCA) and Granada Islamic School in Santa Clara, which draws a large, ethnically diverse (Sunni) Muslim population from the region, in addition to the oldest mosque founded in the Bay Area by Muslim immigrants, the South Bay Islamic Association (SBIA), established in 1974 in San Jose, as well as a Shia mosque. MCA serves as a central meeting point for Arab Muslim families, in particular, and also Pakistani Americans, and many Arab and South Asian American youth I spoke to had attended Granada. In 1996, the Zaytuna Institute for Islamic Education was established in Hayward; it later moved to Berkeley, where it launched an Islamic college which is nationally renowned. Major Muslim civil rights and advocacy organizations were also established in the area, such as the first chapter of the Council on American-Islamic Relations (CAIR), and the Islamic Networks Group, which was established in 1993 in San Jose, in part to counter the intensified Islamophobia surrounding the first Gulf War. Silicon Valley is home to prominent Muslim religious and advocacy institutions that have provided a social and political context for the activism that has emerged in the 9/11 generation.

There are also many nonreligious national or pan-ethnic organizations such as the AACC in San Jose, the Afghan Coalition in Fremont, the multimillion-dollar India Community Center in Milpitas—the largest of its kind in North America—and the newer Pakistani American Culture Center, also in Milpitas, that organize cultural and social events or provide community services, in addition to many other social and professional organizations in the South Bay (Vaidhyanathan 2007). San Jose is also home to a Sikh gurudwara (temple), which has organized community outreach events, particularly after 9/11. Sikhs were brutally and lethally targeted in racial violence because they were mistaken for Arabs and Muslims but also due to a rising tide of xenophobia; Sikhs continue to be targeted in northern California and across the U.S., so interfaith and civil rights coalitions have sometimes included Sikhs as well as Muslims, as I will discuss later.

This book is an attempt to look at one slice of the story of these communities in the post-9/11 era, at a moment when notions of "success" or "arrival" collided with a much more fraught narrative of exclusion and experiences of racial and Islamophobic discrimination and violence that troubled the notion of model minorityhood. In a region where a liberal discourse of multiculturalism and "diversity" has often attempted to mask or contain struggles over race and class, this research sheds light on the experiences of immigrant and refugee communities that are both affluent and established, and also struggling and precarious, through the lens of youth.

The Study

This ethnographic study is based on field work in 2007–2011 in Silicon Valley and Fremont/Hayward in northern California. It focuses on college-age Arab, South Asian, and Afghan American youth, between eighteen and twenty-three years old, who came of age in the post-9/11 era and who live in the greater San Jose area and in Fremont/Hayward. The study uses interviews and participant-observation to offer insights into how a "political" community was mobilized by specific groups of youth in the post-9/11 moment in response to various aspects of the War on Terror. It examines how the micropolitics of specific regional and social contexts can illuminate larger structural processes in order to shed light on questions of state power in a particular historical moment, and as such it is a local case study, not a generalizable report about Muslim American youth or South Asian, Arab, and Afghan American communities at large. In my previous work on the impact of 9/11 on Muslim American youth (Maira 2009), I focused on a group of immigrant high school students in New England, who belonged to a very small, working- to middle-class, recently arrived South Asian immigrant community in a predominantly white city. That ethnographic study explored how they expressed their political subjectivity outside of organized politics, in ways that were shaped by their sense of vulnerability and of being relatively new to the U.S.

This research in California was an opportunity to think about post-9/11 politics not just in a different regional context, but also among a group of young people who were slightly older and mostly in college (and thus could be considered young adults), were U.S. citizens and were born or had lived for several years in the country, and were largely middle to upper-middle class. Nearly all participated in some kind of ethnic or religious group on or off campus, and many were involved in organized activism; I discuss how they engage in "ordinary" politics, as well. I focused primarily on Muslim American youth in this research, given the intensified scrutiny of Muslims in the post-9/11 era, but I also interviewed non-Muslim Arab Americans and Indian Americans as well as older activists from these communities of various religious and national backgrounds, including with secular orientations, in order to understand a range of political views and experiences. I should note that in

the book I use "Muslim American" in instances when I am referring specifically to Muslim American youth and communities and ethnic/national labels
when I am denoting a larger category not specifically restricted to Muslims or
Muslim Americans; this may seem obvious, but given the common conflation
of Muslim with Arab, and the invisibility of Arab Christians, I think this is
important to acknowledge.

This ethnography is also to some extent a comparative study, as it explores
the experiences of three different groups with unique class and immigration
trajectories and distinct historical experiences. I do not do justice to these par-
ticularities within the scope of this book, as each group's experiences merits a
detailed study of its own. However, it is apparent that young people brought
to political debates and organizing their specific histories and cultural and
political connections to other places as well as overlapping concerns, idioms,
and imaginaries. I draw on the stories of these youth as important interlocu-
tors in producing this political analysis, although their critiques may be expressed in a different idiom, and put them into conversation with the debates
in the scholarly literature.

For this research, I interviewed thirty-nine college-age youth (twenty-
three females, sixteen males) who were South Asian (Pakistani and Indian),
Arab, and Afghan American.[5] I also did interviews with about twenty community activists, religious leaders, and youth organizers from these communities, of various ages, in addition to numerous informal conversations with
people from or engaged in work with South Asian, Arab, Afghan, and Muslim
American communities.[6] I attended several community and political events
and visited different community and religious organizations in Silicon Valley
and Fremont/Hayward. During this period as well as for some years before
and after, I myself have been involved in civil, human rights, and antiwar
campaigns related to these communities, particularly between 2003, when
I first moved to the East Bay, and 2005; this was a period when the antiwar movement in the Bay Area was still energized and cross-racial coalitions
focused on post-9/11 civil and immigrant rights issues, not to mention the
Palestine solidarity movement, were very active. The major questions in the
research were thus propelled by my own observations of the challenges, contradictions, and possibilities of the movements in which I was involved, both
peripherally and in a sustained way. I also came to realize that Silicon Valley
was a very different political and cultural terrain for organizing than that of
the metropolitan Bay Area (particularly San Francisco/Berkeley/Oakland).
This research is very much a politically committed project, one that I hope
will be part of an ongoing conversation between scholars and those outside of
the academy, between young activists and students and an older generation,

and between people who find themselves on the same side of the barricade, so to speak, in opposition to perpetual war, ongoing racism, and economic evisceration.

In fact, this study emerged from the many conversations that I had since 2003 with South Asian, Arab, and Afghan American students at UC Davis, many of whom took my courses on Asian and Arab American youth or who came to my office hours to consult with me about student activism or simply share their experiences of growing up in the post-9/11 era. I soon realized that many of these youth were from the South Bay and hung out together, organized together, and had grown up together in Silicon Valley or Fremont/ Hayward. It was apparent that their sense of cross-ethnic affinity was embedded in a sense of cultural and religious affiliation and also, in some cases, in feelings of political solidarity across national and ethnic boundaries. When I embarked on this research, I worked with several undergraduate students from UC Davis who were enthusiastic and able research assistants, and I found myself in the enviable position of being approached by students on a regular basis who wanted to help with the project. Some of them were deeply involved in the social networks of youth from the areas I was studying, while others felt they were on the margins of these circles and hoped the research would help them better understand their own liminal relationship to their "community." It was clear that these youth had deep investments in this research, and felt it was meaningful to them, which only underscored for me the significance of questions of political identification and cross-ethnic solidarity for this generation.

Perhaps one of the most interesting aspects of the research process was a pattern where I or one of my research assistants would interview someone for the study, and she (it was always young women who responded in this way) would then contact me to say that the research seemed fascinating and important and she would like to work with me. It was unexpected and gratifying to see how much this study seemed to resonate with some of these young people, and to know that they were driven by some of the same curiosity as well as urgency that I was in trying to understand the politics produced by youth in this moment. It was also striking that there was clearly a gendered investment in the project and that young Muslim American women, who themselves had been subjected to such intense scrutiny since 9/11, perhaps wanted to reverse the gaze, whether hostile or benign, for once (perhaps this was also why there was also a preponderance of female interviewees, given that women contacted their friends to participate, who tended to be other women, in a snowball effect). This process of moving from research subject to researcher in the project was also very much indicative, I realized, of a self-reflexive awareness among some youth and a belief that in interviewing their peers they would understand their own experiences in a deeper or different way—something they explicitly acknowledged to me time and again.

In this sense, the project turned out to be collaborative and dialogic in ways I had not really anticipated—and it forced me to think deeply about how these youth, who were the object of so much scrutiny, debate, and data collection since 9/11, were perhaps interested in being on the *other* side of the researcher's lens, and possibly in deciding how to use that lens themselves and to represent and translate their own narratives. As this pattern of researched turning into researcher persisted, I started asking my research assistants to write reflections about their own experiences after 9/11 and in relation to the study, to share what they thought was important for me to know. Letting my research assistants do open-ended interviews with youth on their own meant, of course, letting go of some control over what ensued in these conversations, and I would sometimes be amused—and on occasion, frankly, slightly frustrated—that a research assistant would ask questions in an interview about marriage, national stereotypes, or other issues which I did not think at the time were key to the study or proffer generalizations about ethnic groups and their behaviors. In other words, this collaborative process was not without its challenges. Yet obviously, as ethnographers know, these instances of conflicting agendas offered another moment of self-reflexivity where I was being educated about what were, indeed, the issues that these young adults or late adolescents were themselves interested in discussing with their peers or the views they had about different communities; clearly many of these conversations unpeeled different layers of the questions that I should have been asking too. So this is very much a *co-produced* research project, one that would simply not have happened, let alone developed the way it did, without the help of various generations of research assistants, and which is why this discussion cannot simply be relegated to the acknowledgments.

"Learning to Stand Up"

I want to offer here a brief snapshot of a meeting of young activists I attended in Fremont in July 2011 that raised some of the key questions that ripple through this book. The discussion among these youth illustrated to me how cross-ethnic campaigns emerging after 9/11 attempt to grapple with issues of civil rights, warfare, Islamophobia, and political solidarities. The meeting was organized by a young Afghan American activist who belonged to Afghans for Peace, an antiwar group that was trying to organize a leadership training summit, "Learning to Stand Up," in the East Bay to be held that September.

I drove to the meeting in Fremont from my home in Oakland, a route now familiar to me after numerous trips down the freeway to Silicon Valley from the East Bay, often amid snarled traffic on arteries packed with commuters. This time, Highway 880 South was thankfully relatively unclogged and, turning into Fremont on Decoto Boulevard, I was struck by the beauty of the brown hills rising up in front of me to the sky. Fremont is nestled at the foot of the Sierra Hills, and there is a dramatic juxtaposition of the rugged natural landscape with the monotony of shopping malls, fast food restaurants, and tract homes common in East and South Bay towns. The major streets in Fremont are wide and lined with trees, with Asian and Mexican restaurants interspersed between beauty salons, auto body shops, and gas stations. A sign for a Christian fellowship center, proclaiming "The Joy of Life," is followed by one for a trendy-looking South Asian restaurant, "Chutney: Indian and Pakistani Cuisine." Small houses give way to gated communities and low-rise condominiums, rows and rows of identical brown and beige two- and three-story buildings. I was always struck while driving through Fremont by the number of brown faces and particularly by the many South Asians of various ages walking and driving around the streets. Where were all these people from? When did they get here? What were they doing?

The meeting that day was at Suju's Café in a small strip mall, next to an Ayurveda center and across from a Japanese restaurant. The café was packed that afternoon with young people, all of whom were working on laptops and many of whom seemed to be students. There were a lot of youth who looked East Asian, as well as South and West Asian, youth, in their twenties or so. It almost seemed like a library; most people were quiet and intently focused on their computer screens. The young woman who had organized the meeting, Marjan, came in, followed by a young man wearing a baseball cap turned backward and sporting sunglasses. Marjan had long black hair and was wearing a long sleeved black T-shirt, with her eyes lined in black kohl. She swept us all outside for the meeting amid a flurry of arranging chairs and tables for the group in front of the café.

There were about a dozen people in attendance, four young women in hijab, including Sana, a Palestinian American activist; Feryal, a Pakistani American and former UC Davis student; and two young Afghan American women. Aisha, a Palestinian American woman activist who also graduated from UC Davis, was there, as was Sharat Lin, a well-known, older Indian-Chinese American community and antiwar activist in San Jose. There were three youngish white men, one of whom, Hussein, seemed to be a Muslim convert with a small beard, and who greeted us with "A salaam aleikum!" Hussein was wearing a T-shirt in solidarity with Gaza displaying the iconic image of a girl flying with a cluster of balloons in her hand, originally painted on the Israeli Wall by the graffiti artist Banksy. One of the other young white men was with the International Socialist Organization (ISO), and the third seemed to be a student activist from San Jose State University. There was also a young East Asian American woman wearing glasses and a knitted beanie in red, green, and black with a star and crescent, who it turned out was also with the ISO.

Marjan began the meeting, after introductions, by reading out the mission statement of the Muslims for Peace Coalition (MPC), the organization that was sponsoring the leadership training workshop, which stated: "No to war, no to terrorism, no to Islamophobia." The aim of MPC, she said, was to mobilize Muslim Americans to stand up for justice, given their suffering from U.S. wars and Islamophobia, and observed that it had been successful in bringing out hundreds of people in New York. She announced that the organization's framework would be used for the September training summit in the East Bay, following a similar program to be held on the East Coast. Afghans for Peace (AFP), who worked with Afghan Youth Volunteers, a group active in northern Afghanistan, was one of the organizations in the coalition represented by MPC and it wanted to organize a rally on October 7 in the Bay Area, on the tenth anniversary of the invasion of Afghanistan. Marjan noted that AFP's mission was similar to MPC's, but that instead of saying "no to terrorism," since AFP also wanted to challenge state terror, its core principles were "No to violence and extremism, and no to Islamophobia." Hussein pressed her on this point, asking why the organizers couldn't take this approach at the fall workshop as well, if they believed in this critique of the concept of terrorism, as he emphatically did. Marjan said it was important to follow MPC's principles for the conference, even if she herself was an "anarchist," that is, more radical politically. She commented that the Muslim American community was not yet ready to publicly support anything "political," in her view, let alone to challenge the state, and MPC *did* actually want to work with the state. She also pointed out that MPC's mission statement mentioned that the group wanted to work for "our country," even though she herself did not even identify as American.

Marjan's friend in the baseball cap interrupted, saying he wanted to know what exactly MPC meant by working for "civic duties" in its mission statement—did that mean "helping old ladies to cross the street?" There was some laughter around the table, but it was apparent that the discussion of political principles and strategic compromises was getting a bit tense. I commented that perhaps if these issues about challenging state policies or U.S. wars did come up during the workshop, it might be possible to allow airing of these critiques, with which many of the Muslim American youth in attendance might concur, so that the workshop could offer some space to reflect on these issues and so we could work in the cracks and crevices we find in institutionalized spaces. The young Asian American woman nodded. Marjan remarked that, in her view, MPC was the only national Muslim American organization that was even willing to take a critical political stand on these issues. It was apparent that Marjan's own politics were quite different from those of MPC, but she felt she had to stick to its guidelines for the event.

Marjan added that Zahra Billoo, a young Muslim American activist with CAIR in the Bay Area, would be doing a Know Your Rights workshop on the second day of the event. Someone else wanted to know to whom in particular the workshop was targeted, and if it was mainly for students. Marjan responded that it was for anyone who wanted to attend, for the event was based on a "broad notion" of activism; that is, it was not just for "college students," it could be "children, old people." Another person at the meeting wanted to know what the larger objectives of the workshop were. Hussein said, quietly, "I think it's trying to engage the average Muslim around socially conscious issues." Marjan added that the focus was on civil rights, based on the agenda set by MPC. There was some debate about this approach around the table, as well.

A back-and-forth discussion then ensued about whether to invite "big name" speakers to attract people to the event, since some, like Aisha, were concerned that it might be difficult to get a good turnout and pull it off successfully in a couple of months. One young Afghan woman in a silver-gray hijab, who was wearing sparkling rhinestone jewelry, said that it would help to get Muslim "stars," such as the cleric Sheikh Hamza Yusuf, if they wanted youth to come out, because MPC was not yet known in the Bay Area. Feryal seemed to disagree with her, saying that there were many "local gems" who were not as well-known and who should be given a chance to speak, given that the purpose of the event was to develop community leadership. Sana finally offered to try to contact Imam Zaid Shakir and Dr. Hatem Bazian, two well-respected Muslim community leaders from the Bay Area who are popular on the lecture circuit and among Muslim American youth. Lin gently commented that it would be important to try to build the organization "organically" and to create a grassroots base embedded in the local community. Marjan, who seemed tired by this point from fielding critiques and anxious to figure out the logistics of the event, observed that she was not the leader of the program, and wanted everyone to take leadership and help make the event happen.

This discussion gave me much food for thought as it encapsulated some of the major debates about strategic and radical approaches to political organizing after 9/11 and hinted at the tensions related to questions of rights-based activism and political inclusion in communities that felt vulnerable due to state scrutiny of their politics. Could one publicly challenge "state terror" if one was defined as an object of the War on Terror and community members were anxious about surveillance and backlash? What were the limits of Muslim American activism and who got to decide this? Should young activists look for guidance from established institutions and invite celebrated Muslim American figures or create an alternative leadership structure? What did it mean to be a radical Afghan Muslim American anarchist trying to do transnational solidarity work with Afghanistan if state terrorism could not be challenged? These questions about political mobilization and efforts to politicize a community for whom politics is equated with "radicalization," and thus criminalized by the state, were especially acute for youth at the meeting because some of the young activists present would indeed be considered politically radical, within a progressive-left lexicon, including Marjan. But there was also the question of how to draw people to an event in an area saturated with political conferences and talks, as well as faith-focused events and NGO-sponsored workshops, and whether and how to draw on established Muslim American community leaders who have a huge following among the younger generation and have risen to national and international prominence since 9/11.

Primarily, however, the debate that erupted around the table in the Fremont café was about the limits of possible and "proper" politics by Muslim American youth, and how to define "terror" in a context in which the U.S. state was also inflicting violence on civilians from Iraq to Afghanistan. Was this an issue that could be addressed openly in a leadership workshop for Muslim Americans, in a climate of heightened surveillance of Muslim American youth organizing? Could the problems facing the Muslim American community after 9/11 be addressed through a framework of civic integration or civil rights? Clearly, some in that multiethnic group of activists wanted to push for a more critical approach that challenged the leadership of an older generation and the liberal discourse of "civic duties" and inclusion for Muslim Americans. Marjan herself spoke at an October 2011 rally in Fremont on the anniversary of the invasion of Afghanistan, fiercely criticizing the liberal discourse of antiterrorism, peace, and dialogue.

The chapters that follow delve more deeply into the questions that young Afghan, South Asian, and Arab American activists continue to grapple with as they build and participate in cross-racial coalitions in the post-9/11 era, trying to use the existing paradigms of civil rights, human rights, women's rights, and gay rights while working against the grain of a dominant discourse of rights, liberal democracy, and proper political subjecthood.

The Book

The young people I spoke to in Silicon Valley were engaged in various forms of political activism and coalition building focusing on different, overlapping axes of mobilization in post-9/11 politics that pose thorny dilemmas, as the vignette above suggests. I found that their political mobilization generally pivoted on three nodes: civil rights, human rights, and women's rights and gay rights in the context of the post-9/11 culture wars. The main arc of the book focuses on these three major sites of post-9/11 youth activism and discusses the attempts by South Asian, Arab, and Afghan American youth to engage with, or rethink, these frameworks at a moment when rights-talk has become an alibi for war and imperialism and a core element of political activism.

Chapter One provides an overview of the particular racial and economic landscape of Silicon Valley, interrogating the narrative of Silicon Valley and the Bay Area as a liberal multicultural oasis buffered from Islamophobic backlash as well as the contradictions of this exceptionalism. It discusses the notion of 9/11 as a crucible for politicization for South Asian, Arab, and Afghan American youth and the line between "good" and "bad" Muslim Americans that regulates political subjecthood. Chapter Two explores the politics of the new Muslim American counterpublic that has been formed on the terrain of "Muslim civil rights" since 9/11 and also produced through interfaith alliances, and how a politics of recognition and religious multiculturalism shapes cross-ethnic and cross-class coalitions. It demonstrates that civil liberties is a powerful framework in U.S. politics that young Muslim American activists have adopted but which has confined their resistance, in many instances, to a domestic discourse of inclusion that excludes a critique of the global War on Terror and U.S. imperialism, undermining the possibility of other kinds of solidarities.

Chapters Three and Four both focus on the deployment of "human rights" by youth in political engagement with issues of imperial warfare, national sovereignty, and democracy, and the ways this produces cross-ethnic alliances and transnational solidarities but also encounters with repression and censorship. Human rights activism has emerged as a dominant paradigm for global politics, including in the context of U.S. wars and U.S.-backed occupations from Iraq and Afghanistan to Pakistan and Palestine. In Chapter Three, I discuss how many of the youth I spoke to found that the resort to human rights failed in their solidarity activism focused on Palestine, in particular, a contradiction that reveals the deeper limitations and exceptions of human rights politics in the global war on terrorism. Chapter Four then explores how an institutionalized paradigm of human rights and humanitarianism has been used to legitimize the U.S. invasion of Afghanistan as well as Obama's "Af-Pak" doctrine, obscuring the long history of U.S. and Western imperial interventions. I discuss how the narratives of Afghan and Pakistani American youth shed light on Af-Pak as an imperial geography and zone of degraded sovereignty and exceed a liberal human rights discourse.

Chapters Five and Six together explore the post-9/11 culture wars focused on women's rights, gay rights, and Islam, and the ways in which Muslim American youth wrestle with imperial feminism and homonationalism in a climate of permanent surveillance. Chapter Five examines how cultural debates often mask the work of neoliberalism and a politics of class that underlies notions of success and achievement for college students and trajectories of professionalized activism or risky politics in the post-9/11 moment. In Chapter Six, I discuss what it means for Arab, South Asian, and Afghan American youth to come of age in the surveillance state and in the context of the regulation of Islam in the culture wars. Their surveillance stories reveal the scrutiny, policing, and disciplining of their politics, and the self-regulation of "moderate" and "radical" politics as defined by the counterterrorism regime, but I found that young people also attempt to engage in forms of countersurveillance, contributing to what I call "surveillance effects."

Finally, in the Conclusion, I explore what the concept of democracy might mean for young people in a post-9/11 era when liberal democracy has become an alibi for imperial intervention and when uprisings for democracy in the Arab world, in which youth were prominently involved, have challenged U.S.-backed regimes. Democracy has been a key trope in the post-9/11 culture wars and a core component of Western modernity, legitimizing a late imperial project in conjunction with the framework of human and civil rights, women's rights, and gay rights. Reflecting on expressions of solidarity with Egyptians and Arab youth in Tahrir Square at public events in Silicon Valley, I discuss whether there is indeed a notion of democracy that can be excavated from or redefined in struggles against imperial racism, violence, and annihilation.

All these chapters explore how to define the object of struggles for "justice," in a moment when the vocabulary of progressive and left movements seems to be either co-opted or depleted. What we can learn from the political imaginaries of those whose politics are viewed as the most suspect and so are the most fragile, and who also must be the most resistant? The politics of youth who are targets of the War on Terror are, in the words of an Afghan proverb recounted for me by a young Afghan American woman, "more delicate than a flower, yet harder than a rock." These are the political paradoxes and struggles of youth whose stories I wish to tell.

1

The 9/11 Generation in Silicon Valley

The events of 9/11 and their aftermath generated some major shifts in identification and politics for South Asian, Arab, and Afghan American communities and for Muslim Americans at large. First, 9/11 was a watershed moment in the political engagement of South Asian and Middle Eastern communities and was experienced as a political catalyst that propelled these groups into the public square and compelled them to produce and participate in cross-ethnic and interfaith alliances. At the same time, a younger generation of Muslim Americans became increasingly engaged with Muslim identity as a basis for affiliation and mobilization and drawn to a framework of pan-Islamic solidarity. In Silicon Valley, these shifts have occurred in a region where difference and inclusion are overwhelmingly defined by an ideology of multicultural diversity and liberal tolerance and the mythology of the American Dream. The Islamophobic backlash generated contradictions for this imaginary of the greater Bay Area associated with pluralism and mobility, including for Muslim youth who are considered objects of the War on Terror.

In this chapter, I provide a brief overview of Silicon Valley and its cultural geography, including its class schisms, as contexts in which these youth grapple with cultural and religious discourses about belonging, affinity, and border crossing. I then explore the implications of the narrative of Silicon Valley as an oasis of multicultural tolerance for young people's responses to the events of 9/11 and their analysis of Islamophobia and racism. 9/11 was seen as a crucible for a turn to Islam and greater pan-Islamic identification among some Muslim youth from Arab, South Asian, and Afghan American communities, while there is also an acute awareness of racial, national, and class politics that variously converge and conflict with the desire for an "authentic" Islam. These sometimes competing narratives of true or necessary collectivity, belonging, and affinity have profound implications for a politics of solidarity and subversion in the post-9/11 era. They are shaped by a longer history of racial and class tensions as well as cross-ethnic and transnational alliances and solidarities in Silicon Valley, a valley of dreams and repressed nightmares.

Silicon Valley/Silicon Curtain

Silicon Valley is a fascinating site in which to investigate the political responses of communities targeted in the War on Terror because, in part, of its demographic diversity and migration patterns in a region celebrated for its presumed multicultural inclusion and model minority success. San Jose, the urban hub of Silicon Valley in Santa Clara County, has the largest Arab and Indian American communities in the Bay Area and the neighboring cities of Fremont and Hayward are home to the largest Afghan community outside Afghanistan.[1] In fact, a stretch of Fremont Boulevard in Fremont is (unofficially) known as "Little Kabul," and the Afghan population has historically been concentrated in the Tri-City area of Fremont–Union City–Newark and in Hayward, from which many commute to work in Silicon Valley. It is striking that given the significance of the war in Afghanistan so little serious work has been done on Afghan Americans in Fremont/Hayward and, in general, negligible research has been done on youth from South Asian, Arab, and Afghan American communities in Silicon Valley.[2]

Arab and South Asian immigrant communities in the South Bay are part of a highly ethnically diverse region—though there is a notable dearth of African Americans. San Jose has a very large Latino/a population, including a historic presence of Mexican immigrants, and a significant South and Southeast Asian American, especially Indian and Vietnamese immigrant, population. San Jose's Vietnamese American community (10.6% of the city's population) is the largest Vietnamese population outside of Vietnam, and there are also sizeable Chinese American and Filipino American communities. The population of San Jose is almost exactly one-third Asian American and one-third Latino/a, with approximately 40% whites and a miniscule 3–4% African Americans in 2010, a distribution that is close to that of the population of Santa Clara County, which has a larger white population and slightly smaller Latino and Black populations.[3]

The Indian American population has emerged as the fastest-growing community in San Jose (approximately 44,000 or 4.6% of the city's population in 2010), even though South Asians here are more dispersed and less concentrated than in Fremont, where many live in the same neighborhoods and even the same apartment complexes.[4] The Pakistani community in the city of San Jose itself is much smaller (approximately 2,000 in 2010) than the Indian American population, and the Bangladeshi and Sri Lankan populations reportedly miniscule.[5] Santa Clara County has the largest Arab population in the Bay Area, according to the 2000 U.S. Census (the largest group is Egyptian, followed by Lebanese, Palestinian, Syrian, and Iraqi). Exact demographic data on the Arab population, however, is difficult to obtain given that it is not included as a separate racial category in demographic data, since the Census categorizes Arabs as whites and Arab is a category listed only under ancestry; nor are Afghans listed as a separate category or in demographic data for Asian Americans. The Arab American Cultural Center of San Jose estimated that there are approximately 30,000 Arab Americans in the greater San Jose area during the time of this research. Many Arab and South Asian Americans live in the more affluent suburbs around San Jose, and also in towns extending up the peninsula toward San Francisco. As the high-tech industry expanded, it drew many Arab and South Asian scientists, engineers, and professionals who eventually moved out of urban areas into wealthy suburbs such as Santa Clara, Campbell, Cupertino, Los Gatos, and Saratoga.

The Afghan population in San Jose is very small, with an official estimate of only 813 (Ahuja, Gupta, and Petsod 2004), and Afghan Americans tend to be concentrated in less expensive cities and towns, such as Fremont and Alameda. The director of the Afghan Coalition in Fremont estimated that the population of Afghan Americans in Fremont was about 15,000 in 2008. Fremont also has very large Chinese, Indian, and Filipino American populations in a city that is almost half Asian American.[6] The Indian American population in Fremont has grown rapidly to become the second largest in California in 2010, after San Jose's, though it constitutes a much larger proportion in the city, almost a fifth (18.1%, or 38,711) in 2010.[7]

Many people I spoke to who were not from Silicon Valley were surprised to learn about the large concentration of Arab Americans in San Jose, including Arab Americans themselves. This is probably because Arab communities have historically been more visible in San Francisco, where they own many small businesses such as convenience stores and liquor stores and where they are also actively engaged in the liberal political and cultural milieu of the city. Yet the concentration of Arab Americans in Silicon Valley is not surprising, given that San Jose is actually the largest city in the nine-county Bay Area, and the third largest in California with a population of almost one million people (958,789 in 2011); it is the tenth-largest city in the United States. But of course the more important issues underlying this growth, both of the city and of these immigrant communities, is tied to the story of Silicon Valley, home to the computer industry and to corporations such as Cisco Systems, IBM, and eBay, the three largest high-tech employers in San Jose, as well as to six universities and colleges, including San Jose State University.[8] It is this economic context that has drawn Arab and South Asian immigrants, in particular, to the larger San Jose area or Santa Clara Valley, an area that has been mythologized as the "Valley of Dreams" (Pellow and Park 2002). Images of South

Asian capitalist entrepreneurship color the public imagination of Silicon Valley, yet the mythology of the American Dream was ruptured for Muslim South Asians (especially Pakistani Americans) who became "enemy number one" after 9/11, not to mention Arab Americans, as well as Sikh Americans mistakenly targeted by the racist backlash.

The much celebrated success story of Silicon Valley masks the presence of communities that are economically struggling and obscures a more complex, and much less publicized, class and racial politics. This is what some call the "Silicon Curtain," which masks "the oppression and immiseration of thousands of workers and residents" by a self-image of "progress" and prosperity produced by public relations firms determined to sell the American Dream (Pellow and Park 2002, 3). On the one hand, the median household income in San Jose in the period 2007–2011 was $80,764 (with a mean of $102,220), and in Fremont it was $98,513 (with a mean of $114,684).[9] On the other hand, racial segregation divides the affluent areas of Palo Alto and the foothills of Silicon Valley from the "flatlands" populated by people of color in East Palo Alto, Mountain View, and San Jose. By the mid-1990s, economic inequality across race, class, and gender was wider in Silicon Valley than in other parts of the United States (Pellow and Park 2002, 67–68). Writing about the transformation of Silicon Valley in 2013, George Packer observed that homes in Palo Alto cost more than $2 million on average, yet there had been a 20% increase in homelessness, noting, "After decades in which the country has become less and less equal, Silicon Valley is one of the most unequal places in America."[10]

In fact, Asian Americans and Pacific Islanders are among the groups whose median household incomes are below those of Santa Clara County in general, and many, including South Asians, work in low-wage manufacturing jobs.[11] The notion of the "model minority" Asian American, or immigrant entrepreneur, is a classic trope in Silicon Valley that has colored the image of South Asian immigrant communities in particular. It is indeed true that there are relatively affluent, technically skilled South Asian and Arab American professionals in Silicon Valley.[12] Yet during the early 2000s, the economic downturn and the slump in the high-tech industry had impacted Silicon Valley, and its effects were visible in the layoffs and outsourcing of jobs, which, combined with the later housing market crash and subprime mortgage crisis, produced even deeper economic insecurity among these communities in the South Bay during the recession years.[13] While home foreclosures in Silicon Valley dropped by one third from 2008 to 2011, median household incomes also dropped to the lowest levels in eleven years in 2011, with African Americans and Hispanics suffering the most, and the percentage of families on food stamps in 2012 had doubled since 2000.[14]

The Silicon Curtain and the nightmares it conceals is thus the story of Silicon Valley that remains largely untold. Ash Kalra, the first—and only—Indian American city council member in San Jose, observed that there are "a lot of working-class neighborhoods" that coexist with "extremely wealthy neighborhoods" and that San Jose has done "a poor job of helping to integrate the lower-income workforce into the success that has been created through Silicon Valley." A tent city erected by the homeless actually sprang up near the San Jose airport, one of sixty encampments that mushroomed in Santa Clara County in the wake of the "great recession" of 2008.[15] Kalra pointed out that the high cost of living in Silicon Valley, which has persisted beyond the dot-com crash, has meant that those earning lower salaries often end up commuting from towns further away with cheaper housing, such as in the Central Valley, traveling almost two hours each way to work in jobs in the high-tech industry. Furthermore, the freeways have destroyed many immigrant communities as houses were torn down to build the maze of interstate highways that have come to characterize the region (Pellow and Park 2002, 64). Silicon Valley is not a fixed spatial location, but a place that draws residents and workers from various locations who are necessarily mobile and often precarious as well as one in which many struggle to survive.

The high-tech industry has shaped the racial geography and political culture of Silicon Valley, and it has also influenced the social and cultural experiences of immigrant and Muslim communities in this area, before and after 9/11. So while there are affluent Arab and South Asian professionals in Silicon Valley, they remain relatively invisible and there is not an urban infrastructure or cultural landscape that provides a context for the active and visible staging of ethnic politics as in San Francisco. Vic Zikoor of the Arab American Cultural Center (AACC) in San Jose commented on the difficulty of constituting an Arab American "public sphere" in Silicon Valley, including at AACC events, given that people in the area live in dispersed communities and often commute long hours so they are often "stressed by work and traffic." Silicon Valley's "spatially isolated and spread-out residential patterns, its shopping strips and malls, its auto gridlock, its rapid demographic turnover, and the rampant individualism among its most talented workers" is for some an obstacle to forming a "close-knit civil society" (Cohen and Fields 2000, 191).

I discussed these contradictions with Ragini Srinivasan, a young Indian American who grew up in San Jose, and who was editor of a local Indian American magazine, *India Currents*, at the time we spoke. I met her at a café in a Santa Clara mall and she astutely observed over lunch that the strange paradox of Silicon Valley or the "South Bay" is that it is a "place of excess" and also "lack," which she associated with a missing "urban energy." In her view Silicon Valley has "excess money, excess immigrants, excess space, excess traffic" but is "missing some sort of dynamism," despite its many "cultural institutions, and . . . thinkers and start-ups and entrepreneurs," due to its suburban character. The lack of urban culture in this social and cultural landscape, with its tract homes and strip malls, shapes the ways that particular groups insert themselves into and mobilize in the cities and technoburbs of Silicon Valley and Fremont/Hayward, which are lacking in urban density and where public culture is based largely on consumption and strip malls. The public culture of Silicon Valley is often contrasted to San Francisco and Oakland/Berkeley, which are indelibly associated with histories of radical protest cultures, particularly the antiwar, Black Power, ethnic studies, feminist, and queer movements. Yet this genealogy of Bay Area radicalism sometimes overshadows the realities of activism, the burgeoning nonprofit industry, and consumerist liberal multiculturalism that has transformed the area. The seductive romance of the 1960s often thwarts a discussion of contemporary police brutality (except in horrifying moments such as the murder of Oscar Grant in Oakland), the mammoth prison-industrial complex, gentrification, and the flight of people of color from Berkeley/Oakland. Yet there is indeed traffic between the "city" (San Francisco) and the East Bay and South Bay, and social networks that connect them, within the limits of a challenging terrain where class and racial segregation and limited public transit are often deeply confining.

The suburban character of Silicon Valley and Fremont/Hayward inflects the possibilities of protest culture and youth activism and of reshaping political geographies. Cities have historically been associated with the space of protest politics and with providing a geography for revolt and resistance. According to Masao Suzuki, a Japanese American community activist who has been involved in organizing with Muslim and Arab American communities in Silicon Valley, San Jose is "not really a city" and he underscored that it has a conservative political environment, shaped by a largely professional class of high-tech workers and large immigrant communities, in which public political mobilization is not easy. As Suzuki noted, the antiwar rally in San Jose against the U.S. invasion of Iraq in 2003 was ten times smaller than the huge march in San Francisco. Yet in 2006, he recalled, the May Day immigrant rights march in San Jose that galvanized Latino communities, in particular, was the third largest in the U.S., so the region has seen upsurges in particular political movements since 2001.[16] Various forms of urbanism and suburbanism give rise to different kinds of social struggles, movements and nonmovements, or acts of political encroachment by the oppressed and invisibilized, which can emerge in spaces where spectacular public protest may seem unlikely (Bayat 2013, 13). The larger issue that I explore in this book is how the politics of this region and possibilities for cross-ethnic solidarity are deeply imbricated with a culture of neoliberal capitalism and multicultural recognition that has generated sometimes acute tensions for South Asian, Arab, and Afghan American youth after 9/11, and that emerge from the liberalism of race politics as well as persistence of racial and class divides in northern California.

De-Bugging: "Success" and Solidarity in the South Bay

The contradictions between idealized narratives of liberal "diversity," achievement, and self-reinvention in Silicon Valley and the realities of the conservative political culture in this hypercapitalist region need to be situated in the history of the production of "Silicon Valley" as a space emblematic of technological "progress" and cultural heterogeneity. The label "Silicon Valley" was first used in 1971 by local government and business officials to promote Santa Clara Valley as it shifted from a region known for an agricultural industry to one with a growing technology industry, fueled by the military and defense research (Pitti 2003). The area's first high-tech companies actually emerged in the late 1930s, and Hewlett Packard was founded in 1937 by two Stanford University graduates as Silicon Valley became a significant site for the emergence of the "military-industrial-university complex," with collaboration among the military, federal government, local municipalities, and universities (Cohen and Fields 2000; Pellow and Park 2002, 59–60). The presence of Stanford University in Palo Alto played an important role in developing what came to be known as the "showcase region of late capitalism," as did the military contracts awarded to the university and local industries beginning in World War I and continuing through World War II and the Cold War; this military-industrial-academic collaboration contributed to the celebrated and "mythic characterization of the region as a brave new world" (Cohen and Fields 2000; English-Lueck 2002, 7–8).

This mythologized history of Silicon Valley—and California in general—that enshrines individual entrepreneurship and a "heterogeneity of classes, ethnicities, national cultures, self-identified subcultures, and organizational cultures" (English-Lueck 2002), masks what historians of the region describe as, in the words of Stephen Pitti (2003), the "Valley's often forgotten poverty" (4). Simmering racial and class conflicts have erupted at various moments alongside struggles by marginalized, indigenous, and immigrant communities. Major strikes and labor unrest have marked the racialized class tensions in Silicon Valley between the largely Latino/a and Asian American agricultural workers and corporations. These emerged in the shadow of the entrepreneurs and settlers who invaded and devastated this region since the genocidal violence against its indigenous (Muwekma Ohlone/Costanoan) population beginning in the eighteenth century, the Gold Rush, and continuing racist and anti-immigrant policies (Pellow and Park 2002, 50; Ramirez 2007, 8, 40–57).

The transition in the Valley from agricultural production and fruit canneries, which historically employed Latino/a, Asian, and immigrant workers, to the technology industry during the Cold War led to increased unemployment and a widening gap between rich and poor. Since the 1970s, Mexican immigrants and Latinos, as well as Asian and African Americans, have generally provided low-wage labor for the assembly and service work that was "integral to the emergence of modern San Jose, a 'new western city' characterized by the prevalence of both high-tech skilled jobs and blue-collar wealth," invisibilizing the presence of the working poor (Pitti 2003, 3, 176). In fact, in 1982, the U.S. Commission on Civil Rights found the San Jose workforce "sharply divided along ethnic, sexual, and educational lines" (Pitti 2003, 177). The much vaunted ethnic and national diversity in Silicon Valley was created by high-tech capitalism as employers lobbied for H-1B visas to "import skilled labor from India, China, Canada, the Philippines, Taiwan, Korea, Japan, the UK, Pakistan, and Russia" (English-Lueck 2002, 21). Many H-1B programmers, as well as assembly-line workers, also lived and worked in Fremont, where housing and rentals were relatively cheaper during the 1980s and 1990s. This period coincided with a large influx of Afghan refugees fleeing the Soviet invasion and civil war in Afghanistan who settled in Fremont and Hayward, creating an enclave of refugees largely excluded from the prosperity of the high-tech boom in Silicon Valley.

Even scholars who highlight the capitalist "parable of meritocracy" and "tales of bootstrapping" in this "land of liberal thoughts, multicultural restaurants, and invent-it-as- you-go-along traditions" acknowledge that this "culture of opportunity," shaped by a high-tech industry that presumably valued inventiveness and diversity, was riven by class divisions created by the recruitment of different forms of labor to drive this aggressively expanding industry (English-Lueck 2002, 25). For example, while European, Israeli, and some Asian engineers had prestigious, high-salary positions, Latino/a, Asian American, and African American workers and immigrants—documented as well as undocumented—worked in low-paying manufacturing jobs as well as in the "vast informal economy . . . of late night software developers and corporate piece workers" (English-Lueck 2002, 18). The increasing shift to temporary workers and home-based piece work relied on the curtailment of worker rights and repression of labor organizing, as part of an "underground" economy of "cheap labor" populated by immigrants, refugees, and people of color (Pellow and Park 2002, 2, 163).

South Asian immigrants belong to both the affluent as well as exploited classes of labor, as observed by Raj Jayadev, an Indian American community activist and labor organizer who was an assembly line worker at Manpower Inc./Hewlett Packard in the 1990s. Jayadev was involved in a historic campaign organizing low-wage assembly-line workers at Hewlett Packard in the late 1990s, as the dot-com bubble burst. He observed of the workers hidden behind the Silicon Curtain:

> The fact that there was a South Asian working class here—and not just taxi drivers—was news. . . . the South Asian entrepreneurial class was getting established, so they did not welcome that. The South Asians working in that industry didn't want to know that. I was working in assembly work, doing early morning shifts [at HP]. . . . The South Asian community, African immigrants, such as Somalis, were in that industry . . . There was a slippage in class for some of these guys, they had degrees in engineering but they couldn't apply it here and it was very shocking for them.

Jayadev commented to me that many Indian and Pakistani immigrants with technical and educational qualifications "came here to be part of the tech industry, not for putting stuff in boxes" and "would come in" to work "as if they were office workers, in ties and shirts," struggling with downward mobility. The campaign with temporary technology workers became the subject of a documentary film, *Secrets of Silicon Valley* (1999), which "debugs" the myths of Silicon Valley as a "new business frontier" and a "new Western city" (Pitti 2003, 4), a place where the American Dream of autonomy, private property, and capitalist success and California-style self-reinvention can be achieved.

Jayadev's astute comment on class "slippage" provides the context for the difficulties he faced organizing South Asian workers in Silicon Valley who "didn't come to this country as working-class immigrants; they didn't want to associate with the working class or with the movement." Yet he said that when a Punjabi (Indian) woman worker's paycheck was "shorted" (cut), many South Asians working "at the back" in hi-tech warehouses became involved in organizing and in campaigns focused on health and safety issues, underscoring the invisible working class and hidden poverty of Silicon Valley. After the dot-com crash, Jayadev was also involved with the Immigrant Support Network, which mobilized H1-B workers against the restrictions imposed on this class of contingent labor that was vulnerable to economic recession and industry layoffs, exacerbated by the immigration policies of what was then the INS (Immigration and Naturalization Service)—hence the ironic twist in the acronym of the campaign's name (ISN). The HP and ISN campaigns built on earlier campaigns by Latino/a service workers who organized at Apple in the mid-1980s and who also were in the leadership of the campaign against California's anti-immigrant Proposition 187 (Pitti 2003, 193). Yet in a context where South Asian and Arab immigrants, and less so Afghan Americans, are wealthy entrepreneurs who are also the ones engaged in exploitative class relations with workers from their own ethnic communities, as Jayadev observed, the story of cracks in cross-class solidarity is a largely secret one as well.

These less well-known stories of the hidden class and immigrant politics of Silicon Valley highlight two issues salient for this book: one, that exploitation and marginalization in Silicon Valley occurs within, not just between, ethnic and racial groups, given that many of the successful and upwardly mobile entrepreneurs are South Asian, and sometimes also Arab, immigrants. In 2007, 52% of founders or CEOs of technology and engineering companies in Silicon Valley were immigrants, and Indians were the largest foreign-born group of founders of technology companies.[17] Afghans, who came to this area largely as refugees and not as economic migrants, have not moved as easily into this elite or upwardly mobile class as they generally did not have the social capital or language and technical skills to enter, let alone succeed, in the high-tech labor market (Omidian 1996). Many in the first generation of Afghan refugees in Fremont/Hayward worked as taxi drivers or small business owners, while some were unemployed and on public assistance; their children, as they became young adults, often worked in real estate during the boom years of the late 1990s. Mohammad Qayoumi, an Afghan engineer and president of California State University–East Bay in Hayward at the time we spoke, said that hundreds of Afghan American young adults were "caught in the windmill" of the housing boom; he commented that the "subprime [mortgage crisis] was a huge tragedy" for the Afghan community, with many losing work and homes. So eviction, debt, and class divisions are key issues that shape the coming of age of the 9/11 generation in Silicon Valley.

The second important issue Jayadev's narrative highlights is the history of coalition building and progressive movement building in the region that has challenged the powerful status quo in Silicon Valley at various moments, or at least disrupted its official narratives. For example, he recalled that Indian (mostly Punjabi), Arab, and Ethiopian immigrant taxi drivers organized wildcat strikes in San Jose in the 2000s. In a moment of economic recession and a climate of nativist and anti-Muslim hostility that put immigrant workers in the "crosshairs" of public suspicion, cab drivers held a memorial procession of cabs to San Jose, during a work slowdown protesting the shootings and murders of three Indian Sikh taxi drivers in the Bay Area in 2003.[18] Multiethnic organizing among workers and youth in Silicon Valley has been led by organizations such as Asian Immigrant Women's Advocates (AIWA), the Working Women's Leadership Program (WeLeaP!), and Silicon Valley De-Bug, which have mobilized Latino/as and Korean, Filipino/a, Vietnamese, and Cambodian Americans, as well as other groups focused on labor issues, racism, and immigrant rights (Pellow and Park 2002, 97, 138, 209).

Clearly, there is a long history of cross-ethnic alliances in this region that, as Pitti (2003) observes, is historically based on "native resistance, working-class political activism, and new forms of cultural politics over the generations" (3). Post-9/11 political movements and coalitions need to be situated in this historical context, as one moment in a genealogy of organizing by previous generations and other communities, including groups of youth and students. For example, Silicon Valley is one of the hubs of urban Native American identity and activism across tribal affiliations and even national borders, according to Renya Ramirez (2007, 55), with organizations such as the American Indian Alliance and Indian Center of San Jose, and campaigns waged against the Fremont Union High School District challenging discrimination against Native American students. This region notably saw the rise of Chicano activism in the 1960s, focused on issues of educational access, worker rights, and opposition to the Vietnam war; Chicano/a student activists who founded the Student Initiative at San Jose State College (later called the Mexican American Student Confederation) issued the first radical manifesto by Mexican American college students (Muñoz 2007, 67,73). Programs established by groups such as MEChA at San Jose State and Student Initiative organized with farm workers and challenged police brutality and racism in high schools and higher-education institutions, in the broader context of student activism and strikes calling for ethnic studies at San Francisco State and UC Berkeley and walkouts at San Jose State in 1968–1969 (Muñoz 2007, 84–85; Pitti 2003, 178–191).

These earlier movements, like those emerging in the post-9/11 moment, were based on global politics and transnational ties, for example, with communities in Mexico and with a Third Worldist politics linking Chicanos with anti-imperial movements in the Caribbean, Asia, and elsewhere (Pitti 2003, 185–187). However, the rise of a new Latino elite and conservative class during the 1980s offers a precedent for contemporary class schisms within South and West Asian immigrant communities that are important to consider in understanding the politics of Silicon Valley, as community activists I spoke to emphasized, belying an easy or romanticized notion of "ethnic solidarity." In the contemporary era, there have indeed been new, progressive cross-ethnic alliances in the San Jose area such as the campaign against racial profiling by the San Jose police department in 2010, organized by a coalition involving Silicon Valley De-Bug (a San Jose youth/community center and alternative magazine founded by Jayadev), as well as the Asian-American Center of Santa Clara County, La Raza Lawyers, African-American Community Services Agency, the San Jose Peace and Justice Center, and the Immigrant Rights and Education Network (Konda and Moore 2009; Weintraub 2010). Yet the general absence of Muslim, South Asian, Arab, and Afghan Americans from some of these local campaigns and cross-racial coalitions, which are not specifically about the War on Terror or Islamophobia, is an issue that is important to consider. In the chapters that follow, I explore the possibilities, as well as limits, of cross-ethnic solidarity among youth from these communities and the difficulties of forging cross-class and interracial alliances in Silicon Valley.

A Multicultural "Oasis"?

Silicon Valley is an interesting context in which to explore the politicization of these youth because most said that they did not experience an intense anti-Muslim and anti-Arab backlash after 9/11, as occurred in other parts of the country, and that they felt protected by the visibility of the large, well-established Muslim and Arab American community and its religious and political infrastructure as well as a local culture of "tolerance." For example, Farid, whose parents were Indian immigrants and whose father had come to do a Ph.D. in California in the early 1970s, grew up in Almaden Valley, a wealthy suburb of San Jose. Farid was a student at Stanford at the time we met at a coffee shop in downtown San Francisco, where he reflected on the impact of 9/11 on the local community:

> At least from my perspective, you're in very much a bubble in the South Bay, where so much of the population is educated. Even if they weren't more culturally astute by virtue of their education, they have to work with a lot of South Asians, so I think they didn't look at— . . . the monolithic view of all South Asians being dangerous. If anything 9/11 called out how backwards the other parts of the country were in terms of their response. And everyone, white, brown, what have you, were sort of looking on in horror in how everyone else was reacting.

Some Muslim community activists I spoke to in the South Bay also noted that the repercussions and scapegoating after 9/11 were not as severe as in other parts of California. Irfan Rydhan, who in 2003 founded *Muslim Round-table*, which aired on a community TV channel in San Jose, said when I met him at the SBIA mosque: "San Jose is such a diverse city. The backlash [after 9/11] was not as harsh compared to places such as Lodi or Yuba City," which he described as more "closed communities."

This sense of local exceptionalism of the South Bay "bubble," due to the liberal tolerance and multicultural diversity of the greater Bay Area, was a common refrain in my conversations with youth and community members in Silicon Valley. In my previous research on South Asian Muslim immigrant youth in New England, in contrast, it was very apparent that Muslim Americans felt much more under siege and very vulnerable, since they were a small minority in a predominantly white city with few community institutions to provide support (Maira 2009a). Several youth I spoke to from Silicon Valley commented that they felt lucky that they lived in such a diverse area where they were relatively buffered from the virulent Islamophobia sprouting in other areas of the nation. For many, California in general, and Silicon Valley and Fremont/Hayward in particular, were viewed as an oasis in a stormy sea of anti-Muslim sentiment and racism. Daoud, a Pakistani American student at Diablo Valley College in San Ramon who is from San Jose, commented, "Thankfully we live in California where people are tolerant and open-minded." Young people who had grown up in San Jose repeatedly told me that they felt that the area was a safe haven where local residents were familiar with Muslims and Middle Easterners. As I noted in the Introduction, there is indeed a large concentration of South Asian, Arab, and Afghan Americans that has lived in this area for at least two or three decades, and it is true that the post-9/11 backlash was not as virulent as it was in other areas and particularly less so than in New York. It is also the case that the Muslim American community in Silicon Valley is generally an affluent one that has established advocacy and civil rights organizations, and there was a great deal of organizing in response to racial and religious profiling by Muslim (and Sikh) American communities, in coalition with liberal and progressive civil rights and antiracist groups, after 9/11.

The sense of being shielded from the larger national phenomenon of intensified Islamophobia and anti-Arab racism even seemed to take the form of a kind of survivor guilt for some youth. One young Iraqi American woman, Dana, who grew up in Los Altos and San Jose and went to college on the East Coast, observed that her politicization after 9/11 was due to an awareness of anti-Muslim/Arab incidents elsewhere and an underlying sense of guilt that she and her family were shielded from this overt discrimination in the Bay Area. Such comments shored up the notion that there was an exceptional experience of inclusion due to the region's liberal multiculturalism within a larger racist and Islamophobic national culture.

The sentiment among youth that, in general, they were exempted or protected from the Islamophobic backlash around the nation was common even among young women who were wearing the hijab when 9/11 happened, and who were prime targets of Islamophobia in other parts of the U.S. (Cainkar 2011). Jenaan, a mixed Palestinian/Korean/white American woman who wore the hijab, was a sophomore in 2001 at San Jose High School, which has a large concentration of Muslim American students. I met her at a café in the Eastridge Mall in San Jose, as throngs of South Asians, youth as well as families with children, milled around outside. Jenaan was wearing a cobalt-blue scarf and jeans, and radiated confidence and passionate conviction. She reflected:

> At school it was very diverse; San Jose High is very diverse compared to most other high schools, so I never really had an issue being a hijabi or wearing a scarf at school. And even outside, I get the stares—of course, that's normal. Some people give me dirty looks but some people are so ignorant, you know. So I never really had a problem with it, and I didn't really felt scared after [9/11]. A lot of women felt threatened, they took off their scarves. I was like, "You know what, I'm strong. I'm gonna keep my faith, I don't care what people think or say."

Jenaan was animated as she talked and vividly recalled the support she received after 9/11:

> I played volleyball, basketball, track . . . so I was definitely very close to the girls I played with as well. And a lot of them were like, "Jenaan, we have your back! If anyone tries to mess with you we'll defend you." I was like, "You know, I'm strong, I can take care of myself but thank you for offering that."

Jenaan acknowledges that she received some "dirty looks," which she describes as "normal" in the experience of a hijabi woman, but she also emphasized that the diversity of San Jose High's student body and the active support of her high school friends made her experience after 9/11 a relatively unproblematic one. If anything, it seemed to affirm for her a strong commitment to her public expression of Muslim identity, which is also a common pattern among Muslim American youth.

However, there was an interesting contradiction in this narrative of "open-minded," liberal multiculturalism expressed by many of these youth, who would, often in the same breath, also comment on an episode of racism that had occurred in their school or neighborhood. For example, Farida, a Pakistani American woman from San Jose who wore the hijab, had studied in an Islamic school till the seventh grade and went to UC Davis where she was active in the Muslim Student Association (MSA). She reminisced about the immediate aftermath of 9/11: "I was a junior in high school and I didn't really have anything happen to me. I've heard about a lot of people who were egged and stuff, but they were mostly from Livermore and other areas where the communities weren't as multicultural. So that's why I don't think I went through as much here in San Jose during high school." Farida seemed to suggest that this "multicultural" space in San Jose was markedly different from towns that were only thirty miles away, such as Livermore, where Muslims were being assaulted after 9/11. Yet in the same discussion, she also recollected:

> I remember the day after 9/11, my dad telling me that things were going to be crazy outside today. And when I got to school nothing really happened until lunch when a kid said, "Oh, I know you did it [the 9/11 attacks]." And I was like, "Okay." I mean, what are you supposed to say to that? . . . But that was about it. The only other thing that ever happened was in the grocery store when this woman told me, "It's because of you that my son's in Iraq." And I was just, like, "No, you can't say that, you don't know anything about me or where I'm from! How are you going to say something like that?" And the grocery manager had to come out and apologize.

Farida's recollections of the Islamophobic accusations that left her speechless and, it seemed, increasingly angry over time also suggest the paradoxical nature of this notion of the multicultural bubble. The liberal "tolerance" of this oasis may have implied a protection against the most violent forms of anti-Muslim harassment or physical assault, but it clearly coexisted with forms of racism that, in some cases, revealed the twisted logic of racial scapegoating and imperial militarism (e.g., that all Muslim Americans were to blame for 9/11 and also for the U.S. invasion of a country, Iraq, that was unrelated to the 9/11 tragedy and attacked and occupied by the U.S. on false allegations of harboring weapons of mass destruction). Given the absurdity of the woman's comment to Farida in the grocery store, perhaps it was difficult to respond by questioning why her son felt obliged go to Iraq with the U.S. military in the first place. Interestingly, Farida eventually went on to do a senior thesis project in college on the impact of 9/11 on Muslim American youth.

Salah, a Syrian American from San Jose, commented that he never felt "singled out" with racist remarks but then corrected himself and recalled going to a barbecue in his neighborhood and getting into a "very heated" conversation with a young white American whom he had grown up with, about "politics and 9/11 and Islam and the Palestinian struggle." The young neighbor said, "If it wasn't for you Muslims, the world right now would be completely at peace," leaving Salah somewhat stunned. Mariyam, who is Libyan/white American and also wore the hijab while in high school, experienced incidents that were much more violent at Santa Clara High School, where she said that other students actually "threw garbage" at Muslim youth.

In fact, undermining the narrative of a multicultural and generally non-racist, if not antiracist, political culture in San Jose, there were several disturbing incidents of Islamophobia and racist violence against Arab, South Asian, and Afghan Americans in Silicon Valley after 9/11. To name just a few, scattered instances: at least three Sikh cab drivers were shot in the Bay Area in the aftermath of 9/11, and two were killed. Mosques and gurudwaras were vandalized and defaced and an Afghan restaurant in Fremont was attacked with bottles and rocks.[19] At San Jose State University, graffiti found in 2003 threatened that Muslims would be shot on campus.[20] In 2006, an Afghan woman who wore the hijab, Alia Ansari, was shot and killed in Fremont while walking down the street with her toddler;[21] the same year, a Sikh man in Santa Clara was stabbed with a steak knife by a man who accused him of belonging to the Taliban.[22] In 2010, almost a decade after the 9/11 attacks, Muslim teachers at public as well as Islamic schools in Sunnyvale and San Jose were assaulted and had their rooms vandalized; a Muslim man wearing a kufi (skullcap) on his way to prayers at MCA in Santa Clara was assaulted on the street and called a "terrorist."[23] Muslim students in high schools in Silicon Valley were threatened and verbally abused, some were spat on, and women had their hijabs ripped off their heads.[24] There were numerous reports of harassment and Islamophobia targeting youth, such as incidents in Fremont of a girl wearing hijab being accused of being a terrorist by her teacher and a boy repeatedly called "sand nigger" and "camel jockey"; in both cases, the school apparently did not respond to the complaints (American-Arab Anti-Discrimination Committee 2008, 55–56). In fact, Salah recalled that the Muslim Student Association at San Jose State set up a program for volunteers to escort female students wearing the hijab if they had to walk outside at night.

In addition to the uneven quality of the shield of tolerance, then, which was thinner in some places within this oasislike space than others (such as San Jose and Fremont), there also seemed to be a tacit acknowledgement among youth that this narrative was, in fact, only that, a *narrative* produced about local culture, racism, and diversity. The myth of liberal multiculturalism as inherently antiracist or postracial deflected critiques of the deeper structures of racism and racial violence that notions of liberal tolerance and postracialism obscure. It is evident, however, that Muslim American youth participated in and co-produced this mythology about San Jose, the Bay Area, or California, and that perhaps this was also an act of discursive and possibly psychic self-defense in the context of the massive scapegoating and numerous incidents of violent backlash after 9/11. It is also true that the experience of post-9/11 harassment was a relative one, and that the Muslim, Arab, and South Asian communities in this area, in particular, had resources and institutions that offered support for these middle- to upper-middle-class youth. But the issue of class-based vulnerability was generally suppressed in these recollections of multicultural tolerance and it seems that the buffering of social capital did not generally register in the collective memory produced about this time and space, a complex issue I will return to later.

Young people, however, did implicitly or explicitly acknowledge the ways in which the edges of liberal multiculturalism were frayed by signs of something more troubling, a deeper suspicion or racialized anxiety about Muslims and Arabs which sometimes surfaced in encounters with others. For example, Daoud went on to observe of the responses to 9/11 in his high school in San Jose where he faced questioning about Islam:

> Sometimes people have malice behind their question, but they still pose it in the form of a question so it gives you an opportunity to clear up any misconceptions they might have. But no, I haven't run into anything that's left any emotional distress on me. I felt some prejudice, but that could've been my own thoughts, I've never had to confront that.

Daoud's statement, like those made by other Muslim American youth in this study, highlighted the uncertainty about what constitutes racial or religious "prejudice" in the post-race era and the extent to which self-doubt about the very existence of racism sometimes crept into these narratives. Racism becomes a potential figment of the imagination and is perhaps simply located in the psyche of the minority individual him/herself; even if Daoud acknowledges having encountered questions driven by "malice," he at the same time disavows having had to confront prejudice to the extent of experiencing "emotional distress." The insistence that racism does not exist in the South Bay in a significant way, accompanied by self-contradictory statements and admissions of racist incidents, is perhaps a defense mechanism of youth in response to a traumatic assault on what had, in many cases, been a relatively comfortable life in Silicon Valley. It is also perhaps the result of the larger shift to postraciality in the U.S. and the effectiveness of propagating a notion that racism is in general "over" and behind us, particularly in liberal multiracial communities such as the Bay Area. The existence of racial diversity becomes an alibi for the denial of racism and the difficulty of then speaking about racism, even if it smacks one in the face (Alsultany 2012).

September 11 as Political Catalyst/Crucible

While some youth acknowledged that the events of September 11, 2001, triggered a spate of racist or Islamophobic incidents, if viewed as scattered and less vicious than elsewhere, the backlash was also understood as generating something positive, provoking an assertion of religious or ethnic identity and political mobilization, particularly among youth. In general, there seemed to be two overarching strands in the claiming of public identity by these youth in the post-9/11 moment that shaped their political affiliations and also alliances. One trend was the intensified engagement with Islam among Muslim American youth, as an identity, a faith, and a basis for public politics and social justice activism. The other move among Muslim as well as non-Muslim youth was an engagement with rights-based politics and movements challenging the nation-state and issues of war, occupation, and imperialism, as I discuss in the following chapters. These two approaches were not mutually exclusive and often overlapped, with many Muslim American youth becoming very involved with civil rights and antiwar organizing while simultaneously becoming active in Muslim student and community groups and pan-Islamic activism.

* * *

This notion of 9/11 as a crisis as producing a necessary public politics, if defensive or reactive, was common among many of the young people to whom I spoke. Amira, who grew up in Fremont and whose father is Pakistani and mother Afghan, said of the post-9/11 backlash: "Well, it kinda made you kind of question, 'Oh why is everyone pointing out my religion?' But it kinda makes you stronger I think. I never received any direct hatred or anything. No one ever really called me out on it." Farida, a Pakistani American woman who grew up in San Jose in a Shia Muslim family, recalled that after 9/11 "more people went to the masjid [mosque]" and "there was the idea that we need to stick together." For Malaika, a young Pakistani American woman who was born in Santa Clara and lived in both San Jose and the East Bay town of Tracy, the backlash after 9/11 led to a defensive assertion of Muslim identity:

> I think whenever there's a time of crisis, your so-called "community" is on the
> defensive, and you yourself—whether you like it or not—are going to be part

of it. So you have that, in terms of defensiveness. A lot of questions that you're asked, you know it's a tragedy and everyone's upset about it, but at the same time it was an opportunity to really give out education. I felt more strong in terms of my Muslim identity.

Malaika was involved in founding a Muslim student organization in her high school just before the attacks of 9/11, and the group did, in fact, organize educational events about Islam such as iftars (fast-breaking dinners) during Ramadan which, Malaika recalls, were attended by about two hundred people. She commented that she became more self-conscious about being Muslim but also felt a stronger connection with the Muslim American community after 9/11, a community that she was herself involved in constituting through her organizing activities as a Muslim activist.

This narration of the post-9/11 moment as a crucible of tragedy through which political mobilization and consolidation of a more public Muslim American identity emerged has been a pervasive theme in discussions of Muslim American youth (for example, Peek 2011). Much of the scholarship on Muslim American community also points to 9/11 as the beginning of a transformation of a Muslim American politics thrust into the public sphere, often with the leadership of a younger generation, and reconstituted through engagement with U.S. politics, domestic and foreign, beyond the realm of (only) faith and religious belief (Cainkar 2011; Bakalian and Borzoghmeyer 2009). Rydhan, for example, noted that SBIA formed a media committee after 9/11 and remarked, "It took 9/11 to do more open houses" at the mosque for the general public. He added that "a lot of youth became more religious, and they wanted to do something for the community." While I was talking with him at the mosque, a Pakistani American woman whose daughter works with CAIR in San Jose joined our conversation and commented, "Muslim youth had to go to the Koran, because they had to do more explanation [of Islam]."

The events of 9/11 and their aftermath intensified the politicization of Muslim American youth in Silicon Valley and propelled a resurgence of Muslim identification and a turn to what some call a "new Islam" in this generation, a scripturalist turn that has been influenced by global shifts in Muslim communities. Research on South Asian and Arab Muslim youth in the U.S. has noted a pattern of privileging Muslim identity over ethnicity or nationality, with young Muslim Americans increasingly identifying as "Muslim first, Arab [or Bangladeshi or Pakistani] second," a phenomenon I noted in my research as well (Kibria 2008, 2011; Naber 2005, 2008). This shift has occurred in the context of a larger debate and internal dialogue about the relationship of Muslim Americans at large to the nation-state and what it means to be an "American

Muslim" or a "Muslim American," and whether it is even appropriate to use such labels given the critique of the U.S. nation-state among those targeted by its domestic and global policies (Abdullah 2013).[25] This self-conscious production of "Muslim" identity is a feature that many scholars comment on as characterizing second or later generations of Muslim American youth who seek to study Islam, partly in response to the questioning they encountered after 9/11, and to "know" it apart from or in distinction to their parents' interpretations or cultural heritage (Muhammad-Arif 2002). Daoud commented, "However as the years went on I've noticed things about me being Muslim became more important and the things I knew about Islam started to become more important because people started to ask questions and I started having more exposure to non- Muslims." Rydhan observed that a "lot of youth became more religious" after 9/11 and those who attended Islamic Sunday schools, including youth in the San Jose area, came to "realize that Islam is different from what their parents practice, so they want to learn about Islam unfiltered by culture, and go to the source."

Katherine Ewing and Marguerite Hoyler (2008) observe of the shift to a "Muslim-first" identity: "Though this rearticulation is a manifestation of a global discursive process that has been developing for decades and can be seen, for example, in the teachings of the Muslim Students Association, many young Muslims link the emergence of their own intentional identity as a Muslim to the aftermath of 9/11 and the war on terror" (82). These shifts need to be situated in the context of the "global debates about Islamic authority and reform," for as some scholars observe (e.g., Grewal 2014, 23, 25, 34), there has been a sense of a "strong crisis" about Islam among Muslim American youth due to the War on Terror and U.S. policies as well as "internal conflicts" produced by the global Islamic revival. Nazli Kibria (2008, 244, 245; 2011, 2) finds that among Bangladeshi Muslim youth in the U.S. and Britain, there has been a turn toward "scripturalism" that she describes as a aspect of "revivalist Islam," partly shaped by Islamic revivalist movements that have influenced youth in groups such as the Muslim Students Association—although she notes that not all youth in these Muslim organizations share the belief in what has been labeled a "resurgent" or "new Islam." But it is apparent that the scrutiny and interrogation of Islam after 9/11 produced a certain kind of Islam in the 9/11 generation, a move that has had important social and political, not just theological, implications. Kibria (2008) notes that among Muslim youth in the U.S., "experiences of hostility and exclusion" after 9/11 propelled a strong sense of pan-Islamic solidarity but also a "return to the 'true' tenets of Islam" as a source of spiritual knowledge, structure, legitimacy, or positive identification (245–247).

The intensified engagement with Islam among young Muslim Americans after 9/11 has converged with a turn to a universalist Islam that can transcend race and ethnicity and that rejects the Islamic practices of the parental generation, associated with un-Islamic cultural traditions and "unlearned 'village Islam'" (Grewal 2014, 74; see also Schmidt 2002, 9). Ali Zamani, an Afghan American refugee from the Bay Area, commented that after 9/11, the younger generation of Afghans is "turning more to Islam as an umbrella than national identity," and that in his view, this shift to greater religiosity cuts across class backgrounds, creating what Ahmed Afzal (2015) describes as a "transnational Muslim heritage economy." There is a notion among some young Muslims that Islam is being purified in the U.S., as they attempt to find an "authentic" religion stripped of the cultural elements and national attachments that they associate with the immigrant generation and homeland folk and mystical traditions, including Sufi Islam or the worship of popular saints (pirs) (Joseph and Riedel 2008, 167; Kibria 2008, 2011). Hisham Aidi (2014, 48–50), writing about transnational Muslim youth culture and politics, traces these currents to the influence of Saudi-backed Salafi clerics, mosques, and schools that have promoted a return to an "authentic" (as opposed to "folk") Islam and a "borderless, transnational" Muslim-first identity that appealed to Muslim youth struggling with marginalization and racism in Britain and Europe in the 1990s. The post-9/11 shift in religious identity has meant that some Muslim American youth end up rejecting national or even racial identification altogether as they challenge the immigrant generation's apparently "ritualistic" and "cultural Islam," a phenomenon that Garbi Schmidt (2002, 4, 9) notes has occurred among Muslim youth not just in the U.S. but also in immigrant communities in Sweden and Denmark. Farah, an Afghan American woman from San Jose who was born in Kabul and lived in Pakistan till she came to the U.S. at age twelve, said, "My parents aren't that religious. They put culture and religion together a lot. I don't like to mix culture as much with religion." Farah, who considered herself "Muslim first" and had been president of the MSA in high school, said she had a "religious connection with Arabs"; her friends were "African Americans, Pakistanis, and Afghans" as well as Palestinian Americans whom she knew through MSA events.

Pan-Islamic identification is viewed by many Muslim American youth as a major vehicle for crossing national, racial, or ethnic boundaries. Bashir, a young Pakistani American who was born in San Jose and has lived in Fremont as well as in Pakistan, was very involved with the MSA at San Jose State. As we had coffee on the patio outside the San Jose State library in downtown San Jose, while students chatted around us, Bashir reflected on the shift away from national identification and toward a pan-Islamic, multiethnic identity:

People have been intermingling in places like MCA [Muslim Community Association] and other places where everyone goes and prays together. There's no "Pakistani masjid." So that's what's happened with me through involvement in the MSA. Now, I feel like I represent the Muslim community, the ummah [community of believers] . . . the groups that I'm associated with are all multicultural. . . . This is also a new phenomenon. It is mostly due to student organizations. . . . But now, people are really associating themselves with Muslims rather than a culture. Culture confines you, but Islam is an umbrella.

It is important, as Kibria (2011) observes, that attention to the emergence of a Muslim-first identity should not obscure the "great variety of religious approach" (71) among Muslim American youth who hold this up as an ideal but whose daily practices and lifestyles are diverse. This ideal of a multicultural pan-Islamic "umbrella" was a theme in many of my conversations with youth who aspired to a "trans-national, trans-ethnic ideal religious community," one partly developed through the teachings of well-known Islamic scholars such as Sheikh Hamza Yusuf, who founded the Zaytuna Institute in the Bay Area and has an international following, doing workshops for Muslim youth in the UK and other countries since 9/11 (Kundnani 2014, 53; see also Schmidt 2002, 8, 12). Arun Kundnani (2014) notes that this "globalized Islamic identity" emerged to replace secular left political identifications in the 1990s for South Asian youth in the UK and Muslim youth in Europe," and "provided a new language for describing injustice" and a "way of filling the void opened up by the decline of the Left" (37–38). In other words, this global shift is a product of a complex array of generational, historical, and geopolitical developments.

The crucible/catalyst narrative suggests that the outcome of 9/11 was a needed and productive, even spiritual, regeneration of the community—if at a huge cost given the racist backlash and construction of Muslim and Arab Americans as national enemies. This narrative, however, fails to challenge the enduring U.S. structure of racial violence and white supremacy by shifting emphasis to the production of public identity and politics of recognition (Rodriguez 2010). Indeed, the crucible/catalyst narrative disavows the ways in which this engagement with a U.S. politics of incorporation is desired by, and compatible with, a national politics of multicultural inclusion and imperial violence, as well as policies of religious multiculturalism, as I discuss in Chapter Two.

It was very apparent that for most youth I spoke to, the questioning, suspicion, surveillance, profiling, and racism they experienced after 9/11, as well as the wars on Afghanistan and Iraq and drone attacks on Pakistan, were a catalyst for an increasing identification with both religious and ethnic/nationalist identities: as Muslim in the case of Muslim American youth, and/or as Arab, Pakistani, and Afghan as well as Iraqi, Palestinian, Egyptian, or Syrian, depending on their ethnic backgrounds (Ewing and Hoyler 2008; Naber 2012; Peek 2011; Schmidt 2002). The tragedy of 9/11 and the Islamophobic backlash became a crucible for the politicization of a new generation of Muslim Americans who became political subjects qua Muslims, what has been described as "Generation M." Rydhan, who began doing the *Muslim Roundtable* talk show on local-access television in San Jose in 2003, commented that there was a "surge" in Muslim youth activism, although he also observed that this "dwindled down to a few, core people" over time, an attrition common in political movements. Majed, whose parents are Palestinian refugees from Jordan and who grew up in San Jose, said:

> I think 9/11 is what made me a lot more interested in politics in general . . . I kind of just started observing and analyzing everything I was reading in the newspapers, what Muslims would say, what the opposite would say. So my thought process changed after 9/11. But I'd hear a lot of stories, about, you know, what was called the INS [Immigration and Naturalization Services]. The detainees. . . . I can remember when I was a junior in high school, I was in Youth in Government, which is a YMCA program. So you go to the state capitol and you propose bills. . . . Mine had to do with the INS and racial profiling. So I was thinking about all those things. I mean, then you had the PATRIOT Act.

Majed, who attended Granada Islamic School in Santa Clara and San Jose High School, came from a family that was involved with the Council on American-Islamic Relations (CAIR), and became very active with the Students for Justice in Palestine (SJP) chapter while at UC Davis. His story highlights the crystallization of awareness of state power and state policies of detention and profiling and also of a "Muslim" politics and analysis of national and world events. Majed's "thought process" shifted after 9/11, focusing while he was still in high school on the desire to combat Islamophobia and racial exclusion by turning to state institutions or legislative processes, a desire inculcated by programs of citizenship education and tutelage run in some cases by (nominally) faith-based programs, such as the YMCA.

There is also a developmental trajectory that is at work here for youth who were in high school during 9/11 and who were grappling with questions of social identity and exploring ethical commitments in their adolescence, a period understood in the U.S. as a time of testing and forming political beliefs. Meena, an Afghan American woman from Newark, thoughtfully reflected on the convergence of the events of 9/11 with her adolescent experience:

When 9/11 happened, I was in high school and I did give speeches about Afghanistan to try to educate others . . . but I don't know if it was because of 9/11 or because of where I was in my life. Naturally, you know, it's the time you try to find who you are and find your roots. So I don't know if it was 9/11 and the wars that had an effect on me or just that I wanted to find . . . my identity and so I tried . . . being involved in different activities and groups.

Meena's comment suggests that for young people who were entering adolescence in 2001, the intense assault on religious, national, and ethnic identities and the war on Afghanistan only intensified questions and explorations of political engagement.

It is important to note, however, that the engagement with geopolitics and an awareness of state policies and state power among Arab, South Asian, and Afghan American youth did not necessarily begin in 2001. Islamophobia and also, of course, racism have a long history in the U.S. and so shape the political subjectivity of Muslim, Arab, South Asian, and Afghan Americans throughout their lives (Malek 2009; Naber 2012; Salaita 2006a). Arab Americans, in particular, have had to grapple for generations with the history of Orientalist representations of the Middle East and Islam and the repression and distortion of Palestinian narratives in the U.S.; this has led to a relationship to the U.S. state and the mainstream public sphere that is necessarily ambivalent and critical, if not oppositional (Abraham 1994; Orfalea 2006). The 1967 and 1973 Arab-Israeli wars, the oil crisis of the 1970s and the Iranian revolution and hostage crisis of 1978–80, the bombing of Libya in 1986, the first and second Gulf Wars, and U.S. financial and military support for the Israeli occupation of Palestine were all events that reinforced a dominant, Orientalist perception of Arabs and Muslims as oil sheikhs, terrorists, and fanatic militants (Alsultany 2012; Shaheen 2001). Afghan Americans have also had to deal with distorted and Orientalist representations of Afghanistan in the U.S. media since the U.S. proxy war against the USSR, although the Soviet invasion of Afghanistan and the depredations of the Taliban makes the relationship of Afghan refugees to the U.S. a much more complex one (see Ansary 2002), as is also the case for Pakistani Americans. Toufic El Rassi (2007) portrays the experiences of Arab American youth grappling with imperial wars and racial violence in his autobiographical graphic novel, *Arab in America*; he recalls that during the first Gulf War, students at his high school yelled that the U.S. would "shoot up towel heads" and there was an "outpouring of anti-Arab sentiment" as well as patriotic fervor (30–32).

It is crucial to note that the post-9/11 period was not a rupture marking a completely new politics for Arab and Muslim Americans in order to de-exceptionalize this narrative of post-9/11 political subject formation. Some youth in the study were already involved in Muslim student associations in their high schools and engaged with the Palestine solidarity movement or aware of Middle East and global politics well before 2001. For example, Marwa, who is Egyptian American and grew up in Fremont, said that one of "the turning points" in her politicization was when she was in eighth grade and challenged her teacher's Orientalist statements about "Palestinians and suicide bombers," which characterized them as "crazy and terrorist." The teacher responded by asking Marwa to do a presentation on the Palestine issue in class, forcing her to take on the role of educator but also galvanizing her to make a public intervention for the first time, a role that she embraced while studying at Stanford where she became actively involved with Palestine solidarity activism.

The 9/11 generation is also enacting continuities as well as discontinuities with the public politics of the immigrant or previous generation of Muslim American activists, who were the founders of organizations, such as CAIR and the Muslim American Society (MAS), that have focused on Muslim civil rights to counter Islamophobia and profiling. Their political activism is not entirely "new" and must be situated in the longer history of political mobilization in these communities, against the grain of the dominant narrative of a post-9/11 political "awakening." Clearly, there are differences in the ways in which politics is framed by immigrant and later generations given their varying relationships to the state and experiences of race and nationalism as well as of public activism. For example, Salima, a Pakistani American who was born in San Jose, has grandparents who came to California in the late 1970s and so is actually third generation on her mother's side. She went to Granada and was very involved with MCA; Salima observed that there are "two different politics" among Muslim American generations:

> I think the first generation is like, "Let's talk about politics that are happening back home. Let's talk about what's happening in Pakistan and India," because that's what they're used to. That's what they wanna talk about, they're like "Oh, let's talk about what's going on over *there*." Second- and third-generation youth talk about American politics: "What's going on *here*? How will this affect me?" So yeah, they're different and I definitely think that they have different views. I feel that for the first generation . . . it's harder for them to understand and kind of relate American politics to themselves. The same thing with the second and

third generation; they have a disconnect with back home because that's not their home. America is their home.

In Salima's view, the emphasis on "homeland" versus "American" politics reflects a deeper difference in the understanding of where "home" is, one which is common among immigrant communities in general who often engage in transnational movements or long-distance nationalism. For example, Naber (2012) notes that Arab Americans in the Bay Area formed pan-Arab, leftist and anti-imperialist organizations in the 1970s, including an Arab student organization at San Francisco State and a Palestine Solidarity Committee, during a period described as the "Arab American awakening" and in the context of pan-Arab movements in their home regions (38–49). But there were also national Arab American organizations that were established in the 1970s and 1980s to mobilize domestic civil rights campaigns in response to Islamophobia and Arabophobia in the U.S., such as the National Association of Arab Americans and the American-Arab Anti-Discrimination Committee.

After 9/11, there was an increasing convergence of political orientations across generations, as immigrant Muslims, Arabs, and South Asians felt compelled to engage even more with the U.S. political landscape—in response to "homeland security" policies, the Islamophobic backlash, and the Orientalism of U.S. mainstream media—and second- or third-generation youth were drawn into the antiwar movement and became more involved with global politics in the Middle East, Afghanistan, and South Asia. Thus the presumed generational bifurcation of politics based on a divergence between homeland/U.S. politics has in actuality been bridged by the "homeland security" regime and by ongoing imperial policies enacted within and beyond the U.S. that have forced a transnational approach, in a sense, linking domestic and global arenas, particularly for those in the bull's-eye of those polices. Yet the issue of intergenerational fissures, conflicts, or continuities has become primary in discussions of immigrant and Muslim American communities, often to the exclusion of experiences of class and race, let alone of U.S. imperialism; in my view, it has been overemphasized in narratives about Muslim American communities and youth, simplifying a complex political history (see Maira 2002, 2009a). What was apparent in this research is the ways in which both first and later generations of South Asian, Asian, and Arab Americans in Silicon Valley were situated in a political field that was marked by the contradictions of post–civil rights era liberal racism and neoliberal multiculturalism, powerful assemblages of ideologies and practices that shaped their political subjectivities and responses to the War on Terror.

"Good" Muslims and "Angry" Politics

One of the most significant, and politically devastating, paradigms that has shaped the political subjecthood of Muslim and Arab American communities after 9/11 is the binary of the "good" and "bad" Muslim, the state's carrot and the stick. After 9/11, the growing discourse of "good" versus "bad" Islam emanating from the Bush administration suggested that it was not Muslims in general who were a "suspect" population in the War on Terror, just the "bad" or "radical" Muslim Americans who supported militant movements or simply opposed U.S. imperial policies. The disciplinary framework of the good/bad Muslim subject regulates what constitutes acceptable politics and youth activism and it is also deeply contested in the post-9/11 culture wars, including by Muslim American youth, activists, and organizations. My analysis of performances of "good" and "bad" Muslim political subjectivities builds on Mahmood Mamdani's (2004) argument in *Good Muslim, Bad Muslim: America, the Cold War, and the Roots of Terror*, where he observes that after 9/11:

> President Bush moved to distinguish between "good Muslims" and "bad Muslims" . . . "bad Muslims" were clearly responsible for terrorism. At the same time, the president seemed to assure Americans that "good Muslims" . . . would undoubtedly support "us" in a war against "them." . . . But . . . unless proved to be "good," every Muslim was presumed to be "bad." (15)

The politics of performing a "good" or moderate Muslim identity is fraught in a context in which the state sanctions liberal civil rights and Muslim American activism while criminalizing other forms of protest politics or political speech as anti-American or pro-terrorist, leading to self-regulation as well as internal divisions within Muslim and Arab American communities (Maira 2009a).

This dichotomy of the "good"/moderate and "bad"/radical Muslim has its inherent contradictions, with tensions emerging on the fault lines of class, nationality, and gender. On the one hand, working-class or less affluent Muslim immigrants were disproportionately targeted as "bad Muslims" in the mass detentions and deportations after 9/11 that targeted the detritus of neoliberal capitalism (Nguyen 2005; Rana 2011; Shiekh 2011). On the other hand, even affluent Muslim American professionals found themselves swept into the dragnet of the surveillance state—hauled off planes, fired from their jobs, or harassed by the FBI—becoming "bad Muslims," if for a moment, and confronting the limited protections of model minorityhood (American-Arab Anti-Discrimination Committee 2008; Jamal 2008). While many Muslim

Americans, both economically successful and struggling, still clung to the defense that they were "good" Muslims—productive, peaceful citizens who believed in the promise of American democracy and capitalist mobility—others became skeptical, and in some cases publicly critical, of the U.S. state, its foreign policies, and the War on Terror. The rupturing of the model minority image of South Asian Americans, and less so of Arab Americans or Afghan refugees, was precipitated by the intensified racialization of Islam after 9/11 as upwardly mobile Muslim Americans slipped over to the "other side" of the racial divide.

Post-9/11 alliances and fissures among Muslim Americans are shaped by the fact that there are some, both in the immigrant and younger generation, who are invested in model minorityhood and the notion that South Asian, Arab, and Afghan Americans are inevitably aligned with the interests of white middle-class America, while others oppose state policies of permanent warfare, neoliberal capitalism, and racial violence. As Bashir commented:

> 9/11 has created many apologetic people, and they don't realize they don't have to [apologize]. There is a very small group of people that are doing these things [terrorist activities] and even within those smaller groups we need to look into and see what's causing these problems. . . . It's creating division. . . . Unfortunately, the apologists are the ones who are educated. And I believe they think that education is what has made them better than others. And they try to, instead of helping others, they stay away.

For Bashir, the problem with Muslim American apologists was that they were apologizing on behalf of entire communities—and often in the name of Islam—for acts of violence that these groups did not commit and they were unwilling to address the political grievances that underlie the "problem" of violence, reinforcing the Orientalist association of violence that inheres in the good/bad Muslim dichotomy. Furthermore, these leaders provide barometers of what acceptable political subjecthood might look like for others in the community, while distancing themselves from those who are targeted as "bad" Muslims. Bashir also hinted at a class critique of the good/bad Muslim framework, pointing to Muslim Americans who become community "leaders" by virtue of their credentials and class status and who exemplify a cautious or conservative politics, abandoning political mobilization on behalf of those most affected by the policing of the War on Terror. Bashir's own father was an engineer but had been unemployed, so his mother and he and his siblings all worked to support the family. At the time I met him, he was working as a soccer coach in the summer and was limping because he had just injured his leg;

he said, "When we are sixteen, we start working. We work and go to school." While class divisions do not always map neatly onto the "moderate/radical" Muslim schism, it is true that, especially in the immigrant generation, class and social capital have marked the leadership of national Muslim American organizations, and that class is imbricated with processes of profiling and surveillance in complex ways.

Some Muslim American community leaders themselves were also very vocal in their critique of the capitulation to the "good/bad" Muslim political paradigm. Samina Sundas, a Pakistani immigrant woman from Palo Alto, launched American Muslim Voice (AMV) after 9/11 and was involved in various issues of Muslim civil rights. When I met Sundas in July 2011 at the small AMV office in Newark, in a building mainly housing technology companies, she was critical of "Muslim organizations that work with the FBI." Collaboration with law enforcement and intelligence agencies and being identified as a "moderate" Muslim is a charged issue for Muslim, South Asian, Arab, and Afghan activists and organizations in the post-9/11 era, one which is at the center of tense debates about where, and whether, a line can be drawn in the sand between strategic self-defense and collusion with the state. Sundas was also engaged in interfaith and antiwar organizing in Silicon Valley and the larger Bay Area; for example, in July 2013, AMV sponsored a press conference at MCA about the verdict in the police shooting of Trayvon Martin, which included the president of the San Jose/Silicon Valley NAACP. But Sundas was frustrated with the lack of cross-class and interracial solidarity, which she viewed as characterizing the older generation of leadership in Muslim American organizations. She said passionately, "When there's an issue related to immigrant rights or police brutality, AMV is the only [Muslim American] organization involved. It's how to be a good Muslim. Someone from Haiti called me to participate in their event and I went and said, 'As a Muslim, I stand with all oppressed people.'" Sundas, who was preparing to do a youth training workshop that day, commented with evident frustration, "There's so much wealth in our community, but not enough understanding."

The idea of a "good Muslim" is turned on its head by Sundas via the notion that good Muslim Americans *should* oppose state racism or violence and social injustice in the U.S. and globally and engage in solidarity with other racial minorities. This view was held by many of the young people I spoke to, who explained their activism and alliances with other struggles through the expression of a progressive notion of Islam that challenged the framework of "good" and "radical" Muslim politics. Aisha, a Palestinian American woman from a refugee family who was involved with SJP as well as antiwar and labor activism, said, "A big part of Muslim identity for me is being political, fighting for social justice." Bashir remarked, "We acknowledge who's radical and who's not, we acknowledge that," suggesting an internal definition of what being radical means. But he also interrogated the meaning of the label "radical" as pinned onto Muslim American youth, in particular, and on the MSA:

> I believe we are being attacked by the neoconservatives and they're attacking the younger generation instead of going after the older people because the idealism of younger generation is— . . . some people translate [that] as radicalism. I mean we're not different from other [student] clubs, we're very politically active and we're trying to raise awareness on various issues, not one, but many, like Palestine. We're trying to be there for the homeless and we're not any different from any other young, idealist people. But just because we have the Muslims [in our group], we are being attacked.

The demonization and state surveillance of political dissent by Muslim and Arab Americans, particularly by youth, has meant that not all are willing to risk becoming a "bad" Muslim and that there is a self-regulation produced by the counter-terrorism regime's focus on "radicalization" of youth.

The dichotomy of "good" and "bad" Muslim politics has had a far-reaching impact on the notion of what constitutes acceptable political subjecthood for the 9/11 generation. Malaika, who was involved with creating an MSA chapter in her high school, said, "When it came to the MSA and the activities we would do, we tried to avoid all politics. We didn't know where that would lead and we wanted to keep it strictly educational." Malaika expressed a fear of engaging with something called "politics," one shared by many Muslim and Arab Americans in a climate where political speech that is critical of U.S. policies can be grounds for suspicion and surveillance and even investigation or prosecution and in a moment when some youth might consider all politics to be "bad," that is, risky. As I will discuss in Chapter Two, educational and outreach programs, as well as interfaith activism, have come to be defined as safe activities that are part of civic life and outside of the realm of recognizable— and criminalizable—"politics" for Muslim Americans. When Malaika went to college in Stockton, she became vice president of the MSA chapter, whose members were largely Pakistani, and also Arab and Afghan, American. She continued to feel anxious about her activism, reflecting, "I really didn't want to make things political, especially because larger universities have activities, rallies; things going on all the time." Malaika reminisced wryly,

> We were a pretty harmonious campus, but I think that was because we stayed away from political issues. I know that the year before I started college [MSA]

had organized an Israel-Palestine awareness week. So MSA and Hillel had worked together, and I think it went over well. But in general . . . we would try and stay away from it [Israel-Palestine]. They tended to center on noncontroversial issues, like Rwanda. I mean, how controversial can you get? But even that was controversial sometimes!

Malaika's story illustrates the tensions that young Muslim Americans experienced in negotiating the boundaries of permissible politics. Events focused on Israel-Palestine, in particular, were considered the threshold of "radical" politics and could be staged only in an interfaith context of Jewish-Muslim "dialogue," as I discuss in the following chapter, while focusing on the humanitarian crisis in Rwanda was safe—though not always. The intense censure of pro-Palestine activism, including on college campuses, indicates the limits of civil rights and the right to free speech in selected instances of solidarity activism. There is a deeply racialized logic at work in institutionalized patterns of repression, embedded in an imperial regime of rights that regulates who deserves rights, civil or human, and which politics is permissible or criminalizable.

Given the social panic whipped up by the state and mainstream media about "radicalization" among Muslim American youth, and the surveillance, incarceration, and deportation of Muslims not just for their political activities, but also ideological and theological beliefs, there is a charged tactical debate for the 9/11 generation about what forms politics should take. Heena, a Muslim American woman whose family is from India and who grew up in San Jose, said that when she went to UC Berkeley, "I didn't feel like it made a difference to be in protests. And I could think of better ways of communicating your point. For me, if you engage in a community and they see you as a person, that's a better way to show what Muslims are about than a protest. I mean, I think that's important too but I think that if you act angry all the time that's going to help anything." Heena felt that while many Muslim American youth became "more outspoken" after 9/11, over time "people were scared of political events backfiring." She commented on protests against the war in Iraq, "Like my freshman year, we organized a big protest but then people used the images of those protests as example of how violent Muslims are. So I think that after that the MSA became less political because of that one incident. But I also think it depends a lot on who's on the board." While Heena was wary of "angry" political expressions and skeptical of the effectiveness of public protests, especially against U.S. wars, she acknowledged that there was a demonization of protests by Muslim American youth as inherently "violent" and threatening—including those, ironically, challenging

U.S. military invasion and occupation. It seems that for many youth, and in U.S. society at large, "politics" is associated with public, organized activism and "radical" politics imagined as "angry"—loud, public, and risky. The crux of this distinction of "radicalism" often rests on the question of violence/ nonviolence, on the one hand, and domestic/foreign policy, on the other. So taking on U.S. foreign policy, particularly challenging U.S. wars and support for Israel, and implicitly or explicitly defending resistance to imperial violence has become a politics coded in the War on Terror as "radical" and potentially "extremist."

The strategic negotiation of how to perform a "moderate" Muslim politics was pervasive among many in the older generation of activists as well. Rydhan, a Pakistani American whose father is the founder of the South Bay Islamic Association mosque in San Jose, formed a media committee at the masjid after 9/11 to train "media experts" as community members were being "bombarded by the media" and also launched the *Muslim Roundtable* show on local community access television. During my visit to SBIA, Rydhan commented: "The media only shows one side . . . extremists like to talk, moderate Muslims don't do that as much." There is a recognition here of the discursive battle being waged not just *about* Islam but *within* Islam for control of the narratives that were being produced about Muslim American identities and politics. For example, one Indian Muslim community activist from Silicon Valley who was involved in the antiwar and Palestine solidarity movements told me, as did others from the community, that MCA had come under surveillance by the FBI; she said that the mosque's executive committee had become careful about not allowing "stray posters" on the premises but also, in her view, "more apologetic" and "cautious" since 2004 given revelations that the FBI had spied on and infiltrated mosqued communities.

The production and self-regulation of a moderate, "safe" Islam has enormous political and social implications for the political subjectivities of South Asian, Arab, and Afghan American youth after 9/11 at a moment when the U.S. has propagated an image of the "correct" Islam compatible with its imperial multiculturalism. Muslims must be made acceptable/assimilable for Western modernity and U.S. liberal democracy, but the U.S. and many Western nation-states are no longer "safe" for Muslims. The production of "moderate" Muslim spokespersons is a process that the state itself is deeply invested in, as the U.S. has promoted and funded "good" Muslim leaders who assert themselves as "peace-loving" and loyal Muslim Americans, a policy that has continued from the Bush to the Obama regime (see Aidi 2014; Dabashi 2011). Moderate Muslims are needed to demonstrate Muslim support of the U.S. regime in the War on Terror and also "neoliberal conceptualizations of 'the human condition,'" according to Ronald Judy (2003, 107), as distinguished from Muslim "extremists" and militants who violently oppose U.S. policies and interventions. For example, the White House National Security Council established the Muslim World Outreach program in 2003 for "transforming Islam from within" by supporting existing "moderate" organizations in Muslim countries (Mahmood 2006). In March 2007, the RAND Corporation, which provides analyses for the U.S. defense and intelligence agencies, issued a report on "Building Moderate Muslim Networks," arguing that the U.S. needed to learn from its experiences in the Cold War and actively, if covertly, support "moderate" Muslim activists and intellectuals in order to counter "radical Islamists" who reject "liberal Western values such as democracy, gender equality."[26] The RAND Corporation and the right-wing Heritage Foundation have also pointed to Sufi Islam as a route to a "modern, democratic Islam" in key locations such as Pakistan, highlighting the ways in which U.S. state agencies and political organizations are involved in the regulation and also production of a "proper" or moderate Islam within and beyond the U.S. (Sheikh 2012, 174–175). This strategy of cultivating local allies to counter "extremists" or Salafists mirrors the Cold War policies of countering Communist influence, but in this case, it is also a project focused on "Islamic reformation" (Aidi 2014, 72). Kundnani (2014) observes that Obama's speech in Cairo in 2009 assumed that "multicultural recognition of mainstream Islam could win over moderate Muslims and help isolate and defeat extremism" through the "language of diversity, reform, and partnership" (74, 81). The inclusion of "good" Muslim subjects is thus necessary to shore up neoliberal democracy, particularly in a moment of imperial decline.

However, the co-optation of moderate Muslim Americans to represent the community has met with resistance and is increasingly and publicly contested by young Muslim American activists. The debate about participation in U.S. state projects came to a head when a group of Muslim American leaders attended the annual White House iftar during Ramadan with Obama in summer 2014, after revelations of the NSA's surveillance of many Muslim American leaders (including some at the iftar) and in the midst of Israel's massacre in Gaza, which Obama defended at the event. A social media campaign calling for a boycott of the iftar and denouncing the Muslim Americans who attended, led mainly by young Muslim Americans, "signaled a generational shift in Muslim American leadership" and a challenge to the established, largely immigrant male, leadership of Muslim American organizations by those "fed up with over a decade of mistreatment" by the state and a conservative advocacy approach criticized as ineffective due to its compliance with the state's expectations of "good behavior."[27]

Given the state's embracing and befriending of "good" Muslim political subjects, Andrew Shryock (2010) points to the costs of an emergent "Islamophilia" that is the flip side of Islamophobia. He notes "the challenge of countering Islamophobic impulses in ways that do not simply invert or reinforce them by cultivating their opposite: the image of the Muslim as 'friend,' as a figure identified with the Self" (9). For Shryock, the question of Islamophobia/Islamophilia is intimately intertwined with notions of modernity, citizenship, and democracy, for the "good" Muslim is one who has been made "safe" for U.S. neoliberal democracy:

> The good Muslim is also a pluralist (recalls fondly the ecumenical virtues of medieval Andalusia and is a champion of interfaith activism); he is politically moderate (an advocate of democracy, human rights, and religious freedom, an opponent of armed conflict against the U.S. and Israel); finally, he is likely to be an African, a South Asian, or, more likely still, an Indonesian or Malaysian; he is less likely to be an Arab. (10)

The argument that Shryock makes about the love for, not just the fear of, the Muslim is given much less attention than a straightforward (liberal/progressive) critique of Islamophobia as a fear of Islam and Muslims.[28] It is important to think about the incorporation, not just exclusion, of Muslim subjecthood and the ways in which the moderate Muslim is defined in national, racial, as well as ideological terms. The binary of the "good"/"bad" Muslim is deeply gendered, for the "good Muslim" is also likely to be female, in addition to being professional or suitably credentialed, given the state-supported, public role for female Muslims who can testify to the repressiveness and misogyny of Islam and provide authoritative rationales for U.S. interventions to save Muslim women (see Behdad 2007; Razack 2008; Sheehi 2011). As I have argued elsewhere, the "good Muslim" female must conform to a set of criteria regulating an American Islam acceptable for an imperial liberal feminism in the post-9/11 culture wars (Maira 2009b; Shryock 2010, 10).

The (self-)regulation of moderate/radical politics as a gendered practice also seemed to surface in my conversations with youth where the critique of, or uneasiness about, "angry" or "controversial" politics was largely expressed by young women. Although I spoke to young men who were themselves not involved in organized activism, very few seemed to feel strongly about distancing themselves from, or at least were willing to articulate a critique of, politics deemed "radical." At the same time, there were also many young women who had searing and direct critiques of U.S. state policies and were engaged in public protests and vigorous organizing. Expressions or narrations of affect

THE 9/11 GENERATION IN SILICON VALLEY | 71

are, of course deeply politicized, particularly in a context in which "anger" or "rage" among Muslim American youth can be placed on a continuum of feelings that is identified with "radicalization" within the taxonomy of the counterterrorism regime.[29] The affectivity of politics is powerfully expressed by African American poet Amir Sulaiman, associated with Ta'leef Collective, whose poem "Danger," which he performed on *Def Poetry Jam*, challenges the threat of "angry" Muslim youth: "I am not dangerous/I am danger/I am not angry/I am anger/I am abominable, idiotic, illiotic, relentless/I'm a death sentence/for the beast and his henchmen/Politicians and big businessmen/ I'm a teenage Palestinian/opening fire at an Israeli checkpoint, point blank, check-mate, now what?" (cited in Malek 2011, 140). Sulaiman, interestingly, was surveilled by the FBI, put on the no-fly list, and went underground for several months after recording this poem.

The regulation of political affect via the good/moderate and radical/angry dichotomy is indeed deeply gendered given that young Muslim American (particularly Arab or Afghan and increasingly Pakistani American) males are most likely to be labeled potential "extremists." Much of the public discourse, as well as some scholarly work, unquestioningly reproduces an Orientalist portrait of Muslim American girls as passive victims of backward, patriarchal "traditions" and disengaged from the sphere of public politics, so less threatening if still suspect. But it is also true that notions of political "radicalism" are almost always gendered, across religious, racial, and national boundaries, and the masculinization of protest politics and militant action in the U.S. and elsewhere could be just as much a factor in this verbal distancing of young women such as Heena from "angry" politics—and also perhaps the unwillingness of some young men to acknowledge their own feelings of fear or skepticism about "radical" protest politics.

I found that discussions among youth about the experiences of grappling with the "political," and of engaging with civil rights or interfaith activism, were infused with feelings of fear, anxiety, desire, and outrage, as well as empathy. In addition to the fear of political retaliation or repression, which is justifiable in the post-9/11 era, state violence and imperial racism sink deep into the crevices of everyday life, shaping intimacy and domestic and social relations, as postcolonial scholars have argued (Stoler 2006). The War on Terror has seeped into and transformed intimate social relations in this generation and it has done so by reconfiguring structures of political feeling and sentiments of dissent, solidarity, and even desire. One young Arab Muslim American woman, who worked at a national nonprofit organization where she did research on Muslims in the U.S., commented to me that the Islamophobia of the post-9/11 era has deeply affected gendered and intimate relations among her generation of Muslim American youth. She made a poignant observation about how some young men seek to find female Muslim partners who are outspoken, even brashly so, to counter the perception that Muslim men are inherently patriarchal and want submissive partners. This is not a bad move, if true, but it also indicates the extent to which the hypervisibility and intense scrutiny of Muslim Americans has (re)shaped sociality and created a self-consciousness about intimate relationships and gendered performances in this generation, which are understood to always be performances on a public stage with a political cost—or a hoped-for political reward. For example, Shabana Mir's (2007) research about Muslim American women college students highlights the ways in which youth are "caught between a dominant student culture" on U.S. campuses, "global stereotypes about Muslims, the Orientalist gaze, as well as 'conservative' and 'liberal' elements within their own communities" (17). Mir found that young Muslim American woman carried a "burden of awareness" about these competing expectations, with some trying to meet the "ideal" image of Muslim femininity in public while self-consciously performing an "ordinary" youthfulness (16–17). As Sirin and Fine (2008) observe, Muslim American youth "live in an echo chamber of stereotypes and surveillance" (178; see also Grewal 2014).

Despite this looking-glass effect of representations and self-representations in post-9/11 political culture, which has created an acute self-reflexivity among Muslim American youth, it was very apparent that some young women I spoke to articulated a deeply critical analysis of U.S. warfare, foreign policy, or racism while claiming to be apolitical. Salima, the young Pakistani American woman quoted earlier, commented, "I'm not into politics, I purposely don't follow politics at all," suggesting the deliberative nature of this choice. However, she then went on to express a critique of the civilizational thinking underlying the premise for the U.S. invasion of Iraq. Yasmeen, an Afghan American woman from Newark, remarked, "I really do not like politics very much so I try not to get involved in many political activities." But, she added, "I did get involved in more school groups and activities," explaining that she participated in an Afghan student group in high school and in both the MSA and the Afghan Students Association while at San Jose State—an engagement that is evidently political, but which she defined as outside the sphere of "official" politics. These youth negotiate what constitutes the "political" and test the boundaries of politics in a context of hypersurveillance of Muslim American youth activism by the national security state. In some cases, the claim of being "not into politics" may be a shield, warding off their own anxieties and perhaps those of their parents or others about the risk of suspicion and criminalization for being a "political" Muslim, Afghan, Pakistani, or Arab (Sirin and Fine 2008).

Some of the young activists I spoke to went through a process of rethinking their own anxieties about political activism in college and afterward, and there is also an issue of psychosocial development at work here for adolescents and young adults. For example, when I spoke to Malaika over tea at an Iranian bakery in a small strip mall in San Jose, she acknowledged that she was "unsure of herself" and her political views when she was in high school. She spoke frankly of her earlier insecurities about political activism and anxieties about "extremist" politics: "I mean, I guess I was afraid. I wasn't so afraid of identifying as a Muslim as I was identifying closely with political causes. . . . I didn't feel that I had the knowledge to feel passionate about them. I only saw people who were so extremist about certain issues. I've always sort of had this idea about being a diplomat, like I'd try to be negotiating, compromising." She learned about CAIR at a Know Your Rights workshop at her high school and, after college, took a job with the CAIR office in the Bay Area, becoming more confident in her role as a community advocate. She commented, "It's funny because I've stayed away from politics for so long and now all of a sudden I'm doing this." When I first met Malaika, in fact, she was speaking on a panel in Oakland linking Japanese American experiences of internment with Muslim American experiences of being denied civil rights. But Malaika viewed her involvement with CAIR, while political, as not "polarizing," because it is a nonprofit organization and so does "not endorse a political position." Her work could still fit within a framework of liberal democratic politics and civic integration that would not be deemed "extremist," focused on issues of immigrant rights, citizenship, racial profiling, and, occasionally, foreign policy issues such as Palestine. As I discuss in the following chapter, the politics of inclusion via civil rights activism becomes a form of "good" politics that is inserted into the grid of intelligibility that distinguishes "moderate" from "radical" politics.

Furthermore, it is striking that there is a generation of young Muslim American women, including hijabi women, who are visibly at the forefront of student and community groups, as was the case for women I spoke to such as Jenaan, Marwa, Aisha, Maliha, Sabina, Dana, and others. If anything, young South Asian, Arab, and Afghan American women often occupy leadership roles in both ethnic and religious student organizations, and this was true across the three ethnic groups I studied. These organizations, and particularly campaigns focused on civil rights, seemed to be an appealing and legitimate space for female leadership, a point I discuss further in Chapter Five. Sabina, a young Indian American woman from Santa Clara, had attended Granada in middle school and was active in both the MSA and student government at her community college. She attended the MSA West conference at UCLA in January 2011 and wrote a thoughtful reflection afterward on the conference theme, "Taking Back Our Narrative" (see figure 1.1), and its implications for Muslim American youth:

> "Taking back our narrative" is an expression of confidence. We weren't allowed to tell our story, we lost ourselves. When we don't control our narrative, we forget ourselves. We cannot be afraid of those who criticize us. After 9/11, our narrative became hijacked. It began to change, some of our people began to accept it. We cannot rely on the concepts, opinions, and stories of the oppressors. Our narrative is to fight against colonialism and oppression.

The theme of self-confidence, defiance, and resistance in the face of racist attacks and colonial violence, and the internalization of racism and Islamophobia by the oppressed, is a crucial trope in this narrative produced by a new generation of Muslim American activists. When we met, Sabina also spoke passionately about what she felt was a "duty as Muslims to inform and educate other students about the injustice happening around the world. Because as an average student going to college, you don't know such things and especially the way the media portrays events in the Middle East." Sabina said she was deeply inspired by African American Muslim speakers at the event, such as Imam Zaid Shakir and Amir Abdul Malik (labeled by some as "radical" Muslims), who exhorted young Muslim Americans to engage in activism against "militarism, racism, and poverty"; to not forget Latinos and Native Americans; and to remember the struggles of those, including the Black Panthers and Martin Luther King, Jr., who had earlier been targeted by the imperial state. Sabina was very moved by this progressive message, and it seemed that the theme of social justice and interracial solidarity was clearly articulated at the conference in the context of the history of oppositional struggles preceding 2001 and extending beyond Muslim and Arab American communities. This is, perhaps, the "radical" message of youth who are connecting antiimperial and antiracist movements locally and globally that is so threatening to the surveillance-security state.

Conclusion

The binary of moderate/extremist minority subjects, layered over a dichotomy of peaceful/civil and violent/uncivil dissent, distorts and diverts attention from the racial violence of the imperial state and perpetual warfare. It thus plays a central role in the political culture of the militarized capitalist state and in the post-9/11 culture wars, reinforcing Orientalist notions of Arab and Muslim militancy and misogyny, delegitimizing dissent, and legitimizing

Figure 1.1. MSA West 2011 conference program booklet

surveillance and racialized wars. As Salaita (2006a, 71–99) argues, an "imperative patriotism" that deems dissent against state policies unpatriotic has long been used by the U.S. state to suppress radical movements such as the American Indian Movement, the Black Panthers, and Young Lords, which were considered enemies of "American values," as well as socialist and leftist critics deemed un-American during the Cold War and the McCarthy era (see Ramos-Zayas 2004; Shrecker 1998). This is the history that perhaps the African American Muslim speakers at the MSA West conference were trying to bring to light for a new generation of Muslim American youth, given their own history of political engagement dating, in some cases, to the 1960s.

After 9/11, the experience of racial profiling drew some youth from immigrant Muslim groups closer to African Americans (Maira 2009a), but there are also ongoing fissures, racial as well as political, based on differences in relationships with the U.S. state and views of its wars in Afghanistan and Iraq, as well as its support for Israel. African American (and other U.S.-born) Muslims can be frustrated that immigrant Muslim communities prioritize issues of Middle East or global politics—Palestine, Kashmir, Bosnia, or Chechnya—over domestic concerns of racial and class exclusion and that immigrants sometimes remain detached from the histories of civil rights movements from which those who arrived after the 1960s have themselves benefited. At the same time, South and West Asian Muslims may chafe at what they view as the preoccupation of African American Muslims with questions of racial justice and national inclusion that in many instances (but not all) represent an "American" or U.S.-centric politics, while evading the linkages between domestic oppression and racial violence overseas (Abdullah 2013, 72). There is of course, an important history of Black radical politics and internationalism that powerfully focused on the nexus between U.S. racism and imperialism, and that continues to provide a powerful legacy symbolized by the figure and legacy of Malcolm X (Daulatzai 2012). In the post-9/11 era of new coalitions and cross-racial alliances, it is generally on the terrain of civil rights activism that young Muslim, Arab, South Asian, and Afghan American activists connect with African American struggles. The deployment of civil rights by the 9/11 generation raises questions, however, about the limits of struggles for political inclusion and the containment of cross-racial and transnational solidarity, as I discuss in the following chapter.

2

The New Civil Rights Movement

Cross-Racial Alliances and Interfaith Activism

Arab, South Asian, and Afghan American youth have been engaging with an emergent Muslim American politics since 9/11 and with activism that is both identity- and rights-based: defined by religious and/or national identities as well as by the paradigms of civil rights, "Muslim rights," and human rights. The frames of this post-9/11 politics bridge the national and the transnational: young activists have made linkages to a domestic history and discourse of civil rights and also invoked the notion of human rights to express solidarity with peoples elsewhere, in Iraq, Afghanistan, Pakistan, and Palestine. In this chapter, I explore the turn to "civil rights" by young Muslim Americans after 9/11 as a political strategy and discourse in response to the War on Terror.

This new post-9/11 civil rights movement emerges from a genealogy of U.S. civil rights, based on race and citizenship, and articulates with a framework of national inclusion that draws on U.S. multiculturalism and the formation of a Muslim American politics that is legible in neoliberal democracy. While the linkage with African American struggles for civil rights may facilitate cross-racial alliances, coalitions are also formed through interfaith programs, which have flourished in Muslim American communities since 9/11 and that, I argue, generate a "religious multiculturalism." There are tensions and contradictions that arise in each of these spheres of political and intergroup solidarity as young people wrestle with the boundaries of sanctioned and not-so-sanctioned affiliations and with what is defined as "proper" politics. This chapter discusses the slippages in civil rights and interfaith activism and the difficulty of forming cross-racial and cross-class coalitions in Silicon Valley, reflecting on what these gaps in political solidarity and tensions suggest for the production and regulation of "radical" or "moderate" Muslim political subjecthood. I situate these political disjunctures and shifts in the context of a post–civil rights moment and the postracial era signaled by the election of Barack Obama, examining what the emergence of "Muslim civil rights" means for the triumphalist narrative of U.S. multicultural democracy in the officially antiracist state.

I begin with an account of an event, "The Unheard Voices of 9/11 Hearing," which was organized during the tenth anniversary year of 9/11 as part of a series of events sponsored by the Sikh Coalition—an advocacy organization focused on civil rights for Sikh Americans, which has an office in Fremont—and other groups, in New York as well as in Silicon Valley. Held in a senior center in Mountain View in August 2011, this hearing focused on the "impact of 9/11 on the rights and liberties of Arabs, Muslims, Sikhs and South Asians" and community members were invited to share their experiences and engage in discussion with public officials and the San Jose police.[1] I want to acknowledge that this report of the event (which occurred while I was overseas) is based on participant-observation by my graduate research assistant, Trisha Barua, to whom I am deeply indebted for her thoughtful observations and ethnographic insights, not to mention her dedicated contribution to this collaborative research project.

"The Unheard Voices of 9/11"

The community hearing, bringing together Muslim and Sikh Americans in the region, was sponsored by the Sikh Coalition (formed in response to the post-9/11 backlash against Sikh Americans, the group organizes educational programs about Sikhism and promotes civic engagement among Sikhs in the U.S.), along with Paul Fong, the Chinese American California state assembly member for the 22nd district (including Mountain View, Sunnyvale, Cupertino, and Santa Clara). It drew a mostly South Asian audience, many of whom were visibly Muslim and Sikh (wearing headscarves and turbans), of all ages, as well as other community members who were largely East Asian or white American. Fong introduced the event by remarking that freedom of religion and the "nation's values" had been undermined by post-9/11 profiling and racism, and that this must be resisted by solidarity in the fight for dignity and mutual respect in order to affirm community and diversity. Amardeep Singh, a well-known Indian Sikh American activist with the Sikh Coalition, expressed his gratitude to the government officials who were present but also insisted, "To this day, there are still children being bullied, there is still workplace discrimination, and there are still hate crimes." He discussed the problem of the profiling of turbaned Sikh males at airports and national borders (what the Sikh Coalition refers to as "flying while Sikh"), and called on the public officials to step up their efforts to defend the civil rights of groups affected by post-9/11 discrimination and scapegoating.[2] According to the Council on American-Islamic Relations (2007), reports of discrimination against Muslim Americans in the Bay Area doubled from 2005 to 2006, and went up by 25% across the nation, continuing a disturbing trend that had begun in 2004 of a rise in incidents of bias and verbal as well as physical harassment of Muslims.[3] CAIR found an increase in incidents of bias and civil rights violations at airports, government agencies, schools, and work places, the largest uptick being in the category of "unreasonable arrests," including detention, surveillance, interrogation, and seizure of property.[4]

The hearing began with a panel on school bullying, a topic that had been in the news in the wake of reports of bullying of gay teenagers, and featured testimonials by Muslim and Sikh American youth who had been bullied for wearing a hijab or a turban, and who had been called "terrorists" by their peers or physically assaulted. These testimonies situated the issue of youth bullying in a framework that took into account issues of religion and race, highlighting narratives "unheard" in the dominant debate about racial and sexual discrimination against youth. Maha ElGenaidi, an Arab American activist with the Islamic Networks Group in the South Bay, complained that these incidents were generally not discussed in stories of school bullying (reports on civil rights suggest that incidents of biased bullying against South Asian, Arab, and Muslim American youth have been on the rise since 9/11).[5] Loubna Qatoumi, a young Palestinian American activist who was at the time director of the Arab Cultural and Community Center in San Francisco, pointed out that schools and playgrounds are politicized spaces; she cited an incident where a Palestinian student who wanted to do a presentation in class on her "homeland" was told by her teacher that Palestine didn't exist. During the discussion, Singh directly addressed the San Jose police chief, Chris Moore, and told him that Sikh and Muslim American students often did not report bullying because they did not have faith that school administrators would support them and were fearful of reprisals.

Other speakers situated the harassment of youth on a continuum with other, more severe forms of racialized harassment, including racial and Islamophobic violence. Several speakers also spoke of workplace discrimination, which Zahra Billoo, a young Pakistani American lawyer who is director of the San Francisco Bay Area chapter of CAIR, observed had actually increased in recent years. For example, Hani Khan, a young Muslim American woman, spoke of being fired for wearing a hijab by Hollister, a store owned by Abercrombie & Fitch, at a mall in San Mateo where she had worked after school.[6] A Sikh American man, Satnam Singh Gill, recounted that when he ran for a position in the Transit Workers Union, flyers with a photo of him in a turban were torn down and defaced. He said simply, "There's no such thing as equal opportunity employment." In another panel on encounters with law enforcement, a turbaned Sikh man, head of a successful financial services company in Silicon Valley, spoke of being regularly subjected to profiling by the police and intense security searches at the airport, which he experienced as personal "violations." In a poignant statement, an Iranian American man commented that everyone he knew had been visited by the FBI at some point and the people in his circle were so afraid of law enforcement that none would attend an event like this; he noted that no one else from *his* community was even present at the hearing that day. Community members, he said, felt "intimidated" and afraid of being used as "political pawns" by FBI agents, who attempted to recruit them as informants. This observation went to the heart of the problems raised by this staging of a "community hearing" when the "community" itself could not be constituted in public, let alone heard, due to the fear of the very profiling and civil rights violations that the hearing was trying to address—it should be noted, in the presence of some of the agents of those very violations.

A well-known Indian American community activist and civil rights attorney from the Asian Law Caucus in San Francisco, Veena Dubal, pointed out that Arab, South Asian, and Muslim Americans were generally afraid to report hate crimes because of the fear produced by increased collaboration between local law enforcement and the FBI, an issue that she had been investigating in San Francisco along with the ACLU and CAIR. Dubal also described post-9/11 domestic intelligence gathering as eerily evoking the infamous COINTELPRO program of repression of civil rights and antiwar activists in the 1960s and 1970s, for the FBI was conducting "low-level assessments" of Muslim American individuals without reasonable suspicion and turning into a "terrorist prevention agency." Shahid Buttar of the Bill of Rights Defense Committee—a grassroots organization addressing issues of surveillance, detention, and torture in the War on Terror—bluntly labeled the FBI a "rogue agency"; he cited the example of the Secure Communities Initiative, an FBI program for sharing data between police departments and immigration agencies, and initiatives to gather biometric data. Raj Jayadev, the Indian American labor and community activist mentioned earlier, spoke about his work with Silicon Valley Unplugged, a youth-run organization and "site of cross-ethnic organizing." He observed that many of the youth involved were too young to have experienced the moment of 9/11 but they did know about and had experienced its fallout, which he described as a state of "fear, distrust, and surveillance." Muslims and South Asians, he said thoughtfully, were "canaries in a coal mine" for government surveillance initiatives, but they could also be the "vanguard of a movement to challenge legal abuse."

Clearly, there were some contradictions that erupted between the different analyses and testimonials offered at the community hearing, between those who understood the problem as one of inclusion (of "unheard voices") and recognition of racial and religious diversity and others who thought that state agencies were "rogue" programs, as well as between those who situated their experience of invisibility or marginalization in the domestic sphere of civil rights and others who saw it implicitly as part of a larger global problem of imperialism and settler colonialism, which caused people, their national homelands, and their stories to "disappear" from the public sphere. The moving, eloquent, and outraged testimonials and critiques offered at this hearing bring into sharp relief many of the core questions in this book: can those who are the "canaries in the coal mine" for the surveillance state and imperial regime also be a political vanguard of resistance, and what does it mean to think of them as such? What are the implications of framing post-9/11 discrimination, racism, and Islamophobia as a problem of "civil rights" and legal equality? Is the turn to legal justice and electoral politics an effective or worthwhile strategy if racism and discrimination, as acknowledged by the activists at the hearing, is built into the legal system and state agencies themselves? What are the contours and limits of interethnic and interfaith coalitions in challenging state discourse about the War on Terror and what knowledge do they produce about the imperial racial state? The tensions underlying the various stories and analyses at the community hearing surfaced in many of the discussions I had with youth in this research and continue to suffuse political organizing and coalitions among targeted communities, as well as the political debates about rights-based politics, that have emerged since 9/11.

Civil Rights Activism

The language of civil rights is one that resonates with the younger generation of Arab, South Asian, and Afghan Americans, who find in it a framework for linking their critique of Islamophobia and racism to a longer history of struggles by other groups in the U.S. (Kibria 2011, 74). For example, Aisha, a Palestinian American woman who grew up in Union City, was very involved with both domestic and global Arab American activism as an undergraduate at UC Davis and after graduating from college. She translated Muslim and Arab American activism into a national discourse of civil rights and observed, "African Americans had their struggle, they fought for their civil rights, and now Muslim Americans have to do the same. I think it's about democracy." This was a common refrain among the youth to whom I spoke. In Lori Peek's (2011) study of Muslim American youth after 9/11, a young woman comments, "I think that every community in the U.S. has had to fight for their rights. The females had to fight for their rights, the African American community too. Now it's the Muslim community's turn to fight for their rights" (50). The denial of civil rights to Muslim or Arab Americans thus becomes not exceptional, but yet another instance of exclusion from the democracy promised by the nation-state that has been experienced by other racialized minorities at various moments in U.S. history—and in particular, by African Americans, who Angela Davis (2012) observes are viewed as the "representative subjects of 'civil rights'" (182).

The turn to civil rights is a powerful theme in the production of cross-racial solidarity and is propelled by pragmatic concerns with addressing discrimination and profiling as well as the political imperative of resisting the abrogation of freedoms in the name of "national security" (Sirin and Fine 2008, 110). On the one hand, the discourse of civil rights that links to Black freedom struggles deexceptionalizes the racial persecution of suspect populations after 9/11. On the other hand, as evident in the "Unheard Voices of 9/11" event, activism focused on Muslim civil liberties has also becomes an opportunity to wage a battle for inclusion into the national community and recognition as political subjects via a discourse of rights, a test of the true nature of American "democracy." Commenting on the shift to greater "civic engagement" and civil rights activism by Muslim Americans, Selcuk Sirin and Michelle Fine (2008) cite a remark by a young Muslim American man that illustrates the ways post-9/11 mobilization shores up a nationalist narrative: "Especially in this nation, when one strives to do something, anything is possible" (110). While not all youth engaged in civil rights campaigns are as celebratory of the American Dream, the turn to civil rights is fundamentally driven by an appeal to the nation-state as the arbiter of rights, individual as well as collective, and often by an assumption that liberal democracy is the horizon of political mobilization in response to Islamophobia and racial violence. For example, a survey by the Muslim Public Affairs Council (2005) found that a full 99% of Muslim American youth believed that national Muslim organizations should "engage in dialogue with the government and the general American public to get our rights," and 94% thought that "Muslims should be involved in the American political process 'even though they may disagree with the government's foreign policy'" (4).[7] The latter finding, demonstrating how young Muslim Americans acknowledge their dissent against the U.S. state's overseas policies while simultaneously looking to the nation-state for the bestowal of rights, hints at the tension in the demand for "rights" circumscribed by national "dialogue" and inclusion. For some youth I spoke to, however, political mobilization is framed in part by the nation-state but not confined by it, as they also engage with a discourse about imperialism and sovereignty—often via human rights—that transcends the issue of domestic civil rights. These conversations with young people in Silicon Valley revealed the contradictions generated by this dual national-global approach and its implications for a critique of civil and human rights.

After 9/11, many national Muslim American organizations that were focused on political mobilization launched or intensified civil rights campaigns in response to the heightened discrimination faced by Muslims, Arabs, South Asians, and "Muslim-looking" people (especially turbaned Sikhs) in the United States. Know Your Rights workshops were organized by coalitions involving Muslim, Arab, and South Asian American activists and lawyers who tried to do grassroots outreach to communities at mosques, gurudwaras, and community spaces, as well as to youth, using pamphlets in different languages, such as a comic book produced by the Midnight Special Law Collective in the Bay Area (see figure 2.1).

Given the mass detentions, deportations, and surveillance in the War on Terror, and the abrogation of constitutional rights under the USA PATRIOT Act and its reauthorizations, this was certainly a necessary and strategic response to the crisis experienced by those defined as enemies of "homeland security" (and I participated in and organized some of these workshops and campaigns myself). For example, the infamous "Special Registration" program established in 2002 required noncitizen Muslim males from twenty-four Muslim countries (and also North Korea) to register with the federal government, as a result of which almost fourteen thousand of those who voluntarily registered were subjected to deportation proceedings (notably, 35% of these were Pakistani) (Ahuja, Gupta, and Petsod 2004). The program sent a chill throughout Muslim immigrant communities, especially among those who were undocumented or working class, which persisted even after it was eventually canceled in 2011. State intelligence gathering and profiling continued, and expanded, with FBI interviews and undercover surveillance that were less publicized and constituted what I have elsewhere called a "Secret Registration" program (Maira 2009a). For example, under the new interagency Joint Terrorism Task Force (JTTF), Iraqis and other Muslims and Arabs were monitored after 9/11 and preceding the war on Iraq in 2003 (Ahuja, Gupta, and Petsod 2004). By 2010, the language of Islamophobia had shifted more consistently toward a focus on the enemy within at a moment when Obama publicly announced his strategy for the Af-Pak war, which, Kumar (2014) argues, necessitated a national and moral panic about "homegrown terrorism" to legitimize this new phase of the War on Terror (172).

The post-9/11 crisis of civil rights made most vulnerable those who were not privileged enough to adequately defend themselves within the U.S. legal system, given the state's newfound powers to *legally* use secret evidence, war-

Figure 2.1. Midnight Special Law Collective's *Know Your Rights* comic book

rantless wiretapping, mandatory and indefinite detention, "extraordinary rendition" (abduction), and torture. Immigrants working in the service sector in public spaces, whether as taxi drivers or gas station attendants, tended to be the targets of the most violent assaults after 9/11, but even professionals and other more privileged Muslim, Arab, and South Asian Americans found themselves at risk of being harassed, losing their jobs, having their bank accounts frozen, subjected to wiretapping, or being taken off planes (Cainkar 2011; Bakalian and Bozorgmehr 2009; Peek 2011). In 2013, CAIR reported that the largest number of civil rights complaints received in northern California were related to employment discrimination against Muslims, followed by complaints about interactions with law enforcement, including interrogations by the FBI or JTTF, profiling, and surveillance; the total number of complaints had increased since the previous year, and included incidents of bullying and harassment of Muslim students at schools, as discussed in the San Jose hearing (CAIR 2014).[8] Thus, the eviction from political community (Razack 2008) or the state of exception cuts across class lines, a point I will return to in Chapter Five, even if it did not always deepen cross-class solidarity.

Prosecution for "material support" of terrorism—which was actually introduced in the 1996 Antiterrorism and Effective Death Penalty Act passed under President Clinton, which also legalized use of secret evidence—became an ambiguous legal dragnet within which many were trapped. Muslim Americans were targeted simply for their charitable donations to Arab or Muslim organizations, or, in the case of one Pakistani American student in New York, presumably for facilitating donations of socks and raincoats to Al Qaeda in Pakistan (Kundnani 2014, 47).[9] Antiterrorism policies thus tightened the noose around transnational Muslim networks and philanthropic activities, as people began to panic about what forms of community were permissible. Discrimination and racialized surveillance occurred at the level of civil society and also the state; while women in hijab were harassed in stores or attacked on the street, young men were surveilled by the FBI and found GPS devices installed under their cars, as did an Arab American student from Santa Clara, and Muslim student groups have been infiltrated by FBI informants, as I discuss in more detail in Chapter Five.[10] CAIR's 2009 report, *The Status of Muslim Civil Rights in California*—which surveys the Bay Area, Sacramento Valley, Greater Los Angeles Area, and San Diego—also noted that cases of anti-Muslim bias and violence included acts of mis-identification targeting those perceived to be Muslim, particularly (turbaned male) Sikh Americans (9, 12).

As being, or appearing to be, Muslim became criminalized, national Muslim American organizations and juridical structures co-produced the notions of "racial profiling" and "religious profiling" as the proper paradigms for redress. The interviews I did with Muslim American youth highlighted how the Muslim institutional infrastructure in some cases morphed into a civil rights infrastructure with programs educating targeted communities about civil and immigrant rights. For example, Farida observed that after 9/11, "there were all those events set up for people to know their rights and stuff. . . . It was hard, people were being held up at the airports. Nobody even knew about the PATRIOT Act. So people had to be informed about that, like this is what is going on." CAIR and other national Muslim American organizations began hosting Know Your Rights workshops and distributing educational materials about civil rights and legal resources. In the Bay Area, Arab, South Asian, Muslim American, and civil rights groups collaborated to provide free legal clinics and produce pamphlets in various languages to advise community members on what to do if an FBI agent came to their door to interview them, how to deal with "Special Registration," or how to respond to interrogations at airports. I want to emphasize that these strategic responses and legal campaigns are not to be dismissed, and they provided a minimal line of defense for targeted communities in addition to collective support; indeed, I participated in some of these Know Your Rights campaigns myself after 9/11. But the question this kind of organizing raises, for me and also others, is: what kinds of political subjectivity are produced for youth by these campaigns? I am interested in interrogating the conditions of possibility of "an increasing inscription of individual lives within the state order" through struggles centered on winning rights, as David Eng (2010, 28) has suggested in his critique of queer citizen-subjects petitioning the state for rights.

Some Arab, South Asian, and Afghan American youth entered the sphere of formal "politics" via civil rights activism as reenacted or re-created by Muslim Americans. For example, Malaika attended a Know Your Rights workshop, conducted by the Sacramento chapter of CAIR at her mosque, while she was a high school student. Having gone on to work with CAIR's civil rights and government relations programs in the Bay Area, Malaika reflected on the group's approach:

> Part of CAIR's mission, in addition to protecting civil liberties and educating people of their rights, is empowering the community. Being politically active and engaged, and then also developing better relationships with public officials. You know, making sure that their voice is heard and that they're also aware of issues. So we're constantly scheduling meetings with city council members, with assembly members, with congressmen. They try to facilitate a regular contact between the two. And then also, we go to [voter] registration drives, have

workshops on an occasional danger, reaching out to the mosque and making sure the community is active.

Civil liberties, in this view, are central to mobilizing and "empowering" the Muslim American community through rights education and giving it a "voice" in the political sphere through engagement with the structure of representative government.

Several local as well as national Muslim and Arab American organizations organized or intensified campaigns for voter registration, political lobbying, and "civic engagement" via electoral politics after 9/11; for example, the Arab American Institute launched an annual "Yalla Vote" campaign, CAIR offers a "Citizenship Curriculum," and the American Muslim Political Coordinating Council engages in political lobbying (Bakalian and Bozorgmehr 2009, 180–182, 216). It should be noted that these campaigns are organized by faith-based as well as pan-ethnic Muslim and Arab American organizations, such as the Arab Resource and Organizing Center (AROC), a grassroots progressive organization led by young Arab American activists in San Francisco that has organized voter registration drives for California elections. In 2010, AROC distributed pamphlets in English and Arabic explaining each of the ballot measures and propositions, with a bilingual motto: "Exercise Your Rights: Vote!" I should also note here that AROC's 2010 campaign also included a call to voters to support a petition for divestment by California public retirement funds from "corporations committing human rights abuses in Israel," so it was focused not just on domestic but also global politics, and linked citizenship with both civil and human rights, an important articulation I will return to later. In general, young Arab, South Asian, and Afghan Americans organized on the platform of civil rights using various strategies and tactics: street protests, public rallies, and alliances with larger immigrant and civil rights movements. What has united both national as well as local civil rights campaigns is the notion that the nation-state should live up its liberal-democratic promise of constitutionally mandated rights and racial and religious equality, whether through channels of participatory democracy or pressure from outside the system. Liberal philanthropic groups and progressive foundations concerned with AMEMSA (Arab, Middle Eastern, Muslim, and South Asian) communities also began to emphasize the need to fund programs "to protect civil rights" and "increase civic participation" in these communities, producing an agenda dovetailing with the civil rights complex (Ahuja, Gupta, and Petsod 2004, 7).

This surge in post-9/11 civil rights activism did, on the one hand, expose the racialized distribution of rights by the state, but, in its reformist variant, it also facilitated a process and discourse of nationalization. For example, a "leader" in the Arab and Muslim American community used a common refrain to describe the mobilization against the post-9/11 assault on civil rights as restoring belief in American justice: "People in the end did not lose hope in the sense of fairness here in the country" (cited in Bakalian and Bozorgmehr 2009, 182). In this narrative predicated on liberal democracy, Muslim Americans are framed as the latest group to fight for inclusion in the nation, and like African Americans, Latinos, and other Asian Americans before them, will become part of the national community through their struggle in the crucible of civil rights activism. The "story of racial and ethnic inclusion," as Nikhil Pal Singh (2004) points out, is central to a redemptive national narrative based on notions of "America's exceptional universalism" and "religious tolerance" (19). The 2008 election of President Barack Obama, an African American from a partly Muslim family, only reaffirmed this narrative of the inclusive and tolerant tenets of the post–civil rights nation, for many Muslim Americans as much as anyone else.

For some youth, however, civil rights was an inadequate or ineffective framework for post-9/11 political activism because they saw the profiling, exclusion, and violence targeting Muslim and Arab Americans as due to a system of racial domination constitutive of the nation-state and its foundational ideology of Manifest Destiny. While some youth I spoke to identified with, or least invoked, a liberal discourse of civil rights, others were ambivalent or deeply skeptical. Yasser, whose father was Pakistani and mother Mexican American, and who attended Ohlone College in Fremont, said passionately:

> Muslims need to start standing up for their opinion and start attacking the credibility of the CIA and the FBI and telling them they're full of shit. Stop being scared! Unite! Who cares if they kill you or you lose your jobs? Or they do all this funny stuff like they did with the Black people and their civil rights movement. If you start standing up, other people will start standing up! If we start standing up, people will follow along.

Yasser linked Muslim American struggles to the state repression of Black activism and critiqued the exceptionalism of U.S. liberal democracy. In his view, the role of the FBI and CIA in the War on Terror needed to be exposed and challenged by a political critique of the state that would link the targeting of Muslim Americans to similar repressive strategies of surveillance and infiltration used against African American civil rights activists. Resistance to state violence and repression must be based on interracial solidarity emerging from a radical genealogy of antistate struggle. Yasser suggested that Muslim

Americans could be a vanguard for resistance, but one at the forefront of a movement that would be willing to challenge the imperial state and risk the loss of employment, financial security, and class mobility, or even life itself. Being a canary in the coal mine thus means rejecting fear, including fear of death and disappearance. This also means rejecting antiracist struggle based on a notion of racial inclusion, for as Yasser said incisively about Obama, the first African American president and the first from a Muslim family:

> He's a good guy, but it's the same thing. They just put a Black guy in the White House, so what? The only way I'll believe that Obama actually did something is if in ten years, I see that America's not being imperialistic to South America by putting interest on them and taking away their money. . . . I read *Confessions of an Economic Hitman* and how America is still collecting interest off of Latin American countries, basically using their resources. And basically because their country is paying so much interest and the leaders are puppets, people are starving and dying. . . . So I'll only acknowledge Obama's success when he fixes it for other people. When the Third World is done suffering from the U.S. hand, the European hand. If you look, America's been interfering with Nicaragua, they went to El Salvador. . . . They attacked Panama in the Gulf War and killed many civilians, they dropped bombs on them. And these are poor people who have nothing. They did the same thing to Iraq, Afghanistan. So this evil approach they have, unless it changes [only] then I can say Obama's a great guy. To me, Obama and Bush are on the same boat. And people say he's so great, they're so stupid. They think one man runs the world. No, it's still the government, still the people standing behind the curtain.

I cite Yasser's critique at length because it emphasizes a systemic analysis of U.S. racism and global capitalism, challenging the notion that the election of one African American president would change the enduring structure of an imperial state and its "evil" military, economic, and political interventions that inflict violence on other countries. In this analysis of imperial violence and impoverishment of racialized, Third World populations, race is not reduced to identity politics nor is solidarity with African Americans embedded only in a politics of recognition via electoral democracy, but also in resistance to a militarized capitalist state. Perhaps partly because of his mixed Latino/ South Asian background, but also partly because of his interest in reading books such as John Perkins's (2004) analysis of globalization and neoliberalism, Yasser offers a transnational, historical analysis linking U.S. wars in Iraq and Afghanistan to earlier interventions in Central and Latin America and critiques the global apparatus of counterterrorism and counterinsurgency. He points to the ways in which U.S. imperial power has rested on proxy wars, covert operations, and client regimes and on neoliberal policies tied to the IMF and World Bank that have imposed and onerous debts on the global South. This is an astute analysis because the U.S. has relied on nonterritorial, secret, and flexible forms of political, economic, and military domination, making U.S. imperialism difficult to name and even more difficult to resist (Kaplan 1993). Yasser's framework shifts the discussion of the War on Terror from the official premise of "regime change" for democracy to the state's desire for economic and political hegemony and to a larger politics of colonial violence and terror.

For Yasser, Muslim Americans must connect domestic repression to global, anti-imperial and anti-capitalist struggles, rather than simply seek inclusion on the national terrain of civil rights. I should note that some community activists I spoke to who worked with Muslim civil rights organizations expressed a similar critique, and struggled with the implications of challenging U.S. imperial policies in the Middle East when doing so tars Muslim activists with the label "terrorist sympathizers." For example, Zarina, a young Muslim American woman who works with CAIR in the Bay Area, said:

> One of the reasons CAIR is targeted is because we were tainted with accusations about being linked to Hamas, just because some people [in CAIR] are Palestinian and have taken positions on Palestine. So are we compromising our civil rights work? . . . But partly, it's about specialization.

In Zarina's view, CAIR has a mandate that suggests that it does not need to enter into global politics but should focus on (domestic) civil rights issues. She commented, "It's a fine line . . . we are called radical, but some call us 'house Muslims'!" While CAIR activists have been attacked by the right, in particular for their position on Palestine, and accused of being supporters of terrorism, they are simultaneously assailed by progressive-left Muslim Americans for transgressions such as collaborating with law enforcement on training workshops (as have other advocacy groups, such as the ADC), echoing Malcolm X's famous critique of the "house Negro" and "field Negro" (Sheehi 2011, 158). The self-consciousness among Muslim American youth I spoke to about the meaning of "radical" politics in the post-9/11 era echoes regulatory polarizations from earlier periods of radical political mobilization in the United States. Zarina recalled that as a teenager she went to protests outside of prisons in California where "politically outspoken" imams were detained, commenting that her own brother had been told not to talk about Palestine at his mosque, but prevailed in his political critique with the support of the congregation. Clearly, the proper focus of civil rights work and issues of censorship and regulation of Muslim political subjecthood are hotly debated in a climate of political repression. CAIR itself, in its 2009 report on civil rights, has noted that underlying the civil rights violations of Muslim Americans is the "critical response by the Muslim community to ongoing U.S. foreign policy related to the Middle East, Asia and Africa, along with strong criticism of domestic policies" (10). In other words, it is the challenge to U.S. imperial policies by certain groups or movements that creates the suspension of civil rights, so this "state of exception" is always global and not just domestic in an imperial state (Agamben 2005; Razack 2008).

However, the official narrative about civil rights struggles in the U.S. is shaped by a civilizing story of the nation as a community of diverse groups of immigrants, each of which ultimately won its struggle for equality and freedom, including Muslim Americans. This narrative occludes the history of dispossession of natives by settlers, the genocidal violence against indigenous peoples, slavery and Jim Crow, the colonial appropriation of other territories, and imperial interventions overseas. The discourse of civil rights tied to "national redemption and moral regeneration" (Singh 2004, 3) selectively embalms the legacy of Black civil rights leaders such as Martin Luther King, Jr., who have come to symbolize the ability of the nation to live up to its mythic ideals of equality and tolerance, and to confer inclusion on groups that engage in peaceful struggles shaped by Christian ethics and liberal democratic politics.

This liberal racial narrative of civil rights has been erected as a front in the U.S. ascendancy to global power in order to undermine radical struggles against U.S. imperialism, and clearly the state's recuperation of civil rights struggles by groups who are targets of the racial state's violence and exclusion is not new. Mary Dudziak (2000) has argued that civil rights legislation and the will to desegregation in the United States during the Cold War was shaped by the need to "sell democracy to the Third World," for "America could not save the Third World for democracy if democracy meant white supremacy" (106, 115). Chandan Reddy (2011) points out that "the state form in the second half of the twentieth century sought to address race by including it in the juridical and liberal forms of egalitarian freedom and its apparatuses" (222–223); so while the state developed new technologies of surveillance and incarceration in the 1980s and 1990s and refined its methods of repression, it was also transformed into a "multicultural" state promoting racial equality and the neoliberal, individual freedom of the market. Other scholars, such as Andrea Smith (2011), have traced the shift from radical movements for racial and economic justice in the 1960s and 1970s to mobilization that resorts to the "liberal multicultural state as that institution that *recognizes* and legitimizes legal and political claims based on gender and race," as exemplified by the movement against hate crimes that seeks protection to be provided by the very state that has historically perpetrated racial violence (232).

The focus on post-9/11 hate crimes and redress through legal equality similarly obscures the logics of white supremacy and class inequality that undergird the ethos of a settler-colonial capitalist state. Critiques that challenge the logics of imperialism, militarism, and capitalism of the racial state, including those offered by King himself in his later years, are dismissively labeled as "radical" and "anti-American"—which, if the U.S. nation-state's constitutive national logics are white supremacy and capitalist order, they are (Singh 2004, 1–6). The election of the first African American president slid easily into a naturalized narrative of American racial "progress" and integration, so that Obama embodied the ultimate realization of King's dream of racial equality. The Obama moment signified the closure of the epoch of civil rights struggle, the dawn of a "postracial" era. And yet, the racial War on Terror continued under Obama with surveillance; racial, religious, and political profiling; and government plans to root out "homegrown" terrorists, while deportations targeting immigrant communities actually increased under the new regime—not to mention persistent police violence against Black males that sparked a mass movement to challenge anti-Blackness under a Black president. Obama ratcheted up the war on Afghanistan, as promised (shifting the theater of war from Iraq), stepped up the drone attacks in northwest Pakistan, and, despite his early promises, did not shut down the infamous prison at Guantanamo—in addition to his failure to pursue prosecutions of individuals culpable for the financial crisis of 2008. While disillusionment slowly set in among supporters of Obama and the early euphoria of 2008 about hoped-for "change" eventually subsided among liberals and progressives, it took a long time to acknowledge that Obama-mania had been partly driven by a current of longing for national redemption—even if his presidential campaign provoked deeply racist sentiments and was itself entangled with expressions of Islamophobia and distancing from Muslims and Arabs (Cole 2011). Yet for many liberal-left supporters of the "Yes We Can" campaign, there was a deep desire to rectify America's image, sullied during the years of the Bush-Cheney regime, and relieve guilt and shame about the war on Iraq, Guantanamo, and Abu Ghraib.

The liberal fantasy of liberation from an earlier, awful era enabled by Obama's election extends what Donald Pease (2009) argues was a neutralization of the radical left beginning under Clinton and co-optation of minoritized movements into neoliberal market rationalities and the multicultural security state (71, 74). Many liberal critics of the neocon regime similarly contrasted Clinton's multilateralism with the Bush doctrine of unilateralist "shock and awe." This liberal exclusion and left neutralization occurred in the Obama era as well, as evident in the "Obama effect" that dampened antiwar and immigrant rights organizing during the early years of his presidency. Liberal exclusion requires a strategy of liberal inclusion by the multicultural, "postracial" state that both targets *and* incorporates Muslim, Arab, South Asian, and Afghan Americans and recuperates their struggles in the post-9/11 moment—as it has incorporated gay rights activism for "marriage equality" through adoption of "queer liberalism" (Eng 2010). In the context of the War on Terror, the staging of multicultural nationalism through a Muslim racial liberalism deflects critiques of the U.S. state's racist and genocidal policies and the hollowness of U.S. rhetoric about democratization and civil rights (Rodriguez 2010).

In the post-9/11 climate, the narrative of exceptionalist U.S. democracy also relied on an Orientalist story of anti-democratic Arab and Asian states and civil rights activism as tutelage in liberal, participatory democracy. This is evident in some accounts of post-9/11 mobilization which suggest that Muslim, Arab, and South Asian American community activists had to "convince immigrants to believe in the American way of activism, advocacy, and mobilization," since they presumably migrated from societies lacking in civil and human rights (Bakalian and Bozorgmehr 2009, 178). This "coming of age" into liberal democracy via a civil rights awakening in the West was contingent, however, on erasing the political histories of immigrants and struggles against imperial interventions and neoliberal capitalism in their home countries.

A liberal nationalist framework of "civil rights" is racialized through its conjuncture with *civility* and with *civilization* and Western modernity itself, especially in the context of the War on Terror. The racialized and colonial logic of the liberal, modern state defines what counts as "civil" disobedience and what is "uncivil" resistance for Arab, South Asian, and Afghan American youth, a logic that seeps into the post-9/11 culture wars and the "clash of civilizations" paradigm, as I discuss in the following chapters. The repression of radical civil rights and anti-imperialist and antiwar struggles since the 1970s and their demonization as anti-American and, paradoxically, proviolence ("militant" or "terrorist"), has been accompanied by the incorporation of new movements for racial, gendered, or sexual justice and freedoms into the framework of individual rights and neoliberal citizenship (Ferguson 2012). There has also been a concurrent shift among some who belonged to radical struggles to participation in institutionalized rights or "social justice" activism and employment in grant-funded, nonprofit organizations, a point of some contention in the Bay Area, which was home to the Black Panthers as well as radical Asian and Arab American movements (Kwon 2013; Omatsu 1994).

I think the debate about the entry of Muslim Americans into the civil rights–industrial complex can be productively addressed by the critique of queer theorists of the costs for progressive activists of prioritizing a "legal equality strategy"; Dean Spade has pointed to the ways in which mobilization for "same-sex marriage recognition"—or what has been dubbed "marriage equality—is unable to produce "meaningful transformative change" because it evades the "broader administrative frameworks that structure the most significant forms of violence" against queers, yet this organizing has consumed most of the resources of queer activism in recent times (cited in Stanley et al. 2012, 120). Eng (2010) observes that queer liberal movements— such as the liberal gay marriage campaign which has been framed as a new "civil rights movement"—are part of the larger shift "from a politics of protest and redistribution to one of rights and recognition, and of lifestyle as choice" (29). This is what Lisa Duggan (2003) has called the "new homonormativity," based on a "neoliberal sexual politics" of "domesticity and consumption" (50). The incisive queer critique is one that needs to be considered in relation to the liberal Muslim civil rights movement as well, while acknowledging that Muslim American activists are responding to forms of racial violence that are overlapping with yet distinct from those encountered by queers and to state polices of surveillance, deportation, or incarceration that have a global reach. At the same time, queer theorists have underscored the ways in which there are similar logics of disposability, domination, and violence that target queers, immigrants, and Muslim Americans in the post-9/11 state (see Tadiar 2013). In a warfare/carceral state that is also a liberal, multicultural state, queers (and both Muslims and non-Muslims) are drawn to the promise of "liberal and martial citizenship" (Reddy 2011, 10).

In the post-9/11 mobilization for civil rights, racial and sexual rights can be linked through Reddy's powerful critique of "freedom with violence," as inscribed in movements for equality that evade state violence:

> "freedom with violence" refers to the way in which socially and institutionally produced forms of emancipation remain regulative and constitutively tied to the nation-state form . . . every movement to validate a claim of social freedom produces a disparate and adversarial claim by the state elsewhere against what it determines to be irrational cultures and practices; thus, it will no longer do to simply claim the strategic use of the US state or its discourse of freedom. (39)

In his analysis of liberal gay rights campaigns, such as the movement for gay marriage and the repeal of "Don't Ask, Don't Tell," Reddy argues that these "reformist" movements and efforts for inclusion of queers in the U.S. military not only reinscribe the liberal, national state as the "ethical fulcrum" for movements for equality, but also end up legitimizing the use of state violence (or counterviolence) against some other group or some people elsewhere. Race becomes a wedge, with gay marriage advocates being pitted against the presumed homophobia of African Americans (or Muslim Americans), gay rights superseding immigrant rights, and movements against anti-Black violence trumping campaigns against anti-Arab violence. Resonating with the critiques of homonormativity and queer liberalism developed and advanced by Jasbir Puar (2007) and David Eng (2010), and by activist collectives such as Against Equality (Weiss 2012) or Queer (In)Justice, Reddy points out that since the politics of racial retrenchment of the Reagan era and the rollback of civil rights since the 1980s, "the state addresses racism through the affirmation and protection of individual rights, while using a juridical rights-bearing subject as a means of silencing all alternative discourses and systemic accounts of antiracism by projecting them as racist" (145). So, for example, since AROC's campaign for voter mobilization in the Bay Area also included a call for divestment from a state engaged in illegal military occupation and human rights abuses, this campaign, like so many other boycott or divestment campaigns targeting the Israeli state, is likely to be called racist (i.e. anti-Semitic). Any movement that challenges the exceptionalism of U.S. imperial democracy is seen as outside the boundaries of liberal political modernity and political recognition.

Muslim American youth have to grapple with fraught political choices that seem almost impossible to navigate in this climate of external and internal regulation of "proper" or safe politics—what statement going beyond the framework of liberal rights will not land you in prison? What action of cross-racial or global solidarity is really worth the risk? Yasser was critical of the MSA on his campus, though he had been involved with organizing events with them earlier, in part, it seemed, due to his general frustration with the politics of the Muslim American community, and in part due to what he saw as the group's lack of energetic commitment and organizing. In his view, their failure was demonstrated by their inability to attract non-Muslims to events— for Yasser, this was important not necessarily because of a belief in interfaith activism, but more perhaps out of a desire to communicate his worldview with a larger audience. The need to go beyond the Muslim American community and enlarge the sphere of mobilization and solidarity is an imperative that has driven many youth to join interfaith programs, which have proliferated since 9/11. The turn to interfaith organizing has occurred in tandem with the turn to civil rights, and both provides sites for the production of a narrative of liberal inclusion and proper political subjecthood for South Asian, Arab, and Afghan American youth.

Interfaith Activism and Religious Multiculturalism

Interfaith programs have become a sanctioned site of public engagement for Muslim American youth, but I found that they exist in an uneasy relationship with cross-racial alliances and anti-imperial, transnational solidarity for several youth I spoke to in Silicon Valley. Since 2001, Muslim Americans have become increasingly active in a growing interfaith movement, including an interfaith youth campaign that emerged on college campuses and has rapidly spread across the U.S. since the early 1990s (Patel and Brodeur 2006; see also Cainkar 2011). Muslim Americans who felt attacked or isolated after 9/11 often threw themselves into organizing interfaith programs in mosques and community centers and, in some cases, found themselves legitimizing acceptable Muslim American identities and "proper" coalitional politics (Afzal 2015). The turn to interfaith politics is part of a national strategy for managing race relations via a discourse of religious inclusion. One Muslim American community leader recalled that he told an advisor to President Bush after 9/11, "The president has to visit a mosque. You have to say 'churches, synagogues, and mosques.' When they say 'Judeo-Christian,' you should say, 'Christians, Muslims, and Jews'" (cited in Bakalian and Bozorgmehr 2009, 181). Organizations such as CAIR and the Islamic Networks Group (ING) in the Bay Area have been actively involved in the interfaith movement; for example, ING does presentations about Islam for faith-based groups and participates in interfaith programs, stating that it "recognizes the need for ongoing interfaith dialogue and cooperation in our increasingly multicultural and diverse society to bring about peace in our neighborhoods, our country, and the world."[11] Inclusion for Muslim Americans is thus framed through religious pluralism and winning political recognition for a faith-based community that belongs to, and is not outside of, the U.S. multicultural state—a demand that in itself is not problematic, but becomes so when expressed in terms that bracket a critique of the state beyond the ambit of religion or culture. The problem is that in the post-9/11 context, as I will demonstrate, the interfaith movement is built on the same tenets of liberal inclusion that contain politics through liberal civil rights activism.

Interfaith "dialogue" projects, which became a popular model for pluralist inclusion in the 1980s and 1990s, involve state interventions in religion and the anointment of selected religious representatives and religious streams, thus promoting certain expressions of Islam and particular Muslim leaders

(Hicks 2013; see also Aidi 2014, 72–74). Kundnani (2014) points that out in the U.S. as well as in Europe, a "state-sponsored Islamic leadership" has been established with the "multicultural recognition" of "new religious identities," not just ethnic or racial identities, describing this as a shift to "multi-faith-ism" that creates a paradox for presumably secular states who now "endorse an official version of Islam" (77). Furthermore, liberal-progressive founda-tions and other groups invest funds in interfaith projects; it is significant that youth are seen as "bridge builders" within this model of civic integration and inclusion, as part of a larger push by Muslim Americans toward "civic engage-ment" (Ahuja, Gupta, and Petsod 2004, 17; Afzal 2015, 168, 173). The goals of the interfaith youth movement are to encourage engagement across religious difference and to create a public place for religious tradition within society through interfaith cooperation (Patel and Brodeur 2006). Interfaith youth programs generally involve various kinds of workshops, forums, and volun-teer activities that include Muslim, Jewish, and Christian youth and attempt to connect the "Abrahamanic traditions" through a paradigm that emphasizes commonalities among the religions of "the book" (i.e., the Bible). Interfaith youth activism has thus become a significant site for alliance building, cir-cumscribed by the parameters of religion, and also a platform for education about Islam.

Interfaith coalitions, I argue, generally represent the boundaries of permis-sible responses to the War on Terror. Drawing on related analyses of "diversity management" in institutions of higher education and policy making (Ahmed 2012, 13, 173), I view interfaith programs as a site of knowledge production about racial institutions and political movements; it is a place where young people grapple with, and even critique, structures of recognition, contain-ment, and transformation. For example, Laila, a Pakistani American who grew up in Fremont and was attending an Islamic school when the attacks of 9/11 occurred, talked about the bomb threats the school received afterward and recalled visits by Jewish Americans to show support as part of interfaith outreach activities. Other youth spoke of how their public expressions of Mus-lim American identity were shaped by involvement or leadership in interfaith programs. Malaika talked about coordinating an "interfaith club council" at her college and organizing events such as a lecture series for "Islam awareness week" and workshops such as one on "debunking stereotypes" about "women in Islam"; she commented wryly that the event was a "boring one, but it was necessary." That is, if (non-Muslim) Americans just knew more about Islam and Muslims, they wouldn't fear, hate, or suspect them.

I am interested here in the conditions of possibility of interfaith activism, and its implications for racial politics and discourse about the War on Terror and political violence. Many interfaith programs propound ideas of liberal "tolerance" and "dialogue" that are deeply embedded in broader assumptions about multicultural/multifaith belonging and neoliberal democracy, having grown out of the Bush administration's effort to push social services out of governmental agencies and into "faith-based initiatives." It is apparent that the growing "interfaith industry" that has burgeoned since 9/11 has drawn on liberal notions of pluralism to produce what I call *religious multiculturalism*. Speaking to youth and activists in Silicon Valley shed light on the erasures and deferrals that are set in motion by the prioritization of interfaith activism since 9/11 in the multicultural, postracial state. In its increasingly liberal, managerial approach since the 1990s, the institutionalized "grammar of diversity" conceals deeper issues of political and economic inequality and focuses instead on cultural, and now religious, "diversity" (Ahmed 2012, 13; Melamed 2011; Shohat and Stam 1994).[12] The irony is, of course, that this liberal multiculturalism is perceived as a failure for both the left and the right; for conservatives and nativists in the U.S. as well as the UK, liberal multiculturalism is blamed for undermining the "civic integration" of Muslims and "providing a space for militant radicals" or even for fostering violence or riots among Muslim youth in recent years (Esposito 2011, xxv; Modood 2002, 206). This is a paradox that inheres in the nature of liberalism, given its attempt to insist on both difference and individualism in the social order.

Religious multiculturalism, or multi-faithism, is sanctioned by the state and buttressed by the simultaneous trend within the Muslim American community, and among youth, emphasizing Islam as a religion that crosses national, ethnic, and racial boundaries and aligning it with liberal democratic multiculturalism. This pan-Islamic universalism contributes to a discourse of pluralism within Islam, but also to a discourse of Islam within religious pluralism. For example, Salima, who had attended Granada Islamic School and graduated from UC Berkeley, described her family's emphasis on belonging to a "diversified masjid" such as MCA. She discussed her own interest in forming a community beyond "just one bubble of friends" confined to one ethnic or racial group, commenting, "We think that's really important because that really shows what Islam is. And it's made up of so many different people, you know, Malaysian, Indonesian, Pakistani, Indian, European. It's just everywhere. . . . So we're all made differently, we all come from different tribes, but you know, we're here on earth to be with each other and to learn from each other." (Salima referenced here the oft-cited aya, or verse, from the Koran: "We have created you in tribes and clans so that you can get to know one another.") There is a religious discourse that shapes the notion of racial pluralism within Islam, and there is also a programmatic dimension to interfaith affiliations. Salima reflected on the impetus for interfaith programs after 9/11 and went on to talk about her involvement in the "Muslim Green Team," focused on volunteerism and environmental activism in Silicon Valley:

> A lot of the Muslim Student Associations . . . have come together and [are] kind of informing the community at large, like, "This is what we're about," or "These are our beliefs and what we don't believe in." Just kind of clearing up the air. So because of 9/11, that really forced us to step forward and be like, "Hi, we're here. We're American, just like you, and this is what our religion is really about."

Salima suggests that these interfaith and outreach activities by youth demonstrated an embrace of both pluralism and Americanness and positioned Muslim Americans squarely within multicultural, neoliberal citizenship, through volunteer activities that present a civic face of Islam. Clearly, the "eviction" of Muslim Americans from citizenship and political community after 9/11, as described by Sherene Razack, warranted a corrective and necessitated organized outreach and alliance building, so these interfaith activities certainly have had many positive effects. But as the CAIR activist from the Bay Area cited earlier commented thoughtfully: "Interfaith alliances have always been a big part of CAIR. Muslim Americans didn't know how to open their doors to others ten years ago. But now the entire focus is on outreach, and in and of itself, it's not the solution. Clearly there needs to be more work done. . . . I think the more institutionalized this outreach is, the less useful it is." This activist's comment hints at the ways that the investment in the "interfaith industry" is presented as the "solution" to the crisis faced by Muslim Americans after 9/11 and so funnels much of the energy and organizing in Muslim American communities into a politics based on liberal, faith-based inclusion.

The interfaith movement has been increasingly institutionalized in liberal spheres such as the academy and nonprofit organizations where interfaith dialogue has been promoted, and also, notably, in programs related to Israel-Palestine.[13] In the case of interfaith (and intercultural) programs involving the triad of Muslims, Christians and Jews, or the dyad of Muslim-Jewish or Arab-Jewish dialogue, analyses of political conflict and structural inequity are displaced outside of the realm of the state to the domain of culture or religion, confined to what Mahmood Mamdani (2004) calls "culture talk." Liberal, religious multiculturalism has been presented as a solution to the problems of Islamophobia, racial violence, and military occupation, obfuscating or containing a critique of the structural and geopolitical imperatives of warfare and issues of race and racism. The "problem" is reduced to issues of interreligious and intercultural fear, understanding, and acceptance that can be resolved on the terrain of culture and faith.

There is a "brick wall" that activists often hit when participating in interfaith activism, using Ahmed's (2012) metaphor for the limits of technologies of diversity management (174); in this case, the wall blocks critiques of state warfare, imperialism, and white supremacy as they relate to the U.S. and its support for Israel. These issues are off limits in the congenial "dialogue" generated by liberal interfaith activism, erased by the "happy point" of intersectionality (Ahmed 2012, 14). I argue that state and public support for liberal religious multiculturalism, manifested in the growing "interfaith industry," is a response generated by the post-9/11 national crisis to contain the possibility of radical political dissent and antiracist mobilization within the grammar of religious diversity. Yet this dissent and antiracist critique has nonetheless been unleashed, including among youth, and sometimes erupts in the interfaith sphere.

Faithwashing and Cross-Racial Alliances: No "Red, Black, and Green"

The investment in religious multiculturalism is often at the expense of critiques that grapple with the racialization of South Asian, Afghan, and Arab Americans, in the context of the racial state and its global interventions, and sometimes also at the expense of progressive interracial alliances. So global solidarity may be expressed through interfaith dialogues about the War on Terror or the occupation of Palestine, but these are framed as intractable conflicts based on religious identity and requiring greater religious understanding and tolerance. However, I found that tensions related to Middle East politics and censorship of the Palestine question often ruptured interfaith coalitions on college campuses, forcing the question of anti-Arab racism to the surface and interrupting a liberal consensus. For example, Jenaan recalled that in the interfaith student group she belonged to at San Jose State, some of the Jewish American students did not want Muslim youth to wear clothing or jewelry with the colors of the Palestinian flag. Jenaan protested:

> I was, like, "This isn't the issue we're discussing. I can wear whatever I wanna wear." But they didn't understand that, they were just, like, "Oh, you can't wear red, you can't wear black, you can't wear green." You know, the colors of Palestine. I was like, "I'm going to wear whatever the hell I want to wear. You can't tell me what not to wear."

The campus interfaith alliance became a repressive site for Jenaan when the expression of her Palestinian national identity was erased and the "issue"

suddenly became one of regulating permissible Arab political identities, however symbolic (arguably Jewish students or members of the Jewish campus organization would not be asked to remove the Star of David, although it is also
an element of the Israeli flag, let alone the colors blue and white; this would
automatically be considered anti-Semitic within U.S. mainstream and liberal
discourse). Jenaan's experience is just one of many incidents in which Palestinian identity or support for Palestinian rights is erased or even attacked
in liberal activist and educational spaces, which are rarely described as anti-
Palestinian or anti-Arab (see Elia 2011; Salaita 2011), as I discuss in greater
depth in Chapter Three. This vignette illustrates how difficult it is for a politicized or nationalist Arab American identity to be inserted into religious
multicultural alliances—as is also true of a politicized or anti-imperialist
Pakistani or Afghan American identity.

Many interfaith youth programs do address the "conflict" in Israel-
Palestine (the word "occupation" is rarely used, let alone "colonialism" or
"apartheid") but only through a model of Jewish-Muslim/Christian dialogue.
Such an approach suggests that this is a problem of religion and not of state
repression, militarism, and racism; there are also intercultural/Arab-Jewish
youth projects focused on Israel-Palestine that are also contained by the limits of liberal multiculturalism, such as Seeds of Peace. For example, Sabina
participated in an interfaith program on Jewish-Muslim relations for high
school students, organized by Abraham's Vision, and recalled that while the
discussion got "pretty heated" when the participants began speaking about
the "Israel-Palestine issue," the coordinators did not want them to get into a
"political discussion" or "arguments" and steered them away from the topic;
she said, in their view, "The point is to use this space as to way unify and see
what are possible solutions for the future. They wanted us to relate our identity being a Muslim or a Jew and why those identities made us sympathize
with this issue. . . . They made it seem so simple and they knew how to speak.
That would make us so mad because we didn't know how to respond."[14] Sabina added that the program received an award from President Clinton, underscoring the ways the U.S. state supports and promotes interfaith projects
that steer youth away from critical political engagement with Middle East
politics and funnels them into depoliticized spaces focused on religious and
cultural identity talk.

Yasmine, an Iraqi American who reactivated the Students for Justice Club
at Foothill Community College to organize events about the Middle East after
9/11, pointed to the contradictions of a model based on dialogue that obfus-
cates or suppresses political analysis and human rights issues, particularly
in the case of Palestine. She felt it was important to "promote unity among

different races, backgrounds," including across religious boundaries, but was critical of a campus club called People for Peace in the Middle East, founded by Jewish American students to promote Jewish-Arab collaboration. Yasmine recalled that when she wanted to show films about Palestine from a Palestinian perspective, she was told by the club that she "should have other films that, like, show the other side." She retorted, "If this was when we had slaves, would you want me to put on the whites' perspective?" The Palestine question is situated within the intercultural and interfaith framework through a discourse resting on the fallacy of neutrality. Intercultural and interfaith dialogue projects generally rely on this fallacy in service of the status quo, regulating political discourse among youth.

Farida, an Afghan American woman from San Jose, said she stayed away from the Palestine-Israel issue because she wanted to take a "neutral standpoint," given that "each side has their faults." While it is not at all problematic to note that the Palestine issue is a complex one involving multiple actors and colliding narratives, in a charged political field in which a pro-Israel narrative has long represented the mainstream of American politics, a "neutral standpoint" is actually a deferral to the norm.

Liberal interfaith dialogues about Palestine or Islamophobia are generally based on a postpolitical model of what Chantal Mouffe (2005) calls "dialogue democracy," which erases antagonisms in the service of a liberal rationalist "consensus"; as she observes: "There is much talk today of 'dialogue' and deliberation' but what is the meaning of such words in the political field, if no real choice is at hand" (2–3). Mouffe locates this erasure of conflict and antagonism to the triumphalism of neoliberal capitalism in the wake of the fall of the USSR, and to the elision of a "struggle between 'left' and 'right,'" displaced by the focus on "third way" politics in the 1990s (see Duggan 2003). Mouffe's critique does not go far enough, however, to show that antagonistic confrontation does, in fact, erupt within this liberal democratic model of dialogue and consensus "beyond antagonism" but is repressed, often violently, by the liberal democratic state.

Intercultural and interfaith dialogue has achieved a preeminent role in the post-9/11 political field as the legitimate frame for discussing political questions, erasing issues of sovereignty, colonialism, and dispossession.[15] This is what one critic has described as an "interfaith Trojan horse" approach for "faithwashing" the politics of "apartheid and occupation" in Israel-Palestine.[16] It is clear that a political approach to modern conflict and warfare in Israel-Palestine, in particular, and also generally in West and Southwest Asia, is elided by focusing on presumably incommensurable cultural narratives and irreconcilable religious differences that breed "hate" between Jews and Arabs or Muslims and non-Muslims. Clearly, not all youth who participate in interfaith programs on campuses or in community settings support a liberal discourse of diversity that entails evading a political critique of dominant nationalisms, and some vigorously challenged this move, as Jenaan's and Sabina's observations suggest. I do want to acknowledge that there are examples of interfaith groups around the country that emphasize cross-racial, grassroots organizing, such as the Inner-City Muslim Action Network (IMAN) in Chicago, which focuses on urban poverty and police brutality and engages in direct services, social justice organizing, and arts programming (see Aidi 2014, 186). There is also a growing progressive interfaith movement that has mobilized in support of the Boycott, Divestment, and Sanctions movement opposing Israeli occupation and racism, including groups, such as American Muslims for Palestine, that were involved with the Interfaith Partners in Action to support the Presbyterian Church's divestment campaign. However, the deflection of radical critique of the state through liberal interfaith activism is important to consider as a sanctioned form of post-9/11 solidarity politics that foregrounds liberal models of religion as the basis of proper political subjecthood in the postracial era. Muslim liberalism thus displaces radical racialism in the multicultural economy of difference.

This deferral of anti-imperial and antiracist politics has to be situated in a context in which, as Salaita (2006a) points out, protests of Israeli state policies, including on college campuses, are viewed as automatically anti-Semitic and outside the bounds of not just freedom of expression but also civil politics. An interfaith approach to the Israeli occupation is permitted because it situates the "conflict" within the bounds of liberal multicultural humanism and beyond critique of Zionism. The suppression of Arab American identity is part of a longer history of repression of Arab nationalism and Arab American politics in tandem with U.S. interventions in the Middle East and support for Israel, which has been well documented (for example, see Abraham 1994; Abu El-Haj 2007; Malek 2009; Orfalea 2006; Salaita 2006a). Given the centrality of the Palestine question for Arab American politics and for pan-Arab activism in the U.S., an Arab American *political* identity fits uneasily within the rubric of ethnic identity politics in the U.S., which can accommodate only a depoliticized and domesticated Arab cultural identity or a depoliticized Muslim American identity (Naber 2008; Shryock 2008, 107–108).

Strikingly, anti-Arab racism often disappears from the litany of "-isms" within liberal antiracist paradigms, which have inched toward incorporating Islamophobia but rarely ever Arabophobia, including in interfaith and intercultural programs. Scholars such as Therese Saliba make the important argument that this is because the U.S. fundamentally denies racism against

Arabs and Palestinians, given its unwavering support for Israel, and so anti-Arabness is illegible, even in liberal antiracist movements (Salaita 2006a; Saliba 2011). The disavowal of anti-Arabness is linked to a longer, complex history of the rise of Zionist discourse and organizing in the U.S., especially after 1967, which I will address in the following chapter (see Feldman 2015). It also emerges from a context in which Arab American "is a racially ambiguous category—what Helen Samhan (1999) has called "not quite white"—but it is also evident that until 9/11, "Arabness" was not legible within a multicultural or even ethnic studies paradigm that has accommodated pan-ethnic categories such as Asian American and Latino/a (see also Abdulrahim 2008; Naber 2000). Instead, it is apparent that in some cases, Arabs are subsumed within the master category of "Muslim" and that the conflation of Muslimness with Arabness has been simultaneously consolidated and unsettled after 9/11.[17] This is one of the tensions that troubles the production of interfaith coalitions that privilege religion and undermines their relationship to antiracist, antiwar movements, including campaigns involving radical Muslim Americans.

"Green Muslim" Activism and Class Fissures

A prominent example of the ways in which an "acceptable" Muslim American youth activism is produced through interfaith activism is interfaith volunteer activities, such as environmentalist programs, which are popular in northern California and also nationally. Mariyam, who was involved in a local chapter of the Muslim American Society since she was in high school, had participated in their interfaith youth projects, which included cleanup programs with the Catholic church and the "Muslim Green Team," also referred to by Salima. The Jewish Federation of Silicon Valley and the Muslim Association of America have also brought Jewish and Muslim American youth together to clean up the Guadalupe River in San Jose.[18] The paradigm of interfaith volunteerism is part of a growing "green Muslim" movement that has connected faith to the concept of environmental stewardship.[19] "Green" activism, it seems, is more easily wedded to liberal social justice models of interfaith youth organizing than antiwar and antioccupation politics—the green of environmentalism is more compatible than the green of Islamism or the green of red-black-and-green Arab/Palestinian nationalism. Such projects are part of a Muslim American environmentalist politics that has been promoted by activists such as Ibrahim Abdul-Matin, a second-generation (Black) Muslim American; his book, *Green Deen: What Islam Teaches about Protecting the Planet*, has inspired regional networks of Muslim Americans who participate in volunteer projects (*deen* is Arabic for "religion"). Abdul-Matin's core mission is to "rebrand" Muslim Americans not as extremists but as environ-mental activists and "moderate" political actors. He states,

> Look, everyone wants to know where the moderate Muslims are. They're every-where. They go to work, they go to school. Frankly, they're boring—which is why the media doesn't do any stories about them. . . . I'm highlighting Sarah the Muslim who believes in recycling. As more and more Muslims come forward, describing the positive ways they are contributing to society—and they are, they're just not advertising it—I believe people will stop focusing on the tiny percentage of Muslims who are extremists. I hope my book will re-label Mus-lims from terrorist to activist or, even better, environmentalists. I want Muslims to be known as the people who save water.[20]

While not all Muslims who engage in cleanup or recycling projects neces-sarily want to be interpellated as "moderate Muslims" who "save water," these emerging forms of activism and especially volunteerism have come to define "moderate" political subjecthood for Muslim Americans. After 9/11, Muslim, Arab, South Asian, and Afghan American youth are expected to perform "good" citizenship, which in this case is defined as "green citizenship." The irony of the dual connotations of "green" do not seem to be lost on some of the Muslim American proponents of this environmental citizenship, as sug-gested by the title of the book *Green Deen*. Abdul-Matin is one of many in a younger generation of Muslim Americans who are self-consciously engaging in "green deen" and public activist projects that they hope will challenge the perception of Muslims as suspect citizens while also critiquing the excesses of a destructive capitalism that has ravaged the planet. While the latter is a laud-able goal, what is striking here is that Muslim American politics is legible only within the national security paradigm that is tied to a neoliberal consensus. There seems to be a hyperawareness among those who participate in these volunteer movements and interfaith alliances that their insertion into these larger political projects involves a strategic self-fashioning as "good Muslims," within the framework defined by the War on Terror.

Many Muslim American volunteer initiatives related to community service that I heard about in Silicon Valley, such as soup kitchens for the homeless, implicitly or explicitly feed into neoliberal citizenship. Social services have been increasingly privatized under neoliberalism as the state shifts the re-sponsibility of social welfare to individual citizens and community initiatives willing to do volunteer or charitable work. Faith-based community service initiatives tied to ideas of entrepreneurship were encouraged by the Bush ad-ministration and have continued to mushroom since 9/11 (Patel 2006, 20).

Neoliberal governmentality thus provides the context in which interfaith programs provide yet another arena for the promotion of the virtues of productivity, autonomy, and self-reliance (Duggan 2003; Harvey 2007; Ong 2006). This is compelling for Muslim Americans who can prove through public community service and volunteer initiatives that they are, indeed, model minorities or virtuous Americans. There are also "green deen" coalitions that are invested in challenging the ravages of neoliberal capitalism as they impact surplus populations and marginalized communities, using a model of racial and economic justice and also "food justice." For example, Muslim Run is one such project sponsored by IMAN in poor neighborhoods in Chicago, and in West Oakland the People's Kitchen, founded by Sakib Keval, a young Muslim (Indian African) American activist, is a community restaurant that focuses on movement building and cultural programs and offers free organic meals inspired by the Black Panther's free breakfast program (though not a faith-identified project). These programs represent what Aidi (2014) describes as the politics of a new generation of "Muslim race activists" who believe that interracial solidarity, including and especially with indigenous (Black) Muslims, is necessary to challenge the imperial state (191).

The young CAIR activist from the Bay Area I spoke to commented that interfaith coalitions are "evolving, now they're focusing on homelessness and poverty, and we need to catch up with that work in the Muslim community." But she also went on to note critically, "The reason we can't fully leverage coalitions . . . the perfect example is labor. Interfaith coalitions can't touch labor." This young woman was frustrated because, in her view, Muslim Americans were not as actively involved in cross-class coalitions as they should be, and she went on to remark on the class schisms among immigrant professionals: "You don't care who cleans your toilet if you're an engineer." At the same time, she acknowledged that Muslim Americans are heterogeneous in terms of class and that there are many Yemenis, as well as Indians, in the Bay Area who work as security guards and belong to unions. The politics of liberal interfaith activism have to be situated within class relations in Silicon Valley, and the ways in which notions of neoliberal autonomy are shaped by discourses of class mobility and professionalism among largely middle- to upper-middle-class youth. I should note that national Muslim American leaders have also directly spoken to the issue of class divisions within and beyond the Muslim American community. Imam Suhaib Webb of the Muslim American Society, who used to work with MCA in Santa Clara, comments: "If we continue to stay on the defensive, failing to offer our support to the poor, the weak, the disenfranchised, and the other problems that plague our communities, we will not be able to pass the test of America" (cited in Gallup 2009, 133). This is a progressive message of solidarity with the poor and disenfranchised—yet one framed as a route to Americanization for Muslims who, according to Webb, must "speak the language of America" (cited in Gallup 2009, 133; see also Aidi 2014, 190).

In general, the investment in interfaith politics and neoliberal self-help projects has overshadowed cross-class alliances among South Asian, Arab, and Afghan Americans in Silicon Valley. Class fissures within and between these groups are partly related to the inequalities of the "digital divide," in a region where the underside of "entrepreneurial freedom" and class and also racial conflict are largely invisible (Pitti 2003, 200). Furthermore, in the discourse about Muslim American communities who are generally viewed through the prism of the War on Terror and a racialization paradigm centered on religion, and to some extent nation, the question of class and the disciplining force of neoliberal capitalism is largely absent. Interfaith and liberal Muslim civil rights activism generally does not make the connection to issues of multicultural capitalism and broader political solidarity that would challenge freedom and selfhood as defined by neoliberalism and free market rationalities. Political formations embedded in a liberal democratic politics of pluralism, volunteerism, and civil rights simply promote "inclusive exclusion," displacing radical solidarities and resistance to imperial policies, state violence, and neoliberal capitalism (Shryock 2010).

Cross-Racial Tensions and Solidarities

The growing interfaith movement, to which many young people have been drawn and into which many Muslim American youth have been funneled, has significant implications for cross-racial and cross-class alliances as well as fissures in Silicon Valley. This was brought home to me in a conversation with Iman, a young Palestinian Muslim American woman who grew up in Santa Clara and attended Granada and then UC Berkeley. Iman, whose family had a long history of involvement with CAIR, observed that interfaith alliances in the local Muslim American community often took precedence over solidarity with other immigrant groups. She lamented the lack of interracial solidarity with Latino youth during the high school walkouts and immigrant rights marches and mass protests by undocumented immigrants in 2006, observing,

> The Hispanic community in my high school was big and they organized a walk-out event when everyone left campus, and that was huge. And it would have been nice if the Muslim community made a bigger effort to participate. Because the Hispanic community in San Jose is huge. But instead I feel like we did out-

reach to like the Jewish community, or the Christian community. And we'd go
to churches and synagogues and that was it.

Iman's comment struck me because it suggested that Muslim American
youth at her high school in Santa Clara, and possibly also the local Muslim
American community at large, missed an important political opportunity to
forge an alliance with the immigrant rights movement in the area, failing to
connect the issues that Muslim (Arab, South Asian, and other) immigrant
communities were facing after 9/11 to those of Latinos and others subjected
to profiling, incarceration, and deportation. Echoing this critique, the CAIR
activist cited previously commented that an interfaith coalition in San Jose
had held public meetings to discuss the appointment of a new police chief,
in the context of campaigns against racial profiling of Latino youth and other
youth of color by San Jose police, but Muslim Americans were "very absent,"
except for an imam from the SBIA mosque who "sat on the Santa Clara
Human Rights Commission." I want to note that issues of police brutality
have indeed been addressed by coalitions involving young Arab Americans
in the Bay Area, who have made linkages between the racialized police practices targeting young men of color in Oakland and in Israel-Palestine, but
these are not faith identified, as in the campaigns protesting the police killing
of Oscar Grant that occurred during the Israeli massacre in Gaza in winter
2009 (see Attia 2011). In general, interfaith and liberal civil rights activism in
Silicon Valley has not always tackled broader questions of police brutality or
immigration policies that are considered outside the bounds of a proper or
"moderate" Muslim American politics.

There is also the vexed issue of alliances and fissures between "immigrant"
Muslims (or Muslims of South Asian, Arab, Afghan, and Iranian origin) and
African American Muslims, in the context of the growing migration of Muslims after 1965 from South and West Asia, including a class of highly educated
professionals (Abdullah 2013; Schmidt 2002). Where does solidarity with Black
struggles fit within interfaith coalitions and within Muslim American youth
activism? Interracial as well as class tensions have marred immigrant Muslims'
relations with African American Muslims, who are the largest U.S.-born group
of Muslims and constitute approximately one third of the Muslim population
in the country (there is also a growing Latino/a Muslim community). Relations
between Black and immigrant Muslim communities are a key issue for Muslim
American youth and a point of contention for Muslim Americans at large.

Some scholars note that immigrant Muslims brought with them their own
racial and anti-Black prejudices (as is the case with many immigrant communities) and sought to distance themselves from Black Muslims as well as local

race and class politics in the U.S. (Abdullah 2013). Furthermore, Sherman Jackson (2011) criticizes Muslim immigrants for "being unwilling or unable to take a firm and principled stand on the matter of race," arguing that they have a "racial agnosia" and believe Islam "simply does not 'do race'" (95). Given that the Muslim American community is a racially diverse one, interracial alliances already occur *within* the community, so that pan-Islamic solidarity through MSAs or other organizations are in most cases already based on cross-racial affiliations, especially in the younger generation. However, the discourse of a universalist, postracial Islam, which exists in these spaces as well, may end up affirming, rather than challenging, the notion of a "postracial" America. This "racial agnosticism" reinforces the mythologies of race neutrality and denial of white supremacy in the U.S. and, in Jackson's view, end ups colluding inadvertently with the whitewashing of U.S. racism (97).

In the greater Bay Area, there are indeed tensions between African American and immigrant or non-Black Muslims. Abed commented to me on these racial cleavages in Silicon Valley, as he had observed them in the community at MCA:

> Zaid Shakir, Amir Abdul Malik, and Imam Siraj Wahaj, they have always related the issues of civil rights of African Americans to the Muslim Americans, and the funny thing is that the largest ethnic group of Muslims is African American. I don't think a lot of people realize that. As a community, I don't think we have done enough to outreach towards the African Americans and to other communities in general. Our only focus is on the desis and Arabs. . . . It sounds like I am bashing on MCA but I love MCA, it's one of the best communities out there.

Other youth, such as Malaika, noted that MCA has done events such as a talk focused on "Malcolm and Martin" (Luther King) to "integrate" African Americans into the community, but they observed that there is frustration and disappointment among "indigenous" Muslim Americans with the racial fissures among Muslim Americans. An older Palestinian American woman from the Bay Area who has been involved with Arab American activism since the 1960s, and who works with Arab immigrants and refugees in working-class neighborhoods in San Francisco, was frustrated with the race politics of the Arab Muslim community. She criticized middle-class Arab Americans who think they are "political," in her words, simply for watching the news on Al Jazeera, and observed trenchantly, "They are afraid of fighting back if something happens to them. . . . Arabs don't know the history of this country, they don't know that Blacks in this country were slaves for hundreds of years, that this country was built on genocide." Her critique of the political quiescence of Arab and Muslim immigrants and their distancing from indigenous and minority communities, on whose backs later immigrants asserted their claims to belonging, fundamentally challenges the history of slavery and genocide of the U.S. state. Thus, the politics of Muslim civil rights activism is, in some cases, vexed by the erasure of longer histories of resistance to disenfranchisement and white supremacy.

Fault lines between Black and immigrant Muslims have also emerged due to racialized hierarchies of religious authenticity. African American Muslims have sometimes been viewed as inauthentic and "improper" Muslims (Curtis 2013, 16). Amir Sulaiman, an African American Muslim hip hop artist, comments on the sentiment among some Muslim Americans that "what makes you Black and American is haram [un-Islamic]" (cited in Khabeer and Alhassen 2013, 301). Naber (2012) acknowledges the racial hierarchies among Muslim communities in the Bay Area, noting that some Arab Muslim youth are critical of the Arab sense of superiority over other Muslims and the "perceived colorblindness" in mosques, while arguing that pan-Islamic universalism is invoked by Arab Muslim youth to emphasize racial equality (131). Jamillah Karim (2009), who explores "new types of interethnic alliances" as well as interracial tensions among South Asian and African American Muslim girls in Chicago, finds that young African American women sometimes feel that South Asian and Arab American Muslims are "privileging (and imposing) Arab and Asian cultural practices associated with Islam" (130, 497). I want to point out, however, that "immigrant Muslims" also include Black African Muslims, and that Arabs/Muslims can also be Black, a point that is sometimes lost in these discussions of racial fault lines that are reduced to simple polarities. For example, when I visited the MCA mosque in Santa Clara one Friday, during the jummah prayers, there was a diverse crowd of people of various ages and ethnic backgrounds milling around, including many Black women and East Africans attending a conference of Ethiopian Muslims. I also want to emphasize that the issue of anti-Black racism affects the relationship between African Americans and immigrant (and other) communities at large, not just among Muslims, South Asians, or Arabs, in the context of white supremacy. Furthermore, the class fissures between African American and upwardly mobile or affluent Asian and Arab American communities, and among immigrant Muslims themselves, inflect interracial tensions but are often insufficiently addressed.

There are also instances of interethnic tensions between South Asian, Arab, and Afghan Americans more generally and other groups in the Bay Area. For example, some older Afghan Americans described conflicts between Afghan youth and Latinos or Chinese Americans in Fremont and

Hayward, particularly among young men in what seemed to be turf wars or, reportedly, among gang-involved high school youth; there have also been reports of gang-involved Indian (mainly Punjabi Sikh) American males in the South Bay and Fremont who go by names such as Santa Clara Punjabi Boys, Aim to Kill, and the All Indian Mob (Fernandez 2000; Omidian 1996, 141). This is not an uncommon story, as minoritized youth from struggling communities jostle with one another in urban areas, but it is important to take note of youth subcultures as a site of both suspicion and contestation as well as affiliation and solidarity.

An interesting conversation I had with Jenaan in San Jose captures the interracial tensions that must be addressed in youth politics:

> J: I'm honestly more comfortable with minorities than I am with white people. I'm a minority so I have something in common with them. But they're usually the ones who say stupid stuff. . . . They're the ones who are like, "Oh, go back to your country!" and I'm like, "Well, look at you. You're *brown*! Why don't you go back to *your* country?"
>
> Q: Right. So what do you make of that, people who experience racism and then turn around and are racist?
>
> J: I think it has something to do with the idea of divide and conquer. Because they don't want to be seen as the enemy so they go and turn it around. They want to be seen as: "Oh, I'm defending America, I don't want to be associated with terrorists." So they try to put all the tension on other people instead of them.
>
> Q: So how do you think Muslim Americans, Palestinians, Arabs, et cetera, have bridged the gap with other minorities? If you had your way would you work through it by framing it around civil rights or around social justice? Or racism?
>
> J: I think it'd be everything: racism, justice, everything. The white man is still in power even though they're not the majority anymore. So a lot of times they'll be like, "Oh, we apologize for this happening," and I'm like, "It's not our fault. Why are you apologizing?

I cite this conversation at length because Jenaan offers an astute—and witty—analysis of the ways in which white supremacy, including in a majority-minority state such as California, is sustained by racial divisions among brown and black groups that are reinscribed and reconfigured at times of national crisis. So after 9/11, while Muslim, Arab, South Asian, and Afghan Americans were *de*-Americanized and had to apologize to be accepted as American subjects, other minority groups were interpellated as newly Americanized, patriotic subjects on the other side of the intensified racial binary of terrorist/nonterrorist (Alsultany 2012; Davis 2012, 112).

Jasbir Puar and Amit Rai (2004) point to the "multivalent racial forma-tions and racial reterritorializations . . . resulting in increasing polarization of model-minority diasporic populations and discourse" after 9/11 and in "a retrenching and resolidification of the discourse of U.S. exceptionalism," ad-opted by those, such as Indian (non-Muslim) Americans, East Asian Ameri-cans, and other minority groups who wished to distance themselves from the new national enemy (81). Malaika remarked that while growing up in Santa Clara, she "also got the typical [comment], 'Go back to your country!'" What seemed to be a predicable nativist remark, in her experience, generally came from other minorities. Malaika recalled that she humorously retorted to an Asian American woman who once made such a comment: "I was like, 'Do you realize you're Asian? . . . in case you missed the memo, but you are!'" These in-cidents are symptomatic of a deeper shift in U.S. race politics in which "privi-leged and stigmatized racial formations no longer mesh perfectly with a color line," so that "black, Asian, white, or Arab/Muslim . . . can now occupy both sides of the privilege/stigma opposition" within the paradigm of cultural and ideological racism (Melamed 2006, 2–3). As the state has officially adopted liberal multiculturalism, figures closely identified with the imperial state and the War on Terror such as Colin Powell or Alberto Gonzalez embody the shift to nonracialism—Jodi Melamed argues this exemplifies not just a new form of racism, but the (attempted) disappearance of race altogether. The displace-ment of race onto "culture" or "immigration" has been described by Etienne Balibar (1991) as a "racism without race" (23). The youth I spoke to found themselves grappling with these shifts in raciality on the ground, with Jenaan observing that the core issue is that of white supremacy, which needs to be addressed, unapologetically, through a framework of antiracism and justice.

At the same time, it is apparent that in the larger Bay Area, there are several sites in which cross-racial affiliations are being produced between immigrant and Black Muslim communities, among youth and more generally, includ-ing on the terrain of civil rights or social justice organizing. At the center of these interracial alliances are charismatic community leaders such as Imam Zaid Shakir, the popular figure on the college lecture circuit who is one of the cofounders of the Zaytuna Institute in Berkeley. Laila, for example, recalled an event organized by the MSA on her campus focused on the war in Iraq, fea-turing Imam Shakir and two Iraq war veterans, as well as a collaboration be-tween MSA and the Black Student Union for Black History Month. For Laila, such events highlighting and creating linkages with African American youth were important because they demonstrated how to "promote more unity" among Muslim Americans, via a critique of war and state violence. The affinity between Muslim American youth from immigrant communities and other U.S.-born Muslim Americans partly grows out of shared cultural and generational experiences and an understanding of being a racial minority and growing up with U.S. racism (Aidi 2014; Daulatzai 2012). This new, cross-racial Muslim youth culture is apparent in the ethnically and racially diverse Ta'leef Collective, a community organization in Hayward that began as a branch of Zaytuna, cofounded by Usama Canon (also a Muslim convert), and is now an independent organization. Canon does work with incarcerated persons and is also an advisor for the Inner-City Muslim Action Network in Chicago. Ta'leef's Friday night halaqas (study circles) are attended by up to three hundred young Muslims every week, and some of the youth I spoke to in the Bay Area participated in these events and identified with the community at Ta'leef. Laila noted the appeal of figures such as Imam Shakir and other U.S.-born Muslim community leaders, such as Usama Canon, remarking, "They know how to talk to us and joke around with us. . . . I think it's appealing to children who have immigrant parents. Desi parents are really strict!" So there is a cross-generational as well as cross-racial connection forged in such spaces.

Ta'leef focuses on outreach to two primary groups, converts to Muslim and young people, that are both marginalized or alienated from the mainstream Muslim American community in various ways. Ta'leef's mission statement notes the intersections between these two "disenfranchised" communities: "By providing alternative social and sacred space, culturally relevant programming and positive companionship, we assist our beneficiaries in holistically practicing Islam in a way that is reconcilable with their social context. We are a collective of teachers, volunteers, and peers who understand firsthand the challenge of living as Muslims in the west and we strive to provide the necessary means to facilitate that reality."[21] So, for example, Ta'leef screens films such as *Wayward Son* about a professional skateboarder who reconciled Islam with his love for the sport (directed by one of its prominent teachers, Mustafa Davis, who also directed *Deen Tight*). Abed, an Egyptian American from San Jose who had attended Ta'leef, commented, "You'll go to one of their events and you'll see a white lady in her blouse and slacks and you'll see another dude with tattoos and a guy with, like, a mohawk and they are all Muslim and they go there because they feel comfortable. You will see people [who were] born and grew up Muslim also going to that community."

The discourse about Ta'leef suggests a certain kind of multiculturalism, one focused not on the "happy point" of liberal multicultural diversity, but on a larger goal, that of producing a more inclusive Muslim community critically situated in a specific local, generational, and political context and not primarily in relation to the nation (see Aidi 2014).[22] The social and political subcultures that crisscross spaces such as Ta'leef illuminate how cross-racial affinities among Muslim American youth have increasingly been produced in the context of youth cultures and new forms of cultural production. This phenomenon is captured by the title of a documentary film about Latino Muslim rapper Hamza Perez, *The New Muslim Cool*, and features in another film about Muslim hip hop, Davis's *Deen Tight* (cited in Chan-Malik 2013). Sohail Daulatzai (2012), in his analysis of Black Muslim youth cultures and hip hop, traces what he describes as the "new imaginative geography of the post-Civil Rights era" that emerged through cultural production and that has linked "African Americans to the Arab and Muslim Middle East" to "an alternative nation" or "postnation" that is both utopian and internationalist (91, 108). Daulatzai argues that Black Muslim rappers such as the Wu-Tang Clan, A Tribe Called Quest, Public Enemy, Ice Cube, Mos Def, and Lupe Fiasco have helped produce a new "grammar of resistance" based on an insurgent Black and Muslim internationalism that critiques U.S. racial violence domestically as well as globally (110).

While Ta'leef may not be explicitly internationalist in its mission, it clearly recognizes that an important element of cross-racial affiliation or solidarity is produced through popular culture, and it has become the hub of a growing Muslim American youth subculture that includes Muslim rap artists, B-boys, and B-girls. Many Muslim American youth I spoke to were fans of Amir Sulaiman, an African American Muslim MC from the Bay Area affiliated with Ta'leef, who is known for his progressive politics and performs at local events. In 2011, Sulaiman collaborated with Arab American rap artists, such as Omar Offendum, on a song in solidarity with the Egyptian revolution and Arab Spring, "#Jan 25 Egypt," with a powerful video that circulated on YouTube featuring footage of young protesters fighting tanks and soldiers in the streets of Cairo.[23] Imam Shakir clearly understands the significance of hip hop and youth culture, for when I interviewed him in February 2011, he observed, "The elders in the community don't understand this identification [with hip hop], they have a more traditional approach. It's through these cultural genres that young people can cross and a common culture is emerging." He noted the "crossing of lines" at the Ta'leef Collective, where Afghan American youth from Fremont and Hayward regularly meet with African American, Arab American, and other young adults.

It is important, at the same time, to acknowledge what Su'ad Abdul Khabeer and Maytha Alhassen (2013) describe as the "limits of 'resistance' in Muslim youth cultures," which they acknowledge have generally marginalized young Muslim women and which may subvert the parental generation's racial but not gender politics (35). Sylvia Chan-Malik (2013) is also cautious about what she sees as a romanticized trope of Islam as always-already resistant underlying some of the emerging work on the Muslim hip hop movement that obscures its "deeply conservative" strands, even while she argues that an "ethos of social, political, and cultural protest" has generally been "at the heart of Muslim identity and culture" (296). Furthermore, Aidi (2014) points to the contentious debates about Muslim rap that has been denounced by religious conservatives as un-Islamic, while Khabeer and Alhassen point out that some musicians of Muslim background do not actually identify as "Muslim" in the growing cultural movement that includes rap, punk, and nasheed music.

Notwithstanding these complex internal conflicts and struggles within Muslim hip hop and youth cultures, there is indeed a growing subculture linking Muslim and African American youth through cross-racial solidarity in the face of counterterrorism and counterinsurgency (Daulatzai 2012; Naber 2012). For Imam Shakir, who had just given a talk about Malcolm X when I spoke to him, hosted by the MSA at UC Davis, racial crossing has a political significance: "When youth begin to identify with the history of the African American struggle or the Chicano struggle, they adopt some of that militancy and it emboldens a lot of Muslim students, it allows them to push back. It is the anniversary of COINTELPRO, and we are identifying with people who were the targets of the FBI. Those people were shot at and their leaders were assassinated; today, it's wiretapping." Echoing this comment, Bassem talked about an event at San Jose State organized by the Black Student Union on "African American-Muslim connections," which featured an African American speaker who is a former Black Panther and who, he said, was viewed by some as "very controversial" because he is "a strong advocate of getting the minorities together against the American occupation of different countries." Clearly, there is a radical Muslim American youth culture, including in pockets of Silicon Valley, that goes beyond a liberal civil rights and interfaith paradigm, and is challenging the longer history of criminalization of targeted groups, such as COINTELPRO's surveillance and the state's violence against the Black Power movement policies—as suggested by Yasser's critique cited earlier—with Malcolm X being a powerful figure of inspiration (see Aidi 2014, 190; Kibria 2011, 74). This youth politics does not exceptionalize the post-9/11 War on Terror's assault on Muslim civil rights in the U.S. or advocate for political inclusion or faith-based recognition

Challenging the parameters of acceptable Muslim American politics and liberal civil rights activism, there were some cross-class and interracial alliances forged by progressive South Asian and Arab American activists that involved Latinos, African Americans, and Muslim Americans in movements focused on immigrant and civil rights in San Francisco and Oakland. There have also been anti-imperial coalitions with antiwar activists and Native Americans, such as those initiated by young activists with the American

Arab Anti-Discrimination Committee (ADC) chapter in San Francisco in the 2000s (an organization that later morphed into the Arab Resources and Organizing Center). One prominent instance of cross-ethnic coalition building in Silicon Valley has been the ongoing solidarity of progressive Japanese American activists with Muslim and Arab American communities after 9/11 in San Jose, as well as in northern California in general, reflective of the larger alliance forged by Japanese Americans across the nation. In most instances, this Muslim/Arab-Japanese American solidarity was forged through a common struggle for civil and citizen rights as enemy aliens in wartime, but in some cases, it also extended to opposing the war in Iraq and supporting Palestinian and Arab American activists targeted for surveillance and deportation.[24] In December 2001, for example, the Nihonmachi Outreach Committee (NOC) jointly sponsored a program with MCA in the South Bay and reached out to the South Bay Islamic Association mosque in San Jose. They invited Muslim American speakers and Palestinian youth to participate and perform dabke at their Annual Day of Remembrance in San Jose, in memory of the Japanese Americans incarcerated in World War II.

Masao Suzuki, a Japanese American from San Jose, commented that many older activists who had been involved with the San Jose chapter of the National Committee for Redress and Reparations, which won reparations for Japanese Americans incarcerated in the concentration camps, felt strongly that "it was clear that the same thing was happening to American Muslims and that it was also an issue of race, because most of those detained after 9/11 were nonwhite and many were immigrants." For Suzuki, "We were doing this work not just for Japanese Americans, but for others." This suggests a broader notion of political solidarity that is illustrated in the NOC flier for the San Jose Day of Remembrance held at a Buddhist church in February 2011; it features photos of Japanese Americans being herded onto trains by U.S. soldiers during World War II, billboards for the infamous 2010 "Burn a Koran Day," and a banner protesting antiterror laws that criminalize Muslims (see figure 2.2). A political line is thus drawn connecting the incarceration of Japanese Americans and the targeting of Muslim Americans through a racial project of exclusion from the nation-state. Abed reflected on the Japanese-Muslim American coalition:

> MCA is connected with the civil rights of Muslims, but I feel they could do a better job with being connected with the civil rights of other groups . . . you have to be able to build a coalition and the only way to do it is you have to go to them before they go to you. The Japanese American community, they have been the ones coming to us, we do go to them but they initiated it with us and we're very thankful for that.

Figure 2.2. Flier for San Jose Day of Remembrance

In other words, cross-racial solidarity with Japanese Americans and other communities, according to Abed, was something that the Muslim American community in Silicon Valley needed to initiate as an ethical principle. Solidarity, he suggests, has to be always already part of one's politics, including civil rights politics.

It was evident that the Muslim American youth I spoke to were generally not as involved in the interethnic coalitions initiated by Japanese American activists as they were in interfaith coalitions, as hinted at by Abed's comment, and it was also apparent that interfaith alliances did not generally stretch to include Buddhists—nor always Sikhs or Hindus. These fissures are partly due to the deeper cleavages between these groups, but also because the NOC's organizing in northern California, as described by Suzuki, did not fit within the liberal multiculturalist paradigm of mainstream interfaith alliances, challenging instead the larger politics of the warfare state and the racialized scapegoating of "enemy aliens."[25] Having said that, not all Japanese American activists involved in the redress movement shared Suzuki's leftist, anti-imperial politics and some framed their demands squarely within a liberal model of civil rights. So the questions that must be asked are: what notions of nationhood and legal justice do Japanese-Muslim American coalitions challenge or reinscribe? And what political work do such coalitional projects do that liberal interfaith alliances do not?

The notion that Muslim Americans, as a group defined by religion, would align themselves with another community defined by race, or generate solidarity based on opposition to the imperial state or class subordination, raises the specter of affiliations with racial minorities or those left behind by the American Dream, a move that challenges white supremacy and the dominant national discourse of capitalist bootstrapping. Liberal civil rights and interfaith activism in the post-9/11 era colludes with the state's push toward particular bases of affiliation and enables certain forms of solidarity and not others.

Conclusion

The multicultural state's paradigm of national security and counterterrorism has defined acceptable Muslim American politics and alliances by South Asian, Arab, and Arab American youth and what forms of mobilization are permissible and promoted. The boundary between "moderate" civil rights and interfaith activism and "radical" Muslim American youth politics is contested in a discursive battle about the meaning of which forms of politics are "civil" and who is human, which subjects deserves solidarity or the recognition of rights, and which groups must be evicted and exceptionalized to save the nation. The turn to civil rights has been accompanied by an engagement with the paradigm of human rights and transnational solidarity with others suffering from U.S. imperial violence elsewhere, as I discuss in the following chapter.

3

Human Rights, Uncivil Activism, and Palestinianization

Mobilization by Arab, South Asian, and Afghan American youth in response to the War on Terror has been framed through the language of civil rights and enacted in interfaith and cross-racial coalitions, and it has also used the language of human rights, often simultaneously, especially in antiwar and antioccupation campaigns. In this chapter and the next, I explore the ways in which young activists grappled with human rights as a universalizing framework that they hoped would connect the domestic assault on civil rights of Muslim, Arab, South Asian, and Afghan Americans to U.S. overseas interventions and occupation, and to global violence, war, and displacement. In doing so, they acknowledged, implicitly or explicitly, that the discourse of civil rights often failed to link U.S. policies of racial profiling, incarceration, deportation, and surveillance to an ongoing imperial structure of repression, containment, and annihilation, within and beyond the nation. The failure of a liberal model of civil rights to account for structural racism and imperial violence drove many young people to express their dissent against the state through a language of human rights, linking their critique to transnational movements waged against imperial warfare, settler colonialism, and neoliberal globalization.

The contradictions generated by civil rights for post-9/11 activism, as discussed in the previous chapter, and by the regime of human rights, as I will explore here, are constitutive of U.S. imperial technologies that shape and produce Muslim, Arab, Afghan, and South Asian political subjects. The containment of politics through rights claims is not new, certainly, and there is a much longer history of tensions in political subjecthood along the axes of civil and human rights organizing, and their divergences, in response to settler colonialism and racial supremacy (see Rodriguez 2010). For example, Black Power movements in the 1960s and 1970s departed from the domestic agenda of the liberal civil rights movements and internationalized the freedom struggles of African Americans during the era of anticolonial movements in the global South, attempting to take it to the United Nations as a human rights issue, so that the "distinction between 'civil rights' and 'human rights'" became a "coded distinction between Cold War liberalism and internationalism" and anti-imperialism (Daulatzai 2012, 37).

Figure 3.1. Amnesty International bumper sticker

The post-9/11 debate about these two approaches, one focused on domestic civil rights and the other on global human rights, parallels the tensions that emerged in the earlier civil rights, antiwar, and Third Worldist movements: between a domestic "rights-equality framework" and a "nationalist-decolonization" movement (Bruyneel 2007, 128). The decolonization paradigm links the struggles of minorities and indigenous peoples within the U.S. to global questions of imperialism and settler colonialism, and not (just) to national citizenship and inclusion. In today's decolonization framework, solidarity with other groups within the nation-state is accompanied by solidarity with other populations globally, with other anti-imperial movements, and with those suffering from the wars and occupations in Iraq, Afghanistan, and Palestine, as well as the proxy war in Pakistan. This internationalist linkage to overseas wars and occupation is generally framed by Arab, South Asian, and Afghan American youth using a paradigm of human rights and driven by an anticolonial and anti-imperial politics, but tensions emerge between these concerns. As I will discuss, this has necessitated grappling, implicitly or explicitly, with issues of race and racialized exceptions in the human rights framework.

This chapter explores whether the language of human rights has actually enabled an effective critique of imperialism, warfare, and occupation for Arab, South Asian, and Afghan American youth. The youth I spoke to revealed through their experiences of political mobilization on the ground that deploying the vocabulary of human rights, in the case of Iraq, Af-Pak, and, especially, Palestine reveals a tension between an institutionalized regime of human rights activism, tied to the international political order, and resistance to imperial models of sovereignty in the global War on Terror and in zones of occupation and colonialism. Their encounters with censorship of Palestine solidarity activism, in particular, revealed the "red line" in human rights campaigns and Muslim American political movements. I will discuss the ways in which this encounter with repression of the Palestine question is a site of political pedagogy and an entry into what I call Palestinianization, for Palestinian as well as non-Palestinian Americans. I am interested in the ways in which the engagement with human rights, as in organizing for Palestinian rights, is a "social process of producing norms, knowledge, and compliance," that shapes political subjectivities and, in some cases, produces political critiques of forms of collective suffering and political justice denied by the institutionalized human rights and humanitarian discourse (Merry 2006, 109; see also Brown 2004).

Human Rights Activism: Solidarity and the Human

Human rights activism, as Wendy Brown (2004) and other critics have observed, has come to represent "*the* progressive international justice project," a moral-political project that offers "protection against pain, deprivation, or suffering" (453–454). Some Arab, South Asian, and Afghan Americans youth I spoke to turned to human rights as a discourse they hoped could raise the question of violence or discrimination against targets of the U.S.-led War on Terror to the level of global humanity, a paradigm that they used for ethical as well as strategic reasons. South Asian, Arab, and Afghan American youth often encountered or deployed human rights in antiwar organizing, in the context of mobilization against the wars in Iraq and Afghanistan, drone strikes in Af-Pak, and Israeli wars and military occupation. For youth who are construed as racialized objects of the War on Terror, the critique of imperial violence in the name of bringing human rights to other populations, elsewhere, highlights the paradox of why there are different civil rights and human rights for different (racialized) populations. The exceptionalism of U.S. racial wars and U.S.-backed military occupation and invasion drove many youth to engage with the human rights paradigm to make the case that the U.S. should be held accountable for its violations of international human rights law, given that there are subjects who do not have rights, such as in Palestine or Afghanistan or even here in the U.S., that the imperial state purports to support.

Human rights was invoked by youth in Silicon Valley in two major arenas of mobilization, both grounded in notions of cross-racial, transnational solidarity: pan-Islamic activism and the Palestine solidarity and antiwar movement. Some were involved in protests organized by the larger antiwar movement, by national progressive-left groups such as ANSWER that are active in the Bay Area, or by South Bay Mobilization in Silicon Valley, but also in events coordinated through mosqued communities and local networks focused on "Muslim rights." Muslim Student Association chapters and other Muslim activist groups have engaged in advocacy for the human rights of Muslims suffering in zones of war and conflict such as Kashmir, Chechnya, Afghanistan, Iraq, Pakistan, and Palestine, with their campaigns overlapping in many instances with those of non-faith-identified antiwar and Palestine solidarity groups. These two strands of antiwar and human rights organizing—issue based and faith based—did not always converge, and while Arab and Muslim American groups (and to a much lesser extent South Asian and Afghan American activists) were involved in antiwar coalitions, there were often distinct, if overlapping, networks of political protest.

Many students I spoke to were involved with both MSA and Students for Justice in Palestine (SJP) groups on their campuses, using the notion of human rights in different ways. Marwa, an Egyptian American woman from Fremont, was actively involved in the Islamic Society and the Muslim Student Awareness Network at Stanford, both of which were ethnically and racially mixed and included students from Pakistan, Nigeria, Syria, Egypt, and Kazakhstan. She said, "We've done things, like, in Africa, all around the world because there are Muslims everywhere." Pan-Islamic solidarity anchors mobilization against military interventions and occupation affecting Muslims around the globe. In the Bay Area, Naber (2012) observes, there was a shift to faith-based organizing among Arab Muslim Americans in the 2000s, based on the notion of "global Muslim social justice," and an increasing "centrality of religion as an organizing framework for Palestine solidarity activism," evident in mass prayers organized by Muslim Americans in the streets of San Francisco during the second Intifada (147–148). During the Israeli war on Gaza in summer 2014, Imam Zaid Shakir and Hatem Bazian organized a similar mass Friday prayer in downtown San Francisco, followed by a march to the Israeli consulate, sponsored by American Muslims for Palestine.

Some youth straddled activism based on a "transnational, coalitional concept of Islam" and non-faith-based political solidarity (Naber 2012, 148). Marwa, for example, was also involved with the Palestine solidarity movement and in a divestment campaign, launched by the Student Coalition against Israeli Apartheid (SCAI) at Stanford in 2007, becoming a part of a cross-ethnic coalition including Arab Americans, African Americans, and Jewish Americans. She remarked, "It's a really beautiful thing, and you see all these people that are about human rights and that care about the situation," reflecting that, in her view, human rights is a "powerful" framework for wider solidarity, because "when you say it's a human rights issue, people are more bound to care than when you say it's a political issue between two countries." The efficacy of human rights, in Marwa's view, is that the notion of the human supersedes the national. In the case of Palestine solidarity activism, many youth hoped that invoking human rights would overcome the dominant paradigm of a civilizational or religious "conflict" between Israel and Palestine, considered two equivalent political entities (even though Palestine is rarely acknowledged by Zionist supporters of Israel as a nation); this ahistoric, and presumably "neutral" approach, evades the history of settler colonialism and state violence in Palestine and reduces it to a primordial "conflict," as discussed in Chapter Two (see Davis 1989; Pappe 2006).

The framework of human rights is often used strategically, to draw attention to the assault on the sovereignty and freedoms of peoples in the context of a globally recognized discourse of rights, in campaigns arguing that Palestinian rights should also be considered human rights. Some youth argued that human rights trumped Muslim rights, such as Aisha, who thought that organizing in solidarity with Palestinians had to transcend pan-Islamic solidarity. Her family was from Gaza, and she reflected on activism in support of Palestine: "I have been thinking about this a lot and I think it needs to be framed as an issue of human rights, a something that affects all of humanity. That is the way we can connect to other people and to different groups." Many young activists echoed Aisha's observations and turned to human rights as a potentially universalist framework that they believed would make legible the suffering generated by U.S. imperial violence and U.S.-backed regimes of warfare and occupation to a larger public and help build cross-racial solidarity. Yet in doing so, they also found themselves facing, in varying ways, the limitations of the human rights paradigm in relation to questions of imperialism and sovereignty, in particular racialized zones of displacement and annihilation such as Palestine-Israel.

Interestingly, some Muslim and Arab American youth said that the Israeli war on Lebanon in 2006 was a catalyzing event that shaped their awareness of global politics, even more than the attacks of 9/11. Since they were only in middle school in 2001 but in high school or college during the assault on Lebanon, they were old enough to grapple with issues such as the unconditional U.S. support for Israel as played out in the battle between Hezbollah and Israel. For many youth from Silicon Valley, the Israeli assault on Gaza in winter 2008–2009 was also a turning point in their political involvement in international human rights, antiwar, and Palestine solidarity campaigns, as was true for many youth across the nation (Barows-Friedman 2014, 38). The concern with human life and human rights in Palestine deeply shaped their cross-racial, transnational solidarity, and anti-imperial politics.

For example, in Silicon Valley and Fremont, there were many large demonstrations in winter 2009 protesting the Israeli massacre in Gaza in which Arab, South Asian, and Afghan American youth were visibly involved. On January 11, 2009, I went to a rally in Santa Clara held on a street corner between the Westfield shopping mall and an upscale outdoor mall, Santana Row, which was attended by a very diverse and multigenerational crowd of Arabs, Afghans, Iranians, and South Asians, as well as white Americans. The previous weekend there had been a rally at the same location, at the corner of Stevens Creek and Winchester Boulevard, during which the protesters, many of whom were youth, had blocked the entrance to Santana Row. They had marched through the manicured streets of the open-air mall and past the elegant designer boutiques and outdoor cafés, to the shock of shoppers strolling by or sipping coffee on the sidewalk. Sabina, a young Indian American from Santa Clara who attended the rally, described it as "very intense. I was at the end of a huge crowd and there were actually police following us. There were bystanders taking pictures and it was interesting going around Santana Row because it was very rich people who have no idea what's going on around the world. They were probably thinking, 'Who are these crazy people screaming?'" The rally, staged in a major shopping area, ruptured the bubble of Silicon Valley, and marked the coming of age of a new generation of activists.

At the rally I attended, a young woman in hijab was standing at the intersection, in the middle of the busy street, waving a large Palestinian flag high in the air. Another young woman in hijab, with a kaffiyeh wrapped around her shoulders, was shouting vigorously through a bullhorn: "Free, FREE Palestine! Stop bomb-ing Ga-za!" There were dozens of children, some of them toddlers and even babies in strollers, with their families and many youth standing on the sidewalks. Many protesters were carrying signs protesting the deaths of Palestinian children in Gaza; at least 1,400 Palestinians had been killed in the massacre, and more than 300 of them were estimated to be children.[1] One woman had pushed her little son to stand in the front of the crowd, which seemed to underscore the poignancy of the deaths of hundreds of Gazan children. Some South Asian activists were milling around the crowd and asking protesters to sign petitions calling on the U.S. government to end its financial and military aid to Israel. Many of the people at the rally were community members who did not look like stereotypical Bay Area "activists," including several middle-aged South Asian and Middle Eastern women dressed in elegant clothes and with coiffed hair and makeup.

It was apparent that this brutal assault on Palestinians, by a state closely allied to and backed by the U.S., that involved the destruction of schools, universities, and refugee shelters (as well as the use of chemical weapons, such as white phosphorus) had compelled many people to come out into the streets who were not part of organized political groups, including women and youth of various ages and backgrounds. When I asked people how they had heard about the rally, a group of South Asian girls in jeans and sweatshirts standing on the sidewalk said they had learned about it through email and Facebook postings. Two students from UC Davis who were at the demonstration, Amira and Azma, said that they had also heard about the protest through Facebook. While the outrage and grief of the crowd was palpable, as was their passionate desire to inject a critique of (U.S.-backed) violence elsewhere into a space of hypercommercialized materialism, I sensed some internal disagreements and ambivalence had cropped up about how to express this critique. One South Asian girl complained to her family about the young Arab American men at the protest who had their faces wrapped in kaffiyehs, concerned that they looked like "terrorists." She said, "This is supposed to be a peaceful protest. I am going to tell the organizers to ask them to take it off!" Her comment expressed unease with public performances of Arabness that evoked racialized images of the "enemy" in the War on Terror, a concern that solidarity should stop short of looking like the enemy. At a protest of the Israeli strikes in Gaza in San Francisco the previous day, I saw Arab American male teenagers with kaffiyehs covering their faces, as if to defiantly and express their solidarity with those engaged in resistance to Israeli occupation and warfare by performing the iconic and highly charged image of the Palestinian fedayeen (guerilla fighters), one that has historically emblematized Arab and Muslim terrorism in the U.S.

The comment by the young protester in Santa Clara condemning images of kaffiyeh-swathed militant "extremists" is embedded in a political landscape where the performance of "moderate"/good and "angry"/bad Islam has shaped the expressions of public protest for Muslim American youth, as discussed in Chapter One. Azma, a Pakistani American woman from Milpitas whose parents met while living and working in Libya, commented to me after the protest, "I thought that I would feel angry when I went there; obviously, we were protesting because we feel anger, but when I went there, it just made me feel really good about myself and I was really happy that we're going to do something and we're all here together. So, people should listen to us." This is an interesting reflection on the politics of "angry" protest and a reframing of the distancing from "radical" Muslim politics, for Azma both legitimizes feelings of outrage at disproportionate state violence against a besieged population and links them to her discovery of the positive affect of solidarity through collective action. Solidarity is a structure of political feeling and can be infused with sentiments of anger, frustration, fear, anxiety, happiness, and empathy (Williams 1977). These emotions are variously expressed and translated into or borne out of political actions, producing the affective moral and political registers of proper subjecthood for Muslim, Palestinian, Pakistani, and Afghan American youth.

The political sentiments of solidarity expressed by the young people on the sidewalk in Santa Clara that day were not shared by all their peers, clearly, and did not necessarily resonate with other Muslim American youth. Azma, for example, was frustrated by her attempts to reach out to others through Facebook to oppose the occupation and wars in Palestine:

> I think that everyone, regardless of whether they're Arab, Middle Eastern, Muslim or not [should be concerned], it's human rights. It really bothers me when I tell people, like I would invite them to a group or something on Facebook, and they just will deny it right away. And I know they denied it right away because I ask them, "Oh, did you look at it [the Facebook group]?" and they'll say, "No, I'm not into that kind of stuff." And it just really bothers me, because how can you not be into a subject that just relates to everyone?

Azma was frustrated that the Palestine question was an ethnically particular, rather than a universal, issue of "human rights" that would cross national and religious boundaries. She was equally upset that social media was a site of denial and evasion, as much as connection and education, for youth who were unconcerned and did not share her outrage. This frustration was echoed by Aisha, who grappled with the absence of interest by others in the dispossession, displacement, and violence experienced by Palestinians. She became aware at an early age of the erasure of Palestine in the U.S. mainstream media due to her own, invisibilized family history. She reflected, "As a child, I was hanging out with my grandpa who was beaten by Israeli soldiers and his leg was injured, his front tooth was broken. . . . I was left wondering why this wasn't on the news, why people weren't talking about it. I felt I was growing up as a second-class citizen; I couldn't engage politically. These issues were real to me, but there was no place in society to talk about it." Aisha's sense of exclusion from citizenship, and from participation in the body politic of the nation, was not just due to the denial of the Palestinian narrative in the U.S. but also the lack of a space to enter politics related to the Palestine question—what Edward Said (2000) famously called the "last taboo" in the U.S. mainstream public sphere.

Other youth argued that defining Arabs as human would challenge U.S. violence in the global War on Terror legitimized by the language of terrorism and counterterrorism, so human rights becomes a language through which to restore humanity. Jenaan recalled conversations she had with people while working at a movie theater in Santa Clara about the revelations of torture of Iraqis at the U.S. military prison in Abu Ghraib:

> I was like, "How can they do that to another human being?" And some people were like, "You know what, I don't care. They're terrorists, they deserve what they're getting." . . . I said, "You know what, the majority of the people there aren't even terrorists. They haven't been charged with anything, but they're being treated like animals." And that kind of shut people up because they didn't think I would retort!

Jenaan had to confront the view that torture is justified because certain racialized bodies classified as "terrorists" are not (fully) human and do not deserve the protection of due process or rights. Commenting on the torture at Abu Ghraib, Angela Davis (2005) asked, "How do we pose questions about the violence associated with the importation of US-style democracy to Iraq? What kind of democracy treats human beings as refuse?" (50). Populations that are disposable are considered remaindered lives that "deserve" torture within the biopolitics of the counterterrorism regime's assessment of human lives and the "democratization" of regions that only understand force, according to Orientalist experts on "the Arab mind" whose work has legitimized U.S. military and counterterrorism policies (see Sheehi 2011; Tadiar 2013, 22).

Jenaan also commented that as a woman who wore a hijab, and who engaged feistily in political discussions, she frequently challenged people's stereotypical assumptions about Muslim women as submissive or voiceless. I met Jenaan at the Eastridge mall in San Jose in the summer of 2008, where we had coffee in the Barnes & Noble bookstore café. Sitting by the window, we could see families walking around outside and many South Asians of various ages, including children and young men in baseball caps, on a weekend outing to the mall. Jenaan, who had graduated from San Jose State and was working in a real estate company in Palo Alto, spoke with passion and sardonic wit. When I asked her what she thought about the war in Iraq, she said with evident frustration:

> I . . . think it was a waste of time, energy, and life. . . . they [the U.S. military] took down Saddam Hussein and now it's still being occupied and people are still getting killed. They keep coming up with stories about how they were

forced to shoot at random people. . . . They're like, "Well, they're getting the terrorists," and 99% of the people there are civilians who are getting killed. They
get so happy because they killed a terrorist when they probably went inside and
fired at someone defending their own house.

Jenaan argues eloquently against the premises of "regime change" for democracy in Iraq and a racialized worldview in which ordinary Arabs defending
their homes are considered terrorists who can be killed, given that counterinsurgency doctrine views the entire population as a site of resistance to
invasion. She may be enhancing the estimates of "collateral damage" to dramatize her observation, but it is indeed the case that there have been many
killings of civilians by the U.S. military, not to mention rapes of Iraqi girls
and women by soldiers. The massacres of Iraqis at Haditha and Fallujah are
just two well-publicized incidents of U.S. atrocities, not to mention the 2007
killing of journalists and civilians in Baghdad that came to light through
the classified materials given by Chelsea Manning to WikiLeaks; the latter
included reports that the U.S. military covered up executions of children and
the elderly and a count of approximately sixty-six thousand violent deaths
of civilians between 2004 and 2009.[2] The fact that this violence disappears
from plain view, like incidents of mass violence against Palestinians that
are often not even called massacres, leads some to focus on a humanist
approach.

Other young people I spoke to were also frustrated with the impunity with
which the U.S. military had killed civilians in Afghanistan and Pakistan in
the name of its relentless War on Terror against Al Qaeda and the Taliban,
as I discuss in the next chapter. For many youth, who had familial and cultural ties in the regions where the U.S. was engaged in military occupation
as well as covert operations, the fact that some human lives were considered
legitimate targets of "extraordinary technologies" of warfare fueled much of
their opposition to the "racial wars" of the U.S. (Reddy 2011, 12). Recall the
comment of General Tommy Frank, who led the invasion of Iraq, that the
U.S. would not do a body count of Iraqi casualties, a deliberate departure
from the policy during the Vietnam war. Civilian groups such as Iraq Body
Count estimated that over one hundred thousand Iraqi noncombatants had
been killed due to the U.S. war beginning in 2003, not to mention the mass
deaths of Iraqis during the U.S. economic sanctions of the 1990s—including a
staggering estimate of half a million Iraqi children.[3] This genocidal violence
targeting an entire society (one that had not attacked the U.S., it must be
noted) was stunning as much for its scale of devastation as for the impunity
of the U.S. military in its occupation and destruction of another, sovereign

nation. As Judith Butler (2009) observes, "grievability is a presupposition for the life that matters"; the differential recognition accorded to the deaths of racially marked bodies is what underlies the politics of "precarity" that shapes the biopolitics of war and the outrage that infuses a politics of solidarity (14). Achille Mmembe (2003) has argued that the management of death, or necropolitics, is apparent in late-colonial policies of determining "who is disposable and who is not" through "the enactment of differential rights to differing categories of people" (26–27), which he frames as a racialized project of Western modernity. Regimes of killing, incarceration, and torture justified by projects of democracy promotion or counterterrorism are intimately and violently linked to the politics of life and death, to the question of which lives can be sacrificed in order to save humanity (Agamben 2005). This logic of disposability underlies the exceptionalisms in human rights organizing that some youth confronted in their solidarity with others, facing occupation, racial exclusion, and also sociocide, in zones of war and colonization.

The Global "Color Line" of Human Rights

The racialized distribution of human rights rests on the racialization of the notion of the human itself, within and beyond the imperial state, for the human who was afforded constitutional rights was "essentially Caucasian, Christian, capitalist, and civil" (Barker 2014, 34); in the settler colony, "Native humanity and human rights are made contingent on the empire's interests," according to Joanne Barker, as "some humans are not, or not enough, human to warrant the recognition, rights, and entitlements of the empire" (39, 44). The paradoxical assault on global humanity and human rights in the name of human rights, as critics such as Randall Williams (2010) have argued, rests on a civilizational logic or global "color line": the institutionalized human rights regime reinscribes an international division of humanity between "the third world individual living within a nation of danger and the first world rescuers residing in a space of safety and enlightened freedom"—a colonialist geography that is deeply racialized and gendered (xv, 28). As Williams (2010,) observes, after World War II, a "liberal model of human rights" emerged as "the privileged discourse for the symbolic articulation of international justice" and framework for responding to violence, increasingly adopted and produced by national and transnational NGOs, such as Amnesty International and Human Rights Watch (xv, xvii; see figure 3.1 preceding). In fact, "human rights have increasingly come to define 'the political'" and provided a dominant "international ethic" for responding to violence since the 1970s and especially after the Cold War through an assemblage of new forms of imperial intervention, such as "just war, preemptive invasions, humanitarian operations" (Williams 2010, xxiv; see also Fassin and Pandolfi 2010). As Neda Atanoski (2013) succinctly states, "Human rights appear as the only ethical politics in the world today" (17).

However, the enshrining of human rights in international legal instruments and the Universal Declaration of Human Rights in 1948, during the period of decolonization in the global South, eclipsed the "dialectic between (imperial) violence and (international) law" (Williams 2010, xxiii). There is thus a historical tension between legally institutionalized human rights and anti-imperial politics. Sally Merry (2006) has tracked the emergence of international law in the context of a long history of (European) imperial expansion and situates the legal human rights apparatus in the international order of sovereign nation-states (103–104). This legal regime of human rights obscures colonial violence through a selective focus on nonviolence and evasion of human rights violations within or by Western nation-states and imperial regimes, in the context of what Richard Falk calls "Western liberal internationalism" (cited in Williams 2010, 16). The slippage of other forms of international solidarity and disappearance of Palestine, Iraq, or Af-Pak from the framework of human rights is not surprising, then, for it illuminates the "oppositional relationship" between the institutionalized human rights regime and decolonizing movements in the global South, particularly those that involve armed struggle, from South Africa to Palestine (Williams 2010, xxiii). The United States' legalization of torture and doctrines of counterterrorism since 9/11 have led to the paradoxical situation, once again, where international human rights law is used to mask the human rights violations of the imperial state or is defied altogether when convenient.

In addition, human rights internationalism" has been "domesticated" by the "discourses of American nationalism and neoliberalism" and has suppressed movements that focus on social and economic rights, as Wendy Hesford (2011, 11, 187) argues. While activists and "Third World social movements" have helped shift human rights frameworks from individually based to collective rights, there persists a "deep division" between the emphasis on civil and political rights (such as free speech and freedom of religion) in the U.S. and other capitalist democracies, and the prioritization of economic and social rights in socialist and developing states (Merry 2006, 105; Bricmont 2007, 83–88). In fact, U.S. neoliberal imperialism has insisted that its version of human rights and economic rights—that is, rights to the free market— must be imposed across the world as the primary route to "freedom," including for those in the impoverished states of the global South who are barely clinging to life itself (Bricmont 2007, 66; Melamed 2006, 17).

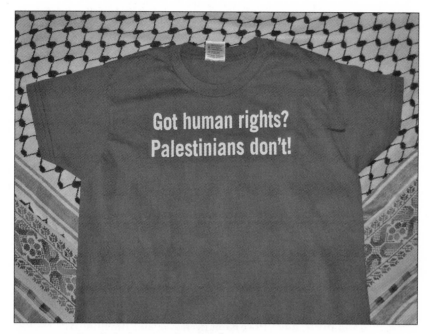

Figure 3.2. T-shirt from 2014 Gaza solidarity events

These critiques, however, do not invalidate the strategic necessity of resorting to human rights in order to speak back to empire, for those who suffer from imperial violence and state terror and deploy human rights as a tool to expose the impunity and hypocrisy of Western regimes. This is, of course, an ongoing debate in many parts of the world, including in Afghanistan, Iraq, and Palestine, where the targets of colonial and settler violence resort to international legal instruments and human rights frameworks, well aware of their exceptionalisms and often with cynicism, precisely because human rights *is*, in fact, the privileged framework for modern politics (Allen 2013). As Hesford (2011) pithily observes, "'Having' a right is of most value precisely when one does not 'have' (the object of) the right" (37). At the same time, the young activists I spoke to realized that there is a deep contradiction embedded in human rights, especially as invoked in the post-9/11 moment, given the absences and repression they encountered in their international solidarity activism related to Palestine, Afghanistan, Iraq, or Pakistan, yet they continued to grapple with rights claims, often strategically, and attempted to find room for dissent within this paradigm. Their experiences suggest, however, that we need to examine the political implications of the exceptionalism of human rights as a failed discourse in the post-9/11 era, such as in mobilization in support of Palestinian human rights.

Palestinianization, Palestine Solidarity Activism, and Arab American Politics

Palestine solidarity activism, including the growing Boycott, Divestment, and Sanctions (BDS) movement in which many youth and college students have been involved in recent years, often relies on human rights discourse, based on the premise that Palestinians do not have the rights that they should and so must assert the right to claim rights (Isin and Ruppert 2015, 180). The Palestine solidarity movement in the U.S. is a transnational human rights movement that extends beyond Arab and Muslim American communities, but it is also a unifying axis for Muslim, Arab, South Asian, and Afghan American politics and a significant crucible for politicization of youth. The cross-racial alliances produced through solidarity with Palestine are not new, given left activism in solidarity with Palestine in the era of Third Worldist politics of the 1960s and 1970s, but the movement declined in the U.S. after the Oslo Peace Accords of 1993, and in the wake of the dissolution of Arab student groups such as the Arab American University Graduates (AAUG), the Organization of Arab Students (OAS), and the General Union of Palestinian Students (GUPS) (see Naber 2012). The Palestine solidarity movement reemerged in the late 1990s after the second Intifada with new formations such as the Students for Justice in Palestine (SJP), founded in 2001, which are multiracial and not based on ethnic/religious identity (see Barrows-Friedman 2014). In the late 2000s, BDS organizing, launched in response to the call for BDS from Palestinian civil society in 2004–2005, was galvanized by the attacks on the humanitarian aid flotilla to Gaza in 2010 and the wars on Gaza in 2008–2009, 2012, and 2014. Indeed, Palestine solidarity activism has increasingly become an important terrain for global justice activism on campuses and among youth, even if it is a highly contentious site of repression and backlash as well.

On the ground, there is an important distinction made between Palestine solidarity activism and *Palestinian* activism—between groups and activists including non-Palestinians in support of Palestinian self-determination and mobilization by Palestinians themselves. New cross-racial alliances, including by younger activists, have increasingly produced a discourse of Palestine solidarity as an issue of racial justice, and not just resistance to military occupation, humanitarian crisis, or displacement. For example, Marwa talked about an African American student who was involved with SCAI, and who had worked for a senator in Washington D.C. and "dealt with the Israel lobby."

She said, "Basically, he sees the racism that still goes on today, you know, against African Americans. . . . And learning about it and just hearing about it [the Palestine issue], he sees major parallels because he says . . . 'I *should* [emphatically] be working for this because it's the same thing.'" The shift to the discourse of racial apartheid and analogies between racial discrimination and segregation by the Israeli state and Jim Crow in the U.S., while heavily contested by supporters of Israel, is an important shift, crystallized dramatically in the Ferguson to Gaza solidarity campaign spurred by police killings of Black males in the U.S and awareness of Israeli collaboration with U.S. police as well as shared experiences of racist state violence. This interracial solidarity has been generated partly by the explicit connections made by the BDS movement to the struggle against South African apartheid, and by the support of major African American left intellectuals such as Robin Kelley, Angela Davis, and Alice Walker (see Davis 1989; Kelley and Williams 2013).[4]

It is important to consider the Palestine solidarity movement as an antiracist movement that crosses boundaries of ethnicity, nationalism, religion, and class, though these various axes of mobilization may be variously highlighted or downplayed depending on the particular group or campaign. While faith-based groups might approach the Palestine issue primarily as an issue of "Muslim rights," which generates an internationalist but not a universalist rubric, Palestinian solidarity and Palestinian activist groups cross religious boundaries and focus on opposition to militarism, dispossession, and, in some cases, apartheid and colonialism through an approach that transcends rights-talk. As discussed in the previous chapter, a liberal interfaith or cross-cultural approach to Palestine solidarity uses a depoliticized model of "coexistence" that evades political realities through faithwashing. Issues of nationalism, race, and religion are variously negotiated in both faith- and non-faith-based forms of organizing in support of Palestine by youth. A Palestinian community activist from the Bay Area, who had been involved in Palestine organizing in the U.S. since the 1970s, observed that while many Arab Muslim youth increasingly mobilized around their religious identity after 9/11, it seemed that Palestinian Christian youth in the Bay Area became more activated around the Palestinian issue. This is a complex issue, but it is true that the leadership of (secular) Palestinian groups in the Bay Area, including the transnational Palestinian Youth Movement, the campaign to commemorate the sixtieth anniversary of the Nakba in 2008, and organizing with local Arab American youth, has visibly featured young Palestinian Christians (mainly women).

Less attention, in fact, has been paid to the politicization of Christian Arab American youth, whose experiences are often lost in the post-9/11 discourse that is heavily invested in the experiences of young Muslim Americans. While the War on Terror compelled some youth to focus on combating Islamophobia and turn to pan-Islamic solidarity, for some Arab Christian youth there was a turn to Arab nationalist politics, in addition to solidarity with Muslim Americans and civil rights activism. Two young women I spoke to, who belonged to the large population of Palestinian Christian families in the Bay Area, reflected on their own trajectories of politicization after 2001. Jenny, who grew up in Morgan Hill, became involved with the Palestine movement and with organizing a recruitment program for Arab American high school youth while at UC Berkeley. She visited Palestine for the first time on her own, because her parents were nervous about traveling through Israeli borders, and commented on her engagement with the Palestine issue with other college students: "I don't know if we'd have done that if 9/11 had not happened." Amalia, a Palestinian American friend of Jenny's who grew up in San Jose, was also involved with both pan-Arab and Palestine solidarity student groups at Berkeley, and remarked, "We definitely wanted to have a voice and presence. We wanted to say, 'We exist, we have a history, you can't erase Palestine!'" The events of 9/11 and the intensification of anti-Arab discourse thus propelled the construction of a defiant Palestinian nationalism. Both Amalia and Jenny also talked about the shift from those in their parents' generation who were hesitant to publicly express an Arab or Palestinian identity—reflected in the non-Arab names they gave their daughters—and wary about the political risks of speaking about Palestine, to their own increasingly vocal and public claiming of Palestinian national identification in their college years.[5]

These intergenerational tensions and transitions are embedded in a longer history of shifts in ethnic and political identification among Arab immigrant communities in the U.S. toward a more public claiming of Arab national identity and mobilization in support of Palestine, especially after the 1967 Arab-Israeli war, and despite ongoing repression of Arab nationalism in the U.S. (Pennock 2014). Arab migrants in the first half of the twentieth century were predominantly Christians from what is now Syria, Lebanon, and Palestine; beginning in the 1960s, there was an influx of Muslim migrants as well as Arab migrants politicized by pan-Arab nationalism and Arab socialism (Naff 1985; Orfalea 2006; Malek 2009). The resurgence of Palestinian activism since 2001 has occurred as a new generation of Arab and Palestinian Americans has come of age, including many whose families are part of the old, well-established Palestinian Christian community in the Bay Area. During the second Intifada in Palestine that began in 2000, solidarity groups and SJP chapters were launched on college campuses, and Palestinian, Arab, and Muslim American youth began mobilizing in coalition with others, as the events

of 9/11 precipitated an intensified focus on the Middle East. These two historical events, in Palestine and the U.S., converged to galvanize Palestine activism
and the focus on human rights in the last decade of the old millennium.

It is striking that the Palestine issue is, according to many I spoke to, a
hub of mobilization for Arabs and Muslims in the U.S. and a focal point for
their political identity (Naber 2012, 146). Bashir observed, "It's the single most
important issue. And sometimes it's not realized how important it is, especially by certain governments. And again and again people say that if this is
resolved, many things will be resolved." As Bashir points out, concern about
Palestine underlies much of the opposition and militant resistance to the U.S.
among Muslims (and Arabs) within the U.S. as well as globally, who are frustrated and outraged at the consistent U.S. support and funding for the Israeli
occupation; this was also a factor in Al Qaeda's rationale for the 9/11 attacks.
The issue of justice in Palestine is a political thread that also links older and
younger generations of Muslim and Arab Americans. A Pakistani immigrant
from Sunnyvale who came to the U.S. in 1967 and was involved with the Pakistani Association of the Bay Area, of which he was once president, as well
as local programs for Muslim American youth, observed eloquently, "Palestine is a core issue on which Muslims tend to agree, there is no difference of
opinion. It [the problem in Palestine] keeps us frustrated. It's a religious, and
a human issue. . . . Palestine is an issue that transcends, whether it's Indian,
Arab, Pakistani. . . . It's a great injustice, and [persists] in the twenty-first century. It's unbelievable." The outrage over the devastation and displacement of
a predominantly Muslim society, and the Israeli regime's control over access
to the third most important site in Islam—the al-Aqsa mosque in Jerusalem—is shared by Muslim Americans across ethnic and national boundaries
and makes this a consistently burning issue for global Muslim rights. For this
older Pakistani immigrant, Palestine was a "human" issue that produces a
consensus among Muslim Americans and has stoked their frustration with
the U.S. state, animating a position of dissent. Marwa also commented on the
way the Palestine question binds the Arab American community and shapes
its political culture:

> All Arabs have this love or care about Palestine. They [Palestinians] have the
> most human rights problems, there's the occupation. Despite all the problems
> between Arabs and such, they all unify on this one topic, it's something that
> brings them all together. If you've looked at history, that's one thing they all
> care about. It's more of a unifying factor to this day; even the way I was raised,
> I remember going to Palestine protests in San Francisco with my whole family
> as, like, a normal thing.

Palestine is a core issue that unites Arabs, through pan-Arab national-ism, and Muslims, through pan-Islamic internationalism and concern about the holy sites of Islam, and is a vehicle to engage with political injustice and human rights activism for youth. Mobilization around the Palestine ques-tion also has implications for the ways in which Arab and Muslim identity is shaped, internally and in relation to larger publics. It is an issue that keeps Muslim and Arab American communities "frustrated," critical, and in opposi-tion to U.S. foreign policy and is a key issue in the Middle East that challenges the official narrative about U.S. interventions for "human rights" and "de-mocracy." As Gregory Orfalea (2006) has suggested, the Palestine movement transformed Arab Americans into a progressive political community with a major political cause that has pitted it against the U.S. state, in particular since the 1967 Arab-Israeli war and the consolidation of the U.S. alliance with Israel. It is the Palestine question that has historically prevented Arab Americans from becoming an assimilable and ambiguously racialized immigrant group or model minority, as has been the case, relatively, for Indian Americans and Pakistani Americans, aswell as Afghan Americans to some extent, until 9/11 (Salaita 2006a). In fact, political solidarity with the Palestinian national struggle is generally illegible in a U.S. public culture that has racialized Arab Americans as a nonwhite population in conflict with hegemonic U.S. politics.

Well before 9/11, Arab Americans have been targets of repression and sur-veillance due to their nationalist politics and organized efforts to challenge U.S. support for Israel. The post-1967 period is often described as an "Arab American awakening" with the flourishing of pan-Arab nationalist, anti-imperialist, and left organizing in the U.S. in the 1970s and 1980s, including an Arab American campaign in Detroit calling on the United Auto Workers to di-vest from Israel after the 1973 Arab-Israeli war—one of the earliest divestment campaigns targeting Israel (Abraham 1983; Haddad 1994, 79; Malek 2009, 69). It is the question of Palestine that stands at the threshold of cultural and politi-cal assimilation for Arab, and in many cases, (immigrant) Muslim Americans, historically troubling the entry of these groups into easy identification with U.S. imperial nationalism and white middle-class America. This is an impor-tant point that is sometimes overlooked by those who focus exclusively on the events of 9/11 as the impetus for politicization and the context for repression of Arab and Muslim Americans. Linking the post-9/11 backlash to the Palestine question and the long history of anti-Arab racism helps situate what is usu-ally glossed simply as Islamophobia within the deeper structure of repression linked to the U.S. state's involvement in the Middle East and to Arabophobia.

Although the Israel-Palestine "conflict" (or colonial question) is so cen-tral to the War on Terror—and fuels so much of "anti-American" militancy as well as counterterrorism operations in the U.S. (see Said 2000), decades of misinformation and censorship related to Israel-Palestine, coupled with heavily Orientalist media representations of Arab militancy and Islamic fanaticism, have obscured the political realities and histories of the region. Over and over again, the young people I interviewed said that they realized early on in their lives that their peers simply knew very little about West Asia, including about Israel-Palestine. This also means that the solidarity with the Palestinian struggle in Arab and Muslim American communities animated a pedagogy of political protest for youth as they confronted the embargo on open discussion of Palestine. Marwa reminisced about her early encounters with anti-Palestinianism in school:

> When I was in eighth grade, one of the turning points of my life was . . . one of our teachers was . . . talking in class—and this is a private school, you're not supposed to talk about your political views and stuff like that—he was talking about Palestine and he was saying stuff about Palestine and suicide bombers, which I don't support, but like he made it sound like Palestinians are crazy and are terrorist. So I was only in eighth grade and I spoke out—because I am crazy—and I was like, "Uhhh, I think you're wrong!" And then we kind of battled him out in class and then he was like . . . "I'll give you twenty minutes in class next week to do a presentation." And I was like, "Okay!" And I started doing the presentations, which really started my activism.

This early experience of being catapulted into political debate and activism due to racist and Orientalist assumptions of Palestinian/Arab irrationality and violence is common among many Arab and Muslim American youth and has persisted over time (Salaita 2006a). Toufic El Rassi addresses his politicization as a young Lebanese American in his witty and poignant autobiographical graphic novel, *Arab in America* (2007), recalling how high school teachers and students used slurs such as "towelheads" and displayed anti-Arab cartoons during the first Gulf War (9–30). Similar experiences of anti-Arab racism targeting youth have been documented in the Bay Area as well, despite its veneer of liberal multiculturalism and progressive pedagogy. The Arab Resource and Organizing Center did a survey of Arab American high school youth in 2009–2010 in the San Francisco Bay Area through their Arab Youth Organizing (AYO) program. They found that nearly half of youth had heard racist remarks in high schools about Arabs and 8% had actually been suspended or punished because they became upset about offensive views expressed about Arabs or Muslims, particularly after the war on Gaza in 2008–2009; several reported incidents of censorship in the classroom, and

76% said that they had not been taught anything about Arab history or culture that year.[6] Clearly, the engagement of Arab American youth with global politics did not begin after 9/11 but must be situated in the longer history of unconditional U.S. support for the Zionist state, ongoing U.S. interventions in the Middle East, and the cultural racism that has bolstered support for Israel in the U.S. public sphere, including the mainstream media's relentless stereotyping and criminalization of Arabs and Palestinians (Alsultany 2012; Sheehi 2011).

Given this historical context, I argue that we need to consider the process of *Palestinianization*, or politicization around Palestinian identity and struggles, as a site of racialization that is endemic to U.S. national culture due to the alliance between the U.S. and Israel and the suppression of the Palestinian national struggle as a struggle for racial justice. Palestinianization is a process that overlaps with the antiracist and antistate politics of other groups subjected to racial violence, displacement, and genocide by the U.S.; it is not an exceptional site of counterhegemonic race politics, of course, but it is one that has been heavily repressed in the U.S. and also (as a result) has been much less discussed and theorized in U.S. scholarship. Palestinianization is a process that non-Palestinians and non-Arabs also experience, as they challenge U.S. collusion with Israeli settler colonialism and warfare, and subsequently encounter repression and demonization. I draw this concept of Palestinianization from June Jordan's (2007) simple yet profound statement, originally published in 1985, on the Israeli invasion of Lebanon and the massacre of Palestinian refugees in Sabra and Shatila camps in 1982: "I was born a Black woman/and now/I am become a Palestinian" (400). This statement suggests something subtly but importantly different from the activist credo "We are all Palestinian"; it evokes an individual transformation and an active process of "becoming" a Palestinian through confronting U.S. and Israeli racism and imperial violence and making the connections among these colonial pasts and presents. Jordan's statement, which I read as a poetic expression of Palestinianization, is also a window into the ways in which becoming "a Palestinian" means staking out a racial politics, and not just a politics based on the rights discourse of Western modernity.[7]

While the representations of Arab/Muslim terrorism that youth such as Marwa encountered in her high school classroom are deeply racialized, and can also lead to Palestinianization, the question of race is seemingly difficult to use as a framework for Palestine activism in the U.S. This is a thorny question that I will explore more in Chapter Five and that is situated in debates about the core nature of the Israeli state and its policies toward Palestinians and Arabs, which are generally not read through the lens of race in the U.S. (see Lubin 2014; Saliba 2011). The politics of "the Israel-Palestine conflict," as it is often ambiguously called, is indeed related to the racialization of Arabs and Muslims in the U.S. as well as in Israel-Palestine, as it is to Western colonial modernity and post–civil rights racial liberalism (Feldman 2015). The definition of Palestinians as subjects who are not worthy of civil or even human rights has been consolidated through the permeation of Zionist discourse in U.S. public culture, including in liberal domains, and unwavering U.S. support for the Israeli state. This has created tensions in how a pro-Palestinian politics should be imagined in relation to racial justice models and how alliances with other progressive and antiracist movements should be crafted, for Arab as well as South Asian and Afghan American youth, whether Muslim, non-Muslim, or secular.

Given the embeddedness of the Palestinian liberation movement in pan-Arab nationalism as well as its link to pan-Islamic solidarity, it is an issue that can propel Arab Muslim youth toward greater identification either as Arab or Muslim, or both. Dana, an Iraqi American from San Jose who went to college on the East Coast, observed that students on her campus moved between the Islamic Society, the Society of Arab Students, and the school's Palestine organization, with South Asians and Arabs being variously more involved in one organization or the other, depending on ethnic and social networks. Distinctions of being "too secular" or "not religious enough" influenced the shifting affiliations of students with these campus organizations and youth subcultures, creating hierarchies of belonging and identity. These tensions among various groups or subcultures did not seem to be as prevalent at San Jose State, according to Salah, perhaps because there was no Arab American student organization, in fact, only a Middle Eastern student club, which he described as "definitely a falafel club, very social," with "no politics." There was a Muslim Student Association and a political organization called Students for Change at the time, but it could also be that the absence of a specifically Arab student group was, in fact, due to the much greater interest and investment in organizing with the MSA. Youth from San Jose who went to UC Berkeley also spoke of religious divisions among the Arab American students and tensions between religious and secular approaches to campus organizing, though these categorizations are, of course, complex and fraught.

It is important to acknowledge that the terms "secular" and "secularism" are imbricated with Western projects of Enlightenment modernity and doctrines of liberal democracy (Asad 2003; Mahmood 2006). In the post-9/11 moment, the debates about secularism have tended to center on Islam and Muslims as objects of secularization regimes. This discourse, however, has tended to pit the "Muslim" against the "secular" in often simplistic and troubling ways. It is indeed the case that a certain Western liberal definition of secularity is central to modern notions of citizenship and statehood and has been promoted globally by imperial regimes such as the U.S. in the War on Terror. But it is also the case that the current discourse of secularism enshrines its own paradigm of secularity based on a liberal, Western norm, erasing the genealogy of indigenous secularisms in the global South (Abbas 2014). Critical secularism offers a critique of the project of secularism installed and authorized by the Western nation-state and colonial modernity, and is not predicated on a simple relationship to religious belief alone, but suggests ways of thought that challenge universalisms and offer routes for crossing social boundaries of all kinds (Said 1983; Mufti, 2004). In the post-9/11 moment, Arab, South Asian, and Afghan American youth find themselves wrestling with the fallout of these debates while engaging in mobilization and coalition building on the ground. The rights claims of these movements and alliances, centered variously on civil, immigrant, or human rights, collide with the tensions generated in negotiating what a "secularist" or faith-based political project should look like. These tensions sometimes echo the difficulties of recuperating a notion of nationalism, secularism or feminism that is not complicit with Western, liberal imperial modernity.

In many cases, students I spoke to were simultaneously involved in a range of faith- as well as non-faith-based groups, and a few talked about the contradictions and contestations they had to wrestle with at different moments. Questions arose such as who should and could belong to the group and how political mobilization around issues such as Palestine should be defined—as an issue of global justice, human rights, national self-determination, anti-colonialism, anti-Zionism, and/or oppression of Muslims? Some who were critical of defining Palestine as a "Muslim cause" were also critical of Arab nationalism as a basis for political solidarity. Aisha reflected thoughtfully that after she started taking courses in Middle East studies in college, she began pondering whether pan-Arab nationalism, by "imposing one language," could become "exclusive"; she said, "It makes you know what brings you closer together and what the real divisions are." These debates among youth about organizing in support of Palestine are shaped by larger political and historical shifts related to the rise of Islamist movements in the Middle East since the 1980s, the perceived (and real) failures of postcolonial nationalist regimes, and the role of secularist politics (see Kundnani 2014; Naber 2012). These questions are rife in the context of organizing around Palestine, partly in relation to the division in Palestinian nationalist politics symbolized by the power struggle between (the Islamist group) Hamas and (the secular party) Fatah.

Aisha commented on the ways in which these tensions rippled into campus activism for Muslim and Christian Arab American youth:

> So what does it mean if Hamas is in power [in Gaza]? . . . Christian Palestinians wanted to be active after 9/11 and you also see these Muslims become active after 9/11 and wanting to tackle the Palestine issue. They were used to being attacked, as Muslims, but for Christian Palestinians it was a new experience. They were [also] viewed as not Palestinian enough.

For Aisha, Palestinian nationalism had to be an inclusive, and also progressive, terrain on which to wage the struggle for Palestinian liberation, one in which the authenticity of Palestinian Christians would not be an issue due to a presumption of their not being Arab/Palestinian enough. Her observation that Palestinian Christians evaded the brunt of Islamophobia and Arabophobia until 9/11 may not be fully borne out by the history of anti-Arab sentiment that targets all Arabs, despite the voluntary or involuntary passing by some as white, as my conversations with Arab Christian youth illustrated. However, Aisha's critique suggests that an internal conflation of Islam with Arabness mirrors the problem that Arab Christians encounter in the larger public. In addition to the assumption that Christian Arabs can not be real Arabs, there is an Islamophobic and Zionist narrative that Arab Christians are inherently oppressed by Arab/Palestinian Muslims, which has become the basis for the alliance between evangelical Christian Americans, such as Pat Robertson and Tim LaHaye, and Zionist groups in the United States. The call by American evangelical dispensationalists for the removal of Palestinians through ethnic cleansing or Jewish colonization in order to facilitate the Jewish redemption of biblical Israel, is trenchantly critiqued by Steven Salaita (2008) in his essay "I Was Called Up to Commit Genocide" (33–50). Salaita challenges the presumption that Palestinian Christian victimhood trumps Zionist oppression, and as a Palestinian Christian American, refuses the call to be a wedge between a Christian America and Muslim Palestine that could legitimize genocidal violence against all Palestinians—Muslim, Christian, or atheist.[8]

However, on the other side of challenging right-wing alliances, the youth I spoke to grappled with how to build progressive alliances and joint struggles with other movements *through* Palestine. Both right-wing and liberal-left-progressive coalitions, it should be noted, invoke the discourse of rights as normative claims-making, whether the right of Christians to settle Jewish populations in Israel in order to attain rapture or the right of indigenous Palestinians to live in Palestine. Solidarity with Palestine must be predicated, if it is produced in the true sense of solidarity and shared struggle and not just as a strategic alliance, on a reciprocal understanding of, identification with, and active support of other struggles, whether they are focused on liberation from colonialism and occupation or on racial, social, and economic justice. Several youth spoke directly to this issue, with a few eloquently describing not just an intersectionality of struggles but a deeper analysis of modes of oppression that constitute the political order and also possibilities of what Rancière (2010) describes as "forms of political inscription that (ac)count for the unaccounted" (35). The inscription of Palestine as a global, racial justice issue makes visible the unaccounted for and disappeared Palestinian, as well as the political subject who becomes a Palestinian.

Racializing Palestine and Forging Alliances

Palestinianization occurs not only in the context of national and religious formations. Aisha's entry into Palestine activism as an ongoing, public engagement was through labor organizing in college; she said, "It was a humbling experience: we weren't the only oppressed people in the world! Our strength is from our involvement in coalitions." Aisha talked about how she had few Arab American friends while growing up in Fremont and was not engaged with an Arab American political community. When she went to a large public university, she became involved in a student-labor coalition with service workers "to organize around workers' rights" and she "gained consciousness of these issues through the labor movement and getting involved in interracial organizing beyond Palestine. So I was learning that it was not just Palestinians who are oppressed, this land too was stolen, there's a history of slavery here. We all share histories of oppression and can come together . . . because of our experience of coming from the global South." For Aisha, it was labor organizing and progressive/left coalitions that led her to a broader anti-imperial and anticapitalist politics that challenged the exceptionalism of Palestine, linking settler colonialism and racial violence there and here. Worker rights and indigenous rights were thus articulated within a larger framework of human rights that she hoped would transcend racial and national boundaries, and single-issue- or identity-based movements. Aisha also noted that her involvement in this coalition and in direct action during labor protests in Davis provided a training ground in organizing strategies and tactics and offered a political education that she later drew on in her activism related to Palestine: "There was really amazing politics. . . . There were four hundred people blocking Russell Boulevard. These community activists knew how to talk to the police . . . and what to do when you got arrested. A lot of Palestinians were fired up that day—making that link between local and global oppression."

The Bay Area has been especially fertile ground for these kinds of political alliances between Palestine solidarity activism and other forms of left organizing, and young Palestinian, Arab, and Muslim American activists I spoke to emphasized the significance of these connections. Lamia, a Palestinian American woman from Burlingame, was involved in organizing the transnational Palestinian Youth Network (now called the Palestinian Youth Movement), which spans the U.S. and Europe, and was a member of the General Union of Palestinian Students (GUPS) chapter while she was an undergraduate at San Francisco State University. She remarked that it was through her campus activism that she learned about Palestinian history for the first time and about the relation of Palestinian/Arab communities to other groups through a politics of race and indigeneity: "So that's kind of my experience of GUPS. It's been an amazing thing that's happened . . . learning about other people of color and indigenous struggles. So we wouldn't be prepared to start a Palestinian youth network if I hadn't been through my GUPS experience. It's been very critical for me in understanding myself as a person of color and learning how to organize." Rasha, a young Palestinian American organizer with the youth program (AYO) at AROC in San Francisco, commented that Arab American youth in the Bay Area have a transnational and cross-racial approach to politics, "connecting to issues back home and to ghettoes here, making connections to public school education, so they are equipped to do both local and global politics. The GUPS folks relate to underresourced neighborhoods, to the prison-industrial complex, and they are also active on Palestine." Janaan Attia (2014), writing about Arab American youth organizing in the Bay Area, describes the "growing Arab youth movement" that has been involved in local alliances with other youth of color (although mainly in San Francisco and the East Bay) and in "building the connectedness of oppressions—as in the similarities between the police in Oakland and the Israeli Defense Forces in Palestine" (170). This linkage was highlighted in the protests of the police killing of Oscar Grant in Oakland that occurred during the Israeli massacre in Gaza in winter 2009, and even more dramatically during the protests for Black Lives Matter in 2014–2015 and the Ferguson to Gaza solidarity campaign in response to police violence and militarization in both the U.S. and Israel, during the 2015 war on Gaza. These alliances are part of a national movement of Arab American youth who are inserting themselves into racial justice movements and identifying as "people of color"; for example, Aidi (2014) discusses the campaign in 2010 by young Arab (and Iranian and Turkish) Americans to have the U.S. census classify Middle Eastern and

North African Americans as nonwhite as illustrative of the "racial shift" that is taking place in the new generation of Arab and Muslim Americans, especially since 9/11 (163; see also Saliba 1999).

One of the sites in which the racialization of Palestinians has become visible, and fraught, in the culture wars about gender, sexuality, and Islam is in discussions of gay rights in the U.S. and Palestine. The debate about homosexuality and homophobia in Arab and Muslim societies has provoked controversy as well as cross-racial and transnational alliances challenging the deployment of gay rights against Palestinian human rights. Sabina, the Indian American woman who wrote about "taking back our narrative," told me about at an event at her community college in Santa Clara, organized by an Israeli faculty member, that featured two Israeli lawyers extolling Israel as a state progressive on gay rights. As Sabina described, "It was demonstrating how just Israel was and how it was a normal democratic state. However, Israel clearly is not a normal democratic state." Sabina's incisive critique speaks to the strategy of "pinkwashing" that paints Israel as a queer-friendly nation to bolster the image of a "normal" and just democratic nation-state, not one that is engaged in the longest military occupation in modern history, built on displacement and dispossession, and engaged in racial discrimination against its Palestinian citizens—all processes that harm Palestinian queers.[9] Campaigns waged by Zionist groups such as the Israel Project and StandWithUs, beginning in 2008–2009, have constructed Israel as a "gay paradise" and tolerant haven for Muslims and Arabs oppressed in their homophobic societies, highlighting what Salaita (2011) describes as a "gay-is-modern-thus-modern-is-Israel syllogism," in which gay rights are a signifier of civility, modernity, and Western civilization (95–101). This is a striking example of what Puar (2007) has called homonationalism, a product of "queer liberal secularity" that has helped produce a "sexual exceptionalism" in nations such as Israel and also the U.S., for "an exceptional form of national heteronormativity is now joined by an exceptional form of homonormativity" (2, 13). "Sexual freedom," as Reddy (2011) argues, is "the evidence of civilization and progress" and so can underwrite the "civilizing" and "humanitarian" wars waged by the U.S. and its ally, Israel (17). Sexual rights trump human rights in the "disciplinary liberationist paradigms of gay and lesbian human rights" that draw sensationalist attention to Arab and Muslim homophobia in Iraq, Iran, or Palestine, or incite homonationalism through the photographs of sexualized torture of Arabs in Abu Ghraib, remaking these zones of occupation, warfare, and racial violence into sites that must be liberated by (Western) tolerance and democracy (Puar 2007, 17).

I found that homonationalism, and more precisely *homoimperialism*, has increasingly reshaped the political landscape for Palestine solidarity movements and antiwar activism focused on Iraq or Afghanistan in recent years. In the Bay Area, Muslim American youth and activists I spoke to suggested that queer rights is increasingly the frame through which they are interpellated into liberal/progressive political movements and coalitions in a political landscape that some describe as queercentric—not to underestimate the homophobia that still persists in many forms in the Bay Area. While South Asian, Arab, and Afghan American youth struggle with internal homophobia or sexism within community-based movements, as in all communities and movements, the rise of homonationalist politics has meant that there is a shift to adopting a (liberal) queer-friendly stance that is "good" on "sexual rights" in order to be part of the new, homonormative political order (see Eng 2010). This was brought home to me when a UC undergraduate student, a young Indian Muslim American woman involved with the MSA, asked me for advice on how to organize an interfaith event on queer sexuality. Specifically, she wanted to know if I could suggest an imam who could speak at the event. I was curious as to whether there was a Muslim queer group on campus behind this request, but it turned out that there was none, and this student had been asked to help organize the interfaith queer event by the campus multicultural center. There was going to be a Christian priest, a rabbi, and now all they needed was an imam. I was taken aback, at first, but later realized that this was yet another way in which Muslim American activism is being regulated by the multicultural academy (and in this case also the state, since the event was at a public university), and channeled into interfaith alliances based on queer liberal multiculturalism. So, for example, this particular multicultural center had not hosted any events about Afghanistan or Iraq, let alone Palestine, nor on the racial profiling of Muslim, Middle Eastern, and Arab Americans; at the time it had no Arab American student representative within its multicultural crew. If no imam could be produced for the interfaith event there would be the risk of inciting, yet again, the specter of Muslim homophobia and staging the public failure of Muslim Americans to participate in homonationalist multiculturalism.

There are, of course, Muslim and Arab American queer groups sprouting across the U.S., and the Bay Area has been home to SWANABAQ (Southwest Asian North African Bay Area Queers), but it is important to note the ways in which homonationalism attempts to co-opt what should be queer-led and queer-driven organizing and erases other forms of violence—racial, class-based, or state-sponsored—against queers, thus suppressing a radical queer critique of imperialism and neoliberal multiculturalism (see Stanley et al. 2102). Young activists must reckon with a situation in which a (liberal and juridical) discourse of sexual freedom trumps aspirations to other kinds of freedom, and in which a more radical notion of queer freedom as anti-imperial liberation is considered anti-American. Having said that, pinkwashing has also produced alliances between Palestine solidarity and queer activists, in some cases bringing Arab and Muslim American youth into conversation with queer movements, creating solidarities at the intersections of race, sexuality, religion, and nationalism.

While some observers of post-9/11 politics and coalition building emphasize that these cross-racial or cross-movement alliances are particular to a U.S.-born generation of South Asians or Arabs and not as common in older or immigrant generations, I think this generational difference is sometimes overstated. It is true that second- or third-generation Arab and South Asian Americans have greater familiarity with U.S. race politics, but earlier generations of Arab or South Asian immigrant activists also forged cross-racial alliances with other communities in the U.S., which are often not recognized.[10] In fact, Rasha—whose father was a cofounder of a national coalition involving Palestinians, African Americans, and other people of color in an earlier moment—recalled the grassroots organizing among Arab Americans in the 1970s and 1980s; she talked wryly about the ways in which the "younger generation thinks it's never been done before." Yet it is also important to consider the new political language that the younger generation has deployed in forging alliances, for example, using the notion of being a "person of color" or through an analysis of the "prison-industrial complex," as Rasha observed— but perhaps less so the language of imperialism, not to mention Zionism, which is less palatable to the U.S. public. This is indicative of the rise of political movements since the 1970s and 1980s that have provided analytic frameworks for critiquing white supremacy and global carcerality but have also been constituted through gaps or erasures in the post–civil rights, neoliberal era, one in which the U.S. alliance with the Zionist project has been key to U.S. imperial policy and wars abroad and aggressively defended at home (see Feldman 2015).

It is apparent that deeper alliances between Muslim, South Asian, Arab, and Afghan American groups and broader movements are not always easy to forge in the neoliberal multicultural era and the human rights paradigm does not necessarily generate solidarity with other struggles focused on immigrant rights, police violence, incarceration, and economic justice. This cleavage is a problem for both sides of hoped-for solidarity: for Arab, South Asian, and Muslim Americans and also for Latino/as, African Americans, other Asian Americans, and allies from various movements. For instance, some linkages have been made by groups in the Bay Area, such as Critical Resistance or Education Not Incarceration, between post-9/11 detentions in the War on Terror and the military-prison-industrial complex, situating both in an ongoing regime of incarceration and militarization that is a core strategy of the racial management of populations by the neoliberal police state, but these alliances are not that strong, especially in Silicon Valley. Even in the case of youth engaged with nationalist or race-based politics, the multicultural political apparatus continually constructs movements as discrete and located in ethnically specific communities (see Majaj 1999). There has also been a shift to nonprofit organizations as a structure for community organizing, what Rasha incisively critiqued as the "nonprofit industrial complex," which is very evident in Bay Area activism, which is riven with all the contradictions of trying to create social transformation or radical protest through grant-funded community organizations (Kwon 2013).

Coexisting with eruptions of intraminority tension after 9/11 was a gap between Palestine solidarity activists and other movements due to an intense, or sometimes singular, focus on the Palestine question among Arab and Muslim American activists, at the expense of other issues and a broader global focus. A Moroccan/white American community activist from the Bay Area thoughtfully observed, "It's true that Palestine is at the crux of imperial policies targeting Arab countries. The problem is just that the connections aren't always made through Palestine to other issues." Saliba (2011) is critical of the lack of coalition building among Arab and Muslim Americans, which she attributes partly to the sense of being under siege that makes it "difficult to extend ourselves beyond the borders of our community" (200). The young Moroccan American activist also noted that other Arab human rights issues sometimes fell between the cracks, such as the struggle in the Western Sahara against the Moroccan state. At the same time, the Palestine question has been a central, if not singular, focus for Arab American communities due to the ongoing, unconditional U.S. financial and military support for Israel, despite changes in American political regimes, and the power of the Israel lobby in the U.S. in censoring and attacking pro-Palestinian voices, making this an exceptional subject of silencing of human rights abuses—unlike the case of China, Burma, or Sudan, for instance, or even other U.S. allies such as Saudi Arabia. But this exceptionalism in the case of Palestine also leads to some unevenness in the attention given by Arab and Muslim Americans to other human rights or Muslim rights issues.

Sabina commented on this dissonance: "I feel that the Palestinian issue is very important but there isn't much spotlight on Muslims in India, the Gujarat massacre, or Kashmir. I have never see any protests on the Gujarat genocide and no one really even knows about it. I feel both should be given the same level of attention." Citing the 2002 pogrom against Muslims in Gujarat in western India, which took place with the complicity of the police and functionaries working with right-wing Hindu nationalists, Sabina was frustrated that "these issues are not given much attention at all and a lot of Muslims don't know much," even about anti-Muslim violence in South Asia. There has been activism in the Bay Area, including in Silicon Valley, in opposition to Hindu right-wing nationalism and "communal violence" in India against Muslims and minorities, but it is significant that this has not really involved second-generation South Asian Americans and has been largely led by immigrant South Asian leftists. Sabina was concerned that there was even a certain degree of social capital associated with participation in Palestine solidarity protests, which in her view, were considered "cool" among her Muslim American peers in the South Bay; this is an interesting indication of shifts in political culture in the 9/11 generation, especially given the larger context of demonization of Palestine solidarity activism. But it is not surprising that a politics opposing the status quo—one that is, indeed, defiantly anti–status quo—would be considered rebellious and cool among youth. Abed, an Egyptian American from San Jose who was very involved with the SJP group on his campus and MCA, was wearing a wristband with the colors of the Palestinian flag when we met in February 2011. He observed,

> During jummah, Friday prayers, I mean, we always say, please help the people in Palestine, Kashmir and Chechnya. But nobody ever knows what's going on in either one. Everybody knows what's happening in Palestine, but nobody ever knows what's happening in Kashmir or Chechnya, because we always pray for them but we never know what's going on.

Abed was critical of what he perceived to be a tokenistic invocation of global Muslim solidarity, and also of the relative absence of discussion of the U.S. occupations and invasions of Iraq and Afghanistan. He said, "I feel like those are the two almost forgotten wars," and reflected on Muslim American expressions of solidarity:

> I feel like people have unfortunately become desensitized with what's going on there . . . it's just that its been going on for so long that I feel, I hate to say this, but I feel people have lost hope in sort of saving Iraq and Afghanistan . . . we have been to so many protests for both of those wars, we've spoken out, we've written letters and nothing's changed, what can we do now?

There is a critique of gaps in solidarity here and also a sentiment of despair that these other zones of warfare were "forgotten," a sense of hopelessness that solidarity actions with Iraqis and Afghans in the U.S. are futile in the face of the imperial war machine. I will dwell in the next chapter on what it might mean to describe acts of solidarity as acts of "saving," but Abed was clearly critical of a rhetorical notion of pan-Islamic solidarity as well as deeply concerned with what strategies the antiwar movement could effectively use. From such a perspective, Muslim internationalism seems counterproductive if it is a performances of solidarity that leads to desensitization, but this is also, fundamentally, an outcry against perpetual warfare.

Repression and "Radicalism"

The feelings of frustration, disappointment, and danger associated with political protest focused on global human rights issues was greatest for youth in the case of Palestine activism. This is an important site where human rights organizing and discourse, and their slippages, have shaped political subjecthood for Arab, South Asian, Afghan, and Muslim American youth. Antiwar activism and mobilization for Palestinian rights was deeply imbued with sentiments of fear and anxiety and a politics of risk in a climate of policing and surveillance of political movements related to the Middle East. Several young people talked about the hostility, racism, and silencing they encountered while trying to organize in support of Palestine on their campuses as well as in the larger community. Abed recalled that one of the few incidents of "intolerance" that he had ever experienced in the Bay Area was, in fact, after a protest in San Francisco during the "bombings in Gaza" in winter 2008–2009. He was carrying a Palestinian flag and someone hit him and pushed him over in the street. At Foothill Community College in Los Altos, Abed recalled that other students gave him "dirty looks" when he wore a kaffiyeh in solidarity with Gazans in January 2009. The kaffiyeh may have become a fashion item in early-millennium youth culture, but it is also a racially charged signifier of Arab solidarity associated with the PLO and the Palestinian struggle and, increasingly, with Arab resistance to U.S. warfare and Islamist militancy.[11] The kaffiyeh has evoked racist backlash and denunciation as a "terrorist" signifier when it appears in the public sphere, including when donned by non-Arab celebrities such as Rachel Ray and displayed on the shelves of youth clothing stores such as Urban Outfitters, indicating its powerful condensation of anti-Arab/Palestinian sentiment.[12]

Both Orientalism and Islamophobia acutely shape attempts to delegitimize Palestine solidarity activism in the U.S., which is why this movement is a revealing site in which to understand the apparatus of repression targeting particular forms of human rights activism in the post-9/11 era. Bashir talked about the backlash against MSA organizing in solidarity with Palestine at San Jose State: "We have events for Palestine. Unfortunately, these events have led some people to conclude that these Muslim groups are a terrorist front. It's sad because those people get their news from Fox News and they have strong racism and Islamophobia." Bashir critiqued the demonization of Palestine solidarity activism, which is bolstered by right-wing groups and commentators, pointing to the likes of political pundits such as Glenn Beck and Bill O'Reilly and talk show hosts such as Michael Savage, who have used their national pulpits to attack Palestine solidarity activism and the Palestinian national struggle as forms of terrorism and anti-Semitism. Bashir touches on an important aspect of anti-Palestinianism, that is, the moral panic whipped up about the "radicalization" of Muslim and Arab American youth is often accompanied by the charge that they are automatically anti-Semites if they are critical of the Israeli state's policies. Bashir commented:

> We're not anti-Jewish or anti-Israel as we're called. But the other side has picked up the strategy of labeling. I've actually seen them tell people to use this strategy to call us anti-Semitic or radical. Even the left are called radical. Sometimes we're called terrorist sympathizers. I mean you have to be a strong person to stand up against these people, so there is discouragement.

The label "terrorist sympathizers" ("terror symps" in counterterrorism speak)—or in its more racist variant "Arab sympathizers"—and the conflation of "radicalism" with "anti-Americanism" is fundamentally a tactic of repression that discourages youth from speaking critically of Israel and U.S. foreign policy. It is also a discursive strategy in which support for Israel becomes a litmus test of loyalty to the U.S.; to be anti-Israel is to be anti-American, and since to be anti-Zionist is to be anti-Semitic, being anti-Zionist is also being anti-American and beyond the pale of the multicultural state.

Right-wing Zionist commentators have marshaled the liberal discourse about "tolerance" and inclusion to accuse those who are pro-Palestinian of being inherently intolerant, anti-Semitic, anti-democratic, and anti-American, so that a key tenet of multicultural inclusion is support for Israel. It should be noted that this is not a new tactic of repression of Palestinian rights activism; well before 2001, the infamous case of the L.A. Eight in 1987 involved seven Palestinians and one Kenyan targeted for deportation using the Cold War–era McCarran–Walter Act, which criminalized support for "world Communism" (Cole 2003, 159, 162; Malek 2009). The eight were student activists organizing in solidarity with Palestinians and were later prosecuted on immigration violations, although the FBI admitted that its case against them aimed to disrupt the political activities of supporters of the leftist Popular Front for the Liberation of Palestine (Cole 2003, 162–169). The case against the L.A. Eight activists was reopened after 2001, in fact, and the charges against them were not dropped until a full twenty years after the case began, in 2007. The figure of the "Communist" has been blurred with the "terrorist" since the 1980s, as Reagan framed the "free world's" struggle against the Evil Empire as coeval with the fight against Islamists in Iran and elsewhere and American Zionists produced the discourse of "Islamo-fascism" to suture Arab militancy with totalitarianism in a new "race war" (Feldman 2015, 223). However, this conflation has not been as clearly understood in the case of Palestine solidarity activism due to the invisibility of the Palestinian (secular) left and of leftists and Marxists in solidarity with Palestine, in the U.S. mainstream media and also among progressive movements since the 1970s. A Palestinian or Arab who is also a leftist is thus the ultimately irredeemable enemy of the U.S. capitalist state.

Many young Muslim and Arab Americans who are not "strong" enough, as Bashir suggests, worry about the real threat of vilification and intimidation if they publicly support Palestine and some distance themselves from a politics defined as "radical," which has come to be a dirty, dangerous word associated with "bad" Muslim and Arab subjects. As Bashir points, this defamation of radicalism targets not just the Palestine solidarity movement but the left at large in a post-9/11 moment. As Ali Abunimah (2014) points out, the "war on critics of Israel" is a "war on the left more broadly" (171). This is a crucial issue, for the oppositional politics of Muslim, Arab, South Asian, and Afghan American youth overlaps (but is not identical) with left movements in the U.S., and is in transnational conversation with secular left politics in the Middle East, yet it is often calibrated exclusively in relation to religious allegiance and politics. The machinery of repression counters the threat posed by transnational solidarities by stripping the category "radical" of its progressive registers and reappropriating it through the lexicon of counterterrorism. There is thus an evacuation of the political critique suggested by "radicalism"—whether for the left or the right—which is replaced with the connotation of violence, and also religious fundamentalism, in the security state's vocabulary of "radicalization" and counterradicalization of Muslim American youth.

In organizing in support of Palestinian rights in the U.S., furthermore, the purportedly universalist language of rights operates on highly slippery, if not impossible, ground. The encounter with the apparatus of repression of Palestinian human rights activism on college campuses has also become a key politicizing experience for many youth who are forced to grapple with the limits of civil rights, "academic freedom," and liberal models of multicultural inclusion. Yara, an Iraqi American woman from Los Gatos, organized a film series at Foothill College, screening documentaries about the Middle East such as *Peace, Propaganda, and the Promised Land*. However, a member of the Silicon Valley chapter of Hillel complained to her advisor that the films were "pro-terrorist" and the speakers she had invited were "anti-Semitic"— including, ironically, the Jewish American speakers. Yara also faced backlash to her organizing from other students who accused her of "promoting hate" and being "anti-American," which she felt was contradictory: "I really think it's the total opposite because you're being anti-American for, like, silencing people." Yara turned this allegation of unpatriotism on its head by associating freedom of expression with a genuine expression of American identity, a familiar move enacted within the liberal paradigm of civil liberties. What is more striking about this incident is the ways in which the violence of occupation and dispossession in Palestine was dismissed and suppressed by some students who, paradoxically, cast its critique as an expression of "hate," a coded word that suggests an irrational affect that can spill over into a violent "anti-Americanism," part of the liberal disciplinary discourse of the post-9/11 culture wars that targets selective regions, peoples, and struggles. This is summed up in the stunning question posed in response to 9/11: why do they hate us?

Other young activists also experienced institutional and ideological silencing of Palestinian human rights on campuses in Silicon Valley, which has deformed campus cultures and academic freedom through a highly skewed discourse about Israel-Palestine. When I met Marwa at Stanford in 2008, she showed me an exhibit of photographs about Palestine in one of the campus cafeterias that SCAI had battled the university administration for six months to install, in commemoration of the sixtieth anniversary of the Nakba (or "catastrophe," referring to the displacement and expulsion of over seven hundred thousand Palestinians in 1948). One of the conditions imposed on the students was that they could not have any captions on the photographs displayed in the lounge, only on the images installed inside a small, enclosed room at the back of the cafeteria. This seemed like a highly problematic but also very fitting situation, for it neatly captured the underlying premise that any kind of narrative about Palestinian suffering involving words was too dangerous to display, even at a university. Jenaan recalled that at San Jose State, an antiracist educational program called Tunnel of Oppression that included Palestine as an issue was attacked for being "anti-Semitic" by the Jewish Student Union, which tried to shut it down until an administrator intervened to allow it to continue. As Salaita famously stated, there is a "Palestinian exception to the First Amendment," including and especially in the U.S. academy.[13]

A pattern of systematic repression across the U.S. focused on youth and student activism related to Palestine solidarity and Palestinian rights is unfortunately by now quite well documented (e.g., Barrows-Friedman 2014; Malek 2009, Salaita 2011).[14] However, the impact this has had on youth movements and on Arab and Muslim American political subjecthood has not been taken seriously enough by researchers and educators—partly due to the suppression of critical research related to Palestine. Thea Abu El-Haj (2010) has done important ethnographic research documenting censorship and racism targeting Palestinian American high school students on the East Coast, including incidents where Palestinian flags were banned at international fairs and students were disciplined simply for stating they were Palestinian or even for asserting that Palestine exists. She points out that despite the rhetoric of liberal tolerance and multicultural inclusion in schools, Palestinian youth felt harassed, silenced, and persecuted, including by other youth, in a climate of resurgent nationalism and anti-Arab and Islamophobic sentiment. This suspicion may rest heavily on the racialized and gendered imagery of young male terrorists, but as the stories by youth here poignantly highlight, repression and censorship—as well as anxiety about political activism and fear of backlash—is felt equally by young women. I think this is a crucial point, for too often the issue of gender has been linked to the War on Terror under the assumption that Muslim and Arab men are the only targets of profiling, and that Muslim and Arab women are only the victims of cultural and religious repression and not also targets of state repression.

Silicon Valley, due to the presence of significant Arab and Muslim American communities and a new generation of activists, has seen the emergence of Palestine solidarity activism but also the repression of this movement by a highly organized Zionist presence. Ali, an Indian Muslim community activist who has been involved with South Bay Mobilization, an antiwar group in Silicon Valley, observed that there was a great deal of organizing in solidarity with Palestine at San Jose State between 2006 and 2008 and during the 2008–2009 war on Gaza, with support from local activists including Latino/a organizers and groups such as De-Bug, the community-based organization in San Jose, which works with diverse groups of youth. Ali recalled that students erected mock checkpoints on the San Jose State campus and that the Palestine movement was much more visible and energetic there than at UC Berkeley at the time. However, this led to reprisals and intimidation from Zionist faculty and pro-Israel groups, who attended events about Palestine and tried to shut them down.[15]

At an event with Jewish American solidarity activists sponsored by the MSA in November 2008 at San Jose State, in which Bashir was involved, one

Jewish American faculty member secretly took photos of the activists and students, who were "petrified," according to Ali. Some students realized that the faculty member was photographing them with his cell phone and quickly dispersed. After Ali and SJSU students organized talks on campus by Robert Fisk, the British journalist and author who has written extensively about the Middle East, and Norman Finkelstein, a Jewish American scholar who has published work critical of the Israeli state, the same faculty member "sent a sixteen-page dossier to all faculty," including photos, denouncing these events. According to Ali, he also submitted allegations to the administration that the event organizers "were a terrorist organization and supported Hamas." Bashir, who attended many of these events himself, observed that Muslim American students and solidarity activists were very threatened by these accusations and surveillance activities and felt they were "being attacked" and discredited as terrorists simply for being "young idealist people," but he commented thoughtfully, "It gives us more motivation." Repression can also fuel the urgency of resistance, and greater solidarity, but it is a site where the racialized attack on Muslim and Arab American activism and solidarity movements is acutely visible, if undercritiqued in relation to the U.S. state's policies with respect to Palestinian resistance to Israeli occupation.

In addition, as these stories by young activists illustrate, there is a well-established Zionist political apparatus in Silicon Valley, California, and the U.S. more generally, that silences anti-Zionist critique and targets student groups and the Palestine solidarity movement through racialized allegations that are core to the racial culture wars (Salaita 2006a). To take just one of numerous example of repression of campus activism, the ADL, AIPAC, the Zionist Organization of America, the American Jewish Committee, and the Israeli consulate pressured the UC Berkeley administration to oppose the student-led campaign to pass a resolution to divest from Israel, as public records obtained by students later showed.[16] Accusations of racism, that is, anti-Semitism, are used against Muslims and Arabs as well as non-Muslims/Arabs, including Jews, to suppress a critique of the Israeli state's military occupation, warfare, and racial apartheid, such as in campaigns by the right-wing Zionist group AMCHA, based in the Bay Area. Groups such as AMCHA, the ADL, Campus Watch, and David Horowitz's Freedom Center have blacklisted academics who are critical of the Israeli state, publishing advertisements in the *New York Times* attacking scholars and deploying students to spy on faculty and report on them to these off-campus, nonscholarly, and highly partisan organizations (for example, Dawson 2007).

Activism focused on Palestinian rights in the U.S. is a site where Arab and Muslim American youth, as well as other students, confront the limitations of the liberal discourse of academic freedom, freedom of speech, tolerance, and human rights, which is bound up with a defense of the Israeli state's policies as part of patriotic Americanness and with Orientalist discourses about Islam and gender, Arab culture and terrorism that have been consolidated in the War on Terror. It should be noted that the lockdown on open discussion of Palestine, and Zionism, occurs also in liberal-progressive and left arenas, including in the antiwar movement, which resist patriotic nationalism but which also include left Zionists, and which have generally perceived it as an untouchable issue; this was true especially before the Israeli war on Gaza in 2008–2009, which was somewhat of a tipping point for Palestine solidarity politics in the U.S. (see Elia 2011). The inability of the left to provide an intelligent and mature critique of Zionism, for fear of being labeled anti-Semitic and alienating liberal-left Zionists, is poignantly illustrated by El Rassi's (2007) story of being a college student in an antiwar group, dominated by progressive white American activists who wanted to tackle issues of racism and include people of color. However, when El Rassi suggested they consider the Palestinian right to self-determination, the other activists shut him down by insisting the issue had nothing to do with racism and that its discussion could actually provoke anti-Semitism (109–111). This vignette, sadly, could be a template for the experiences of Arab American progressives as well as supporters of Palestinian rights, of all ages. Furthermore, it underscores the contradiction whereby a racist discourse crushes the attempt to resist anti-Palestinian or anti-Arab violence and racism by deeming that politics racist (i.e., anti-Semitic) itself.

Palestinian Rights Activism and "Uncivil" Protest

The mobilization by youth around international human rights issues in zones of war and occupatioin such as Palestine, Iraq, and Afghanistan is also the link to the infringement of civil rights within the U.S., for the demonization of Muslim and Arab American youth and activists as "terrorist sympathizers" underlies the selective scrutiny of domestic political organizing and "radicalization" in Muslim American communities. What was most striking to me about the narratives of youth and activists in Silicon Valley is that the framework of human rights does not always enable a wider public in the U.S. to identify with the Palestinian victims of occupation, military violence, and racism. In other words, the discourse of human rights does not "work," and does not always translate into solidarity, in the case of Palestine. It is a claim to rights that is inscribed in international law and performed, over and over again, but it is not accepted or realized in certain spaces of exception. For

instance, the deaths of thousands of Palestinians as a result of the disproportionate Israeli military assault on Gaza in Operation Cast Lead in 2008–2009
or Operation Protective Edge in 2014 and the collective punishment of civilians trapped for years in Gaza due to the Israeli blockade would not even
constitute a recognizable claim to "human rights" for many Americans. Israel's many wars on Gaza have been portrayed in the mainstream media as an
act of self-defense by a (Jewish) nation under siege and legitimized by the
discourse of homeland security that has been consolidated in the War on Terror, a war that fundamentally needs to be waged by both the U.S. and Israel
against the threat of Arab militancy and Islamist violence by uncivilized and
socially backward peoples.

As youth from Silicon Valley realized through their many frustrating experiences with censorship and demonization, human rights is trumped by
the discourse of terrorism and counterterrorism when it comes to Palestine
(and also in some cases Iraq and Afghanistan), and by the rationale of national security, American and also Israeli. The notion that Palestinian rights
are indivisibly *human* rights is not legible within a mainstream, U.S.-based
rights framework due to the exceptionalism of Israeli security discourse,
which posits its disproportionate military violence against civilians and violations of Palestinian human (and civil) rights as a defense against terrorism
by the garrison state. No doubt, the legacy of the Holocaust looms large in
these debates and is often the explicit or unspoken narrative that is used to
frame the defense of the Jewish state as well as in certain instances to legitimize its own racial violence and policies of encampment and enclosure
(Finkelstein 2000). However, this dominant discourse about Israel has begun
to shift, if only in small increments, after the killing of humanitarian activists
on the flotilla to break the siege of Gaza in 2010 and Israel's wars on Gaza
in 2012 and 2014, all of which provoked global condemnation and growing
solidarity with Palestine.[17] Scholars have argued that Americans continue
to identify with the Zionist narrative—despite growing criticism of Israel in
the alternative media and by human rights organizations—due to a deeper
national identification with the settler-colonial ideology of Manifest Destiny
underlying the violent founding of both the U.S. and Israel (see Mamdani
2004; Salaita 2006b).

Underlying the lacunae in the human rights project with respect to Palestine, moreover, is the deeper question of the racially defined notion of the
"human" in colonial modernity. Are Palestinians human too? Or is their humanity illegible within a liberal rights framework and the language of social
justice and antiracist redress? Azma commented that she was "surprised" by
the mainstream media's representation of the war on Gaza in 2008–2009,

which killed fourteen hundred Palestinians, including four hundred children, and U.S. support for Israel's rationale that the Hamas rockets fired from the blockaded Gaza Strip were to blame for the war. She said, "I would assume that they would have an Israeli lobby in America and that they would take Israel's side but to condemn Palestinians for starting it really angered me. Humans are dying, you don't compare sides, you know." The disappearance of human life—and death—into the dominant framework of "two sides" of the Israeli-Palestinian "conflict" is part of a necropolitical framework of colonial violence that erases the question of human rights and the right to freedom in this "exceptional" twenty-first-century occupation, the longest in modern history.

In a strange but not uncommon twist, repressive and right-wing campaigns targeting pro-Palestinian student activists and faculty often appropriate the language of civil and human rights and charge that activists and scholars critical of Israel are hostile to academic freedom and the civil and human rights of Israeli Jews and Jewish Americans, and do not deserve the recourse to civil rights or human rights. If Palestinians do not have human rights, or the right to academic freedom—among other freedoms—their supporters must also be denied the right to freedom of expression in asserting those rights claims. For example, this argument was used by the campaigns waged by AMCHA that targeted Middle Eastern/Middle East studies faculty at San Jose State University for doing a workshop on peace building and nonviolence in Israel-Palestine in 2013, as well as faculty and students at San Francisco State for activities related to Palestine.[18] At UC Irvine, off-campus groups such as the Zionist Organization of America and the Jewish Federation of Orange County were on record calling for punishment and prosecution of the eleven students who protested the speech of the Israeli ambassador, a former soldier, after the 2008–2009 war on Gaza. The Muslim Student Association at UC Irvine was suspended, though the group did not sponsor the protest, and ten of the "Irvine Eleven" students, who had staged an act of civil disobedience by disrupting the speech and then walking out of the event and willingly accepting arrest, were not only disciplined by the university but convicted under the California Penal Code (Abunimah 2014, 197–201). The criminal proceedings against the Irvine Eleven had a deeply chilling effect on Palestine solidarity activism across the nation and dramatized the criminalization of student activism in support of Palestinian rights.

Stephen Sheehi (2011) points to infamous Zionist activist David Pipes's Lawfare Project, which has hijacked the "language of social justice" and "human rights" even as it provides "legal, logistical, and financial support to suppress, intimidate, and bankrupt" Muslim and Arab American advocacy groups and activists in lawsuits (143). The Israel lobby has utilized civil rights in its "lawfare" against Palestine solidarity activists and MSA and SJP chapters, having successfully lobbied the Department of Education's Office of Civil Rights to define anti-Semitism as a violation of Title VI protections.[19] The 1964 Civil Rights Act can now be used to deem illegal criticism of Israel as expressions of the "new anti-Semitism" on college campuses and deny federal funding to universities (Barrows-Friedman 2014, 98). This is yet another instance of the right strategically using the language of antiracism to silence critiques of racism or racialized state policies. A California state assembly resolution, HR 35, passed in 2012 under pressure from Zionist groups, targeted pro-Palestine activism and events, including BDS campaigns, on campuses as anti-Semitic and has exacerbated the fear, repression, and self-censorship among students and faculty in the region (Abunimah 2014, 193).[20]

Students involved in the Palestine solidarity movement find that the discourse of and civil and human rights—as well as the right to academic freedom—does not serve them on campuses or public forums where their protests against Israel's (illegal) occupation, or apartheid policies that discriminate by law against Arabs and Muslims, are deemed "hate speech" or inherently anti-Semitic and thus impermissible, if not criminalizable. In April 2013, five students at Florida Atlantic University did a peaceful protest (similar to that of the Irvine Eleven) at the speech of an Israeli military officer, who defended his role in the Israeli war on Gaza. They were put on probation by the university, suspended from campus leadership positions, and required to participate in a training workshop about "difference" so that the incident would not be put on their school records—multicultural pedagogy was used explicitly as a weapon to bludgeon dissenting students into silence. The students concluded, "It became clear to us that the university administration was apathetic to human rights when it comes to those of Palestinians."[21] At Northeastern University, SJP students who staged a similar walkout during a talk by Israeli soldiers in 2013 were condemned by the university and required to create a "civility statement," and the SJP was put on probation (Abunimah 2014, 209–210). The cases of the Irvine Eleven, the FAU Five, and others have become part of a litany of repressive incidents that are used to send a warning message to students and contain campus activism, including rights-based campaigns. In response, students are increasingly resorting to silent protests, with their mouths taped shut to symbolically counter universities' endorsement of talks by Israeli soldiers, members of an occupying military in the context of ongoing wars on Palestinians; in contrast, it was rare for most campuses to host U.S. military officials publicly defending the war in Iraq while the U.S. occupation was in progress and even protesters who have heckled Obama or Bush have generally not been arrested.

The fear that Muslim, Arab, and Palestinian American students at UC campuses have about involvement with Palestinian rights activism and the worry that it will affect their educational and work opportunities has been documented in a report to UC president Mark Yudof in 2012 by a cluster of civil rights organizations (including the Center for Constitutional Rights, the Asian Law Caucus of San Francisco, and CAIR).[22] Having said that, the Department of Education's Office of Civil Rights threw out the Title VI complaints filed since 2011 against three UC campuses since, for allegedly enabling a climate of anti-Semitism due to Palestine solidarity protests, as having no legal basis.[23] The ACLU and Center for Constitutional Rights condemned the lawsuits as targeting student activism and political speech protected by the First Amendment, in effect creating a chilling campus climate for groups such as the MSA and SJP.[24] One of the important shifts in the academic battles about censorship of Palestine is that Zionist organizations have increasingly used the language of "anti-Israelism," a new term coined to replace the alibi of alleged "anti-Semitism," as they realized that many supporters of Palestinian rights, including Jewish American activists, were challenging this tactic; groups such as the David Project have now defined "anti-Israelism" as a form of "bigotry" and "hate speech" rife on college campuses that deserves to be combated by "criminal and civil legal proceedings" (Abunimah 2014, 171).

The recourse by pro-Israel and Zionist activists to civil rights legislation to provide a cover for repression of criticism of Israel co-opts civil rights discourse as an alibi to defend state violence, militarism, and racial discrimination. It also pits U.S. civil rights discourse against the human rights of Palestinians and Arabs. On the one hand, while pro-Israel groups, including the ADL, claim that they are civil rights organizations fighting hate crimes, their focus on civil rights and freedom of political expression is clearly selective. But this partisan focus is generally not known to many who are exposed only to the public face of Zionist organizations such as the ADL, which professes a multicultural humanism in the best tradition of American liberal pluralism, an issue that I will return to in the following chapter (Salaita 2011, 41). On the other hand, the problem is also that campus administrations are not ideologically neutral and while they may succumb to off-campus pressure from well-established Zionist organizations and organized alumni to ward off bad press, it is also true that, in some cases, these appeals fall on sympathetic ears or are received by administrators who are already schooled in the institutional paradigm of what constitutes "acceptable" political discourse about the Middle East.[25] Yudof played a significant role during his tenure as UC president in singling out campus protests of Israel for condemnation, describing them as an anti-Semitic "cancer" spreading across college campuses, and blocking the growing spate of student-led divestment resolutions from being passed by the UC Board of Regents.[26] Students attempting to mobilize around Palestine as an issue of human rights on California campuses thus do so in a context of organized hostility to their claims, which are viewed as "uncivil," a deeply racialized term.

The strategy to apply a presumably universalist language of rights to the Palestinian condition operates on almost impossible ground. The core problem is that the vocabulary of human rights often fails to make legible U.S. military and racial violence or U.S.-backed military assaults and racism legible in the public sphere of politics and the framework of civil rights generally does not apply to the repression of civil liberties or freedom of political expression of pro-Palestine activists, including youth. In some cases, a liberal model of civil rights actually provides an alibi for the failure of human rights discourse, given that criticism of Israel is deemed uncivil, if not automatically anti-Semitic—an affront to the multicultural humanism institutionalized on college campuses that represses critique of Israeli state policies as "divisive" and racist (Salaita 2011). Critiques of racial discrimination and violence by Israel, ironically, are suppressed by casting them as expressions of racism. This inversion of racism is consistently produced within a multicultural politics that obscures state racism and imperial violence, an example of a larger "language disorder" that distorts our lexicon (Melamed 2006, 19); however, the language disorder with respect to the Palestine question has not been sufficiently acknowledged by U.S. scholars writing about antiracism and multiculturalism.

In other cases of repression, it is the language of human rights that trumps civil rights of Palestine solidarity activists, as human rights discourse is available only to Americans or Jewish Israelis presumably at risk from Islamic terrorists or Arab militants—and Americans and Israelis are increasingly conjoined since 9/11 in a unified imperial, civilizational project. The rights of Americans or Jewish Americans facing a presumably existential, and deeply racialized, threat supersedes the civil rights of critics of state violence, including students and youth. While the demonization and criminalization of those who criticize U.S. or Israeli state policies is selective, and particularly targets Arab and Muslim Americans, it is rarely acknowledged as a racial project. Yet there is a deeply racial logic at work in the institutionalized and systemic patterns of repression of the Palestine question and of Palestinian "rights," a logic that is inextricably intertwined with a colonial past and present.

Conclusion

The youth I spoke to engaged strategically with the framework of human rights, while trying to push the boundaries in contexts in which rights-talk was considered permissible in the post-9/11 moment. They inevitably grappled with repression and censorship and confronted the contradictions in a legal paradigm of human rights focused on "autonomy [and] choice" and the limits of the human rights industry that denies autonomy and freedom to certain racialized groups (Allen 2013, 13; Merry 2006, 109). In the case of the Palestine solidarity movement, the paradigm of human rights failed to generate the (local) solidarity that young activists hoped for. However, I argue that this failure reveals a crucial critique of the politics of human rights as it has shaped modern governmentality and the hinge between imperial sovereignty, democracy, and surveillance. These young people enact what Rancière (2004) describes as the political subjectivization of those who can "confront the inscriptions of rights to situations of denial; they put together the world where those rights are valid and the world where they are not. The put together a relation of inclusion and exclusion" (304).

In his essay "Who is the Subject of the Rights of Man?," Rancière undoes the tautological bind created by Hannah Arendt, who argued that rights belong to those who already have rights; instead, Rancière suggests that rights belong to those who "can do something with them to construct a dissensus against the denial of rights they suffer," to engage in politics (306). This allows us to view youth who challenge the denial of rights to Palestinians by deploying rights-talk as not necessarily dupes of a false "rights consciousness." Rather, they are political subjects who are testing the claims of rights discourse and exposing its paradoxes and gaps, thus challenging the comfortable consensus around liberal democracy, civil liberties, and human rights related to U.S. imperialism, and the Zionist project. Similarly, Lori Allen (2013) argues that the "deep cynicism" about human rights among ordinary people as well as human rights workers in Palestine, where "lost faith flourishes," is a "form of awareness and a motor of action by which subjection and subjectification are self-consciously resisted or at least creatively engaged" (16, 21). It is the exceptions of rights that these young people expose that produce a political dissensus against the War on Terror, and the wars, occupations, and invasions conducted in the name of human rights in Palestine, Iraq, Afghanistan, and Pakistan.

The following chapter explores questions of human rights and transnational solidarity as they animate the political geography of the border region that has come to be named "Af-Pak," a strategic battlefront for the U.S. and a site of humanitarian warfare that bridges the Cold War and the War on Terror. Why is it that solidarity with Palestine, even if highly contested in the U.S., is visible while solidarity with Afghanistan has been so invisible, despite the direct and indirect U.S. interventions in that country over decades? Linking Palestine to Af-Pak through the exceptionalisms of human rights and cartographies of colonialism, I will demonstrate, is crucial in order to understand the nature of the U.S. imperial project as a flexible empire and to grapple with its decline and possible defeat.

4

More Delicate than a Flower, yet Harder than a Rock

Human Rights and Humanitarianism in Af-Pak

It is important to understand the deployment of human and civil rights as it shapes a politics of repression and regulation in the current moment and as expressive of a late imperial condition characterized simultaneously by multiculturalism and by economic crisis and imperial decline. This chapter explores the ways in which youth in Silicon Valley attempted to address questions of human rights, and especially humanitarianism, in the context of the U.S. war and occupation in Afghanistan and Obama's focus on the Af-Pak border for a project of rescue and nation building. Expanding on the previous chapter's analysis of the failures of human rights to reveal the suffering and violence experienced by Palestinian due to U.S.-backed occupation and Israeli wars, I address the critiques of Afghan and Pakistani American youth of U.S. wars, covert interventions, and drone strikes in South and Southwest Asia. Their critiques suggest notions of sovereignty and self-determination that are concerned not just with the integrity of the nation-state, but with indigenous survival and freedom from imperial violence.

These challenges to the U.S. military interventions in Afghanistan and Pakistan, which were intensified by the Obama regime, highlight the absence of a real anti-imperial critique of the U.S. occupation of Afghanistan and of an "Afghan solidarity movement" that is anything like the vigorous, if highly embattled, Palestine solidarity movement in the United States. What does the absence and the invisibility of Afghan Americans in general in the U.S. tell us about the imperial formation developed in the perpetual war waged by the U.S. in Afghanistan? Afghan Americans are invisibilized in the public sphere, including as U.S. imperial subjects, and an Afghan-centered narrative about U.S. military interventions in Afghanistan (past and present) is missing, including on college campuses. I argue that Afghan Americans are erased by a dominant discourse of humanitarianism that is deeply racialized. It is striking that Afghan American youth, like Iraqi and Palestinian American youth, are not considered neoimperial or imperial subjects within the context of U.S. multiculturalism that pivots on ethnic and racial identities, erasing the question of empire. I discuss why Afghan Americans are generally not even considered ethnic subjects within the lexicon of multicultural inclusion. This chapter also reflects on the painful narratives of loss and survival by Afghan refugees in Fremont and Hayward the missing subjects of U.S. and Western colonialism. Their stories infuse the complexities of belonging in the U.S. for Afghan American youth and shed light on why Afghanistan is such an important site at which to consider U.S. empire and the violence of human rights.

Humanitarian Warfare/Wars for Human Rights

One of the ways that the imperial state attempts to resolve the contradiction between its self-image of promoting democracy, human rights, and civil rights, while denying these same rights to citizens and immigrants domestically and to "enemy" populations overseas, is by adopting the framework of human rights and humanitarianism—that is, the battle for human rights and "democratization" justifies imperial interventions, repression, violence, and annihilation. The notion of humanitarian wars is invoked by a global institutional apparatus to insist on the rescue of racialized subjects who must be saved by Western military intervention, direct or indirect; humanitarian imperialism; and neoliberal capitalism (Bricmont 2007; Melamed 2006).

Farid, whose family is from northwest Pakistan, was managing an auto body shop in San Jose, where he grew up, when I spoke to him in June 2008. We sat down to talk in his office and he said incisively: "The day that the Virginia Tech shooting happened, the U.S. shot a missile into Afghanistan and it accidentally missed and hit an elementary school in Pakistan, and 148 kids five years and younger died. But nobody mentioned that because 32 people died here."[1] Farid was frustrated that such mass killings of even young children on the Af-Pak border—despite U.S. administration claims that the Af-Pak war was being precisely waged with drone missiles and "smart" weapons—were eclipsed in the U.S. mainstream media by acts of violence targeting Americans, whether college students in Virginia or embassy workers in Kabul.[2]

It is striking that there has been relatively little focus in the U.S. on human rights violations in Afghanistan and also Pakistan in the mainstream media—increasing only after several years of U.S. occupation and covert operations—as well as on college campuses and, until recently, even in the antiwar movement (Scahill 2013). While peace activists came out in large numbers against the U.S. invasion of Iraq in 2003, Afghanistan was seen as the "just war" in response to 9/11, and later "Obama's war" to root out Al Qaeda. As Jean Bricmont (2007) argues in his scathing critique of "liberal imperialists" who support U.S. military intervention overseas in the name of democracy, the "supposed need to defend human rights by military means is indeed the ideological Trojan horse of Western interventionism within the very movements opposed to it in principle" (21). Relatively few protests focused on the violation of human rights of men, women, and children during the U.S. "troop surge" (read: reinvasion) and secret operations inside Afghanistan, as well as drone attacks in Pakistan, particularly in the first decade or so after the U.S. invasion (Gould and Fitzgerald 2011; Kohlatkar and Ingalls 2006). Arguably, protests of Israel's wars and occupation in Palestine are much more visible in the U.S., even if they are often viciously attacked, and there is an organized infrastructure for Palestine solidarity activism. This is a complex issue, but the relative invisibility is partly due to the marginalization and small numbers of Afghans and Pakistanis in the U.S., relative to the larger and older Palestinian and Arab American communities who have established political institutions and networks, and also due to the powerful pro-Israel lobby in the U.S. that has helped focus attention on Israel (see Mearsheimer and Walt 2007). There is also an ongoing national struggle in Palestine that has historically created alliances with international solidarity and left activists, unlike in the case of Afghanistan where, by all accounts, international solidarity has largely emerged from Islamist networks due to the nature of the contemporary Afghan resistance and the crushing of the Afghan left (Fitzgerald and Gould 2009).

The relative absence of Afghanistan in the national and local antiwar movement was commented on by several youth. Yasmeen, an Afghan American woman from Newark, near Hayward, had participated in protests in Fremont against the treatment of Afghan refugees in Iran and said she was frustrated by the lack of focus on Afghanistan. She remarked in June 2007, "It seems that there really was not much attention focused on Afghanistan; first, it was Iraq and now, it is Iran. I feel Afghanistan just got pushed aside and nobody really knows what is going there." Amira, who is Pakistani/Afghan American (and who was at the Palestine solidarity protest in San Jose described in the previous chapter) was actively involved in the Afghan Student Association at UC Davis. Her Afghan mother lived as a refugee in Pakistan, as part of the large Afghan refugee community in Peshawar, where she met and married her Pakistani father. Amira said that when the U.S. attacked Afghanistan in 2001, "My family was like, 'Oh, they're invading again.' For them, it was a relapse of back when they left the country [during the USSR invasion]. So, it was always under invasion by other people. They were mad because it's always under invasion, since the 1970s I think." Amira refers to the USSR invasion of Afghanistan in 1979, but it is apparent that for Afghan refugees there is a long memory of foreign occupation and colonization of a region that has been viewed as a buffer zone between rival imperial powers since the nineteenth century. Amira's comment alludes to the ways in which the U.S. war on Afghanistan was a continuation of the old and new Great Game played by imperial powers such as Great Britain, the USSR, and more recently the U.S., which drew the Russian military into a proxy war with the U.S.-backed mujahideen in Afghanistan in the 1980s.

Farida, a Pakistani American woman, commented on the rationale for the U.S. war on Afghanistan as retribution for the 9/11 attacks, waged against the Al Qaeda fighters who were being harbored by the Taliban regime: "9/11 was horrible, but do two wrongs make a right? . . . I totally thought the Taliban needed to be out. They were a horrible form of government that wasn't Is-lamic at all. But I didn't think that they really needed to randomly bomb civil-ians. And I thought it was so stupid that they'd send care packages right after bombing [Afghaniastan]!" Farida, who clearly opposed both the Taliban and the U.S. invasion, critiqued the logic of humanitarianism used by the U.S. military in dropping care packages after attacking Afghan civilians. Meena, an Afghan American, lived in Newark when I met her but grew up in Milpitas in the South Bay, and had lived for a year in Afghanistan when her family moved back in 1992. She spoke of how her father had been politically active in Afghanistan and involved in underground organizing during the Soviet invasion, and observed with some anguish,

> The only good thing about America going into Afghanistan was that they took out the Taliban, but they were the ones that put the Taliban in there in the first place. So my point . . . is they destroy, then they come in and try to be the heroes like they're doing in Afghanistan, right now! But I honestly do not see any positive changes because how could anything good come from one country being totally dependent on another?

Meena touches on the cruel irony of the U.S. waging war against a regime that emerged from the groups that the CIA had helped arm and train to fight the Soviets during the Cold War. She was vehemently opposed to the notion of the U.S. as a heroic savior that could somehow legitimize or erase the devastation that it had inflicted directly and indirectly in Afghanistan, through previous wars and covert interventions as well as counterinsurgency operations to reengineer Afghan society. The story of the U.S. role in creat-ing the mujahideen and sponsoring the "jihad" that helped bring down the USSR has been repressed in the mainstream sphere and the U.S. was, once again, cast as humanitarian savior, this time of the unfortunate Afghan and Pakistani victims of the groups spawned by the mujahideen. In fact, Atanoski

(2013) makes the important point that "the buried memory of the Soviet-Afghan war (1979–89) reaffirms U.S. morality in the Middle East at present" (105) a war that Reagan framed as a humanitarian crusade to save indigenous Afghans from Communism, in the wake of the bitter legacy of the Vietnam war. The forgetting of previous wars in Afghanistan speaks to what Yến Lê Espiritu (2014) describes as the "highly organized and strategic forgetting of the Vietnamese people" (18), another refugee community that also remains unrecognized as a people, or even as humans, devastated by war.

Meena raises an important issue about Operation Enduring Freedom (the official name for the U.S. war on Afghanistan launched in October 2001), that of self-determination and sovereignty, for she was opposed to the dependent status of a "liberated" Afghanistan that is in reality a client regime of the U.S., backed by a U.S. and allied foreign military presence. Echoing this view, Azma said of the U.S. mission to "help" Afghanistan and Pakistan:

> We don't have the right to be telling people how to live their lives, and trying to impose our own customs on them, because they might be Third World countries, but they were doing well enough to get by without American assistance.

Azma alludes here to the imposition of an imperial feminist discourse of women's rights as a justification for the invasion of Afghanistan, pointing astutely to another set of rights, that of nations to be free of imperial intervention and occupation under the guise of "assistance." These young women implicitly critiqued the benevolent imperialism of the U.S. and what Didier Fassin (2010) calls the ascendant moral economy of humanitarian intervention that obscures questions of national sovereignty. Furthermore, there is no "abstract, rights-bearing subject" (Davis 2005, 93). In the War on Terror there is a racialized and gendered investment in the production of subjects presumably in need of rights, or whose rights must be defended, and those who can bestow rights, with the help of violence or occupation if necessary.

As Rancière (2004) has argued, there is an inherent paradox in the right to have rights, as suggested by Hannah Arendt, for if the "rights of man" are essentially the "rights of citizens" then those who are in need of rights, such as stateless refugees, do not have recognized rights; it is only the citizens of internationally recognized states who (already) possess rights and can adjudicate them for those who are rightless. Rancière argues further that if rights are "actually empty" then they are "sent abroad" to become "humanitarian rights," the rights of others, elsewhere (307). Furthermore, as Atanoski (2013) observes, "Humanitarian violence is justified through cultural narratives of creating an afterlife for those lives freed through rights and recognition, so that they may participate in and emerge as properly human through the liberal rule of law and free-market development" (8).

"What Part of My Life Should I Start With?"

I want to note that the U.S.- and NATO-led invasion and occupation of Afghanistan was a controversial and contested issue within the Afghan community in Fremont/Hayward, and the young Afghan Americans I spoke to had mixed opinions about this war. Some supported the U.S. invasion because they opposed the Taliban regime, while others, like Yasmeen, Meena, and Amira, were more skeptical or firmly opposed to the war. The split in political opinion is not surprising given that Afghans in the U.S., and in Fremont/Hayward, have come in different waves and with varying political allegiances in Afghanistan and in relation to the United States. Most are refugees who fled during the Soviet invasion or subsequently, from the Talibanization of Afghanistan and regimes of terror and misogyny led by warlords, including the U.S.-backed Northern Alliance, which provides a context for their support of the U.S. intervention (Joya 2009). Yet there are also many in the Afghan American community who are critical of the U.S. invasion of Afghanistan and some who are sympathetic to the Islamist resistance. The politics of refugee communities related to homeland regimes tend to be intensely polarized, for the notion of the U.S. as a place of refuge often infuses their relationship to the U.S. affectively, if not just ideologically, and shapes their stance on U.S. foreign policy, as evident in the case of Cuban, Vietnamese, Cambodian, and Hmong American communities (Nguyen 2012). In the second generation, who may not be refugees themselves, critique of the U.S. sometimes shifts due to their different relationship to the U.S. state—and despite the broader public's intense commitment to the notion of the U.S. as a benevolent empire. As Aisha said of second-generation activists in different immigrant and refugee communities, "It is a common story, our parents were scared to speak up . . . because they didn't want to be ungrateful to the country they came to as refugees or for economic opportunity."

While I found that there were few public events related to the war in Afghanistan in Fremont/Hayward during the period of my research, on the tenth anniversary of the U.S. invasion in October 2011, an antiwar protest was held in the heart of "Little Kabul." The rally was organized by Afghans for Peace, an organization led by a young, second-generation Afghan American woman and in solidarity with Afghan Youth Peace Volunteers, an Afghan organization. The slogan of the "Afghanistan Peace Day" and march was, "We say YES to peace, justice and civil rights. We say NO to war, terrorism and

Islamophobia," underscoring a transnational framework linking global warfare and domestic civil rights. I noticed that the Afghan Student Association at UC Davis, in which many young Afghan Americans from Fremont/Hayward were involved, also began to organize more events on campus focused on Afghanistan after 2004, including fundraisers for Afghan projects. Some Afghan American youth observed to me that their family members and other Afghans began to travel to Afghanistan, to visit, work in NGOs, or get married as part of a larger transnational relationship that has intensified since 9/11 (Maiwindi 2005, 31).

A former Afghan Student Association president from Fremont, Fareed, who was probably in his early thirties, said that at CSUEB, where there is a large concentration of Afghan students, involvement by Afghan American students declined after 9/11 because "some don't want to align themselves with Afghan activities." For example, Faiza, an Afghan American woman from San Jose, said, "I'm not really political, I don't care about all this—it's more international. I like thinking more of . . . humanitarian things, like AIDS, poverty, or health-related things." There are many factors underlying this distancing from Afghan politics, according to Fareed, who worked in a real estate office in the East Bay; he had been involved with the Society for Afghan Professionals, which organized mentoring and tutoring programs for Afghan American high school youth in the Bay Area. He said thoughtfully about the politics of the older generation of Afghans:

> After the 1990s, the collapse of the Soviet or Communist bloc was seen as due to a war that the Afghans fought. . . . We did something that gave people a better life. There has been a shadow over that since 2001. Afghans feel it was a betrayal; we don't support the U.S. in all their activities, but we fought with them and helped break their enemy. But it changed after 9/11. Many people don't talk about it. Some older Afghans went through some bad times in Afghanistan, so they feel reserved, they don't talk about these issues openly.

The U.S. invasion of Afghanistan is experienced by many I spoke to as a betrayal by the U.S. of Afghans' own desires for freedom and stability. Afghan Americans live in the "shadow" of the Cold War battles that some in the older generation feel they helped fight on behalf of the U.S. against communism, a war that played a role in the downfall of the USSR. This is why Afghanistan is so central to what Atanoski (2013) calls the U.S. project of "postsocialist imperialism based in humanitarian ethics" (3). Like Vietnamese refugees, Afghans embody an antisocialist humanitarianism needed by the United States. Afghans are, in a sense, both the ultimate liberators and the primal enemy for postsocialist imperialism and, as a nation, they seem to have both "won" and "lost" simultaneously.

The racial and class struggles of the older generation provide an important context for the invisibility and relative isolation of the Afghan refugee community in the Bay Area. Meena, who had been involved with a community research project focused on Afghan refugees in Fremont/Hayward, reflected on her conversations with elderly Afghan women:

> I have always felt that the Afghan community is in dire need of assistance of all forms. . . . This community not only carries the trauma they dealt with from Afghanistan's political uproars but . . . many of the Afghans I interviewed are secluded from the American society, lonely, and insecure. . . . They seem to feel they don't even have a right to give their view on the question about rearing children here in the American society because the children will do whatever they please. . . . They also felt that they have no say in anything else either. They seem to be just waiting for their death and have given up on their lives. The only hope they have is for their children to come here or other siblings from overseas. Besides this hope of being reunited with their family, they don't seem to have any other desire for life or for living. They just cry and say, "I've been through a lot. What part of my life should I start with?"

Meena's moving reflection on the sorrow of Afghan refugees who have been displaced and dispersed is crucial in reframing the discourse of humanitarianism by illuminating the grief of dislocation and a tragedy that is unmourned by the larger public—the sentiments of devastation that are washed away by imperial discourses of nation building and regime changing, of wars for democracy and liberation, of collateral damage and counterinsurgency (see Omidian 1996). As a daughter of refugee parents, Meena is sensitive to their frustration that they do not even have the "right" to raise their children as they wish, and that they are also unheard and illegible subjects in the larger U.S. public sphere. Which part of their lives should these refugees indeed narrate, for whom, and to what end?

Meena's narrative is moving, and striking, because it does not claim any redemption in the U.S. for Afghan refugees, whom she describes as "waiting for their death," and because she implicitly questions the need for refugee narratives and hints at a refusal to produce them. In this light, I heed Espiritu's (2014) call for a "critical refugee studies" that conceptualizes refugees not as objects of study, but as representing paradigms for a "new politics" and "alternative memories as well as epistemologies," as embodied, sentient beings (3, 10). The point is not simply that the traumatic history of the Afghan refugee community is untold in the U.S, but that the biopolitics of sovereignty means that Afghans will always remain invisible as racialized subjects of colonialism, neocolonialism, and imperialism. Afghan resistance to the Soviet empire, and earlier, to British colonialism is often, if grudgingly, cited to demonstrate why the U.S. will also fail in Afghanistan, which is described as the "graveyard of empires"—alluding to the Great Game that began in the nineteenth century with the Anglo-Afghan wars and implicitly invoking the history of multiple colonial invasions (Bashir and Crews 2012, 4). The absence of an Afghan-centered narrative about U.S. imperialism, and the general invisibility of an Afghan national identity within the rubric of U.S. liberal multiculturalism and racial categories, is necessary for maintaining the fictions about the various wars to liberate, protect, and save Afghans from various foreign forces—and from themselves—as part of the "perpetual military occupation of Afghanistan" and project of "perpetual supervision" (Atanoski 2013, 103).[3] "Afghan Americans" may occasionally appear as ethnic subjects and increasingly become legible within a multicultural politics of recognition, particularly as a new generation of Afghans comes of age in the U.S., but they are rarely, if ever, considered imperial subjects; the same is true of Iraqis, living in Iraq or in the heart of U.S. empire.

Furthermore, Qayoumi said that many Afghan refugees, particularly the older generation who came in the 1980s during the Soviet occupation, assumed that they would return to their country, and while they are "in this country physically, they are back home mentally," living an affective transnationalism, while others struggled with trying to find jobs in the U.S. labor market. A young Afghan American professional, whom I spoke to at the financial office where he worked in Fremont, said that many "Afghans don't want to involve themselves with politics because they are tired of war." The fatigue with invasion, occupation, and displacement in a refugee community fleeing war was apparent in these conversations with Afghans of different generations and shapes the political and affective landscape in which Afghan American youth responded to the U.S. invasion and subsequent developments in Afghanistan. Mariyam, a young woman whose parents were refugees living in Pakistan and Germany before they were resettled in the U.S. in the 1980s, said, "My parents don't want us to talk about politics. They lost family in the war. My mother's family is very pro-U.S, though I compare [the U.S. invasion] to the Soviet invasion and I find it very ironic. . . . Yet they feel it is better under the U.S. and criticize the Russians." Maliha, who was active with the Afghan Student Association and had worked with Afghan refugees in the Sacramento area, thought that "the younger generation is more critical of the U.S." Mohammad Qayoumi, who was president of California State

University–East Bay (CSUEB) in Hayward at the time I spoke to him (and then became president of San Jose State), commented that Afghan American youth vary in their knowledge of Afghanistan and languages such as Pashto and Dari. However, he remarked that some also receive a poor public school education in Fremont/Hayward and are not completely fluent in English either, so they are "looked down upon" in their different worlds and some end up becoming "pariahs" or drifting toward gangs in the Fremont area, struggling with economic pressures and part-time jobs (see Omidian 1996). The precarity of an economically struggling community is thus a major factor in considering what political activism means to Afghan American youth.

The ambivalent politics and class struggles of Afghans in the Bay Area may underlie the relative absence of Afghan-led progressive groups and community institutions compared to the more upwardly mobile and publicly visible Arab and South Asian communities, who tend to dominate local Muslim and community or political organizations. However, Nargis, an Afghan American attorney and community activist in the Bay Area, said that many Afghans in the region have a "very high level of political engagement" and are actively engaged with projects and political parties in Afghanistan, given the ongoing U.S. military presence in the country. For example, one young Afghan American activist was connected to Afghan Peace Volunteers in Afghanistan, a progressive antiwar group that works with youth as well (see figures 4.1 and 4.2).

Nargis observed that young Afghans are also "very connected" to Afghanistan, but this transnational politics is not always legible in the United States. Afghans have suffered from thirty-five years of foreign intervention, she remarked, so they have "complex stories" about homeland and U.S. politics and there is no "cohesive political narrative in the Afghan community." Nadia Ali Maiwindi (2005) observes that decades of war have led to deep divisions within the Afghan American community "based on ethnicity, geography, religion, political affiliation" that have "plagued" activist spaces, yet after 9/11, she notes, "The level of activism in the Afghan-American community grew exponentially. . . . Afghans joined existing groups, created new ones, and became first-time activists" (30–31). Nargis succinctly commented to me, "Every space with Afghans in it *is* political." It is also crucial to consider the possibility that "politics" can be expressed through a refusal of or ambivalence about official politics. Most Afghan American organizations, other than student and professional associations, seemed to be focused on social services and humanitarian programs, likely because these were the activities that were acceptable forms of organizing in the U.S. for a community linked inextricably and directly to the specter of "anti-American" terrorism, and also due to the class struggles of Afghan refugees.

Figures 4.1 and 4.2. Afghan Peace Volunteers' antiwar and Borders Free campaigns

Yet there is a glaring absence of a critical, or actually any, research literature on Afghan Americans as political subjects, which is one reason I dwell on
the stories that came out of my research in Fremont/Hayward, in addition to
the ways in which the Afghan American case illustrates the painful paradoxes
of U.S. humanitarian imperialism.[4] I argue that the story of intergenerational
and diaspora/homeland politics of the Afghan refugee community must be
situated in this history of what Ann Stoler (2013) calls imperial debris, or "the
uneven temporal sedimentations in which imperial formations leave their
marks," as survivors of imperial wars are left behind to ponder their living
death (2). Meena's reflections hint at a history of colonialism and resistance
or the "ghosts" of unspeakable haunting in the traces of everyday life (see
Gordon 1997). She recalled that one Afghan female refugee cited an Afghan
proverb: "Daily living has made me more delicate than a flower, yet harder
than a rock." This poetic statement illustrates, through an image that captures
beautifully the paradoxical conjuncture of painful fragility and staunch resilience, the "less perceptible effects of imperial interventions and their settling
into the social and material ecologies in which people live and survive" (Stoler
2013, 4). It captures the affective dimensions of dispossession and loss of those
displaced by imperial interventions, but also in its complex allusion to tenu-
ousness and steadfastness—what Palestinians refer to as "sumood"—evokes
the tension in anti-imperial solidarity as enacted in the heart of empire, a
thread that spans generations and that youth grapple with in their daily lives
as well.

Af-Pak: A Country Invented for a War

Some in the younger generation of Afghan Americans, like Meena, Amira,
and Yasmeen, grappled with the meaning of the traces of imperial violence
in their own responses to the U.S.-led War on Terror and the simultaneous
absence yet haunting presence of Afghanistan in the United States. Afghanistan reappeared in the 2000s through the new term "Af-Pak," a region named,
or invented, for a war. "Af-Pak" has been used since 2008 to describe the
theater of war highlighted by Obama, who in 2009 shifted the major front of
the global War on Terror from Iraq to the Afghan-Pakistani border region,
now "imagined as continuous war zone" (Bashir and Crews 2012, 2), where he
claimed the source of terrorism against the U.S. was based. Obama's "Af-Pak
strategy" was based on an escalation of war on Afghanistan and drone strikes
on Pakistan—including secret operations—to rehabilitate the tarred image of
the U.S. empire in the wake of the failures thus far in Iraq and Afghanistan
(Kumar 2012, 131, 161).

The U.S. invention of Af-Pak was based on a counterinsurgency and counterterrorism strategy, developed by the architects of military doctrines in the
region such as Richard Holbrooke and General David Petraeus, that conjoined Afghanistan and Pakistan into a "single theater of war" (Bashir and
Crews 2012, 2). In doing so, it inadvertently invoked the colonial partition
of South Asia by the British empire in 1893 based on what was known as the
Durand Line, which sliced through Pashtun communities that were divided
between what came to be the independent nation-states of Afghanistan and
Pakistan (Bashir and Crews 2012, 5). The partition of the Pashtun homeland,
opposed by Afghanistan since its creation, has been a source of warfare and a
festering wound for those on either side of the 1,600-mile frontier (Bashir and
Crews 2012, 3; see also Tarzi 2012). The unresolved question of the Durand
Line, never formally accepted by Afghanistan, has been a source of instability
for the region that haunts the War on Terror today. In fact, Elizabeth Gould
and Paul Fitzgerald (2011) note that the U.S. military refers to the Durand
Line as the "Zero Line," which they describe as the "vanishing point for the
American empire . . . It is the line where America's intentions face themselves"
(21–22). Af-Pak, it seems, has been acknowledged by the U.S. military itself as
not just a quagmire, where the attempt to rewrite the defeat in Vietnam has
instead inscribed another failure, but also a zone where it has met its nemesis.
If it was the Afghan invasion that helped bring about the end of the USSR,
the longest U.S. war in history has also been an element in the decline of U.S.
empire.

As Amin Tarzi (2102) points out, the Af-Pak border divides a region that
has "multiple, partial sovereignties," a condition constitutive of imperial zones
(18). Many Afghans in Fremont/Hayward and Silicon Valley came to the U.S.
from Afghan refugee communities in northwest Pakistan, centered in Peshawar, that were formed in the wake of colonial partitioning and imperial wars,
and they and their children have ties to these borderlands (as do Pakistanis
from this region), even if these transnational connections are politically as
well as emotionally fraught. The creation of Af-Pak is thus the other side of
the British policy of divide and rule; the melding and partitioning of nations
are both imperial strategies of creating colonialist geographies for regions
and peoples who can be dismembered, destroyed, and renamed at imperial
will. Afghans generally disappear in the borders between West, Central, and
South Asia, and fall between the cracks of U.S.-based ethnic classifications
of Middle Easterners and South Asians. Given Afghanistan's liminal location
between South and Central/West Asia, it is often not included in South Asia,
partly as a result of Cold War cartographies that continue to divide and partition Asia (so that West Asia becomes the "Middle East").

The U.S. adopted British colonial conceptions of Afghanistan so that the racialized lens of tribe and religion is still used to understand Afghanistan and its people rather than modern concepts of nationalism and national sovereignty (Bashir and Crews 2012; Tarzi 2012). The Af-Pak borderlands have been associated with deeply Orientalist imaginaries of militant and misogynist fighters and hardy Pashtuns that continue to shape Cold War anthropology and the Pentagon's Human Terrain Systems focused on the region (Fitzgerald and Gould 2011, 12; González 2009; Hanifi 2012, 94–98). Persistent Orientalist representations of an "untamable," backward country have also suppressed the history of Afghan modernity and secularity, which was crushed by the interventions of the U.S., Pakistan, and other states interested in Afghanistan as a strategic site during the Cold War (Gould and Fitzgerald 2011, 13).

Furthermore, Obama's Af-Pak strategy coincided with the ratcheting up of the domestic war on "homegrown terrorism" and focus on the behavioral and cultural proclivities of Muslims, Afghans, Pakistanis, and Arabs presumably prone to "radicalization," within the U.S. as well as in West and Southwest Asia (Kumar 2012, 159–161). The Af-Pak strategy is thus also a mapping of enemies, internal and external to the nation, that reflects imperial policies in the age of Obama, which saw a doubling of the rate of drone strikes over that of the Bush regime and heightened war on Afghanistan as well as domestic counterradicalization operations. Covert operations, surveillance, drone warfare, and secrecy are all part of the "stealth technologies" constitutive of Obama's empire (Atanoski 2013, 204). The "dronification of state violence" and extrajudicial targeted killings in Af-Pak and elsewhere increased steadily under the Obama regime (Shaw and Akhter 2014). In 2010, for instance, the president approved 122 drone strikes in Pakistan, decreasing them only as the condemnation of drone warfare by antiwar groups, such as Code Pink, began to grow and after public protests and die-ins at air force bases deploying drone missiles.[5] As Shahzad Bashir and Robert Crews (2012) observe, "Drone warfare epitomizes the 'sophisticated technology of the modern, civilized West' unleashed from Nevada or Florida against the backward Taliban (who emerged only in the 1980s)" (2).

The aftermath of 9/11 and the war on Afghanistan propelled new alliances between Afghan, South Asian, and Arab American youth and created a loose community of concern and solidarity, political as well as religious, focused on the wars in Afghanistan and Iraq and the U.S. proxy war in Pakistan. Laila, for example, commented when I spoke to her in spring 2009, that the U.S. had "actually bombed [Pakistan] 38 times since August" of 2008 and that she would discuss the drone strikes with her Palestinian friends, who opposed them as well. Other Pakistani American youth, such as Sharif, who grew up in Los Gatos, said that the U.S. war on Afghanistan was "pointless" and "people are dying for no cause." Sharif's grandfather was actually Afghan, and he commented on the phenomenon of intermarriage between Pakistanis and Afghans, as well as among Arabs and Indians, suggesting the intimate and familial relationships that also bind these communities together.

So while "Af-Pak" did not always provide an explicit rubric for youth activism against the War on Terror, it provided an implicit paradigm for emergent cross-ethnic coalitions and political solidarity linking communities who have been torn apart by colonial and national borders. Laila was involved in fundraising on campus for humanitarian relief in Afghanistan and in Gaza; for her, the affinity with Afghan and Arab American youth was built on a shared interest in "politics and religion." While for some youth, solidarity was expressed through humanitarian projects, many (also) framed their opposition to the Af-Pak war and U.S. drone strikes through opposition to imperial intervention. Farid was critical of the role of foreign powers in undermining the sovereignty and stability of both Afghanistan and Pakistan; he said,

> Both countries over there, they've never had a chance to have people leave them alone and worry about themselves, so there's always something going on there. Like how Afghanistan had something going on with Russia, and then the refugees came to Pakistan, and Pakistan had to take care of them. You know, when we should've been worrying about ourselves, but you know, the refugees, you can't do anything, you help them.

The Afghan refugees are perceived as a burden for the Pakistani state, if one that it was obliged to carry in this view—a perception that fueled some tension between Afghan and Pakistani communities, apparently more so in the older generation. But Farid's primary frustration was with the assaults on sovereignty of both these frontline states in the Cold War.

The U.S. conveniently evaded the question of national sovereignty during its 2001 invasion by claiming that Afghanistan was a "failed state" and producing an (imperial) humanitarian and feminist discourse of rescuing Afghan women from the Taliban. After 2007, Pakistan increasingly became the central battlefield for the War on Terror as the Taliban and Al Qaeda supposedly fled across the Afghan border into the Northwest Frontier Provinces (now called Khyber Pakhtoonkhwa) and the Federally Administered Tribal Areas (FATA) of Pakistan. The Pakistani military was called upon to fight militants who were in many cases also Pakistani, leading to a spate of increasingly dramatic attacks and bombings in cities across Pakistan. This was accompanied by the covert but increasingly controversial drone war waged by the U.S. in northwest Pakistan, which by November 2011 was estimated to have killed 2,300–3,000 people, of which at least 175 were children.[6] While I was doing research in Lahore, Pakistan, in 2009–2010, I found there was growing outrage among Pakistanis—particularly among those who could not afford to live in gated communities or flee the country—with a proxy war that was seen as undermining national sovereignty and provoking a bloody blowback against ordinary Pakistanis.

From Ghazni to Hayward: Neoliberal Humanitarianism

The ascendant moral economy of humanitarian intervention obscures issues of sovereignty, (neo)imperialism, and colonialism in Pakistan, Iraq, Afghanistan, and Palestine.Humanitarianism provides a core element of modern governance and global politics and, according to Didier Fassin (2010), the moral logic of humanitarianism has provided a "new repertoire for public action at both the international and local levels," involving states, NGOs, and legal regimes (274). Humanitarianism has justified contemporary wars (selectively) based on the "right to intervene," or what has been codified by the United Nations as the "responsibility to protect" (RTP), considered not just a right but a moral duty—as evident in the U.S. "intervention" in Kosovo, the invasions of Iraq and Afghanistan, and the NATO role in Libya (Fassin and Pandolfi 2010; Weizman 2011). Didier Fassin and Mariella Pandolfi (2010) argue that "a break with the doctrine of sovereignty" emerged, particularly in the late twentieth century, because the paradigm of humanitarian interventionism privileged "the protection of peoples" at the expense of state sovereignty, as enshrined in international law (10). This is why the Non-Aligned Movement rejected the "right" of humanitarian intervention and there is an ongoing contestation of the role of agencies representing modern humanitarianism in zones of warfare and occupation, such as UN relief programs for Palestinian refugees, in relation to a politics of sovereignty (Allen 2013; Bricmont 2007, 98; Feldman 2012).

While humanitarian interventionism is not a new paradigm, it is important to note the ways in which states of emergency and disaster and conceptions of the "victim" have come to frame contemporary wars as well as the contemporary ethics of liberalism (Fassin and Pandolfi 2010).[7] Nguyen (2012) observes that the notion of helping or giving the "gift of freedom" to others who "appear to be insecure, illegible, inadequate, illegal, and illiberal" partitions "the world into spaces commensurate or incommensurate . . . with the rule of liberalism" (15). It is not just the imperial state or neoconservatives that have increasingly adopted a rationale of liberal humanitarianism, but this normative rationality has become a condition of possibility for politics in the U.S. more generally, across the ideological spectrum. Bricmont (2007) points out that since the defeat in Vietnam, the U.S. increasingly used the "political ethic" of human rights to legitimize its military interventions, a rationale adopted by liberals (on both sides of the Atlantic) who supported the "new American wars" in Yugoslavia, Afghanistan, and Iraq (18).

Liberals and progressives, and even leftists, take on causes that are primarily humanitarian and that displace anti-imperial and anticapitalist resistance. In fact, since the fall of the USSR and the official end of the Cold War, the rise of humanitarian NGOs has led to the emergence of a politics of solidarity, or solidarity in lieu of politics, according to Rony Brauman: "As the tide of ideology retreated, humanitarian action gradually came to occupy the space left by politics, supplying a concrete content for the ideal of solidarity" (cited in Fassin 2010, 273). This is one of the political challenges that Arab, South Asian, and Afghan American youth face in their mobilization, particularly that framed as humanitarian "solidarity activism," in the post-9/11 moment. "Freedom" is something certain deserving others, outside the U.S., need and which is wrapped in the discourse of the freedom of the market or bestowed by military intervention.

However, I would argue, as Fassin (2010, 273–274) does, that the shift to humanitarianism is not necessarily an evacuation of politics, but rather a consolidation of a particular form of neoliberal, internationalist politics, one that is not entirely new, but is increasingly constitutive of the paradigm of war in the new global order, and also seeps into the politics of resistance to militarism and warfare. In the case of post-9/11 politics and youth activism, it is crucial to examine the tension that arises from a humanitarian logic that drives both imperial invasions and neoliberal restructuring as well as grassroots mobilization. Humanitarian campaigns often draw young people who are not involved in formal political organizing (for example, the "Kony 2012" video about violence in Uganda that went viral and appealed to masses of American youth before its political deceptions were revealed, and perhaps even after). If U.S. wars are described as campaigns for saving humanity by bestowing on others neoliberal democracy, women's rights, and gay rights, oppositional movements are also framed in many cases as campaigns for rights and rescue.

A fundraiser for Afghanistan that I attended in Hayward brought home to me some of the subtle and not so subtle aspects of the humanitarian logic of redemption and reconstruction in relation to Afghan Americans and the War on Terror at large. In June 2011, the Hayward-Ghazni Sister Cities Committee hosted ten Afghans from Ghazni and Kabul who were touring the U.S.

on a visit sponsored by the U.S. embassy in Kabul and the Ghazni Provincial Reconstruction Team. The event featured talks by the visiting Afghan leaders and included an Afghan dinner; the proceeds were to support the committee's program for Afghan widows in Ghazni. This event was significant given the relative paucity of public events focused on any issues related to Afghanistan in the Bay Area, as I noted earlier. The fundraiser was held in Hayward City Hall, a domed building in the quiet town center. Inside the rotunda, a screen had been set up in front of a staircase winding up the side of the rotunda, and probably not accidentally, a YouTube video of Bruce Springsteen's "Born in the USA" was being projected on the wall as guests entered. No one seemed to notice or remark on the virtual American flag fluttering behind the podium that had been set up on the staircase. The audience for the event was mixed, with a few Afghan women in embroidered kurtas (shirts) chatting with the mostly white crowd. The organizers of the event from the Sister Cities Committee seemed to be mainly white Americans and some Afghans as well as an older South Asian Muslim man. One of the committee members, an older white woman, had draped a bright green and shocking pink silk shawl over her head, which she took off after a while; it was not clear what either gesture suggested, but it was perhaps not unrelated to the fact that both the visiting Afghan women had covered their heads, one with a green hijab and the other with a white chador. Solidarity as a public act can clearly be performative, embodied, as well as appropriative.

The event opened with remarks by the president of the committee, an Irish American man who emphasized the group's work in building relationships with Muslims. His commentary seemed to emphasize the interfaith nature of the program, rather than American-Afghan cooperation or even solidarity. The chair of the committee, an older white man who was a board member of the Afghan Coalition in Fremont, offered an Islamic invocation, commenting jovially that people knew him as the "Christian mullah" and that he was committed to "building bridges between Christians and Muslims." The first speech was by the newly appointed president of San Jose State, Mohammad ("Mo") Qayoumi, followed by a talk about the history of Ghazni by an older Afghan archaeologist, who spoke of how the country's culture had been targeted for destruction for over thirty years and needed to be safeguarded.

It was striking that the subsequent talks by the visiting Afghans consistently emphasized the need for economic aid and U.S.-sponsored neoliberal development in Afghanistan, with no mention of national sovereignty or even democracy. Instead, the senior advisor to the Afghan president on urban development and national reconstruction, an older man with a turban, said that the solution to Afghanistan's problems rested on a "three-legged stool": economic development, security, and a "clean government" free of corruption. He declared that Afghans were grateful for the U.S. and NATO presence in Afghanistan, although a military presence alone was not a solution. The advisor also observed that poverty drove most Afghans toward the Taliban, the message clearly being if that if Americans could provide aid, the problem of terrorism could be eliminated through neoliberal governance. The two Afghan women speakers echoed this theme; one of them, a member of the Afghan Parliament, talked at length and said that it was U.S. tax payers who had helped the Afghan people, including Afghan women. The other Afghan woman spoke of the need to focus on women and education, and to use development to "defeat the Taliban." The mayor of Ghazni, dressed in a simple business suit, remarked how glad he was to visit Hayward, a "very green" city where Afghan Americans seemed to be happy with the services provided by the city. He then outlined several projects under construction and in need of funding in Ghazni, including a vocational institute and a prison.

This event illustrated for me the ways in which Afghanistan, and the Afghan war, has been (re)framed—including by Afghan elites and government officials—through a discourse of gendered humanitarianism and neoliberal governance that evades questions of occupation, war, and sovereignty, not to mention issues of multinational privatization, NGOization, and the global prison industry. The talks in Hayward demonstrated how an analysis of state power is evacuated and replaced by a discourse of state building focused on foreign aid, interfaith solidarity, and liberal rights—which includes supporting widows and building prisons, with no mention of *how* Afghan women are widowed and *who* is incarcerated in Afghanistan or why. The problem of the Taliban becomes a purely economic issue to be addressed by neoliberal development—the speakers were careful not to use the language of sectarianism or fundamentalism, perhaps strategically, let alone offer a critique of geopolitics or foreign military intervention.[8] While militarization was not viewed by all the Afghan speakers as a solution to the crisis of a nation destroyed by decades of war—as hinted at by the Afghan archaeologist—they performed a plea for a neoliberal model of good governance and development, and empowerment for women, that would bring Afghanistan into the world order and liberal democracy. There was no mention by any of the Afghan speakers of the failure of delivery of funds for reconstruction by Western donors (even if this was very much on their minds), let alone of the misogynist and violent warlords—other than those associated with the Taliban—and the racism, misogyny, and violence of U.S. and NATO troops. In addition, the greetings of the "Christian mullah" and emphasis on interfaith solidarity, not to mention the adoption of head covering by some of the non-Afghan women at the event, highlighted the ways it is not just Islamophobia but also Islamophilia that shapes the public discourse about the Muslim friend or foe. As Andrew Shryock (2010) argues, Islamophilia is founded on assumptions about what constitutes "the values of the good Muslim and those of the good citizen of the liberal democratic state" (10), as discussed in Chapter Two, so that diversity and solidarity are translated through religious tolerance and inclusion.

Given the invisibilization of Afghan Americans, even during the U.S. occupation of Afghanistan, it is notable that they only appear as token representatives of a nation in need of aid and as faces of grateful allies in the War on Terror. The performance of neoliberal humanitarianism, co-produced by Afghan subjects and laced with references to women's rights, produces Afghanistan as another nation to be remade in the image of Western liberal democratic capitalism, so that Ghazni could one day look more like Hayward, it is hoped, if with centuries-old monuments. Never mind that Ghazni was a market town established even before the Persian empire and a trading center during the Islamic period, as the Afghan speakers pointed out, or that Hayward is currently an economically depressed city where Afghan refugees and Latino immigrants as well as other residents struggle to find jobs, despite the beautiful new city hall building.

The language of postconflict state building in post-2001 Afghanistan has been shaped by a discourse "codified by experts and international aid agencies," according to Astri Suhrke (2011), resting on "human rights, the rule of law, security sector reform and a market-based economy" and drawing on a multinational apparatus for "peace building" developed in Cambodia, Kosovo, Bosnia, and El Salvador in the 1990s (7–8). The fundraiser actually took place at a moment in which the counterinsurgency doctrine of "winning hearts and minds" in Afghanistan through development, with collusion between the NATO coalition and the "aid lobby" including NGOs, had already failed (Suhrke 2011, 10, 57). Suhrke observes that by the mid-2000s, foreign donors had created a "rentier state unparalleled in the history of Afghanistan and nearly unique in the world of international assistance," riddled with problems of corruption and lack of accountability that frustrated local Afghans (12, 125). The consolidation of this aid regime is part of a larger international project that has eroded national sovereignty and created a racialized and hierarchical apparatus of humanitarian aid workers and agencies in "conflict" zones.

It is very possible that the visiting Afghans, some of whom politicians themselves, were well aware that the event in Hayward was a strategic staging of "good" Afghan subjects worthy of humanitarian aid that required a discourse legible to a liberal American audience. The event organizers seemed aware of the presence of Afghan Americans in Hayward, but Afghan American youth were absent. While the figure of the refugee, living in Hayward or Fremont, was missing in the discourse of this event, the language of "sisterhood" between cities seemed to suggest that Afghans could be part of an American family of adopted kin—especially women—who could be saved, subjects who understood and desired all the things the U.S. could offer. Nguyen (2012) writes of South Vietnamese refugees in the U.S. as the "former stranger turned friend" who deserve U.S. benevolence, and who express "gratitude and love" for their liberation from Communism (136). However, in the case of Afghanistan, those who were befriended in an earlier moment (the mujahideen) could turn into foes of the U.S. while there are new Afghan friends and family members, in Hayward or Ghazni, fighting old and new foes. Sisterhood, like transnational solidarity, can emerge in unexpected places but through familiar gestures when one is at war.

It is also striking that despite the heavy investment in humanitarianism as the "correct" ethos defining relationships between American and Afghans, some humanitarian projects in select regions of warfare and occupation are considered suspect or even illegal, most notably in the case of Muslim-led relief organizations focused on Palestine, but also Afghanistan, Pakistan, and Kashmir.[9] For example, after 9/11, Muslim charitable organizations focused on international relief came under state scrutiny and have been prosecuted for alleged material support to groups classified as terrorist organizations, such as Hamas. The Bush regime shut down the Holy Land Foundation for Relief and Development (HLF), the largest Muslim charity in the U.S., which provided aid to Palestinian refugees and supported schools and hospitals in the West Bank and Gaza; the Global Relief Foundation, which focused on Kosovo, Chechnya, Afghanistan, Pakistan, and Kashmir; and Help the Needy, which delivered aid to Iraq during the devastating sanctions (Nimer 2005; Sheehi 2011, 156–158). Notably, the solidarity campaign in support of the five Palestinians charged in the HLF case was dubbed "Restore Our Freedom to Give," underscoring the politicized divide in the "giving" of charity and the right to philanthropy, where some refugee populations or disaster zones are considered undeserving of humanitarian aid—and seemingly deserving only of the gift of war, occupation, and destruction—since they are on the wrong side of the racialized division between terrorist/civilized.[10]

I think it is important to theorize the *racialized* and *gendered* dimensions of the biopolitics of humanitarianism more explicitly than Fassin does, and to draw on postcolonial and feminist critiques to understand the ways in which the politics of race, gender, and religion are central to both state and NGO projects of humanitarianism, as evident at the Hayward fundraiser. Fassin and Pandolfi (2010) make the crucial argument that the humanitarian state of emergency helps produce the deferral or suspension of national sovereignty, with the help of NGOs whose involvement in zones of conflict or postconflict plays a role, if ambiguously or indirectly, in normalizing these states of exception for nation-states with degraded sovereignty (see also Allen 2013). This predicament is apparent in the ways in which Afghanistan has to a large degree been visible in the U.S. not as a country under imperial or neocolonial occupation but only as a region of salvation, in need of rescue, aid, and reconstruction.

The runaway success of the novel *The Kite Runner*, by Khalid Hosseini (2003), is testament to the hunger in the general U.S. public for a narrative of redemption that would legitimize the U.S. and NATO occupation in Afghanistan, which was well underway when the book was published and which was beginning to generate some unease in the general public, if not opposition. The Afghan American author is, in fact, from Fremont, which provides some of the local context for the novel and its narrative of Afghan/Muslim gender persecution and sexual perversity. Feelings about the book were mixed among the Afghan American youth from the Bay Area to whom I spoke and some, such as Meena, were deeply skeptical of the book's representation of Afghanistan and the war, and of its ethnographic authority for American readers. There was also frustration among Afghan Americans with the fact that aid for reconstruction in Afghanistan was limited and had not been delivered as promised by the international community after 2001 while there was a public push for recruitment of Afghan translators by the U.S. military. For example, Mariyam mentioned that several of her family members had worked as translators in Afghanistan, because it was "easy money"—attractive for those struggling with employment in an area with a high cost of living— but "Pashtuns here feel you're a traitor" for working for the U.S. military.

While having dinner one evening at a popular Afghan restaurant in Fremont, Salang Pass, I was struck by a large U.S. military poster near the entrance with text in Farsi and images of U.S. soldiers in combat gear, advertising positions in Afghanistan for translators with knowledge of Pashto and Dari. The Afghan waitress told me that the poster had been brought by someone from the military and the program offered $250,000 a year for work as an interpreter. She also noted that three people whom she knew from the restaurant had gone to Afghanistan as military translators and had been killed there. The discourse of militarization infiltrates even Afghan restaurants and social spaces, emphasizing that Afghanistan is a region that must be fortified and saved with the help of native experts. There is hope that some customers and community members might be "good" Afghan subjects who are willing to sacrifice themselves for the U.S., for a sum, in order to fight "bad" Afghan and Muslim terrorists.

The waitress commented that it was sad that the U.S. was spending so much money on such a program while, for one million dollars, they could provide many Afghan families with schooling, health care, and water. She also pointed out that many U.S. agencies doing "reconstruction" in Afghanistan were linked to U.S. government officials, commenting wryly, "Cheney has a business there, he is making money off this. It's a business!" Such comments by Afghans are erased from the public discourse, however, which can recognize Afghans only as either foot soldiers or sources of local and linguistic knowledge for the U.S. military. The logics of humanitarianism and militarism work in tandem to erase Afghans as racial let alone imperial subjects and to evade questions of sovereignty and self-determination in Afghanistan and Pakistan.

Sovereignty: Imperial and Otherwise

"Af-Pak" represents a colonial form of degraded sovereignty: a place that does not exist on the modern map but has been invented by an imperial geography of domination and civilization in which the vocabulary of sovereignty is reinvented through the language of "failed states"—a failure that imperial powers help produce and then use as the rationalization for invasion and occupation. It is important to grapple with questions of sovereignty and self-determination that are occluded or distorted in the War on Terror, and situate them in relation to issues of imperialism, settler colonialism, indigeneity, and racial violence. The U.S. invasion and occupation of Afghanistan and proxy war in Af-Pak, including extrajudicial targeted assassinations and covert or special military operations inside Afghanistan as well as Pakistan, are all examples of what Stoler and McGranahan (2007) describe as the state of deferred sovereignty of imperial formations: the "conditions of delayed sovereignty" and "deferred autonomy" that are at the heart of a U.S. model of empire and constitutive of U.S. imperial sovereignty (8; see also Hardt and Negri 2000). These "proliferating zones of degraded legal rights" (Stoler 2006, 97) are not exceptional but, in fact, are intrinsic to imperial formations that constantly and creatively produce their own states of exception, so that "a fundamental violence of empire is lodged in opaque and changing vocabulary" (Stoler and McGranahan 2007, xii). New designations for colonized territories—trusteeships, protectorates, commonwealths, and "unincorporated" territories—have historically been produced by the U.S. as a manifestation of these imperial formations; according to Stoler and McGranahan, technologies of imperial governance are marked by a "politics of dislocation, processes of dispersion, appropriation, and displacement. They are dependent both on moving categories and populations. Not least, they are dependent on material and discursive postponements and deferrals: the civilizing mission, imperial guardianship, and manifest destiny are all promissory notes of transformation" (8).

The concept of "Af-Pak" is a notable example of this sort of shape-shifting imperial formation, and has emerged from the long history of imperial interventions undermining Afghan sovereignty. The vocabulary of "terrorists" used to describe former Afghan "freedom fighters" who were allied to, and feted by, U.S. regimes during the late Cold War, also reveals the shifting and self-contradictory lexicon of empire through the lens of Af-Pak. Several young people I spoke to challenged the contradictions of this imperial vocabulary in the War on Terror. Bashir, who was born in San Jose and whose family belongs to a tribal community from the northern Khyber Pakhtoonkhwa area, found himself rethinking his understanding of the Taliban through the prism of local and tribal—not just national—sovereignties after he returned to Pakistan. At the age of five, he moved with his family to their village in the Attock district of northern Punjab, where he lived for eight years before returning to the U.S. He reflected, "I went back to Pakistan in 2005, and I really started talking to people . . . and I do recall that a lot of people are for the Taliban . . . I mean here, when you say that word, people get scared over here and think it's a terrorist group. But it's actually a whole big tribe. It's a movement. If you live there, you realize that most of these people are just ordinary people." Bashir pointed out that support for the Taliban among those who live in Af-Pak, and consider it a movement of "ordinary people" who are a part of tribal and local communities, was not unusual in a region that was being attacked and devastated by the U.S. and its proxy force, the Pakistani army. He commented:

> This was a very normal thing. They see the attack on Afghanistan as an attack on everyone and many of these people think that it's very unjust. And when 9/11 happened, they wanted a trial, they wanted to punish the people that did this. But they feel like they were betrayed and, like, their voices were not heard. Because they were also trying to help the United States. And so, the day the U.S. attacked Afghanistan, they turned around.

Bashir alludes to Taliban leader Mullah Omar's call to the Bush administration to supply evidence of the linkage of Al Qaeda to the 9/11 attacks so that Osama bin Laden and any others legally responsible could be put on trial.

This was a response in keeping with a state assuming itself to be sovereign and part of the international legal order, notwithstanding the Taliban's internal brutality against its own people and its well-documented misogyny. However, the U.S. regime rejected compliance with international law and nullified the sovereignty not just of the Taliban regime, but of the state of Afghanistan itself, in order to bomb it back to the "Stone Age."

Echoing the comments of some of the Afghan Americans I spoke to, Bashir also pointed to the sense of betrayal felt by Pashtuns on both sides of the Af-Pak border and by Afghans who had supported the U.S. and provided foot soldiers in the war against the USSR, but whose communities were devastated by the U.S. invasion after 9/11. I should note that the War on Terror is a deeply contested and divisive issue in Pakistan and among Pakistani Americans and many have views very different from Bashir's, with some liberal-progressive activists and intellectuals publicly supporting the U.S. military intervention. The Taliban indeed instituted policies that have wreaked havoc in both Afghan and Pakistani societies, while their relationship with the Pakistan military is highly murky. In the case of Pakistan, the civilian casualties of the drone attacks and the covert presence of U.S. security contractors and intelligence operatives inside Pakistan (for example, the bizarre Raymond Davis case in Lahore) have inflamed opposition to the U.S. and its presence in the region but have been ignored in the U.S. by the discourse of counterterrorism and counterinsurgency.[11]

Some Pakistani American youth—as well as Afghan and Arab Americans—I spoke to in Silicon Valley, such as Yasser, were critical of the Taliban "because they treated the women badly and the Afghan people badly, they disrespected other religions." At the same time, Yasser vigorously rejected the official premise of the U.S interventions in Af-Pak as a humanitarian or democratizing mission:

> I know the U.S. helped train the Taliban . . . along with the Pakistani ISI and all these kinds of different factors. So I don't think the U.S. is handling it [well], they're after the uranium in the mountains, they're after making that [oil] pipeline, they're after all these kinds of things and I don't think they really wanna help Afghanistan. . . . I also think they're trying to destroy Pakistan. They have Punjab, Northwestern Frontier, Sindh, Baluchistan, and they're trying to find differences now so that Pakistan can break because there's a nuclear bomb. . . . And Israel and America, you can tell that they're love buddies, just by their financial aid money, we give [Israel] more financial aid than the poor people of Afghanistan and Iraq, and here we are doing [them] a favor.

Yasser referred to the role of the U.S. and the Pakistani intelligence agency (ISI) in fostering and supporting the Taliban, and pointed to the ethnic and national divisions within Pakistan that have put pressure on the Pakistani state as it dealt with U.S. condemnation of its nuclear program. He also spoke about the U.S. interest in minerals in Afghanistan, alluding to the plans for a Central Asia Gas (CentGas) oil pipeline from Turkmenistan through western Afghanistan to Pakistan, a project of the U.S. corporation UNOCAL (later acquired by Chevron).[12] Yasser seemed well aware of the possibility of U.S. covert operations and the designs of U.S. corporations allied with the neoliberal capitalist state that were obscured by the narrative of humanitarian intervention in Afghanistan and Pakistan.[13]

The question of national sovereignty in Af-Pak raised by Yasser, Bashir, Amira, and others is erased by the discourse of benevolent imperialism and counterterrorism. The U.S. has used its power as a sovereign state to inflict spectacular—as well as covert—acts of violence on Afghanistan, and later Iraq and Pakistan, generating civil wars and supporting client states friendly to the global order of neoliberal capitalism.

As Yasser sardonically comments, while Operation Enduring Freedom was framed as doing the Afghans a "favor," the U.S. continues to send massive financial aid to Israel rather than to the country it helped destroy. The logic of humanitarianism in the War on Terror is rife with paradoxes that reformulate the logic of sovereignty and self-determination. U.S. humanitarian imperialism has a long genealogy; in the contemporary era it was the face that Clinton gave to the post–Cold War liberal empire in the 1990s, with the sanctions and attacks on Serbia, Sudan, and Iraq (Bricmont 2007).

The national sovereignty and self-determination of Afghans, Pakistanis, and Iraqis—not to mention Palestinians—is considered either illegitimate or of lesser importance within the biopolitical settlement of counterterrorism and "homeland security." There is a fundamental tension here in the notion of whose "homeland" is being defended or liberated that underlies the paradox of sovereignty in the War on Terror, a contradiction that troubled many of the youth I spoke to and that surfaced in their reflections. For many of its critics, the notion of national sovereignty is a limited or problematic framework that is tied to the nation-state, and to totalizing epistemologies of the sovereign embedded in Enlightenment modernity and Western colonialism. David Strang (1996) points out that that the lexicon of sovereignty and states emerging from a Westphalian conception of nation-states is tied to an imperial logic in which "non-Western sovereignty was actively delegitimated" through a self-referential system of recognition that determined which forms of sovereignty were acceptable in the international order (22–25). Strang posits that this racial logic gave way to a "moral imperialism" at the turn of the twentieth century, when Western powers rationalized their infringements on non-Western sovereignty as the actions of a civilization "outraged" by acts of barbarism (31), in order to protect the rights and sovereignties of European colonizers against the sovereignty and freedom of "the darker nations" (see Prashad 2007). The U.S., argues Mimi Nguyen (2012), is a "supersovereign" power that considers itself above international laws that defend national sovereignty and human rights by postulating that it is an "empire of humanity" (29).

Sovereignty in the War on Terror must be situated in relation to the history of the U.S. as a settler colony and "transnational garrison state" and its racial wars and genocidal violence against indigenous peoples and (at least nominally sovereign) nations (Bello 2010, 311). Donald Pease (2009) argues that the imperial interventions in Afghanistan and Iraq reenacted foundational acts of settler violence against uncivilized peoples that are constitutive of the "Homeland Security State":

> In Iraq and Afghanistan the emergency forces of the state openly reperformed the acts of violence that the myth of Virgin Land had formerly covered up. Operation Infinite Justice [later renamed Operation Enduring Freedom] quite literally depopulated the Afghani landscape so that it might be perceived as a blank page onto which to inscribe a different political order. . . . By way of Operation Infinite Justice and Operation Iraqi Freedom the Homeland Security State restaged the colonial settlers' conquest of Indians and the acquisition of their homelands. The terror and the killing became the Homeland Security State's means of accomplishing anew the already known telos of U.S. history as the inaugural event of America's global rule in the twenty-first century. (172)

Pease's argument linking the invasions of Iraq and Afghanistan to a (repressed) history of settler-colonial violence against indigenous peoples in the U.S. is important because it highlights the ways in which a settler-colonial logic consistently reframes conquest and genocidal violence as acts of self-defense, reversing the relationship between perpetrators and objects of violence and resorting to the rationale of Manifest Destiny or a moral crusade. I think that the recovery of this repressed memory of foundational violence and the genocide of indigenous peoples through the War on Terror is more ambiguous than Pease suggests—notwithstanding the explicit allusions in the U.S. military's use of phrases such as "killing Indians in Iraq" and its labeling of bin Laden as Geronimo in the targeted assassination in Pakistan in 2011. But Pease's analysis is crucial for reframing the War on Terror in relation to settler colonialism and points to the constitutive logic of imperial sovereignty that must make other nations fit for modern statehood and neoliberal democracy. The mainstream discourse of counterterrorism and counterinsurgency in the case of Afghanistan, Iraq, Pakistan, and Palestine relies heavily on the notion that these places are incapable of democratic self-governance and undeserving of national sovereignty, and must be civilized by the U.S. and Europe or its proxy forces. This logic of imperial sovereignty has produced ambiguous zones of sovereignty both outside and within U.S. borders, for the indigenous sovereignty of tribal nations exposes the "contradictions of American colonial rule" and imperial democracy in liberal settler colonies (Bruyneel 2007, xvii; see also Povinelli 2006).

Sovereignty is a primary frame of meaning-making in a global order, and represents "the potentiality to suspend what Arendt calls 'the right to have rights' and thereby denationalize, depoliticize, and decide on states of exception," according to Kalpana Seshadri (2008, 47). The security state apparatus that has been expanded and refined since 9/11 has created a global order based on a state of emergency that constructs subjects fit for surveillance, dislocation, incarceration, torture, and death. Regimes of incarceration and torture justified by projects of "democratization" or counterterrorism are intimately, and violently, linked to the politics of life and death, to the question of bare life: lives that can be killed without being sacrificed as key to the exercise of modern democracy and sovereign power (Agamben 1998, 83). So the question of self-determination is not simply a national political question, but a biopolitical question of who determines which selves can be eliminated or put at risk of death and which must be saved or let die (Foucault 2003).

As Achille Mmembe (2003) argues, the right "to kill or to allow to live constitutes the limits of sovereignty," which is constitutive of "state power in modernity" and is tied fundamentally to Western colonialism (11, 7). He thus extends Agamben's analysis of homo sacer by locating it not in the exemplary site of the camp, in Nazi Germany, but in the colony: "the site where sovereignty consists fundamentally in the exercise of power outside the law" by Western colonial modernity and where "the violence of the state of exception is deemed to operate in the service of 'civilization'" (Mmembe 2003, 23–24). Mmembe demonstrates that it is crucial to insert race and colonialism into an analysis of the state of exception as a technology of Western modernity, enacted in the colony "as a terror formation"; in this zone of "necropower," he argues using the case of occupied Palestine, the management of death is apparent in late colonial policies of determining "who is disposable and who is not" through "the enactment of differential rights to differing categories of people," justified through racialized imaginaries of the savage and uncivilized (26–27). The disappearance of human rights for some peoples—as in the case of the right to self-determination in Afghanistan or Palestine—occurs through a colonial and racial logic that deems mobilization in support of these rights to be acts of solidarity with terrorists, extremists, and the uncivilized. So the young people I spoke to had to grapple with this gap between official rights-talk and national rights, in a context in which defending human rights or sovereignty for colonized and occupied populations is policed and surveilled, as I will discuss in Chapter Six.

In the context of the decline of U.S. economic hegemony and sovereign power globally, and the rise of new powers such as Brazil and China, there has been a shift from national sovereignty to the modality of global sovereignty, which overrides national autonomy and rests on a neoliberal model of human rights expressed "through the concern and care for life: the competition state, free trade, good governance, the promotion of democracy, and international law" (Seshadri 2008, 43). Kamala Visweswaran (2010) observes that the "conflict between the recognition of civil rights or liberties in the national realm and human rights in the international realm" is intrinsic to a "juridical formation consisting of flexible networks of authority and sovereignty" linked to the "institutions of the new world order," such as the IMF, World Bank, GATT, and NAFTA, as well as human rights NGOs such as Amnesty International and Human Rights Watch (192). So while the U.S. state, in particular, still wields its sovereign power globally and through military force, abstract, liberal models of "cosmopolitan sovereignty" (Mouffe 2005, 2), have emerged that are tied to notions of "global civil society" and obfuscate the violence of imperialism and global capitalism. The problem, as Chantal Mouffe argues, is that the discourse of a world order "beyond sovereignty" shapes a political field that is presumably also "beyond left and right," that is, a depoliticization of a public sphere ruled by the dictates of individual free will and market democracy (2).

As Seshadri (2008) suggests, the contemporary model of global sovereignty produces rightless subjects who are displaced due to the ravages of war and neoliberal capitalism, and who then must be saved by the very same global sovereign order in order to be brought back into organized political community, with the use of force in some instances (50). This tautological logic of what I would call *imperial sovereignty* rests on the depoliticization of displaced or stateless lives, whose predicament is removed from the realm of political economy or colonial domination, as in the case of Iraqis, Afghans, Palestinians, and Pakistanis. In a world order where to be human is to have citizenship, the contradictory existence of stateless and displaced subjects, such as Palestinians, Afghan refugees, and Pashtuns in Af-Pak, reveals how the biopolitics of citizenship and state underlies the exceptionalism of human rights regimes (Seshadri 2008).

The paradox is that self-determination and sovereignty have become pressing questions in contemporary sites of imperial violence at a moment when the notion of national sovereignty and the exclusions and violence of the nation-state have been thoroughly critiqued—and when anticolonial struggles are simply understood to be over, in a presumably postcolonial moment.[14] Judith Butler argues that the preoccupation with the heuristics of "sovereignty and bare life" risks reinscribing the logic of sovereignty (and rights) as the only way to understand the workings of "contemporary power"; she suggests it is important to expand our analysis of "states of dispossession," such as in Palestine, while still keeping sight of the ways in which U.S. sovereignty has made illegitimate the sovereignty of other nation-states and "sovereignty is invoked, extended, deterritorialized, aggregated, abrogated in the name of sovereignty as well as against the name of sovereignty" (in Butler and Spivak 2010, 42, 105). Sovereignty is indeed key to current thinking about the nation-state and citizenship, and to the exclusions and violence of nationalism, but it is important not to romance the subject of sovereignty but also not to uncritically embrace the "post-sovereign" (Butler, in Butler and Spivak 2010, 41, 102). I think this is an easy move for those who reside in sovereign states and enjoy the benefits of recognized belonging in the world order, in my view. As Gayatri Spivak points out, rights have been eroded for populations who live in "free market managerial states" and postcolonial states that can offer no "robust citizenship for the people down below" (in Butler and Spivak 2010, 90). Thinking through the biopolitics of sovereignty from the perspective of imperialism and global capitalism reminds us that it is also an instrument of life and death that obliterates self-determination for indigenous and disposable populations and annihilates racially marked others.

Conclusion

Critical theorists have explored notions of self-determination not tied to the form of the nation-state and alternative notions of sovereignty that are based not on territorial, heteronormative models of belonging nor on reactionary nationalist counternarratives to imperial sovereignty (Butler and Spivak 2010, 108; Smith 2011, 241–242). Some have offered conceptions such as the "third space of sovereignty" articulated in indigenous politics in North America and "inassimilable to the institutions and discourse of the modern liberal democratic settler-state and nation" (Bruyneel 2007, xvii). Mark Rifkin (2012, 3, 4) reimagines sovereignty from an indigenous (and queer) perspective as "sensations of belonging to place and peoplehood excluded from settler governance" that are "not recognized as sovereignty within the administrative grid that shapes the meaning of self-determination under settler rule" (3, 4). These conceptions rely not on a liberal notion of self-sovereignty predicated on Enlightenment reason, individual autonomy, free will, and neoliberal choice, but on a radical sense of freedom to determine the conditions of collective, not just individual, existence beyond the dictates of Western modernity, liberal governance, and property (Mmembe 2003, 13; Povinelli 2006, 4). Rifkin (2012) articulates an "erotics of sovereignty" that is embedded in affective and sexual selfhood and entangled with "unacknowledged survivals, unofficial aspirations, and the persistence of pain" (31).[15]

While the young people I spoke to did not articulate these alternative frameworks of sovereignty—and did not explicitly use the vocabulary of sovereignty in most cases—they grappled with the notion of the sovereign, and some were deeply concerned about questions of sovereignty and self-determination in relation to the erasure of rights and the annihilation of other peoples. Their critiques raise important questions about imperatives for survival and selfhood in the context of imperial violence and racial wars. The assault on nonimperial and indigenous sovereignties occurs through a racialized and gendered discourse that legitimizes violence to rescue others in backward, patriarchal, and homophobic societies. In the following chapter, I discuss the ways in which the humanitarian project drives some of the charged debates in the post-9/11 culture wars and explore what they mean for youth who grapple with surveillance of movements challenging U.S. imperial power and neoliberal democracy.

5

Coming of Age under Surveillance

Surveillance Effects and the Post-9/11 Culture Wars

Technologies to regulate "radical" Muslim Americans and repress "extremist" Muslim and Arab American youth and enemy subjects, within and outside the U.S., are used by the national and global security apparatus as part of an expanding culture of surveillance and securitization. Imperial technologies of surveillance, repression, and regulation produce subjects, and politics, to be monitored and contained even while other forms of political subjecthood and alternative notions of politics bubble up from below. As they came of age in the post-9/11 era, the youth in this book struggled with the surveillance, policing, and disciplining of their politics and activism, particularly of political mobilization that challenged the state's attempt to incorporate and promote "moderate" Muslim politics, and the exceptional censorship and demonization of the Palestine solidarity movement by the state and by Zionist groups. This repression in the domestic War on Terror often remains invisible, however, for it is conducted through covert means, such as the use of undercover FBI informants, infiltration, and entrapment. Obama's counterterrorism program drew on counterradicalization practices in Britain in a transnational circuit of ideas and policies that focused on "criminalization of ideological activities," and on surveiling and entrapping Muslim American youth (Kundnani 2014, 9, 13).

This chapter demonstrates how surveillance is key to the post-9/11 culture wars, even if this is not acknowledged, as the counterterrorism regime targets, and also produces, gendered and racialized bodies as objects fit for surveillance. The central tropes of the post-9/11 culture wars are those of liberal democracy and freedom, embedded in contestations over Islam, gender, and sexuality. I argue that these culture wars are also *racial wars* and *class wars*, masked by the language of liberal multiculturalism and colorblind "diversity" and staged through interfaith projects, as discussed in the previous chapters. In these post-9/11 cultural, racial, and class wars, technologies of surveillance produce a "state of conscious and permanent visibility" of the objects of the War on Terror that has shaped the political culture of young people from targeted communities and produced self-surveillance and self-regulation (Foucault 1995, 201). This chapter explores how some youth reframe and resist surveillance through tactics of countersurveillance, which include individualized and dispersed practices in their daily lives that subvert surveillance through "quiet encroachments" (Bayat 2013, 46), as well as an increasingly professionalized activism that rests, sometimes uneasily, within the framework of neoliberal capitalist democracy.

Surveillance is fundamentally a technology of disciplining and managing racialized populations within neoliberal capitalism, and a racialized mode of governmentality for the imperial state. I argue that the culture of surveillance is related to the exceptionalist discourse of U.S. democracy and sovereignty, on the one hand, and to neoliberal governmentality, on the other, both of which are deployed to resolve the tension that emerges between the police state's repression and notions of American "freedom" in the War on Terror. This tension is negotiated by those who experience the brunt of policing and the contradictions of "democracy" in their daily lives, through sentiments of fear and anxiety but also defiance or outrage. Surveillance is a product of modernity, and a "central component of the modern state and the institutions of industrial capitalism," so while postindustrial and postmodern forms of capitalism and technology produce new methods of surveillance, it is fundamentally a disciplinary practice of modern governmentality, not just a product of technology (Lyon and Zureik 1996, 3, 11). As Foucault has argued, technologies of surveillance produce the regularization, and not just disciplining, of populations through classification, data collection, and simulation (cited in Puar 2007, 115; Simon 2005, 16). For Foucault (1995), "surveillance is permanent in its effects" (201); I am interested here in exploring how what I call "surveillance effects" are produced in the post-9/11 moment for those who are constructed as racialized and gendered objects of permanent surveillance.

While it is commonplace for liberal/progressive critics to criticize post-9/11 surveillance in the War on Terror as the repressive tactics of a new McCarthyism, scholars such as Athan Theoharis (2011) argue that the regime of counterterrorism and preventive surveillance that expanded after 9/11, under Bush as well as Obama, actually has roots that precede the McCarthy era, tracing it to the post–World War I repression of "subversive" movements. Programs created by FBI director J. Edgar Hoover used "ideological and associational criteria" for surveillance and infiltration that expanded in the 1950s and 1960s to contain leftist, antiwar, and Black Power movements. There is a long history of surveillance of Arab and Muslim Americans, which began after the 1967 Arab-Israeli war and involved cooperation between U.S. agencies and Israeli intelligence, increasing during the Iranian hostage crisis and later during the first Gulf War as Iranians and Arabs were increasingly profiled as terrorists (Kumar

2012). After 9/11, electronic surveillance was authorized under the PATRIOT Act and in intelligence law, including by Obama, as evident in the (passing) controversies over the expanded and mass surveillance secretly authorized under the Foreign Intelligence Surveillance Act (FISA). In other words, surveillance is constitutive of the imperial state and its secret wars necessary to project "democracy," while it represses dissent domestically as well as globally.

I think it is important to consider the work of surveillance in shaping the everyday political culture of the national security state, as it has evolved since the Cold War and in the context of what has been described as a "new Cold War," as well as the many hot wars waged by the U.S. from Iraq to Afghanistan. As the national security state developed since the 1950s, the "protracted afterlife of the Cold War" has animated what Jodi Kim calls the Cold War as a "structure of feeling," and what I have described as "imperial feelings" or the affective dimensions of U.S. empire as a way of life—sentiments of fear, anxiety, ambivalence, hatred, or desire (Kim 2010, 4; Maira 2009a; Williams 1980). Surveillance is one arena—and a primary one for those who are the targets of the homeland security state—where imperial feelings are produced, managed, challenged, or repressed in the long War on Terror. Talking to Muslim Americans and Arab, South Asian, and Afghan American youth, who were aware that they were targets of permanent surveillance, made me realize the ways that strategies of living with, accommodating, or resisting surveillance are now part of the coming-of-age experiences of the 9/11 generation. It is this aspect of the cultural and social impact of surveillance that I think needs greater attention, as revelations of new forms of surveillance and old and new covert programs proliferate. What does it mean for young people to live in the *everyday of surveillance*?

Surveillance Effects, Surveillance Stories

Nearly all the young people I spoke to talked about the climate of surveillance and the chilling effect it had on the possibilities of dissent and understandings of what it meant to be "political" and also "social." Arab, South Asian, and Afghan American youth have grown up in a climate in which they have to self-consciously regulate, or renarrate, their social and political lives (see Sirin and Fine 2008). They live in a moment when the state engages in warrantless wiretapping, monitors private emails and Facebook, and infiltrates mosques and activist groups with undercover informants, so it is not just those who are involved with formal political organizations who have reason to be fearful, or at least self-conscious, about the production of selfhood and sociality (MacArthur 2007; Maira 2007).

Laila, for example, had attended an Islamic school in Fremont, which received threats after 9/11 and where the teachers were mostly Arabs and Afghans. She recalled that when students were discussing the war in Iraq in class, "The teacher yelled at us and said, 'Don't discuss it! Especially in school because it's not safe.' . . . Like, they really prevented us from discussing it. I don't know if this is true but we've made jokes that it's because our mosque was taped." In this case, the fear of surveillance, whether the school or mosque were actually surveilled by the FBI, effectively shuts down discussion or debate about the state's War on Terror and the U.S. invasion of Iraq, regulating permissible political speech for Muslim American youth. It also forces the objects of surveillance to confront the fact that they live in a "military-spy state" (Mendieta 2011, 2) where freedom of expression is racially distributed. Laila and her teachers acknowledged a reality that was so chilling it perhaps had be dealt with through jokes that were only partly humorous.[1] These are the jokes of the 9/11 generation—an ironic discourse about surveillance that some might assume circulates only in Communist regimes, overseas dictatorships, and the "unfree" world—yet that are very much a part of the educational, political, and simply coming-of-age experiences of Muslim American youth today (Sirin and Fine 2008).

The social and cultural registers through which surveillance becomes a part of daily life—normalized, even as it is resisted—are what I would describe as *surveillance effects*. Surveillance effects shape political culture and also ideas of selfhood, producing objects of surveillance and subjects of surveillance as well as of self-surveillance. These effects bridge the psychic and political ripples generated by the War on Terror for those living in the neoliberal military-spy state. Surveillance effects echo the disciplinary technologies of "state effects," that is, the state attempts to secure an image of itself as unitary, discrete, and all-powerful, despite contradictions to these state effects in everyday encounters with the state (Mitchell 2006). Technologies of control, containment, and regulation operate in the surveillance-security state through policies as well as representations of surveillance as "an all-encompassing, impenetrable, and infallible surveillance structure" (Puar 2007, 152). This leads to self-regulation, and self-censorship, and in some cases citizens disciplined by neoliberal governmentality accept that they must sacrifice their freedoms for the sake of defending the nation, believing that "national security" is, indeed, their own security. This is despite the massive insecurity experienced in the middle and working classes during and since the recession, not to mention the insecurity of racialized groups who are regularly subjected to profiling, interrogation, harassment, assaults, and police violence. Some subjects engage in self-surveillance or aid in the surveillance of others, hoping to exit a profiled category through disciplinary inclusion or collusion with agents of surveillance. Yet the effects of this surveillance, through knowledge of surveillance policies as well as stories *about* surveillance and the stories of subjects produced *by* agents of surveillance, help instill fear of the powerful security-state apparatus, thus amplifying its repressive power. However, like the contradictory working of state effects, the surveillance regime also provokes the opposite effect for some, producing challenges to this apparatus of intelligence gathering and disciplining. It helps produce subjects who are aware that they are the exemplary objects of surveillance, because they fit the racial, religious, political, or national profiles currently in place, and who not only reject the rationalizations of national security but also expose the exceptionalist myths of U.S. democracy and "freedom."

Laila's story is about a moment in which the FBI had indeed targeted mosques and student groups in California and across the U.S., producing a heightened awareness and anxiety about political speech, or indeed any kind of speech, in mosqued communities and among Muslim American youth. In 2012, the stunning investigation by the Associated Press of the NYPD's surveillance program revealed that "mosque crawlers" and undercover informants, called "rakers" (generally Muslim or Arab themselves), had been deployed to ferret out suspicious Muslim and Arab Americans, including students and youth, "monitoring daily life in bookstores, bars, cafes, and nightclubs" in "suspect neighborhoods"; this was part of a "human mapping program" in cooperation with the CIA and drawing on Israeli surveillance techniques, with a reach extending beyond New York State (Associated Press 2012, 5). The NYPD also infiltrated the Occupy Wall Street movement and Palestine solidarity rallies during the Israeli war on Gaza in 2009 (Kundnani 2014, 136–138). The revelation of this infamous "demographics unit" triggered outrage among some in the general public and sparked the first mainstream discussion of surveillance since 9/11, which increased with the revelations by WikiLeaks and Edward Snowden's exposé in 2013 of mass surveillance by the secret Prism and XKeyscore programs of the NSA and CIA. But this was really just the "tip of the iceberg," as many in communities that had been targeted by the surveillance state were only too well aware (Kumar 2012, 144). Some youth at campuses that had been surveilled by the NYPD used social media, including Twitter, and subversive humor to challenge this secret program; the Yale MSA created a Facebook page, "Call the NYPD," with photos of Muslim college students holding signs declaring, "I am a . . . Blonde, Call the NYPD" (Khabeer and Alhassen 2013, 308).

The surveillance regime relies on fundamentally racialized and civilizational knowledge production as counterterrorism experts identify markers of "radicalization" that are associated not just with religion and politics, but with sociality and lifestyle (Puar and Rai 2002, 122). Key to counterradicalization and surveillance programs is a focus on "personal relationships within targeted communities," as intelligence agents focus on social networks and mapping social lives, so that "surveillance becomes intertwined with the fabric of human relationships and the threads of trust upon which they are built," undermining both collectivity and solidarity—which is by design (Kundnani 2014, 13). The counterradicalization regime has also constructed a sociopsychological model of how youth, in particular, adopt "extremist" or jihadist politics with the help of the counterterrorism industry—including think tanks, terrorism studies experts, and law enforcement—which has been influenced by Israeli approaches as well as CIA experiences during the Cold War in Afghanistan and Pakistan (Kundnani 2014, 83, 127). Law enforcement agencies, such as the New York City Police Department, have used behavioral models of "radicalization" that propose that this process takes place in four stages: "pre-radicalization, self-identification, indoctrination, and jihadization" (American-Arab Anti-Discrimination Committee 2008, 39). "Pre-radicalization" involves "religion, lifestyle, social status, neighborhood and education," factors that might lead an individual to engage in "religion seeking" and drift toward identification with "militant Islam," perhaps in the context of racism or unemployment. This crisis in identification is acknowledged as emerging from the vicissitudes of post-9/11 Islamophobia or economic struggles, but absent is any acknowledgement of frustration or outrage due to U.S. foreign policy, state violence, and criminalization. Markers of the "self-identification" stage include "urban hip-hop gangster clothes" as well as "traditional Islamic clothing, growing a beard" and involvement in "social activism and community issues" (Kundnani 2014, 134). The internet, in this model, is a "major factor in final, violent radicalization," which can happen quickly and which is generally associated with youth, particularly young Muslim males (American-Arab Anti-Discrimination Committee 2008, 40). It is striking that (Muslim) religiosity and engagement with urban (African American) youth culture are viewed as potential precursors for the final stage of what counterterrorism experts have called "jihadization"—another new term in the post-9/11 national security lexicon.

This stage-based model that presumes to chart the psychosocial, theological, and political trajectory of "jihadization" has been the basis of FBI surveillance and entrapment operations targeting Muslim American youth and youth cultures. While not all counterradicalization experts follow the model used by the NYPD's Demographics Unit, the conflation of "disaffection, youth alienation, radical dissent, [and] religious fundamentalism" is pervasive, as is the assumption that certain youth subcultures (associated with Black youth) lend themselves to the making of terrorists and must be monitored (Kundnani 2014, 120). This surveillance regime has inevitably transformed what forms of religious, political, and even cultural "self-identification" Muslim American youth perform or narrate. The NYPD's report also noted that American Muslims were apparently not as vulnerable to radicalization as European Muslims (American-Arab Anti-Discrimination Committee 2008, 39). A persistent, sweeping distinction has been made between Americans Muslims—depicted as upwardly mobile, highly educated, and relatively assimilated—and European Muslims—portrayed as alienated, disaffected, economically marginalized, and politically radical—particularly in Britain and France.[2] But after the 7/7 bombings in London in 2005, carried out by British Muslim men, the question of "homegrown terrorism" increasingly framed discussions in the U.S. of Muslim American youth, communities, and politics (Muslim Public Affairs Council 2005, 1). In 2007, Senator Joe Lieberman, chairman of the Senate Committee on Homeland Security, held a series of hearings on the "homegrown threat of violent Islamic extremist terrorism," focusing almost exclusively on Arab and Muslim Americans and dwelling on the role of the internet in fostering Islamic "extremism"; in 2011, hearings on radicalization were held by Congressman Peter King (American-Arab Anti-Discrimination Committee 2008, 39).

The U.S. also became involved in programs in Britain and Europe to contain the presumed threat of Muslim youth and to intervene in Muslim communities by promoting "moderate" Muslim artists, including rappers, to counter radicalization (Aidi 2014, 197–198). Muslim youth culture production has thus become a charged site of global surveillance and regulation of permissible politics and identities. In the U.S., the Community Partnership program was established in 2011 to "identify 'credible' voices within the American Muslim community and build an 'Alliance of Youth Movements' as a bulwark against extremism" (Aidi 2014, 214). The consolidation of the image of the "homegrown" terrorist, in contrast to the threatening specter of foreign terrorists, meant that the security apparatus is increasingly involved in defining Muslim American identities and routes of "proper" and improper socialization and politicization. The distinction between "moderate"/good and "radical"/bad Muslim subjecthood in the post-9/11 wars is thus co-constituted with the surveillance regime, which has created a racial and gendered object of surveillance, overlapping with the profiling of Black and Latino youth as deviant threats to the nation.

Digital and social media are primary arenas of surveillance as well as self-surveillance, given the electronic surveillance programs discussed above.

Muslim American youth were highly aware and self-conscious about internet surveillance well *before* the controversy over the NSA spy program and U.S. surveillance in other countries erupted into a national and global scandal. Azma, who had participated in the protests in San Jose against the Israeli war on Gaza in 2008–2009, said that her mother would talk to her on the way to school about critiques of the official narrative about 9/11: "My mom, actually when it [the 9/11 attacks] first happened, she started researching online conspiracy theories. . . . And my dad got really angry at her because he told her that the FBI could be tracking your computer, so don't do that. And so she said that if you don't want me to do it at home, I'll do it at the library, but he's, like, 'No, that's even worse!'" The fear of surveillance becomes internalized so that it produces a regulatory apparatus through auto-censorship, without the need for direct state repression. Those who understand themselves to be the targets of this repression are generally the ones to censor themselves, also an intended surveillance effect. Foucault's (1995) model of the panopticon, a system of surveillance that targets people in plain sight, produces for surveilled bodies—or bodies that *may* be surveilled—the "principles of [their] own subjection" to technologies of management and regulation of population, without the need for coercion. This then produces a blurring of the line between "who is watching and who is being watched," through diffuse mechanisms of control and the "affective resonance" of surveillance effects—fear, paranoia, anxiety, vigilance, frustration, outrage, or bravado (Puar 2007, 129).

I argue that "surveillance stories," such as those narrated by Azma and Laila, help do the regulatory work of surveillance in deepening anxieties and producing self-regulation among those who are the objects of surveillance, by virtue of their race, religion, nationality, citizenship status, or political activities. The point is that the immigrant father who worries that his wife's computer may be surveilled by the FBI or that research on 9/11 at the library is risky is not simply "paranoid," but expressing political subjecthood in a surveillance state, and knowledge of the racialization of panopticism. Undocumented and immigrant youth are also clearly aware that they are objects of surveillance—as are young men of color subjected to daily profiling by the police—in a moment in which Immigration and Customs Enforcement is part of the Department of Homeland Security and immigration officials cooperate closely with local law enforcement. But particularly since Snowden's leaks regarding mass surveillance, which shook the U.S. government and shocked the general public, surveillance stories are now understood as being part of the lives not only of surveillable populations—Muslims, Arabs, Pakistanis, Afghans, Chechens, and so on—but of all Americans: an American story, which is why it was so unsettling for many who had not been as ruffled by earlier revelations of surveillance of Muslim Americans. Surveillance is not a new story, obviously, and reminds those who are old enough to remember COIN-TELPRO and the McCarthy era that the excesses of the FBI and police surveillance were investigated by the Church Committee of 1976 and supposed to have been curtailed by the Handschu agreement of 1985; however, in 2003, these provisions were relaxed, and new programs were created for gathering and sharing intelligence about noncriminal activities and daily behavior.[3]

Furthermore, it is worth pausing to consider Azma's story of her mother's presumably surveillable research on "conspiracy theories" about 9/11. So-called conspiracy theories, as Jodi Dean (2009) argues, can rupture the circuit of racialized surveillance and violence to the extent that they challenge the mythology of the liberal democratic state and suggest, however creatively or fictively, the possibilities that national security is only a cover for the state's strategic interests, allowing publics to consider the notion of secrecy as constitutive of the surveillance-warfare state. That is, the more bizarre "conspiracy" is the actual web of secrecy linking the covert programs and policies of the deep state, which exists as much in the U.S. as in other militarized states branded as repressive, such as Egypt and Pakistan. The unofficial narratives about the "truth" of 9/11 may seem wild and are often unsubstantiated but, at the least, they suggest that truth is often stranger than fiction, as are stories of surveillance.

To take just one example, the Associated Press discovered that the NYPD "trawled daily through student websites run by Muslim student groups at Yale, the University of Pennsylvania, Rutgers and 13 other colleges in the Northeast. They talked with local authorities about professors in Buffalo and even sent an undercover agent on a whitewater rafting trip, where he recorded students' names and noted in police intelligence files how many times they prayed."[4] So the student who worries that her email is being surveilled or the immigrant father who is anxious that his wife's computer searches at the library may be monitored—let alone that an FBI informant may be accompanying his child to go whitewater rafting—cannot be dismissed as "paranoid," for this is an expression of the political subjecthood of life in a surveillance state, and of knowledge of the racialized technologies of panopticism. Conspiracy theories that go against the grain of official narratives, however, are generally dismissed by the intellectual left and evaluated through an ideological and racialized discourse that pins them onto "loony" radicals or peoples from the global South and "undemocratic" areas of the world, all "fringe" elements of modern societies assumed to be bubbling with irrational accounts of state power. Yet power works in mysterious ways and usually at the expense of ordinary lives. Surveillance stories, such as those narrated by Laila and Azma, help do the work of surveillance in deepening everyday anxieties and produc-

ing self-regulation and self-censorship in those who are the objects of surveillance, by virtue of their race, religion, or nationality, but they can also
produce a critical consciousness about surveillance. How then, do cultures of
surveillance, or surveillance effects, shape the politics and daily lives of those
who are produced as objects of the surveillance regimes?

My Friend "Joe" and Me: The Everyday of Surveillance

One of the ways in which political imaginaries, and imaginings of self, are
shaped by surveillance effects is through normalization of surveillance among
its objects (not to mention its agents); this is a social and a psychic shift,
and has a strategic effect. It is striking, and troubling, to note the extent to
which encounters with the FBI have become part of the everyday lexicon
of South Asian, Arab, and Afghan Americans after 9/11, and the degree to
which knowledge of surveillance has become part of social life. FBI agents,
not to mention undercover informants, are now just another set of state officials and agents whom Arab, South Asian, and Afghan Americans, as well as
Muslim Americans more generally, must anticipate encountering at any time.
This routine experience should be considered highly "abnormal" in a liberal
democratic state professing to be the beacon of democracy and civil rights,
needless to say.

Community activists I spoke to recounted stories of FBI agents who regularly, and often overtly, attended Muslim American events and trolled the
mosques in the area. One Pakistani immigrant activist from Silicon Valley,
who had been involved with civil rights and antiwar organizing, told me that
she saw an FBI agent (who went by the name of "Dave") at MCA. She mentioned that FBI agents had apparently been following her around after 9/11.
This surveillance began, she said, after she challenged them at a public event
where agents spoke about how the Bureau was trying to "protect" the Muslim American community. Citing the FBI surveillance and infiltration of the
Pakistani American community in Lodi, California, after 9/11 and cases of
entrapment of young Muslim American men such as Hamid Hayat, she asked
them directly, "Are you trying to resolve a problem or create a problem?" The
FBI agents did not seem happy about this question. The 2005 case of Hamid
Hayat involved a Pakistani informant for the FBI who befriended a young
Pakistani American man from Lodi and urged him to engage in "jihad," a
pattern that has been replicated in numerous other cases of FBI entrapment of
young Muslim men around the country, such as Faisal Shahzad and Shahawar
Matin Siraj (Adams 2010; Kumar 2010); Hayat was eventually found guilty of
"material support" for terrorism and sentenced to thirty-nine years in prison,

and the Lodi community was besieged by the FBI (Maira 2007). The Pakistani activist spoke to me about her exchange with the FBI with aplomb and a sense of humor, but it was evident that she was frustrated and suspected that she was being surveilled because of her activism around civil rights, and also her direct challenge to the FBI in public. Furthermore, when objects of surveillance can turn into subjects of surveillance, as Muslim Americans are recruited as FBI informants, there is increasing distrust and anxiety about who is really who, dissolving the very bonds that targeted communities most need for solidarity and collective mobilization—an intended effect of technologies of surveillance in a politically repressive state.

Another "surveillance story" brought home to me the ways in which South Asians, Arabs, Afghans, and others in the U.S. produce their own knowledge of the military-spy state, which must be considered in addition to official information and exposés about policies of covert surveillance. I met Zahida, an Afghan American woman, who went to high school in Hayward and worked as a realtor in Fremont, at a fundraiser for an Afghan relief program in the Bay Area with which she was involved. I visited her one evening in her home in a low-rise apartment complex in Fremont, where Zahida said 93% of the residents were South Asian. Sipping tea in her living room, decorated with a red-and-orange Afghan rug, the conversation turned to her "friend Joe," an FBI agent who had been contacting Afghan Americans in the area. Zahida said animatedly,

> He talks to everyone, people kept telling me, Joe called me, and I said, "Who's this Joe?" And he was going to the mosque, he was coming to every event and then he wanted to know about my charity. So I got his number and called him up and said, "What is this? Are you following me?" So we met and we talked and he said, "You are the most outspoken woman, so I wanted to talk to you." And one time, he came with his gun and I said, "I don't want you sitting here with a gun, you need to leave that behind!"

As Zahida told me this story, one of her young daughters watched TV and the other served me snacks. While I am not sure how much they were paying attention to the details, neither daughter flinched or batted an eyelid while their mother laughingly recounted her surveillance by agent "Joe." Zahida was alternatively witty and outraged while recounting tales of surveillance, the impact of the U.S. occupation on Afghanistan, and the Afghan community in Fremont/Hayward. She added, "He is Filipino, but I know his real name is not Joe! And now he's following the Somalis." Zahida's surveillance story, which was chilling in its matter-of-factness, as well as others I heard underscore how Afghan, Arab, and South Asian Muslim Americans have come to understand that they are surveillable populations, by virtue of their national and religious identities as well as political experiences or knowledge, and are sometimes surveilled by other minoritized individuals. It also illuminates the ways in which humanitarian projects, such as the Afghan relief program with which Zahida was involved, have come under regular surveillance so that humanitarianism and human rights campaigns focused on certain racialized regions of the world are suspect and criminalized, as discussed in the previous chapters.

As in the case of the Pakistani American community activist, Zahida narrated this story with bravado and emphasized her lack of fear, which had apparently registered with intelligence agents. She managed to flip the experience of questioning/questioned around by contacting the FBI agent herself and challenging the production of objects of surveillance—Afghans, Iraqis, Iranians, Somalis—from communities linked to U.S. overseas wars, occupations, and (proxy) interventions. If FBI agents (or, increasingly, even local law enforcement officers) can engage in preemptive surveillance, then Zahida's story suggests that the objects of surveillance can try and preempt the encounter.

The focus in the War on Terror on preemptive surveillance is based on racialized mappings of communities and the incitement of "terrorist" affiliations and plots through entrapment. These profiling and sting operations are part of a strategy of what is called "preventative" or "anticipatory prosecution" (Sherman 2009). A 2014 study found that "the vast majority of arrests in the war on terror" (between 2001 and 2010) were cases of preemptive prosecution based on "suspicion of the defendant's ideology and not on his/her criminal activity" or incidents where the government manipulated nonterrorist criminal activities; these included cases involving arrests for "material support of terrorism," which criminalize "charitable giving and management, free speech, free association, peace-making, and social hospitality" (Downs and Manley 2014, 1–2). As a result of this pattern of predatory prosecution, or "lawfare," South Asian, Arab and Afghan Americans live in what Nguyen (2012) calls a "preemptive present" of permanent surveillance (167). Zahida tried to preempt the revelation of this present, and called on "Joe" to appear before her, making a disembodied experience of surveillance an embodied one that she could confront and co-produce. The disciplining effects of surveillance regimes are countered through attempts to rescript the theater of the preemptive present, through claiming the intimacy of surveillance effects as one's own ("my friend," the FBI agent). However, this story of surveillance effects still suggests a process of normalization, if a self-protective one, and of regulating one's political subjectivity in relation to the regularization of the "superpanopticon"—the new form of electronic surveillance made possible by technologies that produce new forms of power (Poster 1990).

A Pakistani American professional, Farrukh Shah Khan, who founded the Pakistani American Culture Center (PACC) in Silicon Valley, shared with me his reflections on what it means to live with the panopticon or superpanopticon—which I consider an allegory about the affective dimension of surveillance effects. I met Khan in the small office where the PACC was first housed, a simple two-room suite in an office building in Milpitas, used by the center to host talks and film screenings. He talked about how "scared" the Pakistani and Muslim American community was after 9/11 and how people he knew became "afraid to go to masjids" because they knew that mosques were being surveilled and infiltrated by FBI informants. There was a reshaping of social life and social networks due to these surveillance effects. Khan said he began thinking about the film *The Matrix*, where the hero "escapes capture by 'the system'" with the help of "renegade, or 'good' people." In his view, the security apparatus after 9/11 was a "system trying to track connections with other Muslims," producing a sense of fear and isolation. He said,

> After 9/11, I was sitting in my cubicle and hearing a security guard walking outside, and I would think, they're coming to get me, and I have no one coming to help me. If I had a cop behind me, I would think—if he stops me, this is what I would say. Others were also in this *Matrix*-type situation of targeting by the system, but I was not too much involved in going to masjids. But I would lie awake at night thinking, what if I'm coming back to Florida [where he lived previously], and I'm stopped by the FBI at the airport? I felt so cornered that I decided to fight back. Anything they said, "Don't do," I did! I went public, I started a TV show, I started a business. I felt if I was silent and I disappeared, no one would know. The Matrix image really stuck with me.

Khan's allegory of post-9/11 life drawing on *The Matrix* is a moving one, for he paints a vivid picture of the anxiety and loneliness of Muslim Americans in Silicon Valley, sitting alone in their cubicles and feeling overwhelmed by their powerlessness and subjection to surveillance regimes. Khan argues that there is no escape from the system other than standing in full view of the panopticon. Turning the spotlight on himself, by inserting himself into the media with his own show and organizing public events for the local Pakistani American community, is a tactic of countersurveillance that Khan suggests works on two levels: one, by recording himself before, or at the same time, he assumes he is being recorded or surveilled by the state; and two, by expanding and transforming the audience for his surveillance, he creates a network of support and solidarity that could intervene on his behalf if he were, one day, to be disappeared. Self-surveillance thus becomes a way to counter, deflect, or preempt preemptive surveillance and policing by resisting the very disappearance of the object of surveillance. In a similar vein, the Bangladeshi American artist Hasan Elahi produced a digital art project that poignantly critiques this co-production of the self through surveillance. After he was detained in 2002 and found out he was on a terrorist watch list, he created an online installation that recorded all of his daily activities and whereabouts, titled *Hiding in Plain Sight*. Commenting on this work of surveillance from below, or sous-veillance, Elahi noted that the CIA and Pentagon are some of the visitors to his site: "So I'm looking at who's looking at me looking at me."[5]

In the face of increasing FBI scrutiny of Muslim Americans, and surveillance of Somalis, Afghans, Arabs, Pakistanis, and others in northern California, various campaigns have been launched to challenge superpanopticism and its chilling, regulatory effects on surveillable subjects. For example, a coalition of civil rights groups in San Francisco discovered that the San Francisco Police Department (SFPD) had signed a secret agreement with the FBI in 2007 that assigned local police to work directly with the Joint Terrorism Training Task Force (JTTF) without civilian oversight (Dubal 2012, 47–49). The Coalition for a Safe San Francisco challenged the SFPD and held hearings in 2010 on racial and ethnic profiling and surveillance by the FBI, which included testimonials from local community members (including Arab Americans from San Jose) and ultimately overturned the secret SFPD-JTTF agreement. In San Jose, civil rights organizations spoke out in public forums in 2011 against collaboration between the San Jose police and the Department of Homeland Security; in 2014, the San Jose Peace and Justice Center organized a campaign against the SJPD's purchase of a drone for aerial surveillance, which if deployed would make San Jose the first city in the Bay Area to have a drone flying overhead.[6] These campaigns, framed in the language of civil liberties and antiracism, reveal an archive of "surveillance stories" that has steadily accumulated over a decade and strategies of countersurveillance that are both organized and public as well as private, individualized, and in the everyday of surveillance.[7]

The Surveilled Counter Surveillance

Strategies of countersurveillance have been used by civil rights campaigns and by young people who are the objects of surveillance, making surveillance itself the object. For example, the CLEAR (Creating Law Enforcement

Accountability and Responsibility) Project, based at the City University of
New York School of Law, offers legal representation and consultation to Muslim, Arab, and South Asian communities targeted by national security and
counterterrorism policies and facing requests for FBI interviews, searches
by law enforcement, and border profiling while traveling overseas.[8] Ramzi
Kassem, a civil and immigrant rights attorney who supervises the project, observed that in some cases, clients from communities targeted by law
enforcement videotape the FBI agents knocking on their doors and asking for
interviews, recording and documenting acts of surveillance.[9] Other instances
of countersurveillance have dramatically highlighted the often Kafkaesque
irony and painful absurdity of the reaches of the surveillance regime. One of
the most bizarre cases of surveillance of Muslim American youth occurred in
Silicon Valley in 2010, involving a twenty-year-old Egyptian American college
student from Santa Clara, Yasser Afifi, who became the center of a storm of
outrage over FBI surveillance. A student of business marketing at Mission
College in Silicon Valley, whose father was a Muslim American community
leader and who had lived in Egypt for a few years, Afifi took his car for an oil
change one day to a local garage, Ali's Auto Clinic. To his surprise, he found
a wire sticking out of his car at the back. The garage owner pulled it out and
they found themselves looking at a device connected to a battery pack and
transmitter that had been attached underneath the car.[10]

Afifi went home and showed the strange contraption to his friend Khaled,
who photographed it and posted the pictures online, commenting, "My plan
was to just put the device on another car or in a lake, but when you come
home to 2 stoned off-their-asses people who are hearing things in the device and convinced it's a bomb you just gotta be sure." A reader of the online
post quickly identified it as an Orion Guardian ST820 tracking device. Afifi
contemplated putting it up for sale on Craigslist, but forty-eight hours later,
the FBI came to Afifi's house and interrogated him, asking if he'd ever been
to Yemen for "training." They then demanded the device back, saying, "It's
federal property. It's an expensive piece, and we need it right now."[11] Before
returning the tracking device, Afifi retorted by asking if they had a search
warrant. As he tried to question the FBI agents, it became clear that he had
been under surveillance and his phone and email communications were
probably being monitored (cited in Malek 2011). Video reports of the story
that circulated online, some produced by white American youth, featured
incredulous and shocked commentaries that such surveillance could be directed at a U.S. citizen "just because he was half Egyptian," underscoring the
racial, religious, and national dimensions of the production of citizens and
subjects fit for surveillance.[12]

The GPS incident involving Afifi occurred just after a 9th U.S. Circuit Court of Appeals had ruled that it was legal for law enforcement to place tracking devices on cars without a warrant, even if in a private driveway (this was challenged, and in 2012 the Supreme Court ruled in *United States v. Jones* that the placement of a GPS device was a violation of reasonable expectations of privacy and the Fourth Amendment).[13] The Fred Korematsu Civil Rights Project at the Asian Law Caucus in San Francisco, which works with Arab, Muslim, and South Asian communities, has clients who also reported discoveries of tracking devices under their cars, including a Yemeni immigrant man in the Bay Area (just as the U.S. war and drone attacks against Al Qaeda in Yemen exploded). I recount the case of Afifi here in some detail not simply because it illustrates the extent of intrusion of surveillance technologies into the daily lives of Muslim and Arab American youth, and the intimacy of surveillance and its regularization, but also because it demonstrates the use of technology by youth to investigate the surveillance apparatus themselves. Afifi's encounter with the FBI also demonstrates the extent to which knowledge of civil rights and how to interact with intelligence and law enforcement agents has permeated this generation of Muslim and Arab Americans, who have grown up going to Know Your Rights workshops at mosques and in their communities. Notwithstanding the irony of the FBI's response to Afifi's online exposé, this surveillance story also underscores the production of various affective responses by youth in the numerous news reports and videos about the incident: the tongue-in-cheek, Harold-and-Kumar style bravado and sauciness of Afifi's friend; the outrage of white American youth that other young people could be racially profiled in the U.S.; and the calm but determined expression of Afifi as he recounted the story for media outlets, reenacting a day in the life of a surveilled subject.

Afifi later filed a Freedom of Information Act (FOIA) request with the government to try to uncover the reasons for the surveillance, realizing that he had been tracked for several months, but the file he received revealed nothing. In 2011, CAIR filed a lawsuit against the FBI on his behalf. A video announcing the lawsuit features several young lawyers and advocates talking about the significance of the case, including the young director of CAIR–Bay Area, Zahra Billoo, who remarked that the case was a fight for the civil rights not just of Muslim Americans, but of all Americans.[14] In this video, Afifi looks confident but slightly more tense than in his earlier media appearances; he comments that he knew he must fit some sort of intelligence profile, given that he had sent money and made phone calls to Egypt, where he had traveled and where his younger brothers live. Surveillance effects, and their affective registers, reveal what is at stake here: the livelihood, and lives, of young people and their families who could be in danger if they fit "the profile," as well as the belief that surveillance must be resisted, including through the law. Those who lead legal campaigns countering surveillance such as this see themselves as testing citizen rights and civil rights on behalf of all Americans and in confrontation with the national security state.

There are other cases in which objects of surveillance have exposed agents of surveillance. For example, in Irvine, members of the mosque informed the FBI of an informant who made provocative statements about jihad.[15] Students at UC Irvine have also been subjected to surveillance, an issue that gained greater attention with the Irvine Eleven case in 2009 and the criminalization of Palestine solidarity activists. In the wake of this case, students began staging silent protests nationwide at events featuring Israeli soldiers defending Israeli wars, walking out with their mouths taped, to highlight the repression of critiques of U.S.-backed Israeli state terror and to dramatize the gap in the discourse of freedom of expression and democracy through strategic political performance. So there is a quick education in the methods of the surveillance state that produces new repertoires of creative tactics by youth. There is also an awareness that the surveillance state and regimes of terror are globalized, as Afifi suggests, and that the U.S. and its allies are part of a transnational apparatus of surveillance, policing, and repression that is resisted by global solidarity movements and networks of youth, from Santa Clara to Cairo and from Ferguson, Missouri, to Gaza, Palestine.[16]

There is a gendered politics at stake in post-9/11 surveillance, given the state's investment in policing and profiling Muslim and Arab males in the War on Terror. The focus on the radicalization of young Muslim and Middle Eastern men as threats to "homeland security" means that expressions of bravado, anxiety, courage, or subversive humor are filtered through an often heightened self-consciousness by young men about what it means to embody the terror threat in the U.S. today. Some youth also spoke to me about how young Muslim American women lawyers working on civil rights, in some cases self-consciously, challenge Orientalist notions of Muslim femininities by being visibly outspoken and assertive, yet by doing so they may still be responding to the Orientalist framework of gendered representation (see Mir 2014). The gendered profile of Muslim and Arab terrorism is not watertight as the surveillance state targets young women as well, if less commonly. In 2005, FBI agents raided the bedroom of a sixteen-year-old Bangladeshi girl from New York, Tashnuba Hayder, who had been subjected to electronic surveillance. Hayder was deported after writing an essay on religious views of suicide and visiting radical Islamic internet sites, without any evidence linking her to any terrorist activity. She was detained with another sixteen-year-old

Muslim girl, Adama Bah, an undocumented immigrant from Guinea, who had attended the same mosque and was also interrogated about terrorism (Malek 2011). Hayder's case was the first terrorist investigation that involved a minor, yet these shocking stories receive relatively little attention.[17]

What is striking about this little-discussed case is that the FBI agents who raided Hayder's room (one of whom was a British Muslim woman) posed as youth counselors, and they used her home-school essays as evidence in her arrest, claiming that it was suspicious that the teenager, a devout Muslim who wore the hijab, was a "loner," not involved in typical teenage activities or subcultures. So state surveillance rests also on profiles of youth culture and on sociality, on what it means to be a typical American teenager in contrast to an "anti-American" and "self-radicalized" young Muslim.[18] A teenager's bedroom décor or essays about the Department of Homeland Security (as in Hayder's case) or nonnormative teenage masculinities (as in media representations of John Walker Lindh, the "American Taliban" from Marin County) are all indices of terrorist "tendencies" (Alsultany 2012, 110–111). There is an acute self-awareness, as a result, among young people who are targets of the panoptic state that their every cultural and religious expression is fit for surveillance and scrutiny as signals of whether they meet the definition of proper American youthfulness.

One way that youth who are in the bull's-eye of the surveillance state respond to the perceived stigma of profiling or surveillance as suspect bodies is to turn their experience of surveillance into an achievement—a badge of honor rather than a stigma. Jamil, an Indian Muslim American who was born in San Jose, and whose mother is Indian–South African, had attended Granada and San Jose high school. He then transferred from a community college in the South Bay to a UC campus, and had grown up going to MCA with his friends, which he described as a "home base." Jamil commented on his awareness of post-9/11 surveillance:

> It's definitely crazy at times, like okay, one crazy story—after 9/11, our house was bugged and there was a van outside of our house forever. They rigged the phone lines. Because my dad was involved with CAIR and the family was tied with CAIR because he's a Muslim leader or whatever. And I know a couple of other kids I hung out with, their parents were also really active and they were, like, "Yeah, we also heard it too." So how we noticed it was because on our court, there's only three houses and we know both of our neighbors and we know everyone's car. So there's this weird van sitting in front of our house and . . . we could hear this weird clicking noise in the phone, like, we knew they were listening. After about a year or so they kind of . . . went away, I don't know why.

Jamil's narrative illustrates the attempt by youth to make meaning of "crazy" times and the ever-present possibility of surveillance at your doorstep and in your neighborhood. Even if electronic wiretapping today no longer always produces the proverbial "clicks" on the telephone line, reports have revealed that FBI agents have indeed been stationed in neighborhoods with concentrations of Muslim Americans and targeted community leaders (Maira 2007). It is crucial to read this not simply as an empirical account of knowledge of surveillance technologies but rather as knowledge of the *intimacy* of the state's intrusions into everyday life, perhaps drawing on previous histories of what it meant to be surveilled. Surveillance effects involve attempts to make meaning of and narrate surveillance through sedimented knowledge of stories that have circulated since the McCarthy era, as well as immigrant experiences of surveillance in other countries. Jamil's story also illustrates the awareness of the experience of surveillability, since Muslim American community leaders such as his father, who were publicly engaged in civil rights organizations such as CAIR, were indeed likely to be surveilled. This narrative might be read by some as an expression of post-9/11 paranoid hyperbole, but at a moment when young people were finding GPS devices on their cars, it is apparent that the stranger-than-fiction quality of life in the surveillance state demands meaning-making accounts, searches for explanations in the face of the absence of explanations and the absurdist narratives of profiling and surveillance (Žižek 2002, 9–19).

Jamil went on to recall his experiences at MCA:

> Especially at MCA, when I drove down, on the right pole there was a huge beige box with three or four antennas, and they used to be listening into MCA through that box. My brother used to do rounds at security and he was like, "What is that box?" and they were like, "It must be the FBI." And apparently there was FBI listening across the street. It was actually a good thing because we got a lot of bomb threats, and so we had officers across the street. In a way they were kind of watching our back even though they were listening in on us! I wasn't there [at MCA] that day but my brother was and they had a bomb scare and had to evacuate the entire building. After 9/11, we got all the threatening phone calls and hate messages or whatever. I just heard they brought in the bomb squad. It was just crazy. . . . And it wasn't like a badge of shame it was like, "Yeah, the FBI is listening into *my* house."

Jamil offers a doubly ironic twist on the state's logic of surveillance of Muslim Americans in the War on Terror: on the one hand, that the presence of the FBI, even if covert, could potentially provide security in the face of Islamophobic bomb threats that had been directed at the MCA and other masjids in northern California and across the United States. This, of course, suggests that law enforcement officials would actually spring into action and protect Muslim American communities, but the lightness of Jamil's tone also suggested to me that this was an attempt to reframe and subvert the dominant discourse of counterterrorism with irony, to suggest that it was Islamophobic and xenophobic racists who were the threat to security and not Muslim or Arab Americans.

On the other hand, there is also the subversive logic in which surveillance becomes not a "badge of shame" but a badge of honor, a sign of achievement. So, for Jamil, his family warranted surveillance because of his father's leadership in CAIR, and other youth could also possibly be objects of surveillance because their families were politically "active." This inversion of the stigmatization of surveillance is perhaps also an affective or psychic strategy to deal with the anxiety of imagining oneself as an object of surveillance, by claiming the political agency of surveillance and reasserting the need to continue to engage in dissenting politics, despite and in some cases *because* of the climate of repression after 9/11. Surveillability becomes an index of the political significance of the object of surveillance, an interesting example of the implications of surveillance effects for post-9/11 political subjecthood and Muslim American youth culture. Jamil and other youth renarrated their surveillability as "radical" political subjects, acknowledging the need for public politics and challenging the racialized surveillance regime, but at the same time, potentially normalizing the surveillance regime. These are the paradoxes of surveillance effects for youth coming of age in the military-spy state.

Resistance and Coalitions: Stop the FBI

The proliferating reports of surveillance of Muslim American, antiwar, Palestine solidarity, and also animal rights activists have established the ongoing link between state surveillance and political repression and provoked coalitions to protest surveillance. One of the well-known cases of surveillance that involved antiwar activists from Silicon Valley and that sent ripples of outrage and anxiety through progressive movements across the nation, including among young activists, was the FBI raids and grand jury subpoenas of labor and antiwar activists from Minneapolis, Chicago, and later San Jose. In September 2010, Masao Suzuki, a Japanese American college professor and progressive activist from San Jose, found an FBI agent outside his door, "an African American gentleman" who "flashed his badge" and wanted to talk to him and his wife. Suzuki reminisced when we met in January 2011 at a café in Berkeley that his leftist parents had been targeted during the McCarthy era by the House Un-American Activities Committee, and he had grown up going to anti–Vietnam war rallies and farm worker organizing meetings in the Bay Area. As an adult, he became involved in Japanese American activism and resistance to police repression in Los Angeles. Perhaps this experience with movements confronting the surveillance state since the Cold War put him in good stead, for he refused to be interviewed by the FBI agent and immediately informed his friends, neighbors, and work supervisor that the FBI was asking about him. Suzuki got a phone call in the midst of this outreach from an activist in Minneapolis letting him know that the FBI had just raided the homes of several antiwar activists there. By the end of that day, seventy FBI agents had served subpoenas to activists in Minneapolis, Chicago, and Grand Rapids, and had seized documents, passports, cell phones, and family photos, looking for evidence of "material support to terrorism."[19] In the following weeks, twenty-three antiwar, labor, and solidarity activists who had been involved with organizing related to human rights in Columbia and Palestine had been issued subpoenas to appear before a grand jury.[20]

Suzuki observed that everyone who had been targeted in the first round of FBI raids had been involved in organizing protests against the Republican National Convention in Minneapolis in 2008; other activists who had been targeted had visited Palestine or Columbia and were active in the antiwar and trade union movement. Eventually, they discovered that the Twin Cities–based Anti-War Committee had been infiltrated by an undercover agent who had also later joined the Freedom Road Socialist Organization. The activists, all seasoned left organizers, sprang into action and launched a highly successful campaign, the Committee to Stop FBI Repression, that held meetings and protests across the country, galvanizing a public outcry that included statements by prominent elected officials and local events opposing the FBI raids and subpoenas.[21] The campaign also organized a national conference in November 2011 and helped create a coalition linking the antiwar, labor, civil rights, and Palestine and Colombia solidarity movements. These cross-movement alliances were apparent to me at a regional conference of the Committee to Stop FBI Repression in Oakland in 2011, which was attended by several young Arab, South Asian and Muslim American activists, as well as other progressive-left activists who helped spark a movement against surveillance that grew in subsequent years.

In January 2011, I attended a Stop the FBI rally in downtown San Jose organized by the South Bay Committee against Political Repression, in which Suzuki was a prominent organizer. At the protest, which was held outside the Martin Luther King, Jr., Library at San Jose State, a small but ethnically diverse crowd of various ages chanted slogans as passing cars occasionally honked in support. The Raging Grannies, three older women in whimsical hats, sang satirical ditties about FBI repression—such as "The FBI Is Coming to Town," to the tune of "Santa Claus Is Coming to Town"—led by an Asian American woman wearing a necklace strung with peace symbols. The speakers included a young female MC; an older white labor activist, who made the connection between the FBI raids and the targeting of socialists during the Palmer raids of the 1920s; and Suzuki, who said that the campaign was important for him given the history of profiling of Japanese Americans imprisoned during World War II and the present-day suspicion of Muslim Americans. Sharat Lin, an Asian American community activist who was then director of the San Jose Peace and Justice Center, situated the FBI raids in the context of the U.S. wars on Afghanistan and Iraq, the detention of up to five thousand Muslims in the U.S. after 9/11, and the need for "real democracy" in the United States. It was clear that the protesters were trying to make connections between the domestic and global fronts of the U.S. War on Terror, and also between regimes of repression and surveillance across time. As they marched through downtown San Jose, the Raging Grannies led chants against FBI profiling, yelling, "U.S., hands off Afghanistan! U.S, hands off Palestine! U.S., hands off Yemen!"

This protest was just one of many involving activists from the Committee to Stop FBI Repression in the Bay Area and across the country, some in front of FBI and federal offices, highlighting the local alliances forged by activists in opposition to the surveillance state. However, this movement also highlighted for me the difficulties of mobilization among those targeted most systematically for surveillance and those who did not belong to organized political movements. It was striking that the most well-organized, and perhaps also well-publicized, national campaign against the FBI until that moment was launched by labor and antiwar activists who were largely white Americans, as well as solidarity activists who had been targeted in the Midwest (including Arab American activist Hatem Abudayyah and Vietnamese American Anh Pham). This was not surprising, for these were veteran activists who used their organizing skills and resources to unleash a highly effective campaign that forged alliances between various political and ethnic communities on the ground and made linkages among different forms of state surveillance, profiling, repression, and violence. But I noticed that there were few South Asian, Arab, or Afghan Americans at the rally in San Jose that day, including youth, which was probably due to the hesitation and anxiety about public protest in communities that had been in the crosshairs of the surveillance state for many years. Furthermore, it is important to acknowledge that dissent is manifested not only at street protests, and "politics" must be considered more broadly, especially for youth and in a military-spy state. As Asef Bayat (2013) argues, "non-movements" based on quiet encroachments and "widespread collective (if fragmented) practices" are effective in enabling participants to escape detection in a climate of political repression and hypersurveillance (28–29), as in Egypt or Iran. In the U.S., too, it is crucial to look beyond spectacular protest actions to consider the everyday tactics and affective strategies developed by youth as acts of counter-surveillance.

Surveillance produces politicization in various forms among the 9/11 generation, with young people such as Afifi becoming public activists in legal campaigns challenging surveillance and profiling and many more, such as Jamil and Azma, tracking or on the watch for political surveillance. Young Arab, South Asian, and Afghan American activists were well aware of the impact of surveillance on their own political organizing. For example, Aisha recalled the campus surveillance of student-labor organizing in which she had been involved: "Campus police were out with cameras when we were holding rallies and sit-ins. You wondered how much of it was going back to the administration? SOC [Students Organizing for Change] provided a space to assert ourselves politically but it also revealed repression. Was it going back to the FBI?" Aisha observed that this knowledge of surveillance and repression, by campus police in this case, was in fact a key element in her politicization.

I want to point out that oppositional movements reveal the repressiveness of the state, as in the Stop the FBI campaign, which then helps expose the repressiveness of liberal democracy, so surveillance is an important site of resistance. Badiou (2005) argues that the exposure of repression is crucial for resistance to state power which must be defined, if it is to be resisted:

> [W]henever there is a genuinely political event, the State reveals itself. It reveals its excess of power, its repressive dimension. But it also reveals a measure for this invisible excess. For it is essential to the normal functioning of the State that its power remains measureless, errant, unassignable. The political event puts an end to all this by assigning a visible measure to the excessive power of the State. (145)

This is a twist on Foucault's axiom that where there is power, there is resistance, for Badiou suggests where there is resistance, power and (the extent of) repression is revealed. So what Badiou calls "genuinely political events" produced, for instance, by the mobilization of the Palestine or antiwar movement interrupt state power by revealing the extent of its errancy and the depth of its repression.

While Badiou's argument is important in thinking about the role of countersurveillance, both public and private, in challenging illusions of freedom in liberal democracy and exposing the power of the police state, Aisha and other youth also worried about the practical impact of repression on their lives and education. The measureless repressiveness and invisible excesses of the surveillance state clearly produce fear and have an impact on political organizing and concerns about employment. For example, Aisha wondered of the surveillance of campus protests,

> Was it going back to the FBI? We were getting arrested—would it limit our prospects for getting a job? I know petitions are part of the information age, which means you put signatures, and also photos on the Web. We were part of the radical left but we were also trying to be part of the system, we wanted jobs for our economic livelihood. So we had to be strategic about how to assert our political views, we started signing petitions as organizations rather than as individuals. We were worried about going to graduate school.

Aisha's comments speak to the ways in which students worried about the implications of reprisals for their careers, and also for organizing strategies and methods, concerns not to be taken lightly given the surveillance programs discussed here as well as the profusion of blacklists of faculty and students involved in Palestine solidarity and BDS campaigns. It is apparent that awareness of surveillance has shaped the political culture of student organizing in the post-9/11 era and that there is a cautiousness in this generation, supposedly the pioneers of Facebook activism, about the possibilities that social media offer for both virtual organizing and electronic surveillance (Isin and Ruppert 2015).[22] Abed also described his peers' self-awareness about producing statements or internet postings that could be taken out of context and used against them in the "internet age" of rapid dissemination of information about political campaigns, a double-edged sword that slices through the debates about the potential and pitfall of internet-based activism. Many Muslim, South Asian, or Arab American activists explicitly acknowledged, and often jokingly commented on, possible surveillance of their email communication, internet listservs, and Facebook pages, and some began resorting to face-to-face conversations for planning campaigns or discussing sensitive issues—old-school methods from the COINTELPRO era. One young Palestinian American woman who was an activist with Arab Youth Organizing, said she decided not to use a cell phone or Facebook for six months, because she strongly suspected that she was being surveilled and wanted to get off the grid as much as possible. So, in fact, technology and social media have become a site of danger, of *excessive* knowledge production of surveillance by and about young people who are targets in the War on Terror.

218 | COMING OF AGE UNDER SURVEILLANCE

However, it seemed from my conversations and online discussions with young activists that most simply took their surveillability for granted, and that this was integral to their political subjecthood, not something to be denied, deflected, or deferred. There is no outside to panopticism and the digital panopticon, by definition. In this vein, Jawad Rasul, a New York City college student, spoke publicly about the impact of surveillance by the NYPD on his daily life, as quoted in one report:

> [The] experiences of being trailed by two different informants has changed how he acts in the day to day. To get ahead of those watching him, Rasul says he's tried to be as transparent as he can about his life. "What I do is constantly update my Facebook profile because someone told me that the anti-terror and other law enforcement agencies don't like surprises. So to keep the pressure off me I update everything on my wall with anything I am doing because I know they are most likely watching me.'"[23]

Social networking and social life for youth have been transformed and have to be renarrated and rescripted in the encounter with everyday surveillance. It is apparent that in the post-9/11 era social selves are, to varying extents, co-produced with the surveillance state. But this self-conscious production of selfhood for the military-spy state, it must be emphasized, is deeply racialized. It is a phenomenon that larger publics in the U.S. are generally not aware of, or at least not as willing to resign themselves to if they are knowledgeable about state surveillance, given that it shatters the mythology of U.S. liberal democracy, which must be continually defended, especially in a moment of imperial decline.

The racial dimensions and also imperial politics of surveillance remain obscured in the debate about post-9/11 surveillance. Libertarians vocally oppose surveillance but as an intrusion into individual privacy and an assault on individual freedom, tied to the freedom of the neoliberal marketplace. The incremental revelations of post-9/11 state surveillance have produced unlikely alliances with conservatives in the culture wars but do so often by suppressing a critique of imperial warfare and neoliberal capitalism, and so these alliances remain a fraught if significant site of post-9/11 movement building (Duggan 2003). On the other hand, campaigns such as Stop the FBI and the work of the Defending Dissent Foundation have produced critiques of surveillance that emerge from a defense of progressive-left movements. As a comic book about FBI entrapment in the Defending Dissent Foundation's Dissent and Repression Comic Series states, the aim is to connect various groups targeted by surveillance to build a "culture of solidarity against repression across political boundaries and issue silos by highlighting the shared experience of repression and resistance."[24]

Figure 5.1. *Manufacturing "Terrorists"* comic book, Defending Dissent Foundation

Professional Activists/Professional Terrorists

Surveillance effects include the emotional traumas and triggers, racialized fears, and class anxieties generated by awareness of the military-spy state among youth. Abed, Aisha, and other student activists I spoke to worried about how repression and criminalization of oppositional politics might undermine their educational careers and economic livelihood. These are significant material concerns, especially given that some of the young people I spoke to had parents who were not affluent or were struggling with unemployment, and some worked to support their families. The economic security of middle-class families in Silicon Valley became increasingly tenuous with the housing crisis and recession, especially given the high cost of living in the area. Abed, for example, said that his father was an engineer who had started his own high-tech company but was later laid off from his job as a software manager; his mother, who had studied agricultural engineering in Egypt, was going back to school so that she could get a job. Aisha's father worked as a limousine driver, but eventually she and her mother both had to go to work in order to support the family. The ripple effects of the economic crisis reinforced anxieties about what it meant to be politically active in a culture where progressive activism is generally seen as detrimental to stability and at odds with the demands of the labor market and neoliberal capitalism. Abed, who was a biotechnology major, thought that student activists needed to maintain a careful balance between involvement in political organizing and academic achievement. He commented:

> You see people protesting and then they're, like, "School . . . I don't know about that, I am still floating around, I am in my seventh year of college." And you kind of rub your head and go, "You're kind of the reason why our movement is not going anywhere. . . ." If you want your voice to be heard then be good at what you want to do, whether it's being a mechanic or a doctor. You have got to work hard. People will skip class to go to a protest . . . why would you skip class for that? Yeah, it's important, if you have time, *then* go, but if you have a midterm then you should be studying or you're really going to knock your grade down for a protest that, honestly, is not be going to covered by anybody.

Abed's critique of student activists "floating around" for years on campus and skipping classes in order to attend campus protests, that he worried received little media attention, echoes the refrain heard among parents, immigrant or otherwise, that activism disrupts academic achievement and upward mobility. This is not an uncommon fear among parents across class and racial backgrounds, and particularly in communities that have been subjected to intense state scrutiny, both before and after 9/11. But it is also interesting to note the class anxieties hinted at in Abed's narrative, which pits the ethic of hard work against the ethos of political protest, another form of productive activity but one that risks coming at the expense of educational and class achievement. The choice is to either get good grades or to be engaged in protest cultures. Having said that, colleges do not generally reward students for participation in protest movements nor make it easy for them to juggle the demands of their education and desires to participate in political organizing. The pressures of staggering student debt also weigh heavily on youth who cannot take for granted that they can get any job, let alone as a mechanic or doctor.

The dilemmas for Arab, South Asian, and Afghan American college students who work while struggling to keep up with their studies and participate in activism cannot be taken lightly, especially with tuition and fee hikes in California and the privatization of public higher education across the nation. These conflicts have been exacerbated in the post-9/11 climate of surveillance and repression, in which universities often collude with the military-spy state, through programs of collaboration with the FBI and the Office of the Director of National Intelligence, including those that specifically target students of color for recruitment, heightening the anxieties of Arab and Muslim American Americans as well as undocumented and immigrant students (see González 2014). As Aisha said of student activists who were "getting arrested" in campus protests and under surveillance, "We were part of the radical left, but we were also trying to be part of the system because we wanted jobs for our economic livelihood." Feroze, whose father worked at IBM, observed that the impact of 9/11 and surveillance on Muslim Americans was "tied heavily to class" and economic as well as social insecurity; in his view, "If you're less sure of your status in the community, you're rightfully more paranoid." Activism, furthermore, can require a budget. Billoo said that students who work at part-time jobs, such as at California State University campuses, have to consider whether they can afford to pay to attend student or activist conferences and "can't always be involved in activism." She commented, "Class is a factor but it's complex because it's also about immigration status," pointing out that many Afghan and Yemeni Americans she meets in her work are first-generation immigrants and naturalized citizens, and "there is the fear" of political activity that could be risky.

At the same time, it is apparent that the politicization of the younger generation in Muslim, Arab, South Asian, and Afghan American communities has led to a desire, among some youth, to enter careers other than the valorized professional occupations their parents had long favored, that is, medicine, engineering, finance, and information technology. Instead, many Muslim American youth have become increasingly interested in pursuing law, public policy, and political science, drawn to the possibility that these fields would allow them to understand better the political context that had dramatically altered their lives since 9/11, or (also) aid them in the mobilization for political space and collective rights for their communities. Billoo also spoke of the significant shift in career trajectories among Muslim American youth since 9/11: "There are a lot of people [in the Muslim American community] in their twenties and thirties who are moving away from traditional careers. . . . At the same time, at upper-class mosques, there are parents who want their children to go to Stanford and be a doctor." The class anxieties of immigrant parents and the pressures on second-generation youth for upward mobility and professionalization are well-rehearsed tropes by now, but I think placing these familiar dilemmas in the context of the post-9/11 moment adds another layer of complexity. For instance, Jamil said that he wanted to pursue "civil rights law because that's what's affecting us most, but then after a while of thinking about it, I was like, maybe I don't want to do it just for Muslims but to stand up for all people"; he was also interested in health care law, hoping he could "stand up for people who are just poorer and less fortunate than me." The premise underlying these aspirations is that legal or policy skills, acquired through higher education—and not just through grassroots mobilization— would allow this generation greater participation in political or legal work, and not just in activism "on the side" while working as engineers or doctors, as was generally the case in their parents' generation.

Bashir, whose father was an engineer but who had taken a different path by majoring in global studies and health science at San Jose State, commented on the shift in career interests in his generation:

> This is an engineering school. Sometimes I do feel different here because everyone talks about engineering. There's a tiny minority of people that are going into different majors. And 9/11 has changed that too. The other day I heard a stat[istic] that was shocking to me, that the Muslim community after 9/11 is producing more lawyers than the Jewish community. And many Muslims are going into political science and international relations.

Bashir's comment about the turn to the law in the 9/11 generation of Muslim Americans was echoed by many others. His allusion to Jewish Americans in the legal field can be read, on the one hand, as a comparison with a community that is often paired with Muslim Americans as a point of reference—including by Muslims themselves—partly due to the dyadic religious framework used to discuss Middle East politics. On the other hand, it alludes to the underlying recodification of racism and class imaginaries in the U.S. after 9/11 (Dabashi 2011). The model minorityhood of Jewish Americans is recycled into the liberal narrative of Muslim Americans as an upwardly mobile, hard-working community that has been unjustly persecuted (Menon 2006; Prashad 2012), a representation that is co-produced by Muslim Americans.

The binary trope of Muslim American youth as either "potential jihadis" or "upwardly mobile minorities" is a tension that shapes Muslim American youth culture, observe Khabeer and Alhassen (2013, 299), as well as political activism. I think an important, though less discussed, strand of the culture wars as class wars is the shoring up of the belief in neoliberal democracy among targeted populations in the War on Terror. Narratives about civil rights activism as an assimilative project for "good" citizens contribute to a neoliberal imagining of inclusion, as discussed in Chapter Two, that is important to the state in in a moment of imperial decline. Furthermore, unlike working-class Muslim communities in Europe, who are viewed in the dominant narrative as inassimilable and "radicalized," partly due to their economic marginalization (though rarely due to their postcolonial predicament), the rhetoric of U.S. neoliberal democracy suggests that well-educated, hard-working Muslim Americans will ultimately prevail through the virtue of capitalist entrepreneurship (Aidi 2014). This narrative is also prevalent among some Muslim American community leaders, who emphasize to the public that Muslim Americans at large are patriotic, hard-working, and relatively well-adjusted (or accommodating) to liberal capitalist democracy.

The question of class in relation to the post-9/11 culture wars surfaced in interesting, and sometimes critical, ways among young people in Silicon Valley. For example, Farid, a Pakistani American who had worked in his father's auto body shop since he was fourteen, bought his own garage in San Jose when he was seventeen and said that several of his relatives also started "working young." When I met him at the garage, Farid talked about how he'd failed out of community college and mentioned that his father was eager that he return to college like his cousins who were studying engineering and, increasingly, law, a field that did appeal to him.

However, Farid seemed skeptical, or perhaps tired, by the entrepreneurial and class ambitions of his family. He wanted to retire in Dubai, because he thought that Pakistanis, Indians, and Afghans worked too hard and he imagined the Gulf as a place where (presumably as an affluent retiree) he could "go out and have fun." The prospect of living in Dubai was also enticing because he said he did not want to live in a state that was likely to wage war and "send people out to fight," such as the United States. There was an interesting tension in Farid's narrative of his career aspirations, which moved between critiques of "hard work" and model minorityhood and aspirations to individual entrepreneurship, that seemed to hint at an underlying neoliberal logic of self-reliance and freedom of class (and spatial) mobility. Yet he simultaneously challenged the biopolitical bliss of living in a state of permanent war and seemed to long for life, and leisure, in a less militarized society and an escape from the treadmill. Farid's experience as someone who dropped out of college also suggests the cracks in the story of Muslim, and especially South Asian, American youth as high achievers from families obsessed with education, pointing to the role of labor, which has generally been obscured in portraits of Muslim American youth.

Bashir also discussed with me the ways class pressures affect young men from immigrant communities. He observed that "men are very pressured to provide for our families" and to focus on academic work rather than on political activism, though he noted that his mother was very supportive of his involvement in campus organizing. He said, "I have a lot of passion and wanted to become involved and that comes from my mom." Other youth I spoke to, including young women, talked about their parents' support for their political engagement, suggesting that parental views of political activism did not follow neatly gendered or generational patterns and that class expectations and ideas about activism also varied considerably by family. In fact, since 9/11, it has become apparent that there are several young Muslim, Arab, South Asian, and Afghan American women at the forefront of the new civil rights and antiwar campaigns and movements, on and off campuses. For example, Sabina recalled an inspiring talk that she attended by a Muslim woman lawyer at Zaytuna College about "education" and career choices, commenting, "There are a lot more women involved now. Every conference that I attend, there is at least one woman speaker." Marwa reflected on her reputation as "the activist" at Stanford:

> In my view, my campus is generally a very apathetic campus. We all care about resume building and getting this much money and graduating with this, blah blah blah, which is great but there are so much more important things. So basically, like . . . my whole dorm is completely like that [apathetic], so I am known as the activist. If anyone wants to ask about anything, even if it is something I'm not involved in, they ask me, "So when is the protest?"

It is notable that it was Marwa, an Egyptian Muslim American woman (who wore the hijab), who became the "icon" of student activism, in her own words, contradicting the Orientalist imaginary of inherently passive, repressed Muslim/hijabi women. She also criticized the classed dimensions of the "apathetic" and conservative political culture at an elite campus such as Stanford, which pivots on academic achievement and class mobility, and is self-contained and self-regulating.

Marwa's observation of her iconic status as an activist is interesting to note in a post-9/11 context in which the visibility of hijabi women is upheld by liberal/progressive Americans as an index of the successful entry of Muslim Americans into liberal/progressive politics. A racial, religious, and gendered framework of recognition shapes the entry of the younger generation into campus politics. However, the much-discussed shift toward greater "public" engagement with local and national politics in Muslim American communities since 9/11 generally remains embedded within a multicultural politics of recognition, one that dominates liberal democratic states such as the U.S. (Dean 2009). Countering Islamophobic and Orientalist representations of Muslim women as inherently oppressed, a pivotal trope in the culture wars, necessitates highlighting the public and active role of Muslim American women activists and, in particular, of women in hijab, while evading a discussion of imperial feminism and radical feminism in Muslim and Arab societies. The burden of Orientalism and racism is indeed heavily borne by Muslim American women who cover in various ways (see Cainkar 2011; Heath 2008). When Jenaan went to San Jose City College, she said, "A lot of people would just look at me and not talk. And when I said something they would be like 'Oh, wow, she speaks. Wow, she speaks English.' I'll crack a joke and they'll be amazed that I can be funny." Shabana Mir (2007) notes that young Muslim American women on college campuses are acutely self-conscious about Orientalist imaginaries of Muslim women; as a result, she argues, when in mainstream views, "Muslims became frozen in an Orientalist fantasy, some young women also promoted the frozen fantasy" or remained trapped within it, often attempting to countering this representation by performing the image of the "tolerant" or moderate Muslim (17).

The prominence of young Muslim American women in leadership positions in post-9/11 political activism, on and off campus, is a complex issue riven by class pressures in addition to gendered and racial politics. Yara noted that Arab American men on her campus were not as politically involved because they were busy study engineering and willingly accepted her leadership, yet she also noted, "I'll get upset with them sometimes . . . and I'll be like, 'Hey, you guys should be helping me out,' and they'll totally defend me. They're like my brothers." So the ethnic or religious community, as is often the case, becomes modeled on the notion of family, where women's activism is understood as an act of (political) labor that strengthens, rather than undermines, bonds of community and kinship. At the same time, I want to note that some young women talked about how their parents and, in a few cases, particularly their fathers were extremely supportive and encouraging of their activism and political development, which is not always the case in nonimmigrant families, and which does, indeed, defy the notion of patriarchal Muslim or immigrant men who want women to be submissive and of Arab women overshadowed by men in the public sphere.

Other youth, female as well as male, said their parents discouraged them from being involved in public politics, largely because they were fearful of reprisals and other negative consequences (Sirin and Fine 2008, 97–98). Arab and Muslim American youth, including young women, who were passionate about their political convictions and took a public stand on issues such as Palestine on their campuses clearly risked backlash and stigmatization, not to mention criminalization. Furthermore, their involvement in activism opposing occupations in Palestine, Iraq, and Afghanistan challenged dominant narratives that repress Arab and Afghan national politics in the U.S., producing what could be called a critical feminist nationalism engaging with issues of sovereignty, as discussed in the previous chapter, and one that is erased or maligned in mainstream and liberal feminist discourses in the U.S. (see Kadi 1994; Zaatari 2011). The gendering of classed and political trajectories of Muslim American youth since 9/11 must be situated in the shifts in the political culture not just within Arab, South Asian, or Afghan American communities but also on college campuses and in the general populace in the era of the PATRIOT Act, which has produced fears of surveillance of activism. Yet Muslim and Middle Eastern youth, both male and female, often take the leadership role--and significantly, are also often called upon to do so, if sometimes symbolically or tokenistically--in the context of growing civil and human rights or antiwar movements since 9/11.

While much attention has focused on the overdetermined role of Muslim women in the culture wars and debates about feminism and the War on Terror, as discussed earlier, I think the issue that has been less explored is the connection between gender and neoliberal democracy for Muslim American politics. The self-reflexive and self-conscious production of Muslim (or Pakistani, Arab, or Afghan) identities in the post-9/11 moment is staged on the terrain of neoliberal citizenship and minority subjecthood. The articulation of gender, religion, and class in neoliberal notions of individual autonomy and productivity looms large for South Asian, Arab, and Afghan American youth who are always aware of what their educational and career choices, not just choices of religious practices, signify for a larger public that is schooled in ideas about "model" and not-so-model minorities. As Puar (2004) observes, the "retrenching and resolidification of the discourse of U.S. exceptionalism," and Western democracy, in the War on Terror has produced claims to model minorityhood in groups constructed as enemy aliens (81).

Ideas of "hard work," as discussed by Farid and Abed, feed into the belief that one can be a virtuous citizen fit for neoliberalism, but the entry into "alternative" careers can also denote the liberalism of a community fit for capitalist democracy and the individual freedoms it bestows. Sharif, a Pakistani American from Los Gatos, whose father was a pilot, talked about how young Muslim Americans were doing "stand-up comedy, film, acting" and also entering fields such as "design, law," which were now "an okay thing to do." He commented, "We're getting into places where nobody went and showing people, the more we can get around, the more people will see us and the less stereotypes people will have of us." For Sharif, entering a field such as the arts, or performance, is in part a political move to counter Islamophobia and gain inclusion, rather than simply about upward mobility, and his remarks invoke the spirit of pioneers who break new frontiers and become acceptable, less threatening subjects. Muslim Americans can be lawyers, actors, and fashion designers; they can also be funny. For example, a second-generation Pakistani American, Azhar Usman, is part of the stand-up comedy troupe Allah Made Me Funny, which has performed around the nation as part of a new Muslim American comedy circuit, which includes groups such as Axis of Evil and more recent stand-up comedy stars such as Aziz Ansari, an Indian Muslim American actor who majored in marketing (Chan-Malik 2013, 297). This comedy subculture has produced a genre of subversive humor that tackles Orientalist representations of "the Muslim" or "the Arab" but has remained largely an attempt to produce alternative performances of liberal Muslim and Middle Eastern identities in response to post-9/11 Islamophobia; it generally remains contained by the key tropes in the culture wars even as it purports to challenge them.

Another subcultural trend that has expanded in the 9/11 generation is the adoption of Islamic fashion styles that have proliferated globally and that appeal to young Muslims, especially young women, sometimes labeled "Mipsterz" or "muhajibabes," who want to be hip and "fashion forward" while upholding religious codes of modesty, piety, and propriety (Aidi 2014; Chan-Malik 2013, 297; Lewis 2013). The notion that being Muslim can also be "cool" is often celebrated, in the context of a virulent Islamophobia that leaves no room for Muslim American youth cultural production; the Islamic fashion trend can also be interpreted as an attempt by Muslim youth to reinvent "youthful" styles while expressing religious commitment and displaying religious authenticity, sometimes rejecting the parental generation's presumably un-Islamic traditions (Khabeer and Alhassen 2013, 305–307). There is also a trend of politicized Muslim and Arab American youth style, with young people sporting T-shirts with political slogans or wristbands and necklaces signaling solidarity with Palestine, for example. But these new subcultures must also be situated in the context of commodification and a neoliberal multicultural landscape that valorizes individual expression and "choice," one in which genuinely radical youth cultures are still a threat to be surveilled, contained, redirected, or eliminated (Wilson 2013). Indeed, surveillance remains a core element of the debates about modesty, social conformity, and Muslim American youth cultures.

One way the complex and contradictory reconfiguration of class anxieties in the War on Terror links the post-9/11 culture wars to surveillance and rights-based activism is through the figures of the "professional activist" and the "professional terrorist." On the one hand, it is apparent that in a generation that has grown up experiencing a sense of siege and eviction from rights, there is a drive to be engaged in full-time political work, as, for instance, civil rights lawyers or policy advocates (Razack 2008). Some South Asian, Arab, and Afghan American youth have chosen to be "professional activists," or as some have described it, "professional Muslims." After 9/11, Muslim American identity has become the locus of a professional identity, in a context in which civil rights advocacy and public policy interventions takes place through national and local nonprofit organizations with paid staff positions. The professionalization of Muslim American politics also occurs in a moment in which "social justice" work has become an institutionalized field in the wake of the NGOization of the post–civil rights era. The historical shift to community-based "self-help" programs and single-issue organizations is part of the containment and pacification of the radical streams of movements that emerged in the 1960s and 1970s and the neoliberal privatization of social services since the 1980s (see INCITE! 2007; Ramos-Zayas 2004, 36). So the aspirations to professional activism in the 9/11 generation must be situated in the neoliberal politics that underlie the notion of social justice activism, including civil rights and human rights advocacy, as a "respectable" professional career. This is notwithstanding the important work that has occurred in many campaigns organized by nonprofit organizations where progressive and left activists try to make their political work sustainable, sometimes through grant funding while struggling to "force change beyond the boundaries of liberal equality" (Duggan 2003, xviii; Kwon 2013).

The "professional activist," I argue, needs the figure of the "professional terrorist," as they are engaged with each other through a dialectic steeped in the contradictions of neoliberal imperialism and surveillance democracy. By "professional terrorist," I do not mean militants who get a paycheck for their activities, but the new category of Muslim terrorists characterized as "young, educated, professional men, in the most economically productive age brackets, often employed in fields such as computer programming, business, science and technology and as foreign students" (Rygiel 2006, 148). Rather than being only poor, uneducated males, the 9/11 hijackers and the perpetrators of attacks in Britain, for example, have included young Muslim professionals, scientists, and engineering students. In 2015, there was much anxiety about the fact that Mohammad Youssef Abdulazeez, the young Palestinian Jordanian (and U.S. citizen) who opened fire on a military recruiting center and Navy Reserve center in Chattanooga had an engineering degree from the University of Tennessee. In an interesting twist, however, it appeared that Abdulazeez had actually lost his job at a nuclear power station because he had failed his drug test, raising questions about the conventional profile of the devout-Muslim-turned-extremist.[25] Over the last several years, there has been an increased scrutiny of the very "model minority" professionals and students from the global South who were recruited by U.S. after the Immigration Act of 1965 as technically skilled labor, such as South Asian and Arab immigrants in Silicon Valley. State suspicion in the War on Terror focuses not just on disaffected working-class Muslim immigrants but also those who have been able to infiltrate the "masculinized, 'techno-muscular capitalism'" of neoliberal globalization, and "access a way of life . . . which should normally be reserved for white, professional, western(ized) men," according to Kim Rygiel (2006, 150, 149). There has been an important shift in the class profile of the "terrorist" that has implications for the youth in this study, since many of their parents belonged to this class of immigrants. I would add to Rygiel's argument that although these highly educated, professional Muslim and Arab immigrants from the global South acquired this "way of life," to varying degrees, they were often excluded from hegemonic white middle-class masculinity and sociality. It is this immigrant entrepreneurial class that is now viewed as potentially harboring a fifth column, emerging out of office cubicles and science labs to strike back at the Western nations that previously valorized their economic and technical contributions and now view them as a frightening specter—terrorist professionals or professional terrorists who might dress, talk, and even look (a little) like "us."

The racialized specter of the professional terrorist—the IT professional living in the suburbs—and of the "homegrown" terrorist—the kid listening to hip hop next door or the young wrestler—generates acute contradictions. For one, Muslim, Arab, and South Asian professionals in the U.S. have increasingly been profiled at borders, taken off planes, detained for interrogation, and had their bank accounts or charitable organizations monitored or shut down, as discussed in the previous chapter. For example, Farid, who had to fly about four times a week for his work after he graduated from Stanford, said he had been subjected to additional security searches three quarters of the time since 9/11. He commented that he was even detained once at an airport in Canada for eight hours after flying back from his sister's wedding. Profiling produces the scenario in which the professional terrorist meets the professional activist, as the latter is often called upon to defend the civil rights of professionals caught in the dragnet of the War on Terror and hired to file lawsuits against airlines or the Transportation Security Administration. Given the increased entry of Muslim Americans into civil rights and legal advocacy, and the mushrooming of organizations offering legal aid to Muslim and Arab American communities since 9/11, the professional activist is also likely to be from one of the same groups targeted by the surveillance state. In 2009, Muslim Advocates, a national legal advocacy organization based in San Francisco, issued a report, *Unreasonable Intrusions*, documenting the increasing practice of Customs and Border Protection (CBS) agents "harassing, intimidating, and seizing data" from the cell phones and computers of U.S. citizens and legal residents at airports and land borders. The report includes testimonials by Muslim, Arab, and South Asian Americans of the ethnic, racial, and religious profiling of "innocent travelers." Several of the accounts are by professionals, and some by imams or students, including a handful from Silicon Valley. For example, "Bilal," a software engineer from Santa Clara, was detained for interrogation at the San Francisco airport when returning from India, via Pakistan, and his checkbook and laptop were searched. He was asked by CBS agents why he made donations to his local mosque and why he sent his children to an Islamic school, and his cell phone was seized and returned to him broken. Interestingly, two of the testimonials are by Pakistani American women lawyers and community activists from the Bay Area who were detained and interrogated at airports (Muslim Advocates 2009, 19–27).

The professional activist is, thus, at moments suspected of being a professional terrorist, and subject to surveillance and suspicion of her or his political and religious beliefs as well as work activities, as indicators of "terrorist" tendencies or sympathies. It is important to note that the agents of surveillance and profiling can also be Muslim or Arab American, especially given the recruitment of native informants but also in other contexts; so the racial politics of this encounter between surveiller and surveilled is increasingly fraught. The line between the professional activist and the terrorist professional is blurred, and sheds light on the ways in which the entry of targeted groups into neoliberal capitalist democracy is always suspect. Even as some try to claim belonging in the neoliberal multicultural state through a discourse of productive citizenship or the virtues of "moderate" politics and civil rights activism, Muslim Americans are policed and surveilled by the terror state's own professionals, as part of a radical regime of surveillance and militarization that has expanded in a climate of deepening class insecurity and ongoing racial tensions.

Conclusion

Technologies of surveillance attempt to define, control, and contain Muslim American subjects and Arab, South Asian, and Afghan American politics and youth activism, but they are also technologies that produce objects for surveillance: the terrorist, the activist, the professional with terrorist tendencies. These objects can exceed or slip out of pre-determined categories, such as the professional terrorist—educated, upwardly mobile, and fit for neoliberal democracy. Equally slippery, too, is the figure of the young professional (Muslim, Arab, Afghan, or South Asian American) activist, such as the new generation of lawyers and civil rights advocates, who are viewed as dangerously sympathetic to Muslim causes and regions of the world; however, they are neither easily identifiable as Islamists nor as grungy, hippie leftists or kaffiyeh-wearing "radical" street protesters. Is the professional activist also a subject fit for neoliberal democracy or a source of subversion? Can she or he be an object of Islamophobia as well as of Islamophilia? These questions are contingent and shaped by notions of "moderate" and "extremist" Muslim American politics that regulate acceptable political subjecthood for youth, as they wrestle with educational and class trajectories. In some cases the professional Muslim or Arab American civil rights activist may be incorporated through a project of liberal reform and national redemption, as argued in Chapter Two. While U.S. democracy may be exported overseas to save Muslims, Arabs, or Afghans from themselves, it is also apparent that a new cohort of (Muslim or Arab American) civil rights activists is viewed as saving those excluded from U.S. democracy, and sometimes, is represented as saving liberal democracy itself.

The links between the politics of humanitarianism, rights, and surveillance are often obscured, yet I argue that we must connect these technologies of governmentality in order to understand the War on Terror as an ongoing cultural, class, and racial war. In fact, I would say that the restaging of battles over the meaning of democracy and freedom after 9/11 demonstrates that the culture wars are more accurately described as *civil wars* within the nation—

battles between competing classes to secure power or hegemony, even if without overt violence, though civil wars are imagined to only happen "over there" and no longer here. As a war framed through the Manichean logic of good and evil that draws on the epistemology of the Cold War as well as the War on Terror (Kim 2010, 3), the post-9/11 culture wars are, at root, a battle within the racial state over the meaning of national identity in an era of neoliberal multiculturalism and imperial democracy. This phase of the culture wars has taken place during a period of economic decline in the U.S., and of mounting frustration and anger about the banking system that helped create the financial crisis and home foreclosures, but that was bailed out by the Bush and Obama regimes. There was a spurt, if only briefly, of mass public resistance to this system with the Occupy movement, strikes by public workers and teachers, and student protests in defense of public higher education around the country. The late 2000s were also a period of nationwide rallies and student walkouts for immigrant rights and in protest of police brutality and vigilante violence targeting young men of color, such as Oscar Grant in Oakland and Trayvon Martin in Florida, culminating with the Black Lives Matter movement that erupted as I was finishing this book. These issues of economic security, immigration, policing, and racial violence are all core to the culture wars and overlap in interesting, if often underemphasized ways, with questions of Islamophobia, Arabophobia, militarization, and imperial violence overseas.

Surveillance is key to this project of producing and regulating subjects fit for neoliberal democracy. I argue that surveillance produces the language of democracy just as neoliberal democracy produces and requires surveillance. That is, domestic surveillance and repression and U.S. overseas interventions in the War on Terror are justified through the discourse of saving others for neoliberal democracy. These others, who must be rescued, regulated, and reengineered to enter Western modernity and enjoy its material as well as gendered and sexual freedoms, are *racial* others, and it is a racialized logic of surveillance and containment that fundamentally defines the culture wars. "Uncivil" protests, such as those by Palestinian and Muslim American students opposing imperial violence and U.S.-backed occupation, are policed and criminalized by a surveillance apparatus that includes state agents and partisan organizations that are anti-Arab and/or anti-Muslim, as discussed in Chapter Three, and that invoke a discourse of civility, democracy, and modernity that is deeply racialized and gendered. While some young activists resist surveillance by calling for a rehabilitation of liberal democracy, others attempt to surveil technologies and agents of surveillance. Countersurveillance or sousveillance is, in some cases, driven by the urge to rethink political organizing strategies and frameworks beyond the parameters prescribed by liberal democracy and civil liberties and to create a progressive culture of desecuritization. Surveillance effects are complex, and there is more work to be done on the ways in which they are reshaping political subjectivity in racial, gendered, sexual, and classed terms in the current moment and permeating social life and intimate and family relationships for the 9/11 generation.

The question that looms large here is: if democracy has become the language of the imperial state and its proxy regimes, and if it is tied so closely to the regulation and containment of dissenting movements and to racialized technologies of repression, can it still be a horizon for dissenting movements? Is there still a radical critique that can be waged using the notion of democracy *against* imperial democracy? These dilemmas, always thorny, were unsettled by the massive, insurgent movements for democracy across the Arab world in 2010–2011, as youth, workers, women, and others rose up to challenge and overthrow U.S.-backed dictatorships from Tunisia to Yemen, following the Green movement in Iran in 2009. The aftershocks of the Arab uprisings rippled through the U.S. and into Muslim and Arab American communities in California and also inspired Occupy protesters and public workers on strike across the nation. I conclude, in the following chapter, by discussing post-9/11 youth politics in light of these struggles over the meaning of democracy, imperial and otherwise.

6

Democracy and Its Others

The War on Terror has been fought in the name of "democracy," saving others unfit or incapable of the correct model of democracy required for Western, liberal governance or state building. "Democratization" and "democracy promotion" have been central alibis in U.S. invasions and occupation of other regions, and various forms of military and political intervention, from Iraq and Afghanistan to Yemen and Pakistan. Democracy is thus a core component of Western modernity, legitimizing a late imperial project and globalized surveillance regime in conjunction with the framework of human and civil rights, women's rights, or gay rights. There are moments of tension that rupture exceptionalist mythologies of U.S. imperial democracy, such as the photos of torture at Abu Ghraib or Edward Snowden's revelations in 2013 of mass surveillance in the U.S. and overseas, but racialized targets of the military-spy state live in the everyday of surveillance. U.S. state-sponsored repression of democracy movements elsewhere has also been forced into public view as a paradox to be confronted during the Arab uprisings of 2011–2012. The uprisings against U.S.-backed dictatorships that swept through regions presumably undisposed to democracy stunned American audiences watching televised scenes of youth, trade union workers, women (covered and uncovered), and Arabs of all ages taking to their streets and toppling aging, corrupt leaders who had been propped up for decades by U.S. arms, funds, and propaganda. The media coverage of the mass protests in Tahrir Square broadcast live from Cairo by international news outlets such as Al Jazeera and CNN, coming on the heels of the Jasmine Revolution in Tunisia, riveted American audiences and caught the U.S. administration off guard, shattering its stated agenda for "remaking" the Middle East. Furthermore, the Arab uprisings inspired the outbreak of the Occupy Wall Street protests in 2011 and the global resistance of the "99%," including protests and sit-ins by students on U.S. campuses that erupted as I was completing this research.

Forced to play catch-up with these popular Arab uprisings for democracy, the Obama regime had to confront the contradiction between the official U.S. rhetoric in the global War on Terror of promoting democracy, civil rights, and human rights to create a "new Middle East," as (in)famously stated by Condoleezza Rice, and historical U.S. state support for the antidemocratic, neoliberal regimes in the region.[1] U.S. government officials, as well as mainstream and liberal media commentators, had no choice but to express their support and admiration—however hollow—for these genuinely grassroots movements for democracy, and to implicitly acknowledge that they had been on the wrong side of the struggle for "democratization" in Tunisia and Egypt, not to mention in Saudi Arabia, Jordan, Bahrain, and Morocco, countries where popular protests against U.S.-backed regimes received less far coverage in the U.S. media. The situation in Libya, Yemen, and Syria was (and is) far more complex and less clear-cut, and debates about the counterrevolutions and the U.S. and NATO interventions were difficult and often divisive for progressives and antiwar activists in the United States. But it was apparent that the so-called Arab Spring, and particularly Tahrir Square—as well as the later protests in Gezi Park in Istanbul—had seized the (liberal) American public imagination and the dominant narrative about democracy in the War on Terror had been disrupted, if only for a brief moment.

The Egyptian revolution of 2011, in particular, and the visible presence of young, media-savvy activists such as Wael Ghonim, the Google executive who was one of many young Egyptians involved in the movement, became the symbol for many Americans of the "other" Middle East. These Arab cyberactivists, students, and "professional activists" became counterpoints to the images of Arab and Muslim youth that U.S. publics had long been fed by the U.S. mainstream media, especially after 9/11. Here, there were unarmed Egyptian youth facing down tanks in the streets, clean-shaven computer professionals organizing Facebook campaigns, young women in hijab leading hundreds of their peers in the streets and confronting the police, and nonviolent demonstrations organized in communal encampments. As the Arab uprisings erupted, a budding romance with Tahrir Square emerged in the liberal American media (take the scene of Anderson Cooper of CNN, who got attacked by pro-Mubarak thugs in Cairo, greeting his viewers with "A salaam aleikum" on one of his nightly news shows), among progressive activists (such as public sector workers organizing for labor rights in Madison, Wisconsin, who made direct links to Tahrir Square), and at solidarity protests across the U.S. and in Arab and Muslim American communities in the Bay Area. I want to note here that the label "Arab Spring" is a contested one, as critics have rightly pointed out that it assumes a new or seasonal "awakening" of a population not generally engaged in democratic revolt, erasing the long history of Arab struggles against colonialism, capitalism, and oppression (see Salaita 2012; Shihade 2012). In addition, it is important to grapple with the impact of the radical political vision of these recent revolutionary movements and their attempt to forge a new paradigm for democratic politics, posing a "challenge to traditional political organizing" and traditional definitions of politics itself (for example, see Nigam 2012, 170).

In February 2011, I attended a rally in solidarity with the Egyptian revolution in San Francisco, where an enthusiastic and diverse crowd, including many Arab families and youth, congregated at the Civic Center Plaza across from City Hall. The speeches were MC'd by two young Egyptian American women—one of whom was actually an undergraduate student at UC Davis—as people in the crowd waved Egyptian and Tunisian flags. A young Arab Muslim imam from Sacramento gave a passionate speech about the will of the Egyptian people to demand democracy and the crowd responded vigorously with solidarity chants. This was followed by political songs in Arabic, including ones written by the legendary Egyptian singer Sheikh Imam, led by a local Arab music ensemble. As some children climbed onto the statue in the middle of the square and unfurled the Egyptian flag, a crowd of about five thousand people snaked around the plaza, chanting antiwar slogans, while the activist band Loco Bloco performed Egyptian music and Filipino American youth in red T-shirts played drums. The Egyptian Americans at the rally were brimming with a mixture of relief, optimism, and concern and the spirit of hope, solidarity, and excitement was audible

This was just one of many solidarity rallies with the Arab uprisings that sprang up all over the Bay Area and in Silicon Valley, in which young Arab and Muslim Americans, as well as South Asian and Afghan American youth, were involved. Questions of civil and human rights, Islam and democracy, and neoliberalism and imperialism collided in this fledgling U.S. solidarity movement. These events in spring 2011 raised the question of what democracy means in the current moment, as a shape-shifting object of various forms of mobilization, intervention, and aspiration. Democracy has also been a key trope in the post-9/11 culture wars, raising the question of what the desire for democracy means for youth engaged with cultures of protest.

Given the critique of the turn to rights and liberal egalitarianism I have mapped in the preceding chapters, I want to conclude here by thinking the question of democracy beyond the legal discourse of rights, and beyond the notion of liberal, parliamentarian democracy. What does it mean if democracy, the rationale for imperial interventions and assaults on other people's right to self-determination, is also the primary horizon of liberal or progressive activism and resistance movements? What are alternative frameworks for the political, and of solidarity, for youth at a moment when civil rights, human rights, women's rights, and gay rights have all been complicit in various ways with imperial governmentalities?

"Hack for Egypt"

In May 2011, I attended a very different kind of "solidarity event" related to the Arab uprisings in Silicon Valley, one that demonstrated the ways that "democracy" is a moving target. The Hackathon for Egypt at Stanford University was billed as an "un-conference," a day-long event organized by a group of computer hackers and Stanford faculty, and sponsored by the Center on Democracy, Development, and the Rule of Law (CDDRL), the Liberation Technology Program, and the Peace Innovation Lab at Stanford. It was cosponsored by Cloud to Street, a nonprofit organization inspired by the Egyptian movement to overthrow Mubarak that described itself as an "experiment in international digital activism."[2] The call for the conference stated, "Earlier this year, Egyptians combined technology and political activism to revolutionary effect. After overthrowing a thirty-year dictatorship, they face new challenges to establishing democracy. Can technology help them through the divisive times ahead? . . . Our aim is to build a community to show what digital activism can achieve." The event was a fascinating example of the kind of solidarity projects emerging from the confluence of "hacktivists" (young and older), academics, and hi-tech entrepreneurs in Silicon Valley, all working in sites where democracy is defined, celebrated, and debated. The notion of the "professional activist," discussed in the previous chapter, merged at this event with the notion of the digital activist, showcasing an instance of transnational, techie solidarity politics centered on varied imaginings of democracy, solidarity, and resistance.

The hackathon was held in the d.school (Institute of Design) on the Stanford campus, in a chic, warehouselike space with red vinyl sofas and a large screen at the front of the room. The format of the "un-conference" was designed to connect Silicon Valley programmers with Egyptian activists and engineers and encourage an open-ended, "democratically designed" mix of hacking and activism. The participants that morning were an ethnically diverse crowd of people, some whites and South Asians in addition to a few Arabs—not an unusual mix for Silicon Valley—with many students but also several older people. Nearly everyone present had a laptop; I quickly realized I was the only one writing in an old-fashioned paper notebook and felt acutely out of place, and time. From the screen peered the faces of young Egyptian activists in Cairo who were waiting to talk to the audience via Skype, and in the room were young Egyptians who had come from Cairo, one of whom was the cofounder of the Kifaya movement, Ahmed Saleh, who had been involved in organizing the historic January 25 protest in Tahrir Square.

The event opened with remarks by Ben Roswell, the founder of Cloud to Street, a white Canadian and former diplomat to Afghanistan who had lived in Egypt and was now a visiting scholar at the CDDRL. Cloud to Street was launched by Roswell to support Egyptian activists who were using social media and who, according to the organization's mission statement, had "pioneered new methods of political change for the 21st century. In doing so they have not only transformed their country, but set an example for all countries seeking democratic change."[3] Digital media is not just viewed as a site for producing democracy in this discourse, but Egypt is actually offered as a possible political vanguard for media activism and for the West, rather than the other way around as in typical democracy-speak. Roswell had apparently been involved in organizing a digital town hall at Stanford in March on the Egyptian uprising, featuring young activists from Cairo, and a series of hackathons in solidarity with Egypt in partnership with the Liberation Technology Program. He commented that day that he and a small team had been visiting Cairo regularly since the fall of the Mubarak regime and meeting with Egyptian activists in order to find out how "technology was involved in dramatic change" and what support they could provide for this alternative "democracy promotion" movement. Roswell seemed to resist an overstatement of technology's revolutionary potential, saying, "What's driving their revolution is a huge amount of courage, it's not just technology." But he also acknowledged that the "incredible ingenuity and technological smarts" of the Egyptian activists had contributed to its success. For example, he noted that activists had installed web cameras around the protest camp at Tahrir Square to document violent attacks on the protesters, a strategic form of countersurveillance and one that was probably an important factor in the revolution's early success as images from Cairo were broadcast live to the world.

The goal of the hackathon at Stanford was for hackers to work together to develop digital tools and "apps" to support the democracy movement in Egypt, after presentations, including those by the activists from Cairo. One of the speakers was a young Egyptian American venture capitalist, in a red Egypt-solidarity T-shirt, who talked about being at a meeting at the U.S. State Department concerning the use of social media, on the very day that Mubarak finally resigned. He recollected, "People were floored in D.C. Few of the people there were Egyptian, but they were crying as they watched what was happening in Tahrir Square on CNN. It was bigger than Egypt, what was happening." I was struck by the irony submerged in this observation of U.S. government officials apparently moved to tears by the protests in Cairo, and rejoicing with Egyptians at the fall of the dictator that the U.S. had supported for so long. This comment crystallized for me the staging of a certain romance about the Egyptian revolution at the time, especially at that moment in spring 2011. The image of Tahrir Square had not yet been infused into the Occupy movement that exploded across the U.S., and around the world, later that year (let alone been supplanted in Egypt itself by the conflict between the Muslim Brotherhood, the military, and popular revolutionaries) but it was already apparent that it was deeply, if paradoxically, resonant for many Americans, not just those who were Arab or progressive.

The young Arab American entrepreneur went on to say, "We've already won, in a sense, because *you* are all here today. A big part of what will happen is what you want to do to help. Maybe you can start building some apps that we could use [in Egypt]." I think this seemingly simple statement captures part of what was romantic about Tahrir Square—a political fable of solidarity with a "good" revolution and a nonviolent, grassroots movement involving many clean-shaven youth, not just bearded males, against a "bad" ruler, who was finally acknowledged in the American public sphere as tyrannical, corrupt, and obsolete. The simplicity of this moral allegory about the triumph of the people's will in the struggle for democracy in Egypt resonated also with narratives of the U.S. civil rights movement, in the sanitized history of that struggle as discussed in Chapter Two, and perhaps also with deep-seated national myths of America as a nation founded through the struggle for freedom and not through settler-colonial violence and genocide. But this political romance about Tahrir Square and Arab youth protesters was enabled by several evasions and contradictions pivoting on the trope of democracy.

I argue that this political allegory was effective because it allowed for a double move in the post-9/11 national culture and debates about the War on Terror at that historical moment. On the one hand, it offered a redemptive moment for an American public wrestling with revelations of the violent excesses of U.S. military force from Guantanamo to Abu Ghraib, as well as the failures of the Obama regime in following through on its promises to rehabilitate the view of U.S. democracy and chart a "new beginning," as articulated in the president's "Address to the Muslim World" in Cairo in June 2009.[4] This allowed liberal Americans to express sympathy with the will of "the people" in an Arab nation that was not directly occupied by the U.S. and so alleviated, perhaps, some liberal guilt in response to the War on Terror, if not anxieties about earlier imperial interventions overseas and settler violence at home whose repressed history is negotiated, or possibly recovered, through contemporary acts of U.S. aggression (Pease 2009, 172–173). The participants at the hackathon were assured that their act of solidarity in the U.S. was a sign of victory for the Egyptian movement, and that they could offer something tangible and positive to support this uprising for democracy. On the other hand, this romantic fable wiped clean the role of the U.S. in propping up the very dictatorship that the Egyptians had managed to overthrow, against all odds. It also erased other forms of U.S.-sponsored violence that the protesters in Cairo were challenging, evident in the Egyptian protests in solidarity with Palestine and opposition to Egypt's collusion with Israel that were either evaded or downplayed in the U.S. mainstream media (Abou-El-Fadl 2012). None of these complex issues of U.S. imperialism and U.S.-backed colonial violence that were tangled with the Egyptian revolution were discussed at the hackathon that day.

The racial allegory of Tahrir Square—unlike dominant narratives in the U.S. about Libya, Yemen, Syria, and Bahrain, where the U.S. role was more murky and where protesters were armed—should thus be considered part of the post-9/11 culture wars, shaped by a deeply racialized, gendered, and nationalized politics of solidarity. The Tahrir Square fable about democracy is also a product of late imperial culture under Obama, whose eloquent rhetoric emphasizing the "open hand" of "'mutual respect,' multilateralism, . . . institution building, and dialogue" with the "Muslim world" concealed his administration's escalation of war and covert operations in Pakistan and Afghanistan; extrajudicial assassinations of terrorist suspects, including U.S. citizens; continuing sanctions on Iran; persistent support for Israeli violence and dispossession in Palestine; and expanded surveillance at home (Sheehi 2011, 184).

The redemptive allegory of Tahrir Square, at least as it emerged in the early weeks of the Egyptian revolution, was also a gendered narrative, offering an opportunity to rethink or reinscribe powerful tropes about women's rights, freedom, and progress in the post-9/11 culture wars. The images of Egyptian women—old and young, wearing hijabs, abayas, jeans, T-shirts, or blue bras—on the streets and battling the police demonstrated that Muslim and Arab women could also be legible through the framework of democracy, even if they sometimes looked different and might have wanted different things than what American viewers of the revolution imagined. At the Stanford un-conference, one of the speakers was Sabah Hamamou, a young Egyptian journalist who was wearing a long black skirt and a headscarf with black stars, who founded Masrawyya, a media platform used to broadcast news and images of Tahrir Square that spread virally across the world. She traced the emergence of the protests in Egypt to the year 2003, a moment when the second Intifada in Palestine was just ending and the war in Iraq was just beginning, alluding to the role of the U.S. and Israel in suppressing democracy in the region. I was struck that Hamamou was the only speaker at the event who situated the Egyptian revolution in the context of war and occupation in the region.

Hamamou also stressed that the revolution was not just for human rights embedded in liberal democratic governance but for an alternative political and economic structure that would address the people's "basic needs," such as "healthcare, education." Her talk thus extended beyond the horizon of democracy and civil rights, touching also on the question of economic and social rights and demands for the state to provide a "structure of redistribution, welfare, and constitutionality" that have been eroded in postcolonial states in the global South and by neoliberalism at large (Spivak, in Butler and Spivak 2010, 90). Hamamou's talk was followed by a presentation by an Indian digital activist from the Liberation Technology Program on digital platforms for constitutional reform and a project for web-based discussions of the human rights principles in the Egyptian constitution, convened by Egyptian opposition leader Mohamed ElBaradei. The goal of this crowdsourcing project, the Indian activist said, was that "constitutions could be changed for democracy" and that the uploading of constitutions from around the world on the internet would allow people to think about "different ways to organize political rights around the world."

While the presenters were speaking, the activists in Cairo peeking out from the projection screen appeared disconnected from the proceedings in the room, their faces actually frozen for a while as a young man in the room tinkered with the computer. When it was time for the activists in Egypt to propose their digital projects, their voices could not be heard; one of them finally begin munching on his lunch. Someone in the audience wryly commented, "He's not frozen, he's stoic!" Finally, it turned out that the problem was simply that the volume had been turned down, a simple technical glitch! The voice of Ahmed Boguta suddenly burst into the room from Cairo with a loud crackle. Boguta discussed his proposal for a website and interactive database to monitor the Egyptian parliament and upcoming elections, and inform citizens about the parliament's role and responsibility. Other projects proposed by the Cairo activists also focused on harnessing technology to pave the way for democracy. Abdallah Helmy, of the Revolutionary Youth Union, suggested a mobile phone app that would connect activists to a larger social network and also "raise awareness about civic rights and duties." This was framed as a key issue for a society preparing for electoral democracy after decades of repression and debating the procedural challenges ahead. Rights education is thus central to this discourse of digital democracy and (de)democratization, whether in its liberal or leftist variants, as discussed in Chapter Two.

The Skype talks were followed by presentations by the hackers and activists in the room as people in the audience pitched their ideas, some using a whiteboard. A slightly older white man from the Peace Innovation Lab greeted the room with "A salaam aleikum!" He went on to propose a project to "build apps that incentivize cooperation" that could be used to address "conflicts building between Copts and Salafis [Muslims]" in Egypt. Ossama Hassanein, a middle-aged Egyptian American entrepreneur from Silicon Valley, said he wanted to create a mobile app to generate "apolitical, nonpartisan communities of interest." Hassanein, who was wearing a red T-shirt with the Egyptian flag and the word "Freedom" emblazoned across his chest, was the chairman of TechWadi, a Silicon Valley–based organization of approximately two thousand Arab American entrepreneurs and CEOs. During the break, he told me that he had attended the rallies in solidarity with Egypt in the area but when some in the crowd began chanting slogans against the U.S., he stopped going. One of the last proposals was from Hamamou herself; she remarked, "In 1798, Napoleon went to Egypt and compiled information about Egypt in twenty volumes. I have a dream to do the same with Egyptian stories." She said she wanted to create a database with audio files of Egyptian narratives, about Egypt by Egyptians. However, the audience seemed oblivious to Hamamou's strikingly overt challenge to the imperial and Orientalist desires of Western rulers and experts to document and catalog the colonized. In fact, one of the white male hackers present immediately suggested that her project could be merged with an American documentary film project. The irony of this appropriative response to the anticolonial thrust of Hamamou's archival project was, perhaps not surprisingly, lost on those present. The dominant language of countering sectarianism and creating apolitical communities for electoral participation and reconciliation, as well as market logics of incentivization and interest, instead shaped many of the local presentations while discussions of U.S. foreign policy and U.S.(-backed) repression were almost entirely absent. The talks by speakers from Cairo and Stanford completed, the audience was then asked to start working on projects during the "open space format" in the afternoon, in the presumably democratic spirit of creative collaboration.

Imperial Democracy

The "un-conference" in Silicon Valley, representing the confluence of technology, knowledge production, and global solidarity projects is a fascinating example of one strand of politics that attempts to seize liberal democracy as a platform for mobilization and entrepreneurship. The event staged a certain performance of transnational, digital solidarity that was strikingly disconnected from local solidarity movements, given the absence of Arab American community activists, and featured instead Silicon Valley entrepreneurs and a select group of youth from the area. Also, some of the Arab Americans present had class interests that would probably not be aligned with those of left activists in the streets of Cairo challenging neoliberal capitalism. The racial and class schisms evident at the hackathon were not unexpected, given its location at an elite university in the heart of Silicon Valley, but the event seemed emblematic of a pervasive, liberal discourse of solidarity and rights activism that has emerged in tandem with Obama's War on Terror, and that obscures the difficult and pressing issues of imperial militarism, racial violence, surveillance, and repression. The question of democracy *within* the U.S. was not raised at all by the hacktivists at Stanford that day, nor, of course, the contradictions of U.S. support for repressive regimes, such as Egypt and Israel. The issue of human rights, or even civil rights, seemed to be located over *there*, but not in California or right here in Silicon Valley, where the FBI had been targeting antiwar activists and Muslim community leaders and secretly placing tracking devices on cars belonging to Egyptian American youth. There was no mention at all of the post-9/11 repression, including digital surveillance, that had so deeply affected Arab and Muslim American communities, including young activists.

I do not want to dismiss completely the desires of the various individuals present at the hackathon for real or even "radical" democracy, for there was a diverse group of people in the room, some of whom may indeed have had political orientations at odds with the general tenor of the public discussion, or critiques of the format and nature of the event. When I spoke to one of the event organizers later at Stanford and asked her what the goal of the hackathon was, she was careful not to be "prescriptive" in suggesting a political agenda. She commented that the mission of the CDDRL was "to promote democracy, but not George Bush's notion of democratization. Democracy is different for each place, we want to support what people are doing in different regions." But the fact remains that the focus of "Hack for Egypt" was definitely on democracy outside the U.S., and only on Egypt. The project thus seems to illustrate what Stephen Sheehi (2011) describes as Obama's deployment of "soft power," which has been "a counter-narrative to the hard power of the Bush administration" and co-opted the language of social change movements (for example, the slogan "Yes We Can"); this discourse "promises to assimilate Muslim communities into U.S.-driven and dominated globalization" through neoliberal, democratic reform, backed by coercion and violence (182).

One of the questions the hackathon immediately raised for me was what made Tahrir Square so appealing to a liberal American public as a site for reimagining the future of "democracy" in the post-9/11 era. This imaginary of democracy and rights was constituted through both the form and content of the un-conference as a presumably open, collaborative, and democratic space. The discussions by digital activists of nonviolent conflict resolution, civic education, and democratic "civil disobedience," with the help of technology, represent a "good," acceptable politics for Muslim and Arab subjects globally. This discourse of permissible politics during the early phase of the Arab uprisings did not completely alleviate liberal American fears that the overthrow of Mubarak would allow the Muslim Brotherhood or "bad" Arab and Muslim politics to run rampant in Egypt—as Hassanein's comment about the local solidarity rallies hinted—and that U.S. strategic interests in the region were now going to be compromised. But Tahrir Square as an imperial allegory enshrined good Arab and Muslim activists, entrepreneurs, and youth as partners in the project for global (and digital) democratization.

Tahrir Square also provided a moment of redemption for Arab Americans, in a sense, and many young Egyptian and Arab Americans I met felt a surge of pride, mixed with hope and fear, as the protests overthrew Ben Ali in Tunisia and Mubarak in Egypt. Abed, whose family is from Cairo, talked to me in February 2011 about how he and many others in the Egyptian American community were "embracing their Egyptian pride" since the uprising in Tahrir Square. The frustration and anger among Egyptians with the dictatorship and its collusion with Israel was released, if for a moment, in a surge of genuine and deep hope for change, at last, for Egypt, Tunisia, and the region. Abed also acknowledged that the revolution was being embraced by Americans who were neither Egyptian nor Arab, citing the example of a video that was circulating on YouTube at the time, posted by a white American family who had lived in Egypt; it featured their four young daughters marching with the Egyptian flag in their living room and chanting, "Down with Mubarak!" Abed was cautious, however, about claiming pride in a national identity that would be exclusivist or chauvinistic, pointing to the role of Western colonialism in crafting national identities in the Arab world and insisting that the Egyptian revolution should not take precedence over movements in Tunisia or other Arab nations. This was a desire for democracy and pan-Arab solidarity that I heard from many young Arab American activists and that did not emerge from a conservative nationalism but from a yearning for sovereignty and liberation from the ravages of imperialism and neoliberal capitalism.

Yet the internationalizing of Tahrir Square also created contradictory responses from Arab American youth, who had perhaps become accustomed to Orientalist imaginaries of Arabs and Muslims and who felt redeemed by the shift in representation, if only for a brief moment. Abed said he was happy to see a column in the *New York Times*, written by the ubiquitous journalist

Nicholas Kristof, titled "We Are All Egyptians." Abed read the title as an expression of solidarity with global struggles against "injustice" condensed into the symbol of Tahrir Square—but less so the self-immolation of the Tunisian street vendor, Mohamed Bouazizi, that sparked the uprising in Tunisia. An important trope that made the allegory of Tahrir Square so effective in the early months of 2011 was the image of the Egyptian revolution as a nonviolent movement, based on peaceful protest. The theme of nonviolence also ran through some of the talks at the Stanford hackathon, but Abed pointed out the protests in Cairo did involve violence of various forms and by different groups. Noting that looters had targeted homes and museums and were sometimes armed, Abed was also angry about police brutality against protesters.[5] So while the protesters may have been nonviolent, this was certainly not a bloodless revolution. However, the romance of Tahrir Square at the time allowed for a liberal narrative that evaded the connections between the violence of the Mubarak regime—the physical violence perpetrated by its policemen, spies, and thugs, as well as the social and economic violence it inflicted on Egyptians and others—and the violence of the imperial state that had propped up this and other antidemocratic regimes in the region and around the world.

In Abed's view, Arab and Muslim Americans were not immune to the appeal of a liberal allegory about democracy, which he critiqued as obscuring the question of imperialism and sovereignty. For example, CNN's Anderson Cooper quickly became the American face of this allegory for many viewers of his live reports from Tahrir Square, particularly after he was assaulted by Mubarak's thugs; he became the intrepid white American male hero who was on the "right" side of the war for democracy, and the post-9/11 culture wars, at last. But Abed was skeptical of this Indiana Jones–like tale, observing trenchantly that

a lot of Muslims and Arabs are applauding Anderson Cooper. . . . I give them [CNN] credit, they're doing an amazing job but . . . I mean, Anderson Cooper said, "The Egyptian government is evil, they've been evil for thirty years," and everybody's like, "Oh, mash 'Allah [praise be to God], Anderson Cooper! *Good job!*" Nobody's taking a step back and saying, okay, well, the only reason they have been in power is because of the U.S. government [giving Mubarak] 1.3 billion dollars annually. . . . What bothers me is that the U.S. is meddling in all of this, again . . . and it's not just Obama's administration, this is something the U.S. has been doing since the 1800s, that whenever they see a country of interest . . . maybe there's political change and they are not sure where's it gonna go, they say, . . . "Well, let us help you," and it's just— . . . Keep your hands off other people's business! It's none of their business!

Abed astutely situated U.S. military, financial, and political support for the Mubarak regime, and the Obama administration's concerns about whether Egypt would remain a U.S. ally, in the context of a much longer, imperial history of U.S. and Western intervention in the affairs of other, sovereign nations, often in the guise of humanitarianism. He went on to critique the hypocrisy in official American narratives about spreading "democracy" globally while preserving U.S. strategic interests:

> I don't care how strategic Egypt is, whatever happens it is up to the people. If the people democratically elect the Muslim Brotherhood, then so be it, . . . it's their choice, you can't . . . call for a democracy and then when people democratically elect a certain— . . . Exactly like it happened in Palestine, like in Gaza, Hamas was democratically elected, but we said, "Oh no, we're not [interested in] democracy anymore, we wanna place our own people!" You can't do this, you can't have one hand in front of you and one hand behind your back, and say, "Oh okay, go ahead have democracy, no okay, we're gonna give you *this* option, this is what you *really* wanted to have . . . since you guys are not smart enough to choose the right people, we'll put them in place for you!"

Abed's ironic commentary—prescient in its observations about the election of the Muslim Brotherhood after Mubarak's fall and the U.S. response—was laced with outrage over the selective deployment of democracy as a switch and bait in U.S. foreign policy, as apparent in the American (and Israeli) unwillingness to accept that Hamas was the democratically elected national government in Palestine in 2005.

I cite at some length Abed's critique of the inconsistent and shifting invocations of democracy by the U.S. not only because he was passionate about the events unfolding in Egypt as an Egyptian American student activist, but also because he incisively articulated the problem of imperial democracy, in contrast to the discourse of digital democracy and solidarity at the hackathon. "Democratization" and "democracy promotion," the vocabulary favored by the Bush administration and adopted by the Obama regime, are imperial code words for regime change, the promotion of the free market, and the consolidation of U.S. economic and strategic interests with the help of the U.S. military. In some instances, young people like Abed were able to grasp the colonialist and also racialized logic of democracy as a touchstone of benevolent imperialism. For example, Abed critiqued the colonialist assumption that Palestinians, Arabs, or Muslims were not "smart enough to choose the right people" as their leaders in the eyes of the U.S. state, but he also understood that this image of presumably backward, antidemocratic Arab and Muslim societies was embedded in the "strategic" interests of the U.S. in maintaining its own hegemony and network of client states. The discourse of the post-9/11 culture wars focuses on Muslim and Arab American subjects who must be made "safe" for imperial multicultural democracy by inserting them into the grid of legibility of the "good" and "bad" Muslim or Arab, as discussed earlier. This, then, is what democracy looks like when it passes the test of permissible Arab and Muslim American political subjecthood.

A similar critique of imperial democracy was leveled by youth concerned with the U.S. role in Af-Pak. For example, Meena, a young Afghan American woman, reflected on the War on Terror and said passionately,

> Before all these events took place I already knew that America was bad, because of its history of conquering and destroying for their own gain. In my history classes, America was always portrayed as the big brother that would always help and save others. But I had people that would always educate me and provide me with the truth about America. I believe America goes into a country and forces their beliefs, their culture and their democratic imperialism on other countries. They believe they are spreading democracy and equality but they are only suppressing people. I felt this before all the wars and 9/11, and I feel it even more strongly after these events.

Meena names the contradiction of "democratic imperialism," framing the invasion and occupation of Afghanistan and Iraq within a centuries-long record of imperial expansionism and Manifest Destiny that belies the national mythologies of the American project of liberating racialized "others" well before 2001. Her comment invokes the U.S. rationalization for the brutal war and conquest of the Philippines in 1898 through the colonialist discourse about Filipinos as "little brown brothers" who needed to be saved and civilized. The racialized others of U.S. imperialism—whether they are Filipinos, Vietnamese, Egyptians, Palestinians, Iranians, Afghans, Pacific Islanders, Puerto Ricans, or Native Americans—are understood to be inherently antidemocratic; incapable of Western, liberal, secular democracy; and so outside of modernity and unfit for sovereign self-determination. As Joanne Barker (2014) writes about the colonization of Native Americans, "their rights to the self-determination of their governments, territories, cultures, and bodies" are mitigated by "what kinds of humans they are righted to be or not to be" in modernity and the "imperial conditions in which Native humanity and human rights are made contingent on the empire's interests" (34).

Democracy, Imperial or Otherwise?

The long war against terrorism has been accompanied by racial and cultural wars that involve a battle over the meaning of democracy accompanied by a turn to rights. The dilemma of "democracy" in the current moment is that it has been deployed as an imperial political category throughout the Reagan-Cheney-Bush era of aggressive neoliberal interventionism, as well as during the Obama regime's "open hand/clenched fist" policy of democratization and co-optation accompanied by military force, so it is naturally a suspect word for many on the left (Gaines 2010, 197; Sheehi 2011, 185). This is also true of the notion of "rights," particularly liberal civil rights and institutionalized human rights, as discussed in the earlier chapters, which represent political possibilities as well as failures for young activists. In the post–civil rights era, "democracy" has become a dirty word for some progressives and leftists, sullied by its co-optation by imperial, neoliberal governmentality. As Dean (2009) observes, "When democracy appears as both the condition of politics and the solution to the political condition, neoliberalism can't appear as the violence it is. Right and left share the same rhetoric of democracy. . . . So preemptive war is fought in the name of democracy even as critics of the same war use the terms to voice, to imagine, their opposition" (18). She asks, "Is democracy the fallback position for left politics, all that remains of our wounded and diminished political aspirations? Or does the hope its evocation promises mark instead a pervasive left despair?" (76).

Clearly there are ideological differences in the aspirations for democracy on the right and left. Neoconservatives oppose genuine democracy as a threat to the national consensus, built on neoliberal values of hard work, individual property, and heteronormative reproduction, which suppresses the disruptive question of democracy posed by the progressive-left movements of the 1960s and 1970s (Cruikshank 2000). As Rancière (2006) observes, "good democracy must be that form of government and social life capable of controlling" genuine democratic life and popular political participation, which is viewed as ungovernable (8). Since the 1990s, conservatives have increasingly harnessed this notion of "good democracy" to legitimize the War on Terror and wage the culture wars, which mask the racial and class conflicts of what I argue are actually *civil wars* within the nation, accompanying the wars overseas.

The shifting narrative of democracy is part of a longer process of transformation of the U.S. state into a liberal, officially antiracist state—a process that Alain Badiou (2005) suggests is, in fact, a "lengthy counter-revolutionary intellectual and political sequence" that began in the mid-1970s (xxxiv). On the one hand, Badiou points out that the period since the mid-1990s has been marked by "dramatic reactionary phenomena" including "racism, hostility toward the Arab world, . . . unchained Zionism" and a "violent defense" of U.S. economic interests and neoliberal global capitalism. On the other hand, the "long 'war against terrorism'" has been accompanied by "massive hostility" and growing resistance to U.S. hegemony globally, as well as the eruption of Occupy protests and public-worker strikes at home (xxxv). During this same period, however, the liberal democratic state has been strengthened as the desired locus of political inclusion and recognition, and as the arbiter of rights, as discussed in Chapter Two. So the crux of the matter is not just that Muslim Americans desire political recognition through civil rights mobilization, but that the state *also* desires this movement for rights and democracy (Reddy 2011, 193). The counterrevolutionary national consensus needs people to *need* liberal democracy as the endpoint of their struggles. Yet there are cracks in this consensus about democracy and legal egalitarianism, as groups become aware that the distribution of rights shores up, rather than undermines, racial, class, and social inequalities, as evinced by the experiences of youth discussed in this book, and as internal pressures on the late imperial state mount and its economic and political hegemony weakens globally.

The concepts of democracy and rights—civil, women, gay, or human—are increasingly deployed (and mutated) by the right, but the problem is also that they have been ceded by the liberal-left. As political theorists argue, democracy has come to represent a limited political horizon for resistance to imperialism and neoliberal capitalism not just because it is appropriated and deformed by the right, but because as a liberal political ideal or practice it is actually a symptom of a current impasse in politics (Dean 2009, 76–77). Žižek (2007), however, argues: "The true victory . . . occurs when the enemy talks your language. In this sense, a true victory is a victory in defeat. It occurs when one's specific message is accepted as a universal ground, even by the enemy" (17). Žižek suggests that the universalization of concepts historically associated with the left is a moment of triumph, but I want to point out that the co-optation of these ideals occurs through a blurring and redefinition of their meaning, as when democracy becomes an alibi for totalitarianism and universalism a guise for repression of aspirations for equality and emancipation (Rancière 2006, 12). So when the right uses the language of democracy, or of rights, I think this moment actually has the potential to be a true defeat for the left. Dean (2009) rightly observes that, in certain cases, "When one's enemy accepts one's terms, one's point of critique and resistance is lost, subsumed. The dimension of antagonism (fundamental opposition) vanishes" (9).

The shift to rights-talk is dangerous because it sometimes slips into "assertions of difference" and victimhood as the basis for claims to civil rights or gay rights, succumbing to a liberal multicultural politics of injury (Dean 2009, 5–9). Duggan (2003), however, has a nuanced analysis of the discourse of injury invoked by groups claiming rights as minorities or queers, arguing that this does not necessarily have to represent a politics of recognition, as pitted against a politics of (downward) redistribution. Struggles for racial, economic, or social justice can still offer a powerful critique of the "felicity of inclusion" into the liberal democratic order (Reddy 2011, 181). Reframing Žižek's optimistic pronouncement, it is useful to consider Spivak's (1995) insistence on "the continuing need for collective struggle," given that "there is no victory, but only victories that are also warnings" (xxv). This debate, which is not simply a theoretical one but has real implications for movements and people on the ground, is crucial to the central question posed in this book about the efficacy of rights-talk, because it suggests that there is no easy way out of this political impasse of democracy and rights, but a resolution need not mean either defeatism or triumphalism for those concerned with radical transformation of the social order. The co-optation and deformation of democracy—and concepts such as "radicalism," not to mention human rights, antiracism, feminism, and sexual equality—requires a continuous pressing on these concepts and resistance to their appropriation by those in power. It necessitates collective organizing to challenge the retreat to politics defined as individualized consumption of political ideas and demands, and a constant production of alternative knowledges and imaginaries of change. Furthermore, as the roots of the Arab uprisings should remind us, these alternative imaginaries are indeed being produced in other parts of the world, though they remain largely invisible in the U.S., including even among U.S. progressives, as is particularly true of the repressed histories of the left in Afghanistan and Pakistan.

The caution in allegories about liberal democracy is also fundamentally about the question of the state as the horizon of political struggle, as reflected in the struggles of youth from communities targeted in the War on Terror who turn to civil rights campaigns, attempting to oppose the state by appealing to the state. As Nivedita Menon (2004) has argued, in the context of movements coalescing around women's rights in India, rights-talk has ended up in many instances strengthening the state, through legal discourses, and in particular, the power of Western states shrouded by the discourse of liberal universalism (38, 224). Moreover, she points out that the "continual recourse to the law" and to rights often becomes a substitute for "the other harder option of building a movement for an alternative vision" (6). The experiences of young activists in Silicon Valley demonstrate how a liberal civil rights discourse redirects a radical critique of the state and the institutionalized human rights apparatus suppresses, rather than supports, resistance to violence against racialized segments of humanity. Menon importantly argues that the investment in rights-based activism happens at the expense of developing other forms of resistance. It is worth noting that the critiques of these young people did spill over into radical challenges to imperialism, settler colonialism, global capitalism, and white supremacy, even if they did not use this terminology, in part because it was not as accessible to them as the commonsensical paradigms of "civil rights" or "human rights."

Critical legal studies has emphasized that rights are "unstable and indeterminate," but there are disagreements between those, on the one hand, who suggest that rights-talk is important to expose nationalist rights mythologies and to continue to struggle for rights "in a world of no rights" for disenfranchised and disposable groups and, on the other hand, those who argue that the oppression of these groups has historically occurred *through* the law and that an alternative politics must be imagined and enacted (see Williams 2000; Spann 2000). Angela Davis (2005) argues that it is possible to engage in rights-based activism with a "dual strategy of taking up the law and recognizing its limitations in order to address that which the law cannot apprehend" (94). In this vein, of not ceding but transforming the language of rights and democracy, it is inspiring to consider the statements of youth such as the radical young poet Amir Sulaiman, mentioned in Chapter Five, who reflected on his experience of racial profiling and FBI surveillance:

> My position wasn't "I'm an American and therefore I have the right to speak and I am petitioning for this right." My position was that my right to speak is God-given, that it's a truly inalienable right, and not just because some men agree it's inalienable. I wasn't interested in surrendering that right, and I wasn't interested in humiliating myself in front of people by begging for a right that they neither have the power to give or revoke. (cited in Malek 2011, 145–146)

Sulaiman's articulation of rights as "inalienable" and ontological is profound, and while I depart from a divine justification of rights, I think his unequivocal rejection of the arbitrary power of certain groups of humans to bestow rights on others goes to the heart of the critique of rightlessness by prominent political theorists, articulated here in powerful and unapologetic terms. Sulaiman also offers an important course of action—a call for neither "begging" and "humiliating" oneself to the racist legal apparatus of the liberal democratic state, nor "surrendering" one's right to have rights.

Thinking through the implications of this courageous call for collective defiance, it is important also to consider that the efficacy of rights for resistance movements is being eroded because the public sphere has shrunk as the state has declined in the context of neoliberal global capitalism, as Spivak (in Butler and Spivak 2010, 89) argues. The question of the state is a complex one, and cannot simply be reduced to that of liberal or bourgeois democracy. There is a need for a robust vehicle for redistribution and structure for redress, not just a structure for more "data-basing of human rights, or public interest litigation in the interest of a public that cannot act for itself" (Spivak in Butler and Spivak 2010, 94). So as with the critique of sovereignty, the enduring challenge is: what *kind* of state, and what *form* of democracy? Badiou (2005) critiques "formal democracy, or democracy as a figure of the State," arguing that the figure of (liberal parliamentarian) democracy is a form of state, "a figure of sovereignty or power," and sometimes of coercive power wielded with the consent of "the people," or in the name of citizens, as is obvious in the U.S.-led global War on Terror (78). A key question in the larger debate about the possibilities of direct democracy is where one stands on the desire for "mass political activity not governed by the State, or by the good State" (Badiou 2005, 90). This is where theorists such as Etienne Balibar, who do not wish to give up on "politics on the level of the state, rights, or law" depart from critics such as Badiou—a debate that is at the heart of a thorny political conversation that has a long history, one I will not delve into here.[6]

I want to emphasize that the point is not to rush into post-statism, but to think about what it means to actually engage in the other form of mass politics, the "harder option" Menon alludes to, that is not so readily available or sanctioned by the liberal democratic state but that also requires that we do not abdicate political struggle altogether out of a desire for a "pure politics." As Rancière (2010) argues, those who bemoan the "end of politics" or celebrate the "return of politics" both end up participating in the repression of the political and consolidation of an existing political "consensus" (42). But it this *paradox* at the core of politics in imperial democracy that is crucial. Radical movements need to expose the "incoherence and gap inside the state, between the institutions charged with making laws and those charged with preserving or reinforcing them," according to Reddy (2011, 228), and bringing forth this contradiction is what is so threatening to the neoliberal democratic order. The gaps in civil rights activism that cannot address the criminalization of civil disobedience and denial of civil rights to Palestine solidarity activists, or in human rights talk that cannot account for the imperial devastation in Af-Pak or Iraq, are precisely the site of a dissensus, that is, "the demonstration (manifestation) of a gap in the sensible itself" (Rancière 2010, 38). This is where politics happens as "an intervention in the visible and

sayable," an attempt by the targets of the War on Terror and objects of surveillance to "mobilize" the gap between the promise of freedom by the existing
international legal order and its realization (Rancière 2010, 37; Butler in Butler and Spivak 2010, 68–69). As with all areas of political praxis, this is not
just a conceptual debate but an actual, ongoing struggle on the ground, and
the current struggle being waged by youth and people around the globe in the
gaps between the state, democracy, and rights-talk is a difficult, frustrating,
disillusioning, and risky one.

Arrested and Alternative Politics

I have attempted in this book to show how young people targeted by the
state in the long War on Terror struggle to challenge imperial violence and
racism, in both public and quiet ways, and the ways in which an alternative political language or terrain is often arrested by the available discourse
of rights and inclusion. This *arrested politics* evades the discussion of U.S.
imperial violence and of "genocide as a central modality of U.S. nation-
building and white supremacist globality"; even critical theorizing about the
War on Terror and anti-Muslim and anti-Arab racism sometimes fails to
address how the logic of genocide is used to define the enemy by the "per-
petually genocidal nation-building project" (Rodriguez 2010, 99, 100). It is
important to illuminate how the logic of genocide links the foundational
violence of the settler-colonial state in "zones of death" in the Philippines,
during an earlier colonial encounter, to Afghanistan, Iraq, Pakistan, or Gaza
in late colonial modernity (Rodriguez 2010, 189). As Moon-Kie Jung (2011)
observes, the U.S. is an "empire-state" built on the twin logics of "extermina-
tion and assimilation" where the promise of "'equal' citizenship," coexisting
with "differential access to rights," is a "practice of colonial rule" that undermines processes of decolonization and rights to self-determination (3; see
also Barker 2014). The problem of "post–civil rights multiculturalism" as it
has incorporated Arab, South Asian, and Afghan Americans is that it has
been complicit with an "un-remembering and un-witnessing" of U.S. imperial violence and genocide, as I have discussed earlier, and this has led to
an "arrested raciality" and deformed national politics in immigrant communities, including those from regions devastated by colonial violence
(Rodriguez 2010, 89, 188).

Departing from the trend in most studies of Muslim, Arab, and South
Asian American youth, I suggest a different way to address the dilemma of
democracy and the impasse of rights for the objects of imperial violence,
situating the question of democracy squarely in relation to the foundational

genocidal violence of the empire-state, to a politics of life and death in the settler colony, as well as to the "rule of difference" and inclusion through arrested politics. It is striking that a critique of colonialism, imperialism, and race is also missing from some scholarly and otherwise astute critiques of neoliberal democracy and liberal nationalism (for example, Dean 2009). The question of democracy needs to be considered in the context of imperialism for it to be fully resituated outside of the language of "the enemy," in Žižek's terms, and beyond the framework provided by the liberal-conservative democratic consensus. In a post–civil rights era where all emancipatory concepts seem to have been co-opted or arrested, disappointment, cynicism, fatigue, and fear can paralyze resistance to imperial violence and lead many, not just young people, to disavow militant or radical dissent. This is not the same as signaling "the end of politics," however, a claim that is very much embedded in the shift to postmodern, poststate, and postsovereignty politics, but it is indeed the case that radical politics (in general) is arrested, contained, and crushed at every turn.

This book demonstrates how youth in the 9/11 generation attempt to work their way through an arrested politics and find an alternative political discourse, in a post-9/11 moment of repression, surveillance, and criminalization of "radical" politics and "bad" Muslims, immigrants, minorities, and political subjects. Palestinian, Arab, Afghan, and Pakistani Americans—like Filipino Americans, Cambodian, Vietnamese, and Hmong Americans—are not simply migrants but also refugees, postcolonial, and neoimperial subjects. There is an uneasy negotiation of consent by those targeted by the "apparatus of state coercive power" in the War on Terror, even if arrested politics is not always expressed as what Antonio Gramsci described as "spontaneous consent" (cited in Rodriguez 2010, 76). While the young people in this book did not generally identify with the U.S. nation-building project, and were deeply ambivalent in most cases about the forms of political allegiance demanded of them in the post-9/11 moment, it is apparent also that they did not always think of their own relationship to the U.S. (explicitly) through the lens of imperialism or neocolonialism. Recognition and inclusion through rights is an overpowering political common sense and youth risk being described as "radicalized" terrorist sympathizers if they adopt the vocabulary of anti-imperialism or reject the imperial state's violent humanitarianism. Yet several young people in this book clearly struggled with the gaps between their knowledge of imperial histories and interventions in Afghanistan, Iraq, Egypt, and Palestine and the U.S. narrative of democracy and rights, with some youth explicitly reframing the problem as one of imperial racism and global capitalism.

It should not be surprising that some young Arab, South Asian, and Afghan Americans articulated their response to the War on Terror through the language of multicultural belonging, and a desire for recognition as ethnic and religious subjects, given the commonsensical national framework provided by postpolitical, neoliberal democracy. This is one of the dilemmas of imperial modernity which is constituted by the paradigms of liberal civil rights and multicultural inclusion that young South Asian, Arab, and Afghan Americans must grapple with even while imagining resistance to the War on Terror and challenging post-9/11 racism and repression. As Mmembe (2003) has demonstrated in his analysis of necropolitics, the reinsertion of race and colonialism into a discussion of exceptional state violence makes it apparent that a colonialist and racialized logic of sovereignty regulates the management of life and death in late modernity. Yet this is perhaps the most difficult argument to make in the heart of empire, which is why it is seems almost impossible for many to present the predicament of Arab, South Asian, and Afghan Americans after 9/11 as a problem not of civil or human rights but of self-determination in a condition of late imperialism.

Resistance and Justice in the Age of Obama

How, then, to express dissent in the War on Terror and what is the alternative form of the "political" in a moment in which anti-imperial politics has been arrested and the vocabulary of the left seems to have been in so many cases deformed or defanged by the right? What frameworks can young people use when "democracy" is the language of U.S. statecraft and expansionism, "women's rights" and "gay rights" are the alibis of imperial interventions and occupation, and cultural and religious difference are promoted by the neoliberal, multicultural state, particularly under Obama? For many Americans, as Angela Davis (2012) observes, the election of Obama was used to suggest that "U.S. democracy has reached a zenith, change has come" for the disenfranchised, the deported, the incarcerated, the foreclosed, or the unemployed (179). Obama's presidency facilitated an exceptionalist narrative of U.S. democracy, as Davis suggests, and allowed a nationalist consensus to be rebuilt on the telos of democracy among progressives and leftists, not just among liberal and conservative nationalists. Roderick Ferguson (2010) has thoughtfully commented on what came to be described as the "Obama effect":

> We are now in a moment when our very capacity to question the fact and power of nationalism is jeopardized precisely because of the identity and charisma of

the president, and because of the ways in which power has managed to make minority difference shine in hues we never thought imaginable. (219)

Citing Obama's speech accepting the Nobel Peace Prize in which he made the bombastic, and quite simply offensive, declaration that "the United States has helped underwrite global security for more than six decades with the blood of our citizens and the strength of our arms," Ferguson notes that "the irony of it all is that any black president would have to emerge from a genealogy of freedom severed from peace. Here I don't mean peace as a category of the state but as an actual way of life that cannot be achieved through war" (217–218). Obama had not contributed in any measurable way to peace at the moment of this unexpected award—incomprehensible except as a symbolic expression of the hope of the rest of the world that the U.S. would embark on the path to peace. This condition of what Badiou calls the "democratic peace/war" under Obama was incisively critiqued by some young people, as I have demonstrated in this book. Responding to the contradictions of imperial democracy and the warfare state under Obama requires a committed shift in political thinking, and a shattering of the illusion of racial inclusion as an end to imperial violence and predatory capitalism.

In fact, it was the early phase of the Arab revolutions that galvanized mass movements across the U.S. and brought a different kind of "hope" for an alternative politics to the American liberal-left, for a brief moment. In an only fitting interruption of the racialized, anti-Arab and Islamophobic narrative of the War on Terror, it was Arab protesters that inspired many across the U.S., including youth, to take to their own streets and challenge "the radical redistribution of wealth to the very, very rich and the radical reconstruction of the state into the authoritarian tool for their protection"—the "radical" politics that Dean (2009, 9) observes were actually implemented by the Obama regime. As I have argued in Chapter Five, it is also important to reclaim the meaning of radicalism in the post-9/11 era and situate it in the context of struggles for social transformation, wresting it away from the lexicon of counterterrorism and surveillance. Yet is also true that radical movements such as Occupy did not, in all instances, make the connections to U.S. imperialism or to the violence of the settler colonial state, even if there were some events led by Occupy activists in solidarity with Egyptian and Palestinian struggles, as in the Bay Area. The concept of "occupation" refers to a political tactic but also rests uneasily on the histories and realities of occupied regions in the settler colonial present, from North America to Palestine. In some locations, such as UC Davis, student activists adopted the credo "Occupy/Decolonize" to incorporate this anticolonial critique and when I was in Palestine, I noticed that young activists stenciled the slogans "#Un-Occupy" and "Occupy Wall Street, Not Palestine!" on walls in the West Bank to make the same point (Maira 2013).

These revolutionary acts by youth against the social order reframe the horizon of radical struggles and force us to think not (just) of rights and legal equality, but of justice. Against a liberal or bourgeois parliamentarian notion of consensual democracy as the acceptable object of emancipatory politics, Badiou (2005) poses the notion of equality, not as an "objective of action" but as its "axiom," and emphasizes an "old, worn-out word"—justice (94, 98). For Badiou , to create a rupture in the status quo, "justice" cannot be a state project nor a "category of statist and social order" but must be an "egalitarian moment of politics," one that is crucial and yet also difficult to easily locate in "spectacle" or "sentiment"; that is, one presumably knows what injustice looks like, and it can be dramatized through affective testimonials of suffering, but "justice is obscure" and yet at the core of "principles at work in rupture and disorder" (96–99). For some, this ambiguity in defining justice might be problematic, but it is also true, as Partha Chatterjee (2014) observes in his reflection on democracy's imbrication with modern statecraft: "To embrace politics in its pure uncertainty, its unrelieved dangerousness . . . without the technical instruments of measuring costs and benefits, is terrifying. To seek refuge in history and statecraft is to return to the comfort of the familiar. This is what most of us prefer to do" (175). Furthermore, against a notion of "formal, abstract democracy" confined to electoral politics and "legal equality" in "bourgeois democracy," Angela Davis, drawing on the work of W.E.B. DuBois, has argued for "abolition democracy," which would actually challenge the imperial, carceral state by building alternative social institutions and "insist on economic, racial, gender, and sexual justice and equality" (Davis 2005, 85, 95; 2012, 106).

The principles of justice and of a radical and truly emancipatory or abolition democracy, beyond a liberal, universalist conception of democratic rights, then, offer a horizon for left political movements that do not want to take refuge in the familiar. It is the negotiation of the meanings of justice, of equality not confined to the law, and of collective (not individual) freedom that must drive the rethinking of the discourse of civil rights, women's rights, gay rights, human rights, and even economic rights. In other words, this does not mean "giving up" on a discourse of rights or democracy, but redefining it through a politics that returns to the core question of justice and that is open to the uncertainty, contradictions, and also creativity of imagining and establishing an alternative political order.

Solidarity and Espionage

What, then, does solidarity look like in progressive or radical movements for justice in the context of the domestic and global War on Terror? A common notion is that political solidarity must link preexisting, discrete "communities" and movements, while for others, such as Hardt and Negri (2009), a utopian form of political "love" drives solidarity, transcending racial, national, and religious boundaries. Yet these approaches generally presume that communities are already constituted in predetermined ways, to be connected through affiliations produced through shared struggles and experiences of oppression. Solidarity has also become a notion that can be commodified or packaged in reductive slogans and marketable clichés, something to be celebrated in the heart of empire and in an era of NGOized activism. Solidarity is often understood, including among some of the young people I spoke to, as an expression of affinity among predefined ethnic, religious, and national categories. It becomes inevitable, or desirable, that South Asians, Arabs, Afghans, Muslims and others in the U.S. targeted by the War on Terror build alliances with one another based on pan-Islamic solidarity or civil rights and engage in transnational solidarity based on human rights.

It is important to think about solidarity beyond the premise simply of affinity, sympathy, collectivity, or an affective bond. In fact, solidarity may necessitate a *rupture* of the bonds assumed to be natural in certain preexisting "communities" (uniting professionals, bankers, and government officials across racial lines, for example, or immigrants across class interests) and compel other affiliations that are forged against the group's interests or rethought in new ways through joint struggles (for instance, linking Arab and Latino immigrants or civil rights and prison abolition activists). Solidarity can disrupt the ties that we think bind us. Radical Black intellectuals such as Stuart Hall (1996) and Angela Davis have been critical of the "fiction of black unity" (Davis 2005, 101) as the sole basis for political struggle, a critique that is ever more acute in a moment of multiracial imperialism embodied by figures such as (former secretary of state) Condoleezza Rice and (ex–attorney general) Alberto Gonzalez. Disentangling these fictions and essentialisms is crucial to building unexpected, and necessary, solidarities.

There were difficult tensions in the emerging solidarity movements that I have discussed in the book, and fissures based on national, religious, racial, and class differences. Young people who confronted the meaning of these conflicts realized that, as Bernice Reagon of Sweet Honey in the Rock has succinctly remarked, "You don't do coalition-building in a womb!" (cited in Das Gupta 2006, 300); these youth also had to rethink what, and how, they were resisting. For example, Feroze—reflecting on alliances that were formed between different Muslim American groups, and between Muslim and Sikh Americans, due to shared experiences of post-9/11 profiling—observed, "More so than like coming up with the true bond among us, it was sort of uniting around the common plight. I don't think any of the groups understood each other more in a substantive level. All we understood was there was a common term of conditions that we both face. And I don't know how meaningful that is, circumstances change. The identification is circumstantial." I think Feroze makes a very astute observation, critiquing affiliation across difference based on a shared "condition" of discrimination, exclusion, or violence in a particular historical circumstance as creating unity around a "common plight" but not a "true bond" based on a deeper understanding of others' histories or struggles. Solidarity is always contingent, but Feroze suggests that it cannot be based simply on shared experiences of being taken off a plane, fired from a job for wearing a turban or a hijab, or targeted by the FBI, and on testimonials of experiences that look or sound the same, for these circumstances can, and do, shift. The state is continually selecting different targets for its most intense disciplining and devising new regimes of policing and surveillance. I argue that the "true bond" that would outlive a particular moment is solidarity based on a deeper politics of resistance to the structure of the imperial state and neoliberal capitalism, which produces a politics that is complex, creative, and evolving.

It is useful here to think of Robin Kelley's (1999) concept of polycultural affiliations, which has been further developed by Vijay Prashad (2001)—it suggests ways of generating solidarity by engaging in political struggle based on overlapping cultural processes and intersecting histories, rather than on discrete, fixed identity categories or multicultural fictions of cultural authenticity. This notion resonates with the adage that identity should emerge from one's politics, rather than politics from one's identity. Prashad (2001) argues that polyculturalism provides the basis for a "genuine antiracist struggle" by rejecting both postracialism and colonialist and cultural nationalist conceptions of racial purity and cultural difference (68). Polyculturalism generates new categories, new meanings of identification and difference, and it has emerged in specific local sites among various groups of youth in the context of the War on Terror (see Maira 2009). As Kelley (2012) observes, "Freedom is a process of becoming, of being able to see and understand difference within unity," in order to have a "radical conception of community" based on an emancipatory unity (15). Jasbir Puar and Amit Rai (2004) argue for a notion of solidarity not based on specific identities or a universalizing class analysis that can bridge difference, but on what they posit as "irreducible singularities" that can be mobilized in their intensity and multiplicity to attack the "heart of empire":

> If we can think of solidarity as the communication of irreducible singularities that are no longer specific (i.e., identitarian) or transcended (by the economy), what fuses one community's struggles to another's is the intensity of articulated oppressions . . . and the multiple experiences of becoming-other produced through its processes. We are not then speaking of a solidarity across difference, if by difference is meant something like "community identities"; nor are we suggesting a praxis of resistance that would find both its internal lack and higher transcendence in a utopic synthesis like the overthrow of "post-Fordism." We are speaking of a monstrous experience of solidarity that would be singular and intense and for that very reason multiple (or always miscegenated) and irreducible. (87–88)

Solidarity does not emerge from "natural," predetermined categories or identities, as all these critics suggest, but produces its own others through the linkages of struggles that are constantly shifting and evolving and not without their own contradictions (see Duggan 2003, 88). For instance, Masao Suzuki spoke about how his experience with the Japanese American redress and reparations movement in California, which I touched on in Chapter Two, led to a "sense of solidarity beyond the idea of coalition building," which he defined as "based on mutual interest" in contrast to "support for another group" beyond common strategic needs. He reflected that his involvement with the antidraft movement during the Vietnam war and the movement opposing apartheid in South Africa exposed him to a politics of cross-racial and transnational solidarity that extended beyond the suffering of a particular ethnic or racial group. As Prashad (2000) observes, "That this solidarity requires a tremendous act of production shows it is not 'natural.' That there is a desire to create unity among working class peoples and oppressed peoples of color does not mean unity is waiting to happen" (197). Solidarity is processual, emerging from cultural and historical processes and in the midst of shifting political events, violence, despair, and hope.

In the context of U.S. multicultural nationalism and the desire for political inclusion and recognition, it is important to think carefully about those alliances that are considered "natural" or desirable in contrast to those are presumably difficult to forge or viewed as a threat. As discussed in Chapter Two, South Asian, Arab, and Afghan American youth found that liberal civil rights activism and interfaith solidarity were more intensely promoted and pervasive than other forms of coalition building in Silicon Valley, such as cross-racial and cross-class alliances resisting the state's overlapping regimes of surveillance, incarceration, and deportation that could unite Muslim and Middle Eastern communities with Latinos, African Americans, and Asian Americans, or solidarity linking workers in different sectors in Silicon Valley. Injecting the question of self-determination and sovereignty into opposition to U.S. interventions and U.S.-backed occupations in Iraq, Afghanistan, Pakistan, and Palestine could generate a shared affiliation with Native American communities, and with others opposed to settler colonialism and imperialism. Struggles for indigenous sovereignty and against the carceral state could shift the dominant, acceptable discourses of human rights and civil rights as well as of national (imperial/settler) sovereignty.

This research forced me to think deeply about assumptions concerning which alliances are permissible or possible and which are not, which politics are sanctioned and which are considered dangerous. These questions emerged from a context in which solidarity was also the condition of my research, and the book was driven by my own sense of solidarity and relationships with the young people in this book as well as with the movements in which I was involved as an organizer and ally. These relationships and affiliations evolved and shifted over time, and the conversations I had with youth and others helped provide a window into the contradictions and possibilities faced by participants in movements in the Bay Area, ones that I myself grappled with at various moments. I want to acknowledge that the political work of producing an emancipatory solidarity is very difficult in a multicultural state whose hegemony is reinforced by fragmentation, differentiation, and incorporation. The challenge of mobilizing collectively in the face of hypersurveillance, constant policing, and censorship is enormous, but I would like to suggest that perhaps there are indeed other forms of solidarity that are possible, that already exist but are not yet named—and perhaps it is with good reason that they are not widely identified. Is it even effective for alternative notions of solidarity to make themselves known or reveal themselves within a surveillance state? Is it important, or necessary, for forms of solidarity to be recognized and if so, for what purpose?

Elizabeth Povinelli (2006), writing of queer and indigenous political imaginaries in liberal settler colonial states, suggests that evading recognition or translation is necessary for what she describes as a "politics of espionage." She observes that "the point may well be to reshape habitudes ahead of recognition, to test something out rather than to translate it, *not* to produce meanings that can be translated, or embodiments that can be recognized" (24, 172). In a military-spy state that crushes resistance movements through permanent surveillance, infiltration, and tactics that sow distrust and suspicion, perhaps it is a politics that is *against* the grain of translation, visibility, and recognition that is needed. "Quiet encroachments," rather than spectacular protests, and fugitive knowledges can thrive in the underground and escape detection by the surveillance state, erupting in public when the conditions of possibility are ripe and congealing into visible protest in ways that can catch repressive regimes off guard and create new spaces and new tactics of protest, as scholars have argued about the Arab uprisings (Bayat 2013; Harney and Moten 2013). This approach also offers a politics that could subvert the NGO-industrial complex and community activism or youth organizing funded by nonprofit organizations that in many cases shores up the premise of neoliberal democracy and imperial multiculturalism, or at least, remains safely within its parameters (see Kwon 2013). I have explored the ways in which those targeted by the military-spy state engage in forms of countersurveillance, which involve tactical forms of resisting as well as also surveiling the apparatus of surveillance itself, producing knowledge of the surveillance state. In other cases, young people and community activists have produced political strategies or subjects that cannot be contained within a politics of multicultural inclusion. These tactics and strategies can be thought through a deeper concept of a subversive "politics of espionage" (Povinelli 2006, 163)—subversive because these actions refuse to fall into the trap of multicultural visibility and recognition. As Povinelli points out, the "state represses counterpublics whose challenge can't be neutralized or accommodated within liberal 'toleration'" (163). These refusals and redirections are, strategically as well as ideologically, a "foil" to the liberal settler state's attempts to co-opt or contain resistance by dividing "good" and "bad" minority subjects and regulating and surveiling "moderate" or "extremist" politics (Povinelli 2006, 24).

The idea of "testing," rather than "translating," political subjecthood and refusing a politics that fits within an existing grid of intelligibility suggests a politics of dissent and solidarity that is subversive, unrecognizable, or under the radar of the imperial state. The notion of a shape-shifting solidarity can not be romanticized either—the danger in the post-9/11 moment is also that solidarity movements are somehow expected to deliver a utopian or "redemptive narrative" (Povinelli 2006, 25). Furthermore, given that imperial formations are constantly being remade and based on "moving categories and populations" (Stoler and McGranahan 2007, 8), anti-imperial solidarity is also a moving target and must be contingent, but not reactionary. There is a risk here that flexibility and contingency may dissolve or undermine sustainable political mobilization and effective resistance—a risk that some organizing on the ground are unwilling to take, sometimes understandably—but it is also true that models of solidarity do not have to be immaculately conceived.

There are many historical archives of inspiration that can be adapted and reshaped to respond to a particular local or historical context, as suggested by Suzuki's reflections on the antiwar and antiapartheid internationalism of a different era that provide a collective memory re-created within post-9/11 solidarity and youth activism.

But in addition to risk, there is also sacrifice in solidarity: the sacrifice of particularity for something beyond the boundary, of singularity for something other than universalism. The "true bond" that Feroze describes is true not because it is permanent or universal, but because it is true to its understanding of the moment of struggle and the politics of resisting and transforming structures of power. As Stuart Hall (1996) observed, it is the "articulation, the non-necessary link, between a social force that is making itself, and the ideology or conceptions of the world which makes intelligible the process they are going through, which begins to bring onto the historical stage . . . a new set of social and political subjects" (144). In the struggle for solidarity, and in order to redefine a politics of resistance and dissensus that is not necessarily legible within the framework of the state and liberal democracy, various social forces are articulated with an ideological vision of justice and moments of freedom.

The poetics of this solidarity, which can be powerful but also tenuous, and may falter even as it flourishes in the cracks of empire, is indeed "more delicate than a flower, yet harder than a rock," as the Afghan refugee told the young woman who shared it with me. It is that strange beauty that the stories of and by young people in this book suggest is possible.

NOTES

INTRODUCTION

1 "AMEMSA Fact Sheet," *Asian Americans/Pacific Islanders in Philanthropy*, November 2011. http://aapip.org/files/incubation/files/amemsa20fact20sheet.pdf.

2 I should note that while I did not include Iranian Americans, who are scattered throughout the Bay Area, their experiences are very important to consider in light of these questions and there is a need for more research on Iranian American youth.

3 For example, while 49% of South Asian households in the Bay Area have an income above $100,000, and 26% of Arab and 38% of Iranian households are in this income bracket, only 10% of Afghan households belong to this affluent category. In 2013, 40% of Afghans in the Bay Area had some college education, compared to 78% of South Asians and 62% of Arabs. More Afghans live in Alameda County, where 33% of the Muslim American households have an income below $40,000, compared to 10% in Santa Clara County (Senzai and Bazian 2013).

4 A 2013 study of Muslim communities in the Bay Area (consisting of six counties including Santa Clara County, where San Jose is located, and Alameda County, where Fremont and Hayward are located) found that 37% live in Alameda County and 27% in Santa Clara County (Senzai and Bazian 2013).

5 Of these thirty-nine youth, fifteen were South Asian (eleven Pakistani, four Indian American); twelve Arab (two Egyptian, three Iraqi, four Palestinian, one Lebanese, one Syrian, and one Libyan American); and twelve Afghan American. Three were mixed (two were Arab/white and one was Afghan/Pakistani American); I have included them here in only one category.

6 I use pseudonyms for all the youth I interviewed. I use the real names of the community activists and religious leaders cited here as these are public figures.

CHAPTER 1. THE 9/11 GENERATION IN SILICON VALLEY

1 The Iranian population is far bigger, at 13,467 (Ahuja, Gupta, and Petsod 2004). According to the U.S. Census Bureau, in 2000 there were an estimated 5,911 Arab Americans in San Jose, which is an undercount but slightly more than in San Francisco (2005 American Community Survey, Santa Clara County). In 2010, there were 43,827 Indians in San Jose, and 38,711 in Fremont. Richard Springer, "Indians in California Up Nearly 50%," *India West*, May 19, 2011. http://indiawest.com.

2 Shalini Shankar's *Desi Land: Teen Culture, Class, and Success in Silicon Valley* (Durham, NC: Duke University Press, 2008) is focused on South Asian American

youth culture in Silicon Valley in the late 1990s and on young people's understandings of success, consumption, and desi (pan–South Asian) identity, but does
not address political activism or the specificities of Pakistani and Muslim
American identification.

3 U.S. Census Bureau, Profile of General Population and Housing Characteristics:
2010—Santa Clara County and San Jose City, California, *American FactFinder*.
http://factfinder.census.gov/faces/nav/jsf/pages/index.xhtml.

4 U.S. Census Bureau, Profile of General Population and Housing Characteristics:
2010 Demographic Profile Data—San Jose City, California, *American FactFinder*.
http://factfinder.census.gov/faces/nav/jsf/pages/index.xhtml.

5 U.S. Census Bureau, Race Reporting for the Asian Population by Selected
Categories: 2010—San Jose City, California, *American FactFinder*. http://
factfinder.census.gov/faces/nav/jsf/pages/index.xhtml.

6 The population of Fremont was 48% Asian American, 32% White, 14% Hispanic,
and 4% African American, according to the U.S. Census Bureau in 2006 (Fremont
Data: Ethnicity).

7 U.S. Census Bureau, Profile of General Population and Housing Characteristics,
2010—Fremont City, California, *American FactFinder*. http://factfinder.census.
gov/faces/nav/jsf/pages/index.xhtml.

8 San Jose Department of Planning, Building, and Code Enforcement, Planning
Division, "City of San Jose, Capital of Silicon Valley: Fact Sheets," *SanJoseCA.gov*,
n.d. (ca. 2013). https://www.sanjoseca.gov/DocumentCenter/View/780.

9 U.S. Census Bureau, Selected Economic Characteristics: 2007–2011 American
Community Survey 5-Year Estimates, Santa Clara County, California, *American
FactFinder*. http://factfinder2.census.gov/faces/tableservices/jsf/pages/product-
view.xhtml?pid=ACS_11_5YR_DP03.

10 George Packer, "Change the World," *New Yorker*, May 27, 2013. http://www.
newyorker.com/reporting/2013/05/27/130527fa_fact_packer.

11 Asian Pacific American Legal Center, *The Diverse Face of Asians and Pacific
Islanders in California*. 2005. Los Angeles: Asian Pacific American Legal Center of
Southern California. According to this report, 15% of Pakistanis and 7% of Indians
in the Bay Area (which includes Santa Clara County) were under the poverty line
as of the 2000 U.S. Census.

12 Some striking examples of this "model minority" narrative are the stories of
young entrepreneurs who made millions during the dot-com boom. One such
example is Gurbaksh Chahal, an Indian American from San Jose who sold his
first internet startup, Click Agents, for $40 million at the age of 18 ("Gurbaksh
Chahal: Fox's New 'Secret Millionaire,'" *Young Money*, December 2008/January
2009, pp. 4, 11).

13 See Hamish McKenzie, "Silicon Valley's Ugly Rich-Poor Gap: What's the Tech
World Going to Do about It?," *Pandodaily*, July 8, 2013. http://pandodaily.
com/2013/07/08/silicon-valleys-ugly-rich-poor-gap-whats-the-tech-world-
gonna-do-about-it/.

14 "2013 at a Glance," *Silicon Valley Index*, 2013. http://www.siliconvalleyindex.org/index.php/component/content/article?id=31; "Income," *Silicon Valley Index*, 2013. http://www.siliconvalleyindex.org/index.php/economy/income.

15 "In Silicon Valley, Tent Cities Point to Growing Inequality," *New America Media/ Silicon Valley De-Bug*, March 8, 2013. http://newamericamedia.org/2013/03/in-silicon-valley-tent-cities-point-to-growing-inequality.php.

16 On May 1, 2006, over three hundred thousand mostly Mexican protesters marched to the San Jose City Hall from the predominantly immigrant East Side, as part of a nationwide immigrant rights movement and in opposition to a federal bill, HR 4437, that would make immigrant status a felony (Gleeson 2012, 107).

17 Richard Springer, "Indians Dominate Tech Sector: Study," *India West*, January 5, 2007, pp. A1, A31, A32.

18 Raj Jayadev, "Sikh Cab Drivers Say Racism, Recession Put Them in the Crosshairs," *New America Media*, October 27, 2003. http://news.newamericamedia.org/news/view_article.html?article_id=a5df86f3b625bfca9e3815f58ddfc14d.

19 Jessie Mangaliman, "Officials Decry Attacks on Arab Americans: Muslim, Sikh Communities Seek Help to Halt Violence," *San Jose Mercury News*, September 18, 2001, p. 1A.

20 Julie S. Lyons and Becky Bartindale, "Threats against Muslims at SJSU: The Police Investigate Restroom Graffiti," *San Jose Mercury News*, March 11, 2003, p. B1.

21 John Cote, "Hate Crime Alleged in Stabbing of Sikh," *San Francisco Chronicle*, August 2, 2006, p. B10; Linh Tat, "Community Members Wear Hijabs, Turbans in Solidarity," *Inside Bay Area*, November 14, 2006.

22 Cote, "Hate Crime Alleged."

23 Lisa Fernandez, "Sunnyvale: Man Attacked for Being Muslim, Public Safety Officers Say," *San Jose Mercury News*, June 14, 2010. http://www.mercurynews.com/breaking-news/ci_15295575.

24 Karen De Sa, "Volunteers Set Up Escorts for Those in Fear," *San Jose Mercury News*, September 20, 2001, p.8A; Karen De Sa and Michael Bazely, "Backlash Still Felt among Immigrants," San Jose Mercury News, September 12, 2002, p. A14.

25 A Pew Research Center survey in 2011 found that nearly half of Muslims in the U.S. considered themselves Muslim first and American second, with a higher percentage identifying as Muslim first than in Egypt, Indonesia, Lebanon, and Turkey (cited in Abdullah 2013, 80).

26 "RAND Report Says Cold War Offers Lessons on Engaging with the Muslim World" [press release], *Rand Corporation*, March 26, 2007. http://www.rand.org/news/press.07/03.26.html.

27 See Sahar Aziz, "The New Generation of Muslim American Leaders," *Al Jazeera* (English), July 24, 2014. http://www.aljazeera.com/indepth/opinion/2014/07/new-generation-muslim-american-2014723143141881797.html.

28 See, e.g., CAIR/University of California, Berkeley, Center for Race and Gender. *Same Hate, New Target: Islamophobia and Its Impact in the United States, January*

2009–December 2010. June 2011. http://crg.berkeley.edu/sites/default/files/islamophobiareport2009–2010.pdf.

29 It is interesting, in this context, to note that national surveys of Muslim Americans ask youth about their emotional state, with the 2009 Gallup survey (103) reporting that 26% of Muslim American youth report feeling anger, much more than any other religious group.

CHAPTER 2. THE NEW CIVIL RIGHTS MOVEMENT

1 Event information at "Hearings," *Unheard Voices of 9/11*, n.d. http://unheard-voicesof911.org/hearings/.

2 For Sikh Coalition reports, see "Profiling," *Sikh Coalition*, n.d. (ca. 2014). Originally at http://www.sikhcoalition.org/our-programs/advocacy/profiling. Archived at https://web.archive.org/web/20141008104757/http://www.sikhcoalition.org/our-programs/advocacy/profiling.

3 Mercury News Wire Service, "Anti-Muslim Hate Crimes Reportedly Rise," *San Jose Mercury News*, May 11, 2005, p. 4A; Momo Chang, "Discrimination against Muslims Continues to Rise," *Alameda Times-Star*, September 19, 2005.

4 The CAIR report contrasted with the findings of the state attorney general, whose report compiled incidents investigated by authorities and showed a drop in hate crimes against people of "Middle Eastern" descent, but there is both the possibility that the state report was based on the low number of incidents that are officially classified as hate crimes and that more Muslim Americans are reporting incidents of bias. Nicholas Shields, "Muslim Group Sees Rise Last Year in Reports of Civil Rights Abuses," Nicholas Shields, *Los Angeles Times*, July 28, 2005; Rebecca Lum, "Bias against Muslims on the Rise, Group Says," *Inside Bay Area*, July 27, 2007.

5 See "Post-9/11 Civil Rights and Civil Liberties Priorities for the South Asian Community," *South Asian Americans Leading Together (SAALT)*, December 12, 2008. www.saalt.org.

6 CAIR–San Francisco Bay Area and the Legal Aid Society–Employment Law Center were part of a lawsuit filed by the Equal Employment Opportunity Commission against Abercrombie & Fitch on behalf of Khan (see Council on American-Islamic Relations, 2013).

7 It also needs to be pointed out that the MPAC survey was conducted among youth (fourteen to twenty-five years old) attending the annual convention of the Islamic Society of North America, who were strongly affiliated with Islamic institutions (Muslim Public Affairs Council 2005, 2).

8 In response to incidents of bullying, harassment, and Islamophobia in schools in northern California, CAIR launched the "Muslim Youth at School" project in 2012. See Council on American-Islamic Relations (2013), 17–18.

9 Jeanne Theoharis, "The Legal Black Hole in Lower Manhattan: The Unfairness of the Trial of Muslim Activist Syed Fahad Hashmi," *Slate*, April 27, 2010. http://www.slate.com.

10 Chris Hawley, "NYPD Monitored Muslim Students All Over the Northeast,"
    Associated Press, February 18, 2012. http://www.ap.org/Content/AP-In-The-
    News/2012/NYPD-monitored-Muslim-students-all-over-Northeast; Kim Zetter,
    "Caught Spying on Student, FBI Demands GPS Tracking Device Back," *Wired*,
    October 7, 2010. http://www.wired.com/2010/10/fbi-tracking-device/.

11 Maha ElGenaidi, "Churches & Other Centers," *ING*, 2005. Originally at www.ing.
    org/speakers/page.asp?num=14. Archived at https://web.archive.org/
    web/20070820223315/http://www.ing.org/speakers/page.asp?num=14.

12 As many scholars have argued, multiculturalism was initially a much-needed
    response to Eurocentric narratives of U.S. national culture and the invisible
    hegemony of whiteness, and so in its early years was productive in broadening
    educational curricula circumscribed by a civilizational canon and challenging the
    meaning of American identity—a "strong" or progressive multiculturalism
    (Melamed 2006, 15).

13 The U.S. state has since World War II increasingly adopted an official liberal
    multiculturalism by virtue of which the state is not only the "guarantor of rights"
    but also assumed to be antiracist, even as it directly or indirectly suppresses
    movements that demand genuine racial justice (Reddy 2011, 194, 210).

14 Sabina is referring here to the Unity Program of Abraham's Vision for high school
    students, focused on Jewish-Muslim relations, Islam, and Judaism. See "Course
    Summary," *Abraham's Vision*, n.d. (ca. 2011). http://www.abrahamsvision.org/
    programs/unity-program.html.

15 For example, this issue came to a head in Muslim American media and activist
    circles when a delegation of Muslim American leaders spent a year at the
    Hartmann Institute in Jerusalem. One of the delegates concluded that despite her
    previous reservations about censorship of pro-Palestine viewpoints in interfaith
    programs, the dialogue with Jewish Zionists convinced her to be less critical of
    Zionism, in an article published in *Time* during the Israeli invasion of the West
    Bank and Gaza in summer 2014. Rabia Choudhury, "What a Muslim American
    Learned from Zionists," *Time*, June 24, 2014. http://time.com/2917600/
    muslim-american-zionists/.

16 Sana Saeed, "An Interfaith Trojan Horse: Faithwashing Apartheid and
    Occupation," *Islamic Monthly*, July 1, 2014. http://www.theislamicmonthly.com/
    an-interfaith-trojan-horse-faithwashing-apartheid-and-occupation/.

17 I wish to thank Saree Makdisi for this point about Arabness as dissolving into the
    "master category" of Muslimness.

18 "Jewish, Muslim Teens Worth Together," *Islamic Life*, September 23, 2013. http://
    www.islamiclife.com/health/2013/jewish_muslim_teens_work_together.php.

19 See, e.g., http://green-muslims.org/.

20 Maria Ebrahimji, "Author Wants to Rebrand Muslims from Terrorists to
    Environmentalists," *CNN Belief Blog*, November 16, 2010. http://religion.blogs.
    cnn.com/2010/11/16/
    author-wants-to-rebrand-muslims-from-terrorists-to-environmentalists/.

21 "About Us," Ta'leef Collective, n.d. (ca. 2013). Originally at http://www.taleefcollective.org/?page_id=26. Archived at https://web.archive.org/web/20130214000409/http://www.taleefcollective.org/?page_id=26.

22 While I spoke to youth and also community leaders connected to the Ta'leef Collective, the organization's staff, including Canon, declined to be interviewed. It is possible that this response was due in part to the excessive media attention on Muslim youth organizations and a consequent wariness about their representation at the hands of others.

23 See Omar Offendum, The Narcicyst, Freeway, Ayah, Amir Sulaiman, and Sami Matar, "#Jan 25 Egypt," YouTube, February 7, 2011. http://www.youtube.com/watch?v=sCbpiOpLwFg.

24 See Nikkei for Civil Rights and Redress September 11 Committee, "Building a Movement to End this Illegal and Immoral War," Amerasia 33(3): 11–124.

25 This connection is also powerfully made in the documentary film Enemy Alien (2009), about Palestinian activist Farouk Abdel-Muhti, who was incarcerated after 9/11 and died in prison. Its director, Konrad Aderer, is the grandson of Japanese Americans incarcerated in World War II.

CHAPTER 3. HUMAN RIGHTS, UNCIVIL ACTIVISM, AND PALESTINIANIZATION

1 "Amnesty: U.S, Europe Shielding Israel over Gaza War Crimes," Haaretz, May 27, 2010. http://www.haaretz.com/news/diplomacy-defense/amnesty-u-s-europe-shielding-israelover-gaza-war-crimes-1.292505.

2 "Iraq: The War Logs," Guardian, 2012. http://www.theguardian.com/world/iraq-war-logs; Ryan Gallagher, "Ten Revelations from Bradley Manning's WikiLeaks Documents," Slate, June 4, 2013. http://www.slate.com/blogs/future_tense/2013/06/04/bradley_manning_trial_10_revelations_from_wikileaks_documents_on_iraq_afghanistan.html.

3 Jonathan Steele and Suzanne Goldenberg, "What Is the Real Death Toll in Iraq?"Guardian, March 18, 2008. http://www.theguardian.com/world/2008/mar/19/Iraq. See Iraq Body Count, http://www.iraqbodycount.org/.

4 See also "'African Americans for Justice in the Middle East and North Africa' Condemn Rising Tide of Racism in Israeli Society," Mondoweiss, August 2, 2013. http://mondoweiss.net/2013/08/african-americans-for-justice-in-the-middle-east-north-africa-condemn-rising-tide-of-racism-in-israeli-society.html; Felicia Eaves et al., "African Americans for Justice in the Middle East and North Africa: Solidarity Statement," Pambazuka News, July 26, 2012. http://www.pambazuka.org/en/category/advocacy/83905.

5 See the narratives by Arab American women in Shakir (1997) to situate this generational shift in historical perspective.

6 The AYO survey had 357 participants from San Francisco, Oakland, and a youth conference in Berkeley. See Arab Young Organization/Arab Resource and

Organizing Center, *Teaching Understanding and Representing Arabs throughout History (TURATH).* 2012. San Francisco: AYO/AROC.

7 Lubin (2014) uses Jordan's writing as an example of what he analyzes as an "Afro-Arab political imaginary" challenging "imperialism and racial capitalism" (143).

8 In 2009, the heads of all the churches in Jerusalem issued a historic statement, the "Kairos Document," calling for international solidarity with the "Palestinian people who have faced oppression, displacement, suffering and clear apartheid for more than six decades." It stated, "We address it first of all to ourselves and then to all the churches and Christians in the world, asking them to stand against injustice and apartheid, urging them to work for a just peace in our region, calling on them to revisit theologies that justify crimes perpetrated against our people and the dispossession of the land." "Kairos Document," *Kairos Palestine*, December 15, 2009. http://www.kairospalestine.ps/sites/default/Documents/English.pdf).

9 See the powerful statements at "Statements," *Palestinian Queers for BDS*, n.d.http://www.pqbds.com/about/.

10 For example, as discussed in the Introduction, Yemeni agricultural workers in California were involved in farmworker organizing with Chicano activists and the UFW (see Friedlander 1994). South Asian immigrants on the West Coast in the early part of the twentieth century forged connections with leftist Americans and anticolonial Irish activists through the radical Ghadar movement that challenged the British empire, and Indian Muslim migrants in roughly the same period became a part of social and political networks in Detroit, New Orleans, and Harlem (see Prashad 2000; Ramnath 2011; Bald 2013).

11 A satirical online video addresses the appropriation of the kaffiyeh as well as the racist backlash against it in the post-9/11 moment: KABOBfest, "Keffiyeh Infiltrates Our Nation's Youth," *YouTube*, January 27, 2008. https://www.youtube.com/watch?v=wYj8XSKN8RM.

12 For a report on the Rachel Ray controversy and Urban Outfitters' recall of kaffiyehs from a New York store in 2008, see "Dunkin Donuts Ad Controversy about Rachel Ray Arabic Scarf," *ABC News/YouTube*, June 2, 2008, https://www.youtube.com/watch?v=_FI14XMdTmg.

13 Cited in Samantha Brotman, "Salaita Speaks Out, Warns of a Palestinian Exception to the First Amendment and Academic Freedom," *Mondoweiss*, September 10, 2014. http://mondoweiss.net/2014/09/palestinian-exception-amendment.

14 See also "News & Updates," *Palestine Legal*, n.d. http://palestinelegalsupport.org/news-and-updates/news-updates-archive/.

15 For example, there have been campaigns orchestrated by the virulently anti-Arab organization AMCHA against Muslim and Middle Eastern student groups and faculty. See "Anti-Israel and Anti-Semitic Activity at San Jose State University (SJSU)," *AMCHA Initiative*, n.d. (ca. 2012). http://www.amchainitiative.org/anti-israel-and-anti-semitic-activity-at-san-jose-state-university-sjsu/.

16 Yaman Salahi, "Behind the Scenes with Israel's Campus Lobby," *Al Jazeera* (English), September 26, 2011. http://english.aljazeera.net/indepth/opinion/2011/09/201192384847314840.html.

17 For example, the Goldstone report, controversial among both pro-Palestine and pro-Israel activists, attested that the Israeli military had committed war crimes in Operation Cast Lead in Gaza. See: "UN Fact Finding Mission Finds Strong Evidence of War Crimes and Crimes against Humanity Committed during the Gaza Conflict; Calls for End to Impunity" [news release], *Office of the High Commissioner for Human Rights, United Nations*, September 15, 2009. http://www.ohchr.org/EN/NewsEvents/Pages/DisplayNews.aspx?NewsID=91&LangID=E.

18 Amcha also attacked UCLA faculty for organizing a panel about the war on Gaza in 2009. That same year, a UC Santa Barbara faculty member, Bill Robinson, was accused by Zionist activists of being anti-Semitic for sharing material with his students critical of Israeli state policies; the president of the Anti-Defamation League (ADL) even met with the university administration to demand that Robinson be investigated (Salaita 2011, 60–61).

19 See Nora Barrows Friedman, "Victory for Campus Free Speech as US Dept of Education Throws Out Anti-Semitism Complaints," *Electronic Intifada*, August 28, 2013. http://electronicintifada.net/blogs/nora-barrows-friedman/victory-campus-free-speech-us-dept-education-throws-out-anti-semitism.

20 The text of the resolution, which was opposed by the UC Student Association, is at http://leginfo.legislature.ca.gov/faces/billTextClient.xhtml;jsessionid=d4df7d3510900146efbbc88f1045?bill_id=201120120HR35.

21 Deidra Funcheon, "FAU Students: We Were Punished for Nonviolent Protest," *Broward/Palm Beach New Times*, August 13, 2013. http://blogs.browardpalmbeach.com/pulp/2013/08/fau_student_protest_pealstine_isreal_gruber.php.

22 Ali Abunimah, "Climate of Fear Silencing Palestinian, Muslim Students at UC Campuses, Rights Groups Warn," *Electronic Intifada*, December 4, 2012. http://electronicintifada.net/blogs/ali-abunimah/climate-fear-silencing-palestinian-muslim-students-university-california-rights.

23 See the statement by the Department of Education's Office of Civil Rights dismissing the complaint against UC Berkeley at http://newscenter.berkeley.edu/wp-content/uploads/2013/08/DOE.OCR_.pdf.

24 See "The Systematic Attempt to Shut Down Student Speech at the University of California," *Palestine Solidarity Legal Support*, n.d. (ca. October 2012). http://palestinelegalsupport.org/download/advocacy-documents/FACT%20SHEET%20Shutting%20Down%20Student%20Speech%20at%20U.C._fn_DISTRIBUTE.pdf.

25 For example, in 2009, UC president Mark Yudof condemned an event by the Muslim Student Union at UC Irvine on the "politics of genocide" in Israel and stated, "It is difficult for me to separate my public role as President of a state university from my private life as a Jewish man who is active in Jewish causes and a strong defender of Israel. Permit me now to remove my cap and gown and to exercise my First Amendment rights as a private citizen." This was in a letter

issued in response to pro-Israel critics of the event, and posted at the site of one of them, Scholars for Peace in the Middle East: http://spme.org/spme-research/ analysis/scholars-for-peace-in-the-middle-east-commend-the-university-of-california-president-mark-yudof-for-his-stand-against-anti-semitism/6885/. Yudof also issued a letter in March 2011, singling out as reprehensible examples of hate speech two incidents involving criticism of Israel, and created an advisory council on Campus Climate, Culture, and Inclusion that included a member of the pro-Israel ADL and that met at the Simon Wiesenthal Museum of Tolerance, a notoriously Zionist organization. Mark G. Yudof, "President Youdof Addresses Campus Climate Concerns from Jewish Community," University of California, September 21, 2011. Originally at http://www.universityofcalifornia.edu/news/ article/26327. Archived at https://web.archive.org/web/20131011000213/http:// www.universityofcalifornia.edu/news/article/26327. See also Makdisi 2010..

26 Yudof, "President Yudof Addresses Campus Climate Concerns."

CHAPTER 4. MORE DELICATE THAN A FLOWER, YET HARDER THAN A ROCK

1 While I was unable to confirm this specific incident, which would have taken place on April 16, 2007, 164–195 children were reportedly killed by the 371 U.S. drone strikes in Pakistan between 2004 and 2013, of which 320 took place under the Obama regime. In one infamous incident, in October 2006, a CIA drone attacked a religious school, killing 69 children in Bajaur agency in northwest Pakistan. See Chris Woods, "Drone Strikes in Pakistan," *Bureau of Investigative Journalism*, August 11, 2011 http://www.thebureauinvestigates.com/2011/08/11/ more-than-160-children-killed-in-us-strikes/.

2 The U.S. reliance on unmanned drones as a primary strategy in the war against Al Qaeda and the Taliban was also increasingly and publicly opposed by allies of the U.S. in Pakistan and Somalia, who realized that it was a major source of anger and opposition to the U.S. in the region. See, e.g., Ghada Eldemellawy, "Yemen: The First Step toward Criminalizing Drone Strikes, Obama Take Note." *Al Jazeera* (English), August 2, 2013. http://www.aljazeera.com/indepth/opin-ion/2013/08/201381141830129979.html.

3 Atanoski (2013) also makes the important argument that the U.S. covert interven-tion in Afghanistan in the 1980s allowed Reagan to counter the bitter memory of the Vietnam war by reaffirming the benevolence of the U.S. in "aiding weaker Third World people" resisting Soviet atrocities (106).

4 The little research that has been done on Afghan Americans in Fremont tends to paint a picture of a dysfunctional and divided community hostile to community programs initiated by others on their behalf, neglecting to consider the political history of these refugees and the legitimate reasons for their possible distrust of interventions and organizing by outsiders (Omidian and Lipson 1996).

5 Michael Gordon, "Kerry, in Pakistan, Expresses Optimism on Ending Drone Strikes Soon." *New York Times*, August 1, 2013. http://www.nytimes.

com/2013/08/02/world/asia/kerry-in-pakistan-visit-sees-longer-us-role-in-afghanistan.html?ref=todayspaper&_r=0. For example, thirty-eight protesters were arrested for civil disobedience at the New York Air National Guard Base at Hancock Field in Syracuse in April 2011, some wearing blue scarves in solidarity with Afghan youth; they lay down to block the main road to the base, two of them in wheelchairs. Charles Ellis, "Thirty-One Drone Protesters Found Guilty in DeWitt Court; Four Jailed," *Syracuse.com*, December 1, 2011. http://www.syracuse.com/news/index.ssf/2011/12/update_thirty-one_drone_protes.html.

6 The 175th child, according to the Bureau of Investigative Journalism, was sixteen-year old Tariq Aziz, who had volunteered to help document the civilian casualties of the drone attacks at an assembly of families of those who had been killed in the drone war; on his way home from the jirga in Waziristan, Aziz was killed by a drone, as was his twelve-year old cousin. Juan Gonzalez, Amy Goodman, and Pratap Chatterjee, "U.S. Drone Kills 16-Year-Old Pakistani Boy Days After He Attends Anti-Drone Organizing Meeting," *Democracy Now*, November 7, 2011. http://www.democracynow.org/2011/11/7/us_drone_kills_16_year_old.

7 For example, Jean Bricmont (2007) points out that British imperialists framed their interventions overseas as "moral crusades" in the late nineteenth century (69).

8 In contrast, see the recommendations in Patricia Gossman and Sari Kuovo, "Tell Us How This Ends: Transitional Justice and Prospects for Peace in Afghanistan," *Afghan Analysts Network*, June 2013. http://www.afghanistan-analysts.org/wp-content/uploads/2013/06/TransitionalJustice_execsummary.pdf.

9 As Adil Najam (2006) points out in his study of Pakistani American philanthropy, Pakistanis in the U.S. tend to financially support causes related to community development as well as civil and human rights in Pakistan, issues that humanitarian liberals would presumably support.

10 The Holy Land Five, five Palestinians who were charged with indirectly supporting Hamas by sending charity to Gaza, received sentences of fifteen to sixty-five years in 2009, after one mistrial and a second trial that involved secret witnesses. In 2012, despite a public campaign on their behalf, the five lost their appeal for a rehearing. See the Freedom to Give website: http://freedomtogive.com/.

11 Lee Ferran, "Raymond Davis, CIA Contractor, Appears Defiant before Pakistani Judge," *ABC News*, February 25, 2011. http://abcnews.go.com/Blotter/raymond-davis-cia-contractor-appears-pakistan-court-hearing/story?id=12997942.

12 UNOCAL officials met with Taliban representatives during their visit to Texas in 1997. UNOCAL also hired Zalmay Khalilzad as a consultant before he became U.S. envoy to Afghanistan, and reportedly worked with Hamid Karzai in the same role. "Taleban in Texas for Talks on Gas Pipeline," *BBC News*, December 4, 1997. http://news.bbc.co.uk/2/hi/world/west_asia/37021.stm.

13 As part of the scramble to control the oil reserves of Central Asia, beginning well before 2001, the U.S. government, CIA, and oil companies including Halliburton

(of which Dick Cheney was CEO before he became vice president in the Bush regime), were concerned about establishing an "investor-friendly climate in Afghanistan" for U.S. corporations who were thirsty for lucrative contracts in a country then destabilized by civil war. Tom Turnipseed, "Bush, Enron, UNOCAL, and the Taliban," *Counterpunch*, January 10, 2002. http://www.counterpunch.org/2002/01/10/bush-enron-unocal-and-the-taliban/.

14 The struggles of indigenous peoples to draft a Declaration on the Rights of Indigenous Peoples in the U.N. Human Rights Commission in the 1980s and 1990s illustrates this "impasse," where the demand simply for self-determination, not even territorial sovereignty, is seen as a threat to existing nation-states and settler colonies such as the U.S. (Merry 2006; Robbins and Stamatopoulou 2004, 425).

15 See also Scott Morgensen, *Spaces between Us: Queer Settler Colonialism and Indigenous Decolonization* (Minneapolis: University of Minnesota Press, 2011) for a queer critique of settler colonialism and queer modernities.

CHAPTER 5. COMING OF AGE UNDER SURVEILLANCE

1 This is poignantly enacted in the documentary film *USA mot Al-Arian* (*USA vs. Al-Arian*; dir. Line Halvorsen, 2007), during which the young children and wife of Palestinian activist Sami Al-Arian, who was under surveillance for a decade, listen to the wiretaps (which they presumably obtained through a Freedom of Information Act request) of their phone conversations on DVDs, laughing about recorded conversations of their orders for takeout pizza.

2 A 2009 Gallup poll (Gallup 2009) observed that Muslim Americans were far more likely to be "thriving" and satisfied with their lives than French and especially British Muslims, and even more than those in Muslim-majority countries (though Muslims in Germany apparently had levels of life satisfaction similar to those in the U.S.).

3 See Arthur N. Eisenberg, "Police Surveillance of Political Activity: The History and Current Status of the Handschu Decree," Testimony Provided to the New York Advisory Committee to the U.S. Commission on Civil Rights, *NYCLU*, n.d. http://www.nyclu.org/content/testimony-police-surveillance-of-political-activity-history-and-current-state-of-handschu-de. The 2004 Intelligence Reform and Terrorism Act (IRTA) called for an "Information-Sharing Environment" linking federal, state, and local agencies and the private sector, leading the Department of Homeland Security to launch the Suspicious Activity Reporting (SAR) Initiative to train local law enforcement to engage in surveillance of behavior and report it to a local DHS Fusion Center, which would share it nationally (Dubal 2012, 43).

4 Hawley, "NYPD Monitored Muslim Students."

5 Hana Baba, "Looking at You Looking at Me: Surveillance Protest Art," *SFGate*, April 4, 2012. http://blog.sfgate.com/kalw/2011/04/12/looking-at-you-looking-at-me-surveillance-protest-art/ (accessed July 8, 2012).

6 The San Jose Police Department (SJPD), civil rights advocates and community activists later discovered, already had at least one JTTF officer assigned to the FBI

under a secret memorandum of understanding, who followed federal, not local, guidelines (personal communication with Veena Dubal, August 25, 2013).

7 The SJPD announced in 2011 that it would include Immigration and Customs Enforcement (ICE) officers through a DHS program, Community Shield, and consider participating in the SAR initiative. This came on the heels of a campaign by the Coalition for Justice and Accountability against racial profiling and use of force by the SJPD that resulted in the formation of a city taskforce and changes to urban policing policies in 2010. Raj Jayadev, "Advocates Balk as San Jose Police Consider Fed Surveillance Program," *New America Media*, July 27, 2011. http://newamericamedia.org/2011/07/rights-advocates-balk-as-san-jose-police-consider-federal-surveillance-program.php.

8 "CUNY CLEAR," *CUNY School of Law*, n.d. (ca. 2012). http://www.law.cuny.edu/clinics/clinicalofferings/ImmigrantandRefugee/cunyclear.html.

9 This is also dramatically illustrated in the documentary film *Enemy Alien* (2011), about a Palestinian activist incarcerated in the U.S., in which the filmmaker, Konrad Aderer, and the film itself become the subject of a counterterrorism investigation by the FBI and Aderer decides to secretly record his meeting with Bureau agents.

10 Kim Zetter, "Caught Spying on Student, FBI Demands GPS Tracking Device Back." *Wired*, October 7, 2010. http://www.wired.com/threatlevel/2010/10/fbi-tracking-device/.

11 Ibid.

12 "FBI Caught Spying on Student, Demands GPS Tracker Back." *Daily Conversation/YouTube, October 8, 2010*. http://www.youtube.com/watch?v=2pb1vf_i-VU.

13 However, while the *United States v. Jones* ruling stated that the use of a GPS device constituted a search, it did not state whether such a search required a warrant, leaving this question open. David Kravets, "Supreme Court Rejects Willy-Nilly GPS Tracking," *Wired*, January 23, 2012. http://www.wired.com/threat-level/2012/01/scotus-gps-ruling/.

14 "Calif. Muslim Sues FBI over Secret GPS Surveillance," *CAIR/YouTube*, March 2, 2011.http://www.youtube.com/watch?v=DgZsMsCdlHE.

15 Jerry Markon, "Tension Grows between Calif. Muslims, FBI after Informant Infiltrates Mosque," *Washington Post*, December 5, 2010. http://www.washington-post.com/wpdyn/content/article/2010/12/04/AR2010120403710.html.

16 For examples of the role of foreign states in domestic counterterrorism training in the Bay Area—such as Israeli and Bahraini police units involved in Operation Urban Shield 2011 in Berkeley, which targeted Occupy protesters—see Maira and Sze (2012). The blockade of an Israeli boat at the Oakland port in protest of the war on Gaza in August 2014, in which many young Arab American activists took the lead, also highlighted the cooperation between Israeli military and police and U.S. police in St. Louis County, Missouri, where a young African American, Mike Brown, had been killed by police and militarized police forces had attacked

protesters. See Massoud Hayoun, "Oakland Activists Block Ship for Third Day," *Al Jazeera America*, August 18, 2014. http://america.aljazeera.com/articles/2014/8/18/gaza-oakland-protest.html.

17 Nina Bernstein, "Questions, Bitterness and Exile for Queens Girl in Terror Case," *New York Times*, June 17, 2005. http://www.nytimes.com/2005/06/17/nyregion/17suicide.html?pagewanted=all&_r=0.

18 Ibid.

19 "Timeline of Events," *Committee to Stop FBI Repression*, n.d. (ca. 2012). http://www.stopfbi.net/about/timeline.

20 In May 2011, the federal grand jury investigations targeted a twenty-fourth activist, Carlos Montes, a Chicano antiwar organizer who had been involved in Columbia and Palestine solidarity activism and in protesting the School of the Americas and its role in training the Columbian military and death squads. He was arrested in Los Angeles and questioned by plainclothes FBI agents about his political activism, sparking a round of organizing by the Committee to Stop FBI Repression.

21 "Timeline of Events," *Committee to Stop FBI Repression*.

22 See the Electronic Frontier Foundation's Surveillance Self-Defense Project at https://ssd.eff.org/.

23 Seth Wessler, "Muslim Students Reeling from Shocking News of FBI's Spying," *Color Lines*, February 24, 2012. http://colorlines.com/archives/2012/02/first_came_the_shock_then.html.

24 Quote from back cover of Defending Dissent Foundation, *Manufacturing "Terrorists": The FBI's Entrap and Demonize Strategy* (Dissent and Repression Comic Series). 2012. Washington, DC: Defending Dissent Foundation.

25 Greg Jaffe, Cari Gervin, and Thomas Gibbons-Neff. "Tenn. Gunman Used Drugs, Struggled with Clash of Faith." *Washington Post*, July 18, 2015. http://www.washingtonpost.com/politics/chattanooga-shooter-an-aimless-young-man-who-smoked-dope-and-shot-guns/2015/07/18/c213f6a6-2d7d-11e5-a5ea-cf74396e59ec_story.html.

CHAPTER 6. DEMOCRACY AND ITS OTHERS

1 Condoleezza Rice, while secretary of state, said during a press conference in Tel Aviv in June 2006, during the Israeli bombardment of Lebanon, that "[w]hat we're seeing here, in a sense, is . . . the 'birth pangs' of a 'New Middle East.'" Secretary of State Condoleezza Rice, Special Briefing on the Travel to the Middle East and Europe of Secretary Condoleezza Rice, Press Conference, U.S. State Department, Washington, D.C., July 21, 2006.

2 "Lessons from an Experiment in International Digital Activism," *Cloud to Street*, August 26, 2011. Originally at http://www.cloudtostreet.org/?p=398. Archived at https://web.archive.org/web/20120225075624/http://www.cloudtostreet.org/?p=398.

3 "About: Working to Understand the Intersection of Cyberspace and Political Space," *Cloud to Street*, n.d. (ca. 2012). Originally at http://www.cloudtostreet.

org/?page_id=5. Archived at https://web.archive.org/web/20120225161414/http://www.cloudtostreet.org/?page_id=5.

4 "President Obama Speaks to the Muslim World from Cairo, Egypt," *White House*, June 4, 2009. https://www.whitehouse.gov/video/President-Obama-Speaks-to-the-Muslim-World-from-Cairo-Egypt.

5 In fact, our conversation took place soon after an Egyptian academic teaching at UC Davis, Noha Radwan, had given a televised interview on the *Democracy Now* show from Tahrir Square and subsequently been beaten up by pro-Mubarak thugs.

6 See Bruce Robbins, "Balibarism!," *n+1*, April 5, 2013. http://nplusonemag.com/balibarism.

BIBLIOGRAPHY

Abbas, Sadia. 2014. *At Freedom's Limit: Islam and the Postcolonial Predicament*. New York: Fordham University Press.

Abdullah, Zain. 2013. "American Muslims in the Contemporary World: 1965 to the Present." In *The Cambridge Companion to American Islam*, edited by Julianne Hammer and Omid Safi, 65–82. New York: Cambridge University Press.

Abdul-Matin, Ibrahim. 2010. *Green Deen: What Islam Teaches about Protecting the Planet*. San Francisco: Berrett-Koehler.

Abdulrahim, Sawsan. 2008. "Whiteness and the Arab Immigrant Experience." In *Race and Arab Americans before and after 9/11: From Invisible Citizens to Visible Subjects*, edited by Amaney Jamal and Nadine Naber, 131–146. Syracuse, NY: Syracuse University Press.

Abou-El-Fadl, Reem. 2012. "The Road to Jerusalem through Tahrir Square: Anti-Zionism and Palestine in the 2011 Egyptian Revolution." *Journal of Palestine Studies* 41(2): 6–26.

Abowd, Thomas. 2014. "The Boycott, Divestment, and Sanctions Movement and Violations of Academic Freedom at Wayne State University." In *The Imperial University: Academic Repression and Scholarly Dissent*, edited by Piya Chatterjee and Sunaina Maira, 169–185. Minneapolis: University of Minnesota Press.

Abraham, Nabeel. 1994. "Anti-Arab Racism and Violence in the United States." In *The Development of Arab-American Identity*, edited by Ernest McCarus. Ann Arbor: University of Michigan Press.

Abraham, Sameer Y. 1983. "Detroit's Arab American Community: A Survey of Diversity and Commonality." In *Arabs in the New World: Studies on Arab American Communities*, edited by Sameer Abraham and Nabeel Abraham, 84–108. Detroit, MI: Wayne State University Center for Urban Studies.

Abu El-Haj, Thea R. 2007. "'I Was Born Here, but My Home, It's Not Here': Educating for Democratic Citizenship in an Era of Transnational Migration and Global Conflict." *Harvard Educational Review* 77(3): 285–316.

———. 2010. "'The Beauty of America': Nationalism, Education, and the War on Terror." *Harvard Educational Review* 80(2): 242–274.

Abunimah, Ali. 2014. *The Battle for Justice in Palestine*. Chicago: Haymarket Books.

Adams, Lorraine (with Ayesha Nasir). 2010. "The Trials of Faisal Shahzad." *Granta* 112: 257–269.

Afzal, Ahmed. 2015. *Lone Star Muslims: Transnational Lives and the South Asian Experience in Texas*. New York: NYU Press.

Agamben, Giorgio. 1998. *Homo Sacer: Sovereign Power and Bare Life*, translated by Daniel Heller-Roazen. Stanford, CA: Stanford University Press.

———. 2005. *State of Exception*, translated by Kevin Attell. Chicago and London: University of Chicago Press.

Ahmed, Sara. 2012. *On Being Included: Racism and Diversity in Institutional Life*. Durham, NC, and London: Duke University Press.

Ahuja, Sarita, Pronita Gupta, and Daranee Petsod. 2004. *Arab, Middle Eastern, Muslim and South Asian Communities in the San Francisco Bay Area: An Introduction for Grantmakers*. San Francisco: Grantmakers Concerned with Immigrants and Refugees, and Asian Americans/Pacific Islanders in Philanthropy. https://www.gcir.org/resources/arab-middle-eastern-muslim-and-south-asian-communities-san-francisco-bay-area-introduction.

Aidi, Hisham D. 2014. *Rebel Music: Race, Empire, and the New Muslim Youth Culture*. New York: Pantheon.

Allen, Lori. 2013. *The Rise and Fall of Human Rights: Cynicism and Politics in Occupied Palestine*. Stanford, CA: Stanford University Press.

Alsultany, Evelyn. 2012. *Arabs and Muslims in the Media: Race and Representation After 9/11*. New York and London: NYU Press.

American-Arab Anti-Discrimination Committee (ADC). 2008. *Report on Hate Crimes and Discrimination against Arab Americans*. Washington, DC: American-Arab Anti-Discrimination Committee Research Institute.

Ansary, Tamim. 2002. *West of Kabul, East of New York: An Afghan American Story*. New York: Farrar, Strauss, & Giroux.

Asad, Talal. 2003. *Formations of the Secular: Christianity, Islam, and Modernity*. Stanford, CA: Stanford University Press.

Associated Press. 2012. "AP's Probe into NYPD Intelligence Operations." http://www.ap.org/Index/AP-In-The-News/NYPD (accessed July 8, 2012).

Atanoski, Neda. 2013. *Humanitarian Violence: The US Deployment of Diversity*. Minneapolis: University of Minnesota Press.

Attia, Janaan. 2011. "Inside Out: Youth of Color Organizing from Multiple Sites." In *Arab and Arab American Feminisms: Gender, Violence, and Belonging*, edited by Rabab Abdulhadi, Evelyn Alsultany, and Nadine Naber, 166–173. Syracuse, NY: Syracuse University Press.

Badiou, Alain. 2005. *Metapolitics*, translated by Jason Barker. London: Verso.

———. 2011 [2006]. *Polemics*, translated by Steve Corcoran. London and New York: Verso.

Bakalian, Amy, and Mehdi Bozorghmehr. 2009. *Backlash 9/11: Middle Eastern and Muslim Americans Respond*. Berkeley: University of California Press.

Bald, Vivek. 2013. *Bengali Harlem and the Lost Histories of South Asian America*. Cambridge, MA, and London: Harvard University Press.

Balibar, Etienne. 1991. "Is There a 'Neo-Racism'?" In *Race, Nation, Class: Ambiguous Identities*, by Etienne Balibar and Immanuel Wallerstein, 17–28. New York: Verso.

Barker, Joanne. 2014. "The Specters of Recognition." In *Formations of United States Colonialism*, edited by Alyosha Goldstein, 33–56. Durham, NC: Duke University Press.

Barrows-Friedman, Nora. 2014. *In Our Power: U.S. Students Organize for Justice in Palestine*. Charlottesville, VA: Just World Books.

Bashir, Shahzad, and Robert D. Crews. 2012. "Introduction." In *Under the Drones: Modern Lives in the Afghanistan-Pakistan Borderlands*, edited by Shahzad Bashir and Robert D. Crews, 1–16. Cambridge, MA, and London: Harvard University Press.

Bayat, Asef. 2013. *Life as Politics: How Ordinary People Change the Middle East*, 2d ed. Stanford, CA: Stanford University Press.

Behdad, Ali. 2007. "Critical Historicism." *American Literary History* 20(1–2): 286–299.

Bello, Walden. 2010. " From American Lake to a People's Pacific in the Twenty-First Century." In *Militarized Currents: Toward a Decolonized Future in Asia and the Pacific*, edited by Setsu Shigematsu and Keith L. Camacho, 309–321. Minneapolis: University of Minnesota Press.

Benjamin, Walter. 1988. "Theses on the Philosophy of History." In *Illuminations: Walter Benjamin—Essays and Reflections*, edited by Hannah Arendt, translated by Harry Zohn, 253–264. New York: Schocken.

Bowen, John. 2007. *Why the French Don't Like Headscarves: Islam, the State, and Public Space*. Princeton, NJ: Princeton University Press.

Bricmont, Jean. 2007. *Humanitarian Imperialism: Using Human Rights to Sell War*. New Delhi: Aakar Books/Monthly Review.

Brown, Wendy. 2004. "'The Most We Can Hope for . . .': Human Rights and the Politics of Fatalism." *South Atlantic Quarterly* 103(2/3): 451–463.

Bruyneel, Kevin. 2007. *The Third Space of Sovereignty: The Postcolonial Politics of U.S.-Indigenous Relations*. Minneapolis: University of Minnesota Press.

Butler, Judith. 2009. *Frames of War: When Is Life Grievable?* London and New York: Verso.

Butler, Judith, and Gayatri C. Spivak. 2010 [2007]. *Who Sings the Nation-State? Language, Politics, Belonging* [a dialogue]. London, New York, and Calcutta: Seagull.

Cainkar, Louise. 2011. *Homeland Insecurity: The Arab American and Muslim American Experience after 9/11*. New York: Russell Sage Foundation.

Chan-Malik, Sylvia. 2013. "Cultural and Literary Production of Muslim America." In *The Cambridge Companion to American Islam*, edited by Julianne Hammer and Omid Safi, 279–298. New York: Cambridge University Press.

Chatterjee, Partha. 2014 [2007]. "Democracy and the Violence of the State: A Political Negotiation of Death." In *The Inter-Asia Cultural Studies Reader*, edited by Kuan-Hsing Chen and Chua Beng Huat, 163–177. London and New York: Routledge.

Cohen, Stanley. 1997. "Symbols of Trouble." In *The Subcultures Reader*, edited by Kenneth Gelder and Sarah Thornton, 149–162. London: Routledge.

Cohen, Stephen, and Gary Fields. 2000. "Social Capital and Capital Gains: An Examination of Social Capital in Silicon Valley." In *Understanding Silicon Valley: An Anatomy of an Entrepreneurial Region*, edited by Martin Kenney, 190–217. Stanford, CA: Stanford University Press.

Cole, David. 2003. *Enemy Aliens: Double Standards and Constitutional Freedoms in the War on Terrorism*. New York: New Press.

Cole, Juan. 2011. "Islamophobia and American Foreign Policy Rhetoric: The Bush Years and After." In *Islamophobia: The Challenge of Pluralism in the 21st Century*, edited by John L. Esposito and Ibrahim Kalin, 127–142. New York: Oxford University Press.

Council on American-Islamic Relations (CAIR). 2007. *The Status of Muslim Civil Rights: San Francisco Bay Area—2007*. Santa Clara, CA: CAIR.

———. 2009. *The Status of Muslim Civil Rights in California—2009*. Santa Clara and Sacramento, CA: CAIR.

———. 2013. *Standing Up for Your Rights, Preserving Our Freedom: The Status of Muslim Civil Rights in Northern California—2013*. Santa Clara and Sacramento, CA: CAIR.

Cruikshank, Barbara. 2000. "Cultural Politics: Political Theory and the Foundations of Democratic Order." In *Cultural Studies and Political Theory*, edited by Jodi Dean, 63–79. Ithaca, NY: Cornell University Press.

Curtis, Edward E. 2013. "The Study of American Muslims: A History." In *The Cambridge Companion to American Islam*, edited by Julianne Hammer and Omid Safi, 15–27. New York: Cambridge University Press.

Dabashi, Hamid. 2011. *Brown Skin, White Masks*. New York: Pluto.

Das Gupta, Monisha. 2006. *Unruly Immigrants: Rights, Activism, and Transnational South Asian Politics in the United States*. Durham, NC: Duke University Press.

Daulatzai, Sohail. 2012. *Black Star, Crescent Moon: The Muslim International and Black Freedom beyond America*. Minneapolis: University of Minnesota Press.

Davis, Angela. 2005. *Abolition Democracy: Beyond Empire, Prisons, and Torture*. New York: Seven Stories Press.

———. 2012. *The Meaning of Freedom: And Other Difficult Dialogues*. San Francisco: City Lights.

Davis, Uri. 1989. *Israel: An Apartheid State*. New York: Zed Books.

Dawson, Ashley. 2007. "The Crisis at Columbia: Academic Freedom, Area Studies, and Contingent Labor in the Contemporary Academy." *Social Text* 90 (Spring): 63–84.

Dean, Jodi. 2009. *Democracy and Other Neoliberal Fantasies: Communicative Capitalism and the Failure of the Left*. Durham, NC: Duke University Press.

Downs, Stephen, and Kathy Manley. 2014. *Inventing Terrorists: The Lawfare of Preemptive Prosecution*. Albany, NY: Project Salam and National Coalition to Protect Civil Freedoms.

Dubal, Veena. 2012. "The Demise of Community Policing: The Impact of Post-9/11 Federal Surveillance Programs on Local Law Enforcement." *Asian American Law Journal* 19: 35–59.

Dudziak, Mary L. 2000. "Desegregation as a Cold War Imperative." In *Critical Race Theory: The Cutting Edge*, 2d ed., edited by Richard Delgado and Jean Stefancic, 106–117. Philadelphia: Temple University Press.

Duggan, Lisa. 2003. *The Twilight of Inequality: Neoliberalism, Cultural Politics, and the Attack on Democracy*. Boston: Beacon Press.

Elia, Nada. 2011. "The Burden of Representation: When Palestinians Speak Out." In *Arab and Arab American Feminisms: Gender, Violence, and Belonging*, edited by

Rabab Abdulhadi, Evelyn Alsultany, and Nadine Naber, 141–158. Syracuse, NY: Syracuse University Press.

El Rassi, Toufic. 2007. *Arab in America*. San Francisco: Last Gasp.

Eng, David. 2010. *The Feeling of Kinship: Queer Liberalism and the Racialization of Intimacy*. Durham, NC: Duke University Press.

———. 2012. "The Civil and the Human." *American Quarterly* 64(2): 205–211.

English-Lueck, J. A. 2002. *Cultures@SiliconValley*. Stanford, CA: Stanford University Press.

Erikson, Erik H. 1968. *Identity: Youth and Crisis*. Philadelphia: Temple University Press.

Espiritu, Yến Lê. 2014. *Body Counts: The Vietnam War and Militarized Refugees*. Oakland: University of California Press.

Esposito, John L. 2011. "Introduction." In *Islamophobia: The Challenge of Pluralism in the 21st Century*, edited by John L. Esposito and Ibrahim Kalin, xxi–xxxv. New York: Oxford University Press.

Ewing, Katherine P., and Marguerite Hoyler. 2008. "Being Muslim and American: South Asian Muslim Youth and the War on Terror." In *Being and Belonging: Muslims in the United States since 9/11*, edited by Katherine P. Ewing, 80–103. New York: Russell Sage Foundation.

Fassin, Didier. 2010. "Heart of Humaneness; The Moral Economy of Humanitarian Intervention." In *Contemporary States of Emergency: The Politics of Military and Humanitarian Interventions*, edited by Didier Fassin and Mariella Pandolfi, 269–293. New York: Zone Books.

Fassin, Didier, and Mariella Pandolfi. 2010. "Introduction: Military and Humanitarian Government in the Age of Intervention." In *Contemporary States of Emergency: The Politics of Military and Humanitarian Interventions*, edited by Didier Fassin and Mariella Pandolfi, 9–25. New York: Zone Books.

Feldman, Ilana. 2012. "The Humanitarian Condition: Palestinian Refugees and the Politics of Living." *Humanity: An International Journal of Human Rights, Humanitarianism & Development* 3(2): 155–172.

Feldman, Keith P. 2015. *A Shadow over Palestine: The Imperial Life of Race in America*. Minneapolis: University of Minnesota Press.

Ferguson, Roderick A. 2010. "An American Studies Meant for Interruption." *American Quarterly* 62(2): 215–219.

———. 2012. *The Reorder of Things: The University and Its Pedagogy of Minority Difference*. Minneapolis: University of Minnesota Press.

Fernandez, Lisa. 2000. "Indo-American Youth in Gangs Defy Stereotypes." *San Jose Mercury News*, April 9.

Finkelstein, Norman G. 2000. *The Holocaust Industry: Reflections on the Exploitation of Jewish Suffering*. London: Verso.

Fitzgerald, Paul, and Elizabeth Gould. 2009. *Invisible History: Afghanistan's Untold Story*. San Francisco: City Lights.

Foucault, Michel. 1995. *Discipline and Punish: The Birth of the Prison*, translated by Alan Sheridan. New York: Vintage Books.

———. 2003. "Society Must Be Defended": Lectures at the Collège de France, 1975–76, translated by David Macey. New York: Picador.

Friedlander, Jonathan. 1994. "The Yemenis of Delano: A Profile of a Rural Islamic Community." In Muslim Communities in North America, edited by Yvonne Y. Haddad and Jane I. Smith, 423–444. Albany: State University of New York Press.

Gaines, Kevin. 2010. "Of Teachable Moments and Specters of Race." American Quarterly 62(2): 195–213.

Gallup. 2009. Muslim Americans: A National Portrait. Washington, DC: Gallup, Inc.

Ganguly, Keya. 2001. States of Exception: Everyday Life and Postcolonial Identity. Minneapolis: University of Minnesota Press.

Garrod, Andrew, and Robert Kilkenny. 2014. Growing Up Muslim: Muslim College Students in America Tell Their Life Stories. Ithaca, NY, and London: Cornell University Press.

Gleeson, Shannon. 2012. Conflicting Commitments: The Politics of Enforcing Immigrant Worker Rights in San Jose and Houston. Ithaca, NY: Cornell University Press.

Gokhale, Ketaki. 2007. "Changing Face of Silicon Valley High Schools." India West, January 5, A1, A10, A37.

González, Roberto J. 2009. American Counterinsurgency: Human Science and the Human Terrain. Chicago: Prickly Paradigm Press.

———. 2014. "Militarizing Education: The Intelligence Community's Spy Camps." In The Imperial University: Academic Repression and Scholarly Dissent, edited by Piya Chaterjee and Sunaina Maira, 79–98. Minneapolis: University of Minnesota Press.

Gordon, Avery F. 1997. Ghostly Matters: Haunting and the Sociological Imagination. Minneapolis: University of Minnesota Press.

Gould, Elizabeth, and Paul Fitzgerald. 2011. Crossing Zero: The Afpak War at the Turning Point of American Empire. San Francisco: City Lights.

Gramsci, Antonio. 2000. "Note for an Introduction and an Approach to the Study of Philosophy and the History of Culture." In The Antonio Gramsci Reader: Selected Writings 1916–1935, edited by David Forgacs, 324–347. New York: NYU Press.

Grewal, Zareena. 2014. Islam Is a Foreign Country: American Muslims and the Global Crisis of Authority. New York: NYU Press.

Gumbs, Alexis P. 2014. "Nobody Mean More: Black Feminist Pedagogy and Solidarity." In The Imperial University: Academic Repression and Scholarly Dissent, edited by Piya Chatterjee and Sunaina Maira, 237–259. Minneapolis: University of Minnesota Press.

Haddad, Yvonne Y. 1994. "Maintaining the Faith of the Fathers: Dilemmas of Religious Identity in the Christian and Muslim Arab American Communities." In The Development of Arab-American Identity, edited by Ernest McCarus, 61–84. Ann Arbor: University of Michigan Press.

Hall, Stuart. 1996. "New Ethnicities." In Stuart Hall: Critical Dialogues in Cultural Studies, edited by David Morley and Kuan-Hsing Chen, 441–449. London and New York: Routledge.

Hammer, Juliane, and Omid Safi, eds. 2013. The Cambridge Companion to American Islam. New York: Cambridge University Press.

Hanifi, Shah M. 2012. "Quandaries of the Afghan State." In *Under the Drones: Modern Lives in the Afghanistan-Pakistan Borderlands*, edited by Shahzad Bashir and Robert D. Crews, 83–101. Cambridge, MA, and London: Harvard University Press.

Hardt, Michael, and Antonio Negri. 2000. *Empire*. Cambridge, MA: Harvard University Press.

———. 2009. *Commonwealth*. Cambridge, MA: Belknap Press (Harvard University Press).

Harney, Stefano, and Fred Moten. 2013. *The Undercommons: Fugitive Planning and Black Study*. Brooklyn, NY: Minor Compositions (Autonomedia).

Harvey, David. 2007 [2005]. *A Brief History of Neoliberalism*. New York: Oxford University Press.

Hasan, Asma G. 2000. *American Muslims: The New Generation*. New York and London: Continuum.

Heath, Jennifer, ed. 2008. *The Veil: Women Writers on Its History, Lore, and Politics*. Berkeley: University of California Press.

Hesford, Wendy S. 2011. *Spectacular Rhetorics: Human Rights Visions, Recognitions, Feminisms*. Durham, NC: Duke University Press.

Hicks, Rosemary R. 2013. "Religious Pluralism, Secularism, and Interfaith Endeavors." In *The Cambridge Companion to American Islam*, edited by Julianne Hammer and Omid Safi, 156–169. New York: Cambridge University Press.

Hosseini, Khalid. 2003. *The Kite Runner*. New York: Riverhead Books/Berkley.

INCITE! (Women, Gender Non-Conforming, and Trans People of Color against Violence), ed. 2007. *The Revolution Will Not Be Funded: Beyond the Non-Profit Industrial Complex*. Cambridge, MA: South End Press.

Isin, Engin, and Evelyn Ruppert. 2015. *Being Digital Citizens*. London and New York: Rowman & Littlefield.

Jackson, Sherman. 2011. "Muslims, Islam(s), Race, and American Islamophobia." In *Islamophobia: The Challenge of Pluralism in the 21st Century*, edited by John L. Esposito and Ibrahim Kalin, 93–106. New York: Oxford University Press.

Jamal, Amaney. 2008. "Civil Liberties and the Otherization of Arab and Muslim Americans." In *Race and Arab Americans before and after 9/11: From Invisible Citizens to Visible Subjects*, edited by Amaney Jamal and Nadine Naber, 114–130. Syracuse, NY: Syracuse University Press.

Jordan, June. 2007 [1985]. "Moving towards Home." In *The Collected Poems of June Jordan: Directed by Desire*, 398–400. Port Townsend, WA: Copper Canyon Press.

Joseph, Craig M., and Barnaby Riedel. 2008. "Islamic Schools, Assimilation, and the Concept of Muslim American Character." In *Being and Belonging: Muslims in the United States since 9/11*, edited by Katherine P. Ewing, 156–177. New York: Russell Sage Foundation.

Joya, Malalai. 2009. *A Woman among Warlords: The Extraordinary Story of an Afghan Who Dared to Raise Her Voice*. New York: Scribner.

Judy, Ronald. 2003. "The Threat to Islamic Humanity after 11 September 2001." *Critical Quarterly* 45(1/2): 101–112.

Jung, Moon-Kie. 2011. "Constituting the Empire-State and White Supremacy: The Early Years." In *State of White Supremacy: Racism, Governance, and the United States*, edited by Moon-Kie Jung, Joao H. Costa Vargas, and Eduardo Bonilla-Silva, 1–26. Stanford, CA: Stanford University Press.

Kadi, Joanne. 1994. "Introduction." In *Food for Our Grandmothers: Writings by Arab-American and Arab-Canadian Feminists*, edited by Joanne Kadi, xiii–xx. Boston: South End Press.

Kaplan, Amy. 1993. "'Left Alone with America': The Absence of Empire in the Study of American Culture." In *Cultures of United States Imperialism*, edited by Amy Kaplan and Donald Pease, 3–21. Durham, NC: Duke University Press.

———. 2005. "Where Is Guantánamo?" In *Legal Borderlands: Law and the Construction of American Borders*, edited by Mary Dudziak and Leti Volpp, special issue of *American Quarterly* 57(3): 831–858.

Karim, Jamillah. 2005. "Between Immigrant Islam and Black Liberation: Young Muslims Inherit Global Muslim and African American Legacies." *Muslim World* 95 (October): 497–513.

———. 2009. *American Women Muslim Women: Negotiating Race, Class, and Gender within the Ummah*. New York: NYU Press.

Kelley, Robin D. G. 1999. "People in Me." *Color Lines* 1(3): 5–7.

Kelley, Robin D. G., and Erica L. Williams. 2013. "Madiba in Palestine: Apartheid Died on the Sharp Edge of Principles." *Counterpunch*, December 10. http://www.counterpunch.org/2013/12/10/madiba-in-palestine/.

Khabeer, Su'ad A., and Maytha Alhassen. 2013. "Muslim Youth Cultures." In *The Cambridge Companion to American Islam*, edited by Julianne Hammer and Omid Safi, 299–311. New York: Cambridge University Press.

Khan, Salim. 1981. "A Brief History of Pakistanis in the Western United States." M.A. thesis, History Department, California State University, Sacramento.

Kibria, Nazli. 2008. "The 'New Islam' and Bangladeshi Youth in the U.S." *Ethnic and Racial Studies* 31(2): 243–266.

———. 2011. *Muslims in Motion: Islam and National Identity in the Bangladeshi Diaspora*. New Brunswick, NJ, and London: Rutgers University Press.

Kim, Jodi. 2010. *Ends of Empire: Asian American Critique and the Cold War*. Minneapolis: University of Minnesota Press.

Knight, Michael M. 2004. *The Taqwacores*. Berkeley, CA: Soft Skull Press.

Kohlatkar, Sonali, and James Ingalls. 2006. *Bleeding Afghanistan: Washington, Warlords, and the Propaganda of Silence*. New York: Seven Stories Press.

Kumar, Amitava. 2010. *A Foreigner Carrying in the Crook of His Arm a Tiny Bomb*. Durham, NC, and London: Duke University Press.

Kumar, Deepa. 2012. *Islamophobia and the Politics of Empire*. Chicago: Haymarket.

Kundnani, Arun. 2014. *The Muslims Are Coming: Islamophobia, Extremism, and the Domestic War on Terror*. London and New York: Verso.

Kwon, Soo Ah. 2013. *Uncivil Youth: Race, Activism, and Affirmative Governmentality*. Durham, NC, and London: Duke University Press.

Lesko, Nancy. 2001. *Act Your Age! A Cultural Construction of Adolescence*. New York: Routledge.

Lewis, Reina. 2013. *Modest Fashion: Styling Bodies, Mediating Faith*. London and New York: I.B. Tauris.

Lowe, Lisa. 1996. *Immigrant Acts: On Asian American Cultural Politics*. Durham, NC: Duke University Press.

Lubin, Alex. 2014. *Geographies of Liberation: The Making of an Afro-Arab Political Imaginary*. Chapel Hill: University of North Carolina Press.

Lyon, David, and Elia Zureik. 1996. "Surveillance, Privacy, and the New Technology." In *Computers, Surveillance, and Piracy*, edited by David Lyon and Elia Zureik, 1–18. Minneapolis: University of Minnesota Press.

MacArthur, Andrew P. 2007. "The NSA Phone Call Database: The Problematic Acquisition and Mining of Records in the United States, Canada, the United Kingdom, and Australia." *Duke Journal of Comparative and International Law* 17: 441–481.

Mahmood, Saba. 2006. "Secularism, Hermeneutics, and Empire: The Politics of Islamic Reformation." *Public Culture* 18(2): 323–347.

Maira, Sunaina. 2002. *Desis in the House: Indian American Youth Culture in New York City*. Philadelphia: Temple University Press.

———. 2007. "Deporting Radicals, Deporting La Migra: The Hayat Case in Lodi." *Cultural Dynamics* 19(1): 39–66.

———. 2009a. *Missing: Youth, Empire, and Citizenship after 9/11*. Durham, NC: Duke University Press.

———. 2009b. "'Good' and 'Bad' Muslim Citizens: Feminists, Terrorists, and U.S. Orientalisms." *Feminist Studies* 35(3): 631–656.

———. 2013. *Jil Oslo: Palestinian Hip-Hop, Youth Culture, and the Youth Movement*. Washington, DC: Tadween.

Maira, Sunaina, and Elisabeth Soep, eds. 2004. *Youthscapes: The Popular, the National, the Global*. Philadelphia: University of Pennsylvania Press.

Maira, Sunaina, and Julie Sze. 2012. "Dispatches from Pepper Spray University: Privatization, Repression, and Revolts." *American Quarterly* 64(2): 315–330.

Maiwindi, Nadia. 2005. "9/11 and the Afghan-American Community." In *Shattering the Stereotypes: Muslim Women Speak Out*, edited by Fawzia Afzal-Khan, 29–32. Northampton, MA: Olive Branch Press (Interlink).

Majaj, Lisa S. 1999. "Arab American Ethnicity: Locations, Coalitions, and Cultural Negotiations." In *Arabs in America: Building a New Future*, edited by Michael W. Suleiman, 320–336. Philadelphia: Temple University Press.

Makdisi, Saree. 2010. "The Architecture of Erasure." *Critical Inquiry* 36(3): 519–559.

Malek, Alia. 2009. *A Country Called Amreeka: U.S. History Retold through Arab-American Lives*. New York: Free Press.

———. 2011. *Patriot Acts: Narratives of Post-9/11 Injustice*. San Francisco: McSweeney's/Voice of Witness.

Mamdani, Mahmood. 2004. *Good Muslim, Bad Muslim: America, the Cold War, and the Roots of Terror*. New York: Pantheon.

Mearsheimer, John, and Stephen Walt. 2007. *The Israel Lobby and U.S. Foreign Policy.* New York: Farrar, Straus & Giroux.

Melamed, Jodi. 2006. "The Spirit of Neoliberalism: From Racial Liberalism to Multicultural Neoliberalism." *Social Text* 89 (Winter): 1–25.

———. 2011. *Represent and Destroy: Rationalizing Violence in the New Racial Capitalism.* Minneapolis: University of Minnesota Press.

Mendieta, Eduardo. 2011. "The Politics of Terror and the Neoliberal Military Minimalist State: On the Inheritance of 9–11." *City* 15(3–4): 1–7.

Menon, Nivedita. 2004. *Recovering Subversion: Feminist Politics beyond the Law.* Ranikhet, India: Permanent Black.

Menon, Sridevi. 2006. "Where Is West Asia in Asian America? 'Asia' and the Politics of Space in Asian America." *Social Text* 86 (Spring): 55–79.

Merry, Sally E. 2006. "Anthropology and International Law." *Annual Review of Anthropology* 35: 99–116.

Mir, Shabana. 2007. "American Muslim Women on Campus." *Anthropology News* (May): 16–17.

———. 2014. *Muslim American Women on Campus: Undergraduate Social Life and Identity.* Chapel Hill: University of North Carolina Press.

Mitchell, Timothy. 2006. "Society, Economy, and the State Effect." In *The Anthropology of the State: A Reader*, edited by Aradhana Sharma and Akhil Gupta, 169–186. Malden, MA: Blackwell.

Mmembe, Achille. 2003. "Necropolitics," translated by Libby Meintjes. *Public Culture* 15(1): 11–40.

Modood, Tariq. 2002. "Muslims and the Politics of Multiculturalism in Britain." In *Critical Views of September 11: Analyses from around the World*, edited by Eric Hershberg and Kevin W. Moore, 194–208. New York: New Press.

Mouffe, Chantal. 2005. *On the Political.* Abingdon, UK: Routledge.

Mufti, Aamir R. 2004. "Critical Secularism: A Reintroduction for Perilous Times." *boundary 2* 31(2): 1–9.

Muhammad-Arif, Aminah. 2002. *Salaam America: South Asian Muslims in New York.* London: Anthem Press.

Muñoz, Carlos, Jr. 2007. *Youth, Identity, Power: The Chicano Movement*, rev. and exp. ed. New York: Verso.

Muslim Advocates. 2009. *Unreasonable Intrusions: Investigating the Politics, Faith, and Finances of Americans Returning Home.* San Francisco: Muslim Advocates. https://d3n8a8pro7vhmx.cloudfront.net/muslimadvocates/pages/178/attachments/original/1360963837/Unreasonable_Intrusions_2009.pdf?1360963837.

Muslim Public Affairs Council (MPAC). 2005. *Special Report: Religion and Identity of Muslim American Youth Post-London Attacks.* Washington, DC: MPAC.

Naber, Nadine. 2000. "Ambiguous Insiders: An Investigation of Arab-American Invisibility." *Ethnic and Racial Studies* 23(1): 37–61.

———. 2005. "Muslim First, Arab Second: A Strategic Politics of Race and Gender." *Muslim World* 95: 479–495.

———. 2008. "Introduction: Arab Americans and US Racial Formations." In *Race and Arab Americans before and after 9/11: From Invisible Citizens to Visible Subjects*, edited by Amaney Jamal and Nadine Naber, 1–45. Syracuse, NY: Syracuse University Press.

———. 2012. *Arab America: Gender, Cultural Politics, and Activism*. New York and London: NYU Press.

Naff, Alixa. 1985. *Becoming Americans: The Early Arab Immigrant Experience*. Carbondale and Edwardsville: Southern Illinois University Press.

Najam, Adil. 2006. *Portrait of a Giving Community: Philanthropy by the Pakistani-American Diaspora*. Cambridge, MA: Global Equity Initiative–Asia Center/Harvard University Press.

Nguyen, Mimi T. 2012. *The Gift of Freedom: War, Debt, and Other Refugee Passages*. Durham, NC, and London: Duke University Press.

Nguyen, Tram. 2005. *We Are All Suspects Now: Untold Stories from Immigrant Communities after 9/11*. Boston: Beacon Press.

Nigam, Aditya. 2012. "The Arab Upsurge and the 'Viral' Revolutions of Our Times." *Interface: A Journal for and about Social Movements* 4(1): 165–177.

Nimer, Mohamed. 2005. "American Muslim Organizations: Before and after 9/11." In *Muslims in the United States: Identity, Influence, and Innovation*, edited by Philippa Strum, 5–17. Washington, DC: Woodrow Wilson International Institute for Scholars.

Omatsu, Glenn. 1994. "The Four Prisons and the Movement of Liberation: Asian American Activism from the 1960s to the 1990s." In *The State of Asian America: Activism and Resistance in the 1990s*, edited by Karin Aguilar San-Juan, 19–69. Boston: South End Press.

Omidian, Patricia O. 1996. *Aging and Family in an Afghan Refugee Community: Transitions and Transformations*. New York: Garland.

Omidian, Patricia O., and Julienne G. Lipson. 1996. "Ethnic Coalitions and Public Health: Delights and Dilemmas with the Afghan Health Education Project in Northern California." *Human Organization* 55(3): 355–360.

Ong, Aihwa. 2006. *Neoliberalism as Exception: Mutations in Citizenship and Sovereignty*. Durham, NC: Duke University Press.

Orfalea, Gregory. 2006. *The Arab Americans: A History*. Northampton, MA: Olive Branch Press.

Pappe, Ilan. 2006. *The Ethnic Cleansing of Palestine*. Oxford, UK: Oneworld Publications.

Patel, Eboo. 2006. "Affirming Identity, Achieving Pluralism: Sociological Insights from a Practitioner of Interfaith Youth Work." In *Building the Interfaith Youth Movement: Beyond Dialogue to Action*, edited by Eboo Patel and Patrice Brodeur, 15–23. Lanham, MD: Rowman & Littlefield.

Patel, Eboo, and Patrice Brodeur. 2006. "Introduction: Building the Interfaith Youth Movement." In *Building the Interfaith Youth Movement: Beyond Dialogue to Action*, edited by Eboo Patel and Patrice Brodeur, 1–13. Lanham, MD: Rowman & Littlefield.

Pease, Donald. 1993. "New Perspectives on U.S. Culture and Imperialism." In *Cultures of United States Imperialism*, edited by Amy Kaplan and Donald Pease, 22–37. Durham, NC: Duke University Press.

———. 2009. *The New American Exceptionalism*. Minneapolis: University of Minnesota Press.

Peek, Lori. 2011. *Behind the Backlash: Muslim Americans after 9/11*. Philadelphia: Temple University Press.

Pellow, David N., and Lisa S. Park. 2002. *The Silicon Valley of Dreams: Environmental Injustice, Immigrant Workers, and the High-Tech Global Economy*. New York and London: NYU Press.

Pennock, Pamela. 2014. "Third World Alliances: Arab American Activists in American Universities, 1967–73." *Mashriq & Mahjar* 4: 55–78.

Perkins, John. 2004. *Confessions of an Economic Hit Man*. New York: Plume/Penguin.

Pitti, Stephen J. 2003. *The Devil in Silicon Valley: Northern California, Race, and Mexican Americans*. Princeton, NJ: Princeton University Press.

Poster, Mark. 1990. *The Mode of Information: Poststructuralism and Social Context*. Cambridge, MA: Polity Press.

Povinelli, Elizabeth. 2006. *The Empire of Love*. Durham, NC: Duke University Press.

Prashad, Vijay. 2000. *The Karma of Brown Folk*. Minneapolis: University of Minnesota Press.

———. 2001. *Everybody Was Kung Fu Fighting: Afro-Asian Connections and the Myth of Cultural Purity*. Boston: Beacon.

———. 2007. *The Darker Nations: A People's History of the Third World*. New York and London: New Press.

———. 2012. *Uncle Swami: South Asians in America Today*. New York: New Press.

Puar, Jasbir. 2007. *Terrorist Assemblages: Homonationalism in Queer Times*. Durham, NC: Duke University Press.

Puar, Jasbir K., and Amit S. Rai. 2002. "Monster, Terrorist, Fag: The War on Terrorism and the Production of Docile Patriots." *Social Text* 72 (Fall): 117–148.

———. 2004. "The Remaking of a Model Minority: Perverse Projectiles under the Specter of (Counter)terrorism." *Social Text* 80 (Fall): 75–104.

Ramirez, Renya K. 2007. *Native Hubs: Culture, Community, and Belonging in Silicon Valley and Beyond*. Durham, NC: Duke University Press.

Ramnath, Maia. 2011. *Haj to Utopia: How the Ghadar Movement Charted Global Radicalism and Attempted to Overthrow the British Empire*. Berkeley: University of California Press.

Ramos-Zaya, Ana Y. 2004. "Delinquent Citizenship, National Performances, Racialization, Surveillance, and the Politics of 'Worthiness' in Puerto Rican Chicago." *Latino Studies* 2: 26–44.

Rana, Junaid. 2011. *Terrifying Muslims: Race and Labor in the South Asian Diaspora*. Durham, NC: Duke University Press.

Rancière, Jacques. 2004. "Who Is the Subject of the Rights of Man?" *South Atlantic Quarterly* 103 (2/3): 297–309.

———. 2006. *Hatred of Democracy*, translated by Steve Corcoran. London and New York: Verso.

———. 2010. *Dissensus: On Politics and Aesthetics*, elec. ver., edited and translated by Steve Corcoran. London and New York: Continuum.

Razack, Sherene H. 2008. *Casting Out: The Eviction of Muslims from Western Law and Politics*. Toronto: University of Toronto Press.

Reddy, Chandan. 2011. *Freedom with Violence: Race, Sexuality, and the US State*. Durham, NC: Duke University Press.

Rifkin, Mark. 2012. *The Erotics of Sovereignty: Queer Native Writing in the Era of Self-Determination*. Minneapolis: University of Minnesota Press.

Robbins, Bruce, and Elsa Stamatopoulou. 2004. "Reflections on Culture and Cultural Rights." *South Atlantic Quarterly* 103(2/3): 419–434.

Rodriguez, Dylan. 2010. *Suspended Apocalypse: White Supremacy, Genocide, and the Filipino Condition*. Minneapolis: University of Minnesota Press.

Rogin, Michael. 1993. "'Make My Day!' Spectacle as Amnesia in Imperial Politics [and the Sequel]." In *Cultures of United States Imperialism*, edited by Amy Kaplan and Donald Pease, 499–534. Durham, NC: Duke University Press.

Rygiel, Kim. 2006. "Protecting and Proving Identity: The Biopolitics of Waging War Through Citizenship in the Post-9/11 Era." In *(En)Gendering the War on Terror: War Stories and Camouflaged Politics*, edited by Krista Hunt and Kim Rygiel, 145–167. Aldershot, UK, and Burlington, VT: Ashgate.

Said, Edward W. 1983. *The World, the Text, and the Critic*. Cambridge, MA: Harvard University Press.

———. 2000. "America's Last Taboo." *New Left Review* 6 (Nov./Dec.): 45–53.

Salaita, Steven. 2006a. *Anti-Arab Racism in the U.S.A.: Where It Comes from and What It Means for Politics Today*. London: Pluto Press.

———. 2006b. *The Holy Land in Transit: Colonialism and the Quest for Canaan*. Syracuse, NY: Syracuse University Press.

———. 2008. *The Uncultured Wars: Arabs, Muslims, and the Poverty of Liberal Thought*. London and New York: Zed Books.

———. 2011. *Israel's Dead Soul*. Philadelphia: Temple University Press.

———. 2012. "Corporate American Media Coverage of Arab Revolutions: The Contradictory Messages of Modernity." *Interface: A Journal for and about Social Movements* 4(1): 67–101.

Saliba, Therese. 1999. "Resisting Invisibility: Arab Americans in Academia and Activism." In *Arabs in America: Building a New Future*, edited by Michael W. Suleiman, 304–319. Philadelphia: Temple University Press.

———. 2011. "On Rachel Corrie, Palestine, and Feminist Solidarity." In *Arab and Arab American Feminisms: Gender, Violence, and Belonging*, edited by Rabab Abdulhadi, Evelyn Alsultany, and Nadine Naber, 184–202. Syracuse, NY: Syracuse University Press.

Salime, Zakia. 2011. "Securing the Market of War: The Middle East Partnership Initiative." In *Accumulating Insecurity: Violence and Dispossession in the Making of*

Everyday Life, edited by Shelley Feldman, Charles Geisler, and Gayatri A. Menon, 215–239. Athens: University of Georgia Press.

Samhan, Helen. 1999. "Not Quite White: Race Classification and the Arab-American Experience." In *Arabs in America: Building a New Future*, edited by Michael W. Suleiman, 209–226. Philadelphia: Temple University Press.

Scahill, Jeremy. 2013. *Dirty Wars: The World Is a Battlefield*. New York: Nation Books (Perseus).

Schmidt, Garbi. 2002. "Dialectics of Authenticity: Examples of Ethnification of Islam among Young Muslims in Sweden and the United States." *Muslim World* 92: 1–17.

Secrets of Silicon Valley [film]. 2001. Dir. Alan Snitow and Deborah Kaufman.

Senzai, Farid, and Hatem Bazian. 2013. *The Bay Area Muslim Study: Establishing Identity and Community*. Washington, DC: Institute for Social Policy and Understanding.

Seshadri, Kalpana R. 2008. "When Home Is a Camp: Global Sovereignty, Biopolitics, and Internally Displaced Persons." *Social Text* 94 (Spring): 29–58.

Shah, Nayan. 2012. *Stranger Intimacy: Race, Sexuality, and the Law in the North American West*. Berkeley: University of California Press.

Shaheen, Jack. 2001. *Reel Bad Arabs: How Hollywood Vilifies a People*. Northampton, MA: Olive Branch Press.

Shakir, Evelyn. 1997. *Bint Arab: Arab and Arab American Women in the United States*. Westport, CT, and London: Praeger.

Shaw, Ian, and Majed Akhter. 2014. "The Dronification of State Violence." *Critical Asian Studies* 46(2): 211–234.

Sheehi, Stephen. 2011. *Islamophobia: The Ideological Campaign against Muslims*. Atlanta, GA: Clarity Press.

Sheikh, Farzana. 2012. "Will Sufi Islam Save Pakistan?" In *Under the Drones: Modern Lives in the Afghanistan-Pakistan Borderlands*, edited by Shahzad Bashir and Robert D. Crews, 174–191. Cambridge, MA: Harvard University Press.

Sherman, Jon. 2009. "'A Person Otherwise Innocent': Policing Entrapment in Preventative Undercover Counterterrorism Investigations." *University of Pennsylvania Journal of Constitutional Law* 11: 1475–1500.

Shiekh, Irum. 2011. *Detained without Cause: Muslims' Stories of Detention and Deportation in America after 9/11*. New York: Palgrave Macmillan.

Shigematsu, Setsu, and Keith L. Camacho. 2010. "Introduction: Militarized Currents, Decolonizing Futures." In *Militarized Currents: Toward a Decolonized Future in Asia and the Pacific*, edited by Setsu Shigematsu and Keith L. Camacho, xv–xlviii. Minneapolis: University of Minnesota Press.

Shihade, Magid. 2012. "The Season of Mobilization: The Arab Spring and European Mobilizations." *Interface: A Journal for and about Social Movements* 4 (1): 1–16.

Shohat, Ella, and Robert Stam. 1994. *Unthinking Eurocentrism: Multiculturalism and the Media*. London and New York: Routledge.

Shrecker, Ellen. 1998. *Many Are the Crimes: McCarthyism in America*. Boston: Little, Brown and Company.

Shryock, Andrew. 2000. "Family Resemblances." In *Arab Detroit: From Margin to Mainstream*, edited by Nabeel Abraham and Andrew Shryock, 573–610. Detroit: Wayne State University Press.

———. 2008. "The Moral Analogies of Race." In *Race and Arab Americans before and after 9/11: From Invisible Citizens to Visible Subjects*, edited by Amaney Jamal and Nadine Naber, 81–113. Syracuse, NY: Syracuse University Press.

———. 2010. "Introduction: Islam as an Object of Fear and Affection." In *Islamophobia/ Islamophilia: Beyond the Politics of Enemy and Friend*. Indianapolis and Bloomington: Indiana University Press, 1–25.

Sifri, Randa. 1984. "Arab Culture in the Bay Area." In *Taking Root, Bearing Fruit*, edited by James Zogby, 81–82. Washington, DC: American-Arab Anti-Discrimination Committee Reports.

Simon, Bart. 2005. "The Return of Panopticism: Supervision, Subjection, and the New Surveillance." *Surveillance and Society* 3(1): 1–20.

Singh, Nikhil P. 2004. *Black Is a Country: Race and the Unfinished Struggle for Democracy*. Cambridge, MA: Harvard University Press.

Sirin, Selcuk, and Michelle Fine. 2008. *Muslim American Youth: Understanding Hyphenated Identities through Multiple Methods*. New York and London: NYU Press.

Smith, Andrea. 2007. "Introduction." In *The Revolution Will Not Be Funded: Beyond the Non-Profit Industrial Complex*, edited by INCITE!, 1–18. Cambridge, MA: South End Press.

———. 2011. "Unmasking the State: Racial/Gender Terror and Hate Crimes." In *State of White Supremacy: Racism, Governance, and the United States*, edited by Moon-Kie Jung, Joao H. Costa Vargas, and Eduardo Bonilla-Silva, 229–242. Stanford, CA: Stanford University Press.

Spann, Girardeau A. 2000. "Pure Politics." In *Critical Race Theory: The Cutting Edge*, 2d ed., edited by Richard Delgado and Jean Stefancic, 21–34. Philadelphia: Temple University Press.

Spivak, Gayatri C. 1995. "Introduction." In *Imaginary Maps: Three Stories*, by Mahasweta Devi, xxiii–xxxi. New York: Routledge.

Stanley, Eric A., Dean Spade, and Queer (In)Justice. 2012. "Roundtable: Queering Prison Abolition, Now?" *American Quarterly* 64(1): 115–127.

Stoler, Ann L. 2006. "Intimidations of Empire: Predicaments of the Tactile and Unseen." In *Haunted by Empire: Geographies of Intimacy in North American History*, edited by Ann L. Stoler, 1–22. Durham, NC, and London: Duke University Press.

———. 2013. *Imperial Debris: On Ruins and Ruination*. Durham, NC, and London: Duke University Press.

Stoler, Ann L., and Carole McGranahan. 2007. "Introduction: Refiguring Imperial Terrains." In *Imperial Formations*, edited by Ann L. Stoler, Carole McGranahan, and Peter C. Perdue, 3–42. Santa Fe, NM: School for Advanced Research Press.

Strang, David. 1996. "Contested Sovereignty: The Social Construction of Colonial Imperialism." In *State Sovereignty as Social Construct*, edited by Thomas J. Beirsteker and Cynthia Weber, 22–49. Cambridge, UK: Cambridge University Press.

Suhrke, Astri. 2011. *When More Is Less: The International Project in Afghanistan*. New York: Columbia University Press.

Tadiar, Neferti X. M. 2013. "Lifetimes of Disposability within Global Neoliberalism." *Social Text* 115 (Summer): 19–48.

Tarzi, Amin. 2012. "Political Struggles over the Afghanistan-Pakistan Borderlands." In *Under the Drones: Modern Lives in the Afghanistan-Pakistan Borderlands*, edited by Shahzad Bashir and Robert D. Crews, 17–29. Cambridge, MA, and London: Harvard University Press.

Terry, Janice. 1999. "Community and Political Activism among Arab Americans in Detroit." In *Arabs in America: Building a New Future*, edited by Michael W. Suleiman, 241–254. Philadelphia: Temple University Press.

Theoharis, Athan G. 2011. *Abuse of Power: How Cold War Surveillance and Secrecy Policy Shaped the Response to 9/11*. Philadelphia: Temple University Press.

Vaidyanathan, Nirupama. 2007. "Center of Attraction." *India Currents* 21(5): 11–14.

Visweswaran, Kamala. 2010. *Un/common Cultures: Racism and the Rearticulation of Cultural Difference*. Durham, NC: Duke University Press.

Weintraub, Daniel. 2010. "A Silicon Valley Group Gives Voice to Voiceless." *New York Times*, May 22.

Weiss, Margot. 2012. "Reinvigorating the Queer Political Imagination: A Roundtable with Ryan Conrad, Yasmin Nair, and Karma Chávez of Against Equality." *American Quarterly* 64(4): 845–849.

Weizman, Eyal. 2011. *The Least of All Possible Evils: Humanitarian Violence from Arendt to Gaza*. New York: Verso.

Williams, Patricia J. 2000. "Alchemical Notes: Reconstructing Ideals from Deconstructed Rights." In *Critical Race Theory: The Cutting Edge*, 2d ed., edited by Richard Delgado and Jean Stefancic, 80–90. Philadelphia: Temple University Press.

Williams, Randall. 2010. *The Divided World: Human Rights and Its Violence*. Minneapolis: University of Minnesota Press.

Williams, Raymond. 1977. *Marxism and Literature*. Oxford, UK: Oxford University Press.

Williams, William A. 1980. *Empire as a Way of Life: An Essay on the Causes and Character of America's Present Predicament*. New York: Oxford University Press.

Wilson, Elizabeth. 2013. "'Can We Discuss This?'" In *Modest Fashion: Styling Bodies, Mediating Faith*, edited by Reina Lewis, 158–171. London and New York: I.B. Tauris.

Young, Cynthia. 2006. *Soul Power: Culture, Radicalism, and the Making of a Third World Left*. Durham, NC: Duke University Press.

Zaatari, Zeina. 2011. "In the Belly of the Beast: Struggling for Nonviolent Belonging." In *Arab and Arab American Feminisms*, edited by Rabab Abdulhadi, Evelyn Alsultany, and Nadine Naber, 60–77. Syracuse, NY: Syracuse University Press.

Žižek, Slavoj. 2002. *Welcome to the Desert of the Real: Five Essays on September 11 and Related Dates*. London and New York: Verso.

———. 2007. *Slavoj Žižek Presents Mao: On Practice and Contradiction*. London: Verso.

INDEX

Note: Page numbers in *italics* indicate photographs and illustrations.

insurgent movements, 16

interfaith alliances: and civil rights activism, 95; and coalitional categories, 14–15; and collective mobilization, 3; and cross-racial tensions and solidarities, 107–8, 115, 118; and environmental activism, 106; and "good/bad Muslim" binary, 66; and "Green Muslim" activism, 104; and Palestine solidarity activism, 133, 145

Interfaith Partners in Action, 103

International Monetary Fund (IMF), 90

International Socialist Organization (ISO), 31

Iranian hostage crisis, 60, 195

Iranian revolution, 5, 60

Iraq Body Count, 128

Iraqi immigrants, 21–22

Iraq war: and the Af-Pak war, 164, 174; and civil rights activism, 89, 92; and civil rights/human rights linkage, 120–21; and "color line" of human rights, 131–32; and cross-racial alliances, 77; and cross-racial tensions and solidarities, 112, 116; and decolonization paradigm, 120; and "good/bad Muslim" binary, 67; and Palestine solidarity activism, 127–28; and promotion of political solidarity, 261; and "radicalization" trope, 13; and surveillance of Islamic schools, 197; and "uncivil" protest, 158; and U.S. imperialism, 189. *See also* Gulf Wars

Irvine Eleven, 157, 158, 210

ISI (Pakistani Intelligence), 187–88

Islamic Networks Group, 25, 79, 96

"Islamic reformation" project, 69

Islamic schools: and countersurveillance, 211; and cross-racial tensions and solidarities, 107; and effects of surveillance, 197; and "good/bad Muslim" binary, 73; and interfaith activism, 97–98; and multiculturalism in Silicon

Valley, 51–52; and professionalization of activism, 230

Islamic Society, 122

Islamist movements: and the Af-Pak war, 165, 168; and culture of surveillance, 231; and "good/bad Muslim" binary, 69; and the "Long War on Terror," 4–5; and Palestine solidarity activism, 140–41; and "radicalization" trope, 10; and suppression of political activism, 149, 151; and "uncivil" protest, 156; and "youth as enemy" paradigm, 7–8

"Islamophilia," 70, 182, 231

Islamophobia: and the Af-Pak war, 169; and antiwar activism, 29, 31; and biopolitics of humanitarianism, 182; CAIR programs aimed at, 268n8; and civil rights activism, 81–83, 92; and countersurveillance, 212–13; and cross-racial alliances, 102–3; and culture of surveillance, 231–32; and economic development of Silicon Valley, 48; and effects of surveillance, 199; and frameworks of resistance, 256; and "good/bad Muslim" binary, 70–71, 74; and interfaith activism, 99; and the "Long War on Terror," 5; and multiculturalism in Silicon Valley, 49–52; and the "new order of War on Terror," 2–3; and Palestine solidarity activism, 134, 136, 141; and professionalization of activism, 225, 227; and "radicalization" trope, 12, 15–16; and suppression of political activism, 149–50, 153; and the Unheard Voices of 9/11 Hearing, 79; and "youth as enemy" paradigm, 7

Israel, 5, 21, 87, 95, 123, 147. *See also* Palestine conflict and solidarity activism; Zionism

Israeli Defense Forces, 143

Israel-Palestine Awareness Week, 67

Israel Project, 144

San Jose, California (*cont.*)
   and cross-racial tensions and solidarities, 107–8, 111, 113, 115–16, *117*; and cultural geography of Silicon Valley, 38–42, 265n1, 265n4; and economic development of Silicon Valley, 44, 46–48; and effects of surveillance, 201; and "good/bad Muslim" binary, 65, 67–68, 72–73; and "Green Muslim" activism, 104; and immigrant rights protests, 267n16; and "model minority" narrative, 266n12; and multiculturalism in Silicon Valley, 48–53; and Palestine solidarity activism, 127, 134, 139, 148; and professionalization of activism, 222–23, 225; and resistance to surveillance, 213–15; and suppression of political activism, 150, 152–53; and "uncivil" protest, 157; and the Unheard Voices of 9/11 Hearing, 78, 79; and U.S. imperialism, 186

San Jose Day of Remembrance, 116–18, *117*

San Jose High School, 50

San Jose Peace and Justice Center, 48

San Jose Police Department, 207

San Jose State University, 31, 72, 83, 100–101, 139, 157

Santa Clara Human Rights Commission, 108

Santa Clara Valley, 39–40, 43, 124

Santana Row rally, 124

Saudi Arabia, 235

Savage, Michael, 149

scapegoating, 2, 6, 48–49, 51, 53, 78

Schmidt, Garbi, 57

school bullying, 79

second Intifada, 122, 134, 240

secret evidence, 85

Secrets of Silicon Valley (1999), 45

Section 8 housing, 23

secular activism, 11

secularism, 139–40

Seeds of Peace, 101

segregation, 40, 91

self-surveillance, 194, 197, 200, 207

September 11 attacks, 54–62, 229

Seshadri, Kalpana, 190–91

sexual rights, 144–46

Shahzad, Faisal, 203–4

Shakir, Zaid, 32, 74, 109, 112–13, 115, 122

Sheehi, Stephen, 157–58

Sheikh Imam, 236

Shia Islam, 25, 54

Shryock, Andrew, 70, 182

Sikhs: and civil rights activism, 83, 85; and cross-racial tensions and solidarities, 111, 118; and cultural geography of Silicon Valley, 40; and economic development of Silicon Valley, 47; and multiculturalism in Silicon Valley, 49, 52; and promotion of political solidarity, 259; and "radicalization" of youth, 11; and the Unheard Voices of 9/11 Hearing, 78–79

"Silicon Curtain," 40–41, 45

Silicon Valley, 3, 12, 22, 27, 38–43, 124, 265n3. *See also specific municipalities*

Silicon Valley Community Foundation, 14

Silicon Valley De-Bug, 47, 48

Silicon Valley Unplugged, 80

Singh, Amardeep, 78

Singh, Nikhil Pal, 88

Siraj, Shahawar Matin, 203–4

Sirin, Selcuk, 72, 82

slavery, 91

Smith, Andrea, 91

Snowden, Edward, 198, 234

social capital, 46

social media and networking, 125–26, 200–201, 217–18, 238, 240–42

Society for Afghan Professionals, 169

Society of Arab Students, 139

solidarity politics: and accounts of surveillance, 204, 207; and the Af-Pak war, 163, 165, 168, 174, 176–77; and

ABOUT THE AUTHOR

Sunaina Marr Maira is Professor of Asian American Studies at UC Davis. She is the author of *Desis in the House: Indian American Youth Culture in New York City* and *Missing: Youth, Citizenship, and Empire after 9/11* as well as other works. Maira co-edited *The Imperial University: Academic Repression and Scholarly Dissent.*